D0597035

the Dust of Death

A Critique of the Establishment
and the Counter Culture—
and a Proposal for a Third Way

InterVarsity Press
Downers Grove, Illinois 60515

Cover Art:
A welded steel and canvas
construction, untitled, 1960,
by Lee Bontecou,
courtesy of The Art Institute
of Chicago.

"The Liberal Christ
Gives an Interview" by
Adrian Mitchell is
reprinted (on pages
319-20) from
Out Loud by
permission of Cape
Goliard Press,
London. ***Out Loud***
is distributed in
the United States by
Grossman Publishers,
New York.

ISBN 0-87784-911-0 (paper)
0-87784-956-0 (cloth)
Library of Congress
Catalog Card
Number: 72-94670

Printed in the United
States of America

To Jenny
who loves me
and keeps pace
with me to
"a different
drummer"

Preface

There were beggars in Berkeley. It was a warm October evening in the mid-sixties. With some close friends I had eaten a leisurely dinner in a small restaurant on Telegraph Avenue. We were enjoying our coffee, our minds relaxed and running deep. Suddenly two young men entered the restaurant and toured the tables, hurriedly scraping off the remains left on the plates. Then they slipped outside, sat down on the steps and began to eat, begging for dimes from passers-by as they did so.

Beggars in Berkeley? As a European on my first visit to the United States I was forcibly struck by the incident. China, once, perhaps, where my memory of pre-Mao conditions include a forest of stretched-out arms; India, perhaps, where the sunken gaze of poverty is unique in its depth and its submission; Haight-Ashbury, perhaps, where the boarded-up shop windows stare like the sightless eyes of a self-maimed community. But Berkeley, the so-called freedom lab in the heart of the world's largest educational corporation? The much-heralded pilot plant of simplicity designed to combat materialism and waste? There were beggars in Berkeley.

Certainly it was only an isolated incident. But the impression it left settled as a brooding suspicion that what we were witnessing in this and a thousand similar incidents was the gradual disillusionment of a generation, perhaps even of a culture. Ideals had grown so distant they were barely distinguishable from illusions. Meaning had become a mirage. Eager minds, soaring beyond facts to a super-freedom of fantasy, had plunged earthwards. Even resolute action, which seemed to have rolled the stone almost to the top of the hill, paused for breath only to watch the stone roll backwards. There had been no lack of human thought, action and effort—even blood—all given in generous quantities. But underneath the efforts of a generation lay dust.

Subsequent events and a closer inquiry, far from contradicting this suspicion, have served only to confirm it. The examination of this suspicion and the charting of an alternative is the burden of this book.

Contents

1/The Striptease of Humanism

"I come too early. My time has not come yet. This tremendous event is still on its way."
Nietzsche

"To be a man means to reach toward being God."
Jean Paul Sartre

"In seeking to become angels we may become less than men."
Pascal

"True civilization does not lie in gas, nor in steam, nor in turntables. It lies in the reduction of the traces of original sin."
Baudelaire

"It is becoming more and more obvious, that it is not starvation, not microbes, not cancer but man himself who is mankind's greatest danger."
Carl Jung

"It is in our hearts that the evil lies, and it is from our hearts that it must be plucked out."
Bertrand Russell

"Oh great gods, how far he lies from his destination!"
Fellini, Fellini's Satyricon[1]

Western culture is marked at the present moment by a distinct slowing of momentum, or perhaps, more accurately, by a decline in purposefulness and an increase in cultural introspection. This temporary lull, this vacuum in thought and effective action, has been created by the convergence of three cultural trends, each emphasizing a loss of direction. The first is the erosion of the Christian basis of Western culture, an erosion with deep historical causes and clearly visible results. The second is the failure of optimistic humanism to provide an effective alternative in the leadership of the post-Christian culture. And the third is the failure of our generation's counter culture to demonstrate a credible alternative to either of the other two—Western Christianity and humanism.

The convergence of these three factors in the late sixties marks this period as especially important. What is at stake is nothing less than the direction of Western man. Only a few years ago the dismissal of Christianity was held to be a prerequisite for cultural advance. The decline of Christianity thus represented a cure for man's problems, not a cause. So with the dawning of optimistic humanism the decline of Christianity was welcomed. Its adherents would be the only losers.

But that was yesterday. And contemporary yesterdays have a habit of suddenly seeming a hundred years ago. Today the cultural memory of traditional values hangs precariously like late autumn leaves, and in the new wintry bleakness optimism itself is greying. Now it appears that all of Western culture may be the loser.

My purpose is first to examine humanism, partially as a movement in itself but even more as a backdrop against which to appreciate the need for an alternative; then to chart the alternative offered by the counter culture with all its kaleidescopic variety; and finally, to present a third way as a more viable option in the light of man's current situation. The weaknesses in both humanism and the counter culture are pointed out, not to negate much that has been extremely sensitive and intensely human, but to show the inevitability of their failures. The critique at least serves to illustrate certain mistakes that must not be repeated, and it highlights important questions and dilemmas with which further alternatives must grapple.

A third way is desperately necessary because the present options are growing more obviously unacceptable. And, in fact, there is a Third Way—one which is becoming increasingly welcome to a large number of sensitive searchers and free-spirited individuals who make up a major part of those dissatisfied with things as they are. This Third Way holds the promise of realism without despair, involvement without frustration, hope without romanticism. It combines a concern for humanness with intellectual integrity, a love of truth with a love of beauty, conviction with compassion and deep spirituality. But this is running ahead.

The Rise of Optimistic Humanism

We cannot appreciate the need for the Third Way unless we understand the present crisis of humanism, and this in turn requires a knowledge of its historical background. Sometimes the forerunners of modern humanism are said to be Confucianism and those branches of Buddhism which put an early and distinctive stress on man's responsibility to manage his own life without gods or religion. However, the first milestone on the journey of Western humanism was in the fifth century B.C. in Greece, where for the first time in Europe the use of objective reason freed science and philosophy from the shackles of superstition and religion. The Golden Age of Greece was brief but glorious, and its influence cast a long shadow over the Roman Empire and the classical world. Yet with the advent of Islam and barbarism, except for small pockets of scholars the classical age was swept from the face of Europe.

The Renaissance was the second important milestone on the road to modern humanism, the eruption of the importance of man irreparably severing the intricate unity of the medieval web of life. Along dark, narrow streets appeared light, sunny arcades; beside the impressive heaven-directed Gothic architecture grew humanly scaled towns, buildings, squares and statues; instead of stiff figures and symbolic images, warm, fully-rounded human beings sprang to life on canvas.

The Renaissance was an intoxicating phase of humanism, an explosive confidence of the human mind, the celebration of art, morals, thought and life on an eminently human scale. It was Christendom's twilight toast to the dignity and excellence of man. Making flattering self-comparisons with republican Rome and the Athens of Pericles, the Florentines appointed themselves both executors and heirs of the classical heritage. The scale of Protagoras was to be their scale—"Man is the measure of all things." As Leon Battista Alberti, a typical early Renaissance thinker, expressed it, "A man can do all things if he will."[2]

It was during the Renaissance that the word *humanist* was coined. Initially it only defined a concern for humanity, and many early humanists saw no dichotomy between this and their Christian faith. Yet it was from the Renaissance that modern secular humanism grew, with the development of an important split between reason and religion. This occurred as the church's complacent authority was exposed in two vital areas. In science, Galileo's support of the Copernican revolution upset the church's adherence to the theories of Aristotle, exposing them as false. In theology, the Dutch scholar Erasmus with his new Greek text showed that the Roman Catholic adherence to Jerome's Vulgate was frequently in error. A tiny wedge was thus forced between reason and authority, as both of them were then understood.

It was in fact in a combination of the forward-looking stance of science and the backward-looking glance at classicism (made possible through the new sources, improved texts and fresh interpretations) that the Renaissance found its leading intellectual impetus. Vasari, the Renaissance art historian, asked himself why it was in Florence that men became perfect in the arts and then gave as his first answer: "The spirit of criticism."[3] It was this same spirit of criticism which continued to gather force until it crashed down on Europe in a landslide of unbelief. As the dust settled, the ensuing period was described as the Enlightenment, the eighteenth-century ferment of thought and action which is the third great milestone on the road to modern humanism.

The Enlightenment has its own unmistakable identity, but at the same time it also has an affinity with the Renaissance. Both directly appealed to classical antiquity, deliberately opposed Christianity and consequently accelerated the forces of modernity. But the Enlightenment, with its advantage of distance, could afford to view the Middle Ages through the eyes of the Renaissance, so that there was a detachment and an objectivity impossible for the earlier humanism. If the Renaissance humanists proclaimed a new world, it was because they knew that the old world was irretrievable. But for the men of the Enlightenment the joy of the new world was a result of the triumphs that were predictable from the progress of the scientific intellect. If the legacy of the Renaissance is humanism, then the contribution of the Enlightenment is paganism.

The eighteenth century came in on a wave of irony and satire, exalting the trivial, ridiculing the noble and attacking anything which previous centuries had been taught to believe, revere or love. It was the heyday of the ubiquitous critic, but the chief influence lay not with the popular writers and dramatists (such as Jonathan Swift and Oliver Goldsmith) but with the *philos-*

ophes, the articulate, sociable, secular men of letters who were the heart and soul of the Enlightenment. In 1784, toward the end of the Enlightenment, Kant defined the era as the period of man's emergence from his self-imposed minority. He offered as its motto, *Sapere Aude*! (Dare to know!). It was in the pursuit of this challenge that the powerful combination of British Empiricism and French Rationalism (both extended into the fields of science and political action) changed the face of Europe.

As this occurred, the break between reason and revelation was finalized, and the battle was joined in terms of "Hellene" versus "Hebrew," light versus darkness, reason versus superstition, philosopher versus priest and men of realism versus purveyors of myth. In this battle the impact of the Classical Age was not just antiquarian. The ancients were "signposts to secularism."[4] Across the fog of the Christian centuries, as they saw it, the *philosophes* tried to build a bridge to the Greeks and the Romans. They succeeded in bringing back a great prize—the spirit of criticism. They took pride in the omni-competence of reason, not just because they held reason to be all-powerful, but because they had developed an extreme anti-authoritarian temperament. They asserted their right to use reason to question anything.

As time went on the questions became more far-reaching and the criticisms more uncompromising. In the earlier stages many leading *philosophes* were deists, arguing against theism from a rigid concept of natural law; later on they were atheists, using the arguments of utilitarianism. Within the church, where there was spiritual life it was often inward-looking pietism with no cultural cutting edge, and where there was no spiritual life the bankruptcy was not decently disguised but brazenly advertised by a mixture of internal struggles, bland theologies and dull apologetics. Little wonder that it could be said that for men like David Hume "religion has lost all specificity and authority; it is no more than a dim, meaningless and unwelcome shadow on the face of reason."[5] As the eighteenth century came to a close, all the wisdom and all the wit apparently lay on the side of the Enlightenment. Man was demanding to be recognized as an adult, a responsible being. There is no denying that this was a momentous stage in the journey of the Western mind.

The eighteenth century went out amid wars of revolution and the nineteenth century was ushered in by the campaigns of Napoleon. To the perceptive this was symptomatic of the hidden logic of humanism, but to most men it was only a sign that an age of ideas was ripening into an age of application. Man was not only the measure of the world he knew but the measure of the world of which he dreamed. Relying on its application of reason and science, the nineteenth century could anticipate a rich fund from which to draw its buoyant idealism and robust social enterprise.

If there was any lingering doubt as to whether or not philosophy had transferred its support from theology to humanism, this was finally dispelled for most people when the mechanistic world view of science provided an explanation of the origin and development of the universe. Astronomy and physics had already removed any need for God as a scientific hypothesis, but the turning point came in the nineteenth century when biology added its explanation. Simultaneously the evolutionary theory appeared to demolish Christianity and provide a scientific basis for the philosophy of progress already widely held. Technically, Darwin was not the originator of the idea of evolution but rather the first to give the theory a detailed scientific basis.

The cultural flow at the end of the nineteenth century became a series of whirlpools with many strange currents and cross-currents. From one side of the spectrum of religious thinking came Higher Criticism and liberal theology; from the other side came an extremely reactionary entrenchment within the church. (The Roman Catholics promulgated the dogma of papal infallibility in 1870, while in England Bishop Wilberforce achieved notoriety in his debate with T. H. Huxley.) This period saw the appearance of semi-religions like the Church of Christ, Scientist and the Theosophical Society, and on the secular front it witnessed also the birth of the modern humanist societies.

The Ethical Union was founded in 1896 to federate all the humanist secular societies then in existence. Three years later they launched the Rationalist Press. Both of these remained comparatively small until humanism was popularized in the mid nineteen-fifties. In 1963 they merged to form the British Humanist Association, itself linked with the wider International Humanist and Ethical Union. This marks the fourth milestone on the road to modern optimistic humanism.

Looked at another way, it could be said that after the first slow stage of "cosmic" evolution (inorganic) had come the second stage of "biological" evolution (organic). With the universe "decreated" (Simone Weil), and the West "unchristened" (C. S. Lewis), the third stage, "purposive psycho-social" evolution, could now begin. "We're storming the gates of heaven!" cried German socialist Karl Liebknecht at the end of World War I.[6] He need not have troubled. For most people, heaven had long since been evacuated and Man had come of age. "Man makes himself," said Gordon Childe.[7] "We see the future of man as one of his own making," said H. J. Muller.[8] And Sir Julian Huxley remarked, "Today, in twentieth-century man, the evolutionary process is at last becoming conscious of itself. . . . Human knowledge, worked over by human imagination, is seen as the basis to human understanding and belief, and the ultimate guide to human progress."[9]

If the earlier days of secularism sometimes represented a belligerent all-out anti-God campaign, then Swinburne's "Hymn of Man" ("Glory to Man in the highest! for Man is the master of things") was a typical text—a monumental defiance that was actually a mask for underlying insecurity.[10] Modern humanism is more urbane and self-assured. Typical as a text for this is John F. Kennedy's reputed dictum enlarging on Alberti: "All men's problems were created by man, and can be solved by man." The modern humanist at his best is a man highly educated, deeply aware, tolerant and far-sighted, with clearly defined policies, confident that his philosophy is a relevant way of life and determined to communicate it.

The mid-sixties were the high noon of optimistic humanism. The British Humanist Association, with its distinguished Presidents Sir Julian Huxley and Professor Sir Alfred Ayer and its dazzling intellectual representation, blossomed in public influence and political activity. Around it, the new universities mushroomed like institutional tracts erected on the same beliefs. The crowning proof of man's capability seemed to be the triumph of the moon landing. The gigantic satellite launching towers were hailed by many as technological cathedrals built to the glory of modern man.

As a result, optimistic humanism gained its strength from the confidence that the entire field of human development was now possible within the humanist frame. Julian Huxley claimed that all problems could be solved by humanism and that the whole range of human living could be included within its scope. He predicted that philosophical problems like mind versus matter, social problems like the clash of the two cultures and even international problems such as war would soon be solved. Humanism, he said, would "heal the split between the two sides in the cold war."[11]

Also included was a new concept of religion, distinctively humanist because it was a religion without revelation. In the nineteenth century Auguste Comte had proposed a Religion of Humanity complete with his own suggestion for sacraments, saints and rituals, organized into two thousand churches throughout Europe, with Comte himself the supreme leader. Huxley's version is far less papal and more in line with the urbanity of modern humanism. "Religion of some sort is probably necessary. . . . Instead of worshipping supernatural rulers, it will sanctify the higher manifestations of human nature in art and love, in intellectual comprehension and aspiring adoration."[12] Here is humanism at its highest and most hopeful, attempting to solve all problems and include all human living within its framework, guiding the progress and guarding the evolution of the human race by its own purposive direction.

Time, however, is gradually and cynically stripping this to its essential quaintness. Only the cold-blooded technocrat finds modern war less chilling or its solution nearer. The ideal of human nature "sanctified" in humanist art was already falsified, faltering under the sunken stare of an alienated Giacometti bronze, or strangled by the tortured canvases of Francis Bacon. Evolutionary optimistic humanism is in the process of being betrayed by its own idealism. The humanist artists as its antennae were already into a world which the humanist philosophers and scientists had not yet seen. As with all idealism, its tragedy is the blindness of its heroes; tuned into a world of illusions, they are only too vulnerable to reality.

The Surfacing of Pessimism

Now we can see an important point more clearly. Optimistic humanism was only one stream of secular humanism. Its reverse was pessimistic humanism, and if the optimism was characteristically strong in academic circles, it is now evident that pessimism was more prevalent in the wider reality of life. Pessimistic humanism was always there, like a subterranean stream, murky in its depths and dark in its apprehension of dilemmas. It is this subterranean stream that is now threatening to surface and usurp the dignity and dominance of optimistic humanism.

Again we must go back in history to realize the full importance of this surfacing pessimism. Its genius was to see that behind the apparent stability of the nineteenth-century world in which modern humanism was born stood a different reality. Both Nietzsche and Kirkegaard were men who lived in passionate revolt against the smugness of the nineteenth century, particularly against the cheapness of its religious faith and the brash confidence of its secular reasoning, or generally against its shallow optimism, wordy idealism and tendency to conform. Such a smug world was not just false but dangerously foolish, if the true nature of reality lay elsewhere.

It is amazing that this subterranean pessimism was not taken more seriously earlier. But it was derided as the "Devil's Party"—the poets, philosophers and prophets of chaos and catastrophe—and all too easy to dismiss.[13] Some were ignored. Their repeated warnings were simply relegated to the status of cultural myth having only an innocuous respectability. In 1832 Heinrich Heine had said, "Do you hear the little bell tinkle? Kneel down—one brings the sacraments for a dying God."[14] Nietzsche's later cry of the death of God and his searching diagnosis ("Everything lacks meaning. . . . What does nihilism mean? *That the highest values devaluate themselves.* The goal is lacking; the answer is lacking to our 'Why?' ")[15] were not taken seriously either. After all, wasn't Heine a poet, and wasn't Nietzsche later deranged?

Other warnings were dismissed as only to be expected from the theory or temperament of their particular authors. Repeatedly in the 1930s, George Orwell depicted Western intellectuals as men who in blithe ignorance were sawing off the very branch on which they were sitting. Malcolm Muggeridge in his articles lanced open the "death wish of liberalism." C. S. Lewis carefully made his exposures in "The Funeral of a Great Myth."[16] But the serious disquiet of Orwell, the humorous if testy honesty of Muggeridge and the gentle clarity and utter reasonableness of C. S. Lewis were before their time. They were predictable. They were ignored.

But the rising tide of disquiet cannot now be ignored. It is becoming the accepted mood of much recent judgment, as a hundred illustrations could quickly show. Writing in 1961 specifically on problems of Western culture, Frantz Fanon mocked, "Look at them today, swaying between atomic and spiritual disintegration."[17] In the same context, Jean Paul Sartre challenged, "Let us look at ourselves if we can bear to, and see what is becoming of us. First we must face that unexpected revelation, the striptease of our humanism."[18] These two men could easily be dismissed as pessimistic, prejudiced politically and philosophically, but the disquiet does not stop there. Coming closer to the heart of humanism and speaking almost as an heir to a distinguished humanist house, Aldous Huxley described himself this way: "I was born wandering between two worlds, one dead and the other powerless to be born, and have made in a curious way the worst of both."[19] From the world of science John Rader Platt, the American biophysicist, said, "The world has now become too dangerous for anything less than Utopia."[20] Norman O. Brown, a man famous for the lyrical romanticism of his visions, admitted, "Today even the survival of humanity is a utopian hope."[21]

There can be no stable equilibrium between optimism and pessimism but only an uneasy oscillation between the two. Optimistic humanism is strong in its stress on the aspirations of man but weak in its understanding of his aberrations. Accordingly, it lacks a base for the fulfillment of the former and its solutions to the latter are deficient; thus its ultimate optimism is eternally romantic. Pessimistic humanism, on the other hand, insists on the absurdity of man's aspirations and speaks to the heart of his aberrations, but the price of its realism is the constant pull toward despair. This clear contrast throws further light on the current crisis.

Four Pillars of Optimistic Humanism

Optimistic humanism is being exposed as idealism without sufficient ideals. More accurately, its ideals are impossible to attain without a sufficient basis in truth, and this is just what its rationalistic premises are unable to provide. This is the key weakness of each of the four central pillars of optimistic humanism.

The first pillar is the belief in reason. Here optimistic humanism is forced to its initial leap of faith. It is impossible to prove by reason alone that reason has the validity accorded it by humanism, and the twentieth century has strongly undermined this confidence in two places. Modern psychology has shown that, far from being utterly rational, man has motivations at a deeper level than his reasoning powers, and he is only partially aware of these forces. Much of what was called reasoning is now more properly called rationalizing.

Modern philosophy also has reduced the pretentions of reason. For man, speaking from a finite reference point without divine revelation, to claim to have found a "universal" is not just to be mistaken. The claim itself is meaningless. For most modern men, objectivity, universals or absolutes are in a realm beyond the scope of reason; in this realm there is only the existential, nonrational, subjective understanding of truth.

Both psychology and philosophy have thus clipped the proud wings of rationalism and the unlimited usefulness of reason by itself. By *rationalism* I do not mean "rationalism" as opposed to "empiricism" but rather the hidden premise common to both—the humanist's leap of faith in which the critical faculty of reason is tacitly absolutized and used as a super-tool to marshal particulars and claim meaning which in fact is proper only to the world of universals.

The second pillar is the belief in progress. The orientation toward the future introduced into Western culture by Christian linear teleology was secularized by the Enlightenment. Ostensibly it had been given objective scientific support by the evolutionary theory. It was widely believed that nature was marching forward inevitably to higher and higher views of life (as expressed, for instance, in the philosophy of Herbert Spencer). But this is now being drastically undermined. Many point to evidence of an evolutionary crisis, somewhat tarnishing the comfortable image of inevitable progress with man at the center of the stage controlling his own evolution. Some even predict the extinction of the human species. The details of this we will examine in the next chapter. Here it is sufficient to note that current scientific doom-crying is making inroads into optimism; belief in inevitable progress is not supported by evidence of the past nor corroborated by the present situation and is hardly the united scenario of futurology. This means that optimistic humanism is less and less a belief supported by empirical data. It is becoming more and more an ideology, an idea which is inflated to the status of truth quite beyond the force of evidence.

The third pillar is the belief in science as the guide to human progress and the provider of an alternative to both religion and morals. If "evolution is good," then evolution must be allowed to proceed and the very process of change becomes absolutized. Such a view can be seen in Julian Huxley's *Evolutionary Ethics* or in the writings of Teilhard de Chardin. But in ever more areas, science is reaching the point of "destructive returns"; and the attempt to use evolution as a basis for morals and ethics is a failure. If evolutionary progress is taken as an axiom, then the trend towards convergence (social and evolutionary "unanimization") becomes a value, as suggested by Teilhard de Chardin. But this militates against the value of individuality and can be used to support totalitarianism.[22] Bertrand Russell was typical of a growing majority who admit that science can be no more than neutral and does not speak directly into the area of moral choice.

The fourth pillar is the belief in the self-sufficiency of man. A persistent erosion of man's view of himself is occurring. The fact that man has made so many significant scientific discoveries points strongly to the significance of man, yet the content of these same scientific discoveries underscores his insignificance. Man finds himself dwarfed bodily by the vast stretches of space and belittled temporally by the long reaches of time. Humanists are caught in a strange dilemma. If they affirm the greatness of man, it is only at the expense of ignoring his aberrations. If they regard human aberrations seriously, they have to escape the dilemma raised, either by blaming the situation on God (and how often those most strongly affirming the non-existence of God have a perverse propensity to question his goodness!) or by reducing man to the point of insignificance where his aberrations are no longer a problem. During World War II, Einstein, plagued by the mounting monstrosity of man against man, was heard to mutter to himself, "After all, this is a small star."[23] He escaped the dilemmas of man's crime and evil but only at the price of undermining man's significance. A supreme characteristic of men today is the high degree of dissatisfaction with their own views of themselves. The opposition to determinism is growing not because determinism explains nothing but because it explains too much. It is a clutching constriction on that which man feels himself to be. Arthur Koestler attacks it as "ratomorphic,"[24]

Viktor Frankl as "modern nihilism"[25] and Noam Chomsky as "the flat earth view of man."

Mortimer Adler's *The Difference of Man and the Difference It Makes* is one book which probes deeply in this area and is scrupulously objective in its extensive analysis.[26] He warns that if man continues to recognize no fundamental difference in kind between himself and the world of animals and machines, then his view of himself in terms of his moral dilemma or his metaphysical being must alter irretrievably. Anything left of contemporary concepts of morality and identity will be reduced to the level of the illusory, and the implications for individuals and for civilization are far-reaching.

Thus, in each of these four areas, although optimistic humanism appeals to the highest of man's aspirations, it ignores the full reality of his aberrations. And by contrast, the pessimistic humanism of the existentialist majors on man's aberrations (what it often calls alienations) and allows little place for his aspirations. So the optimist finds himself subscribing to a belief in man which it is increasingly difficult to substantiate. This very irrationality should make it anathema to the rational humanist but the belief cannot be discarded because little would be left of optimistic humanism.

It is a strange but undeniable fact that optimistic humanism appeals generally to a very small sector of society. In the Athens of Pericles it was partly a slave-based population that allowed the intellectuals the time for reflection. In the Italian Renaissance the new ideas were not broadly based and were often restricted to court circles, as at Urbino. During the Enlightenment, philosophers were generally from the privileged if not the aristocratic classes. This characteristic is also perceptible today. An article in the *Humanist Magazine* in 1964 was entitled, "What's Wrong with Humanism?"[27] A long-time humanist complained that modern humanism was "clinically detached from life." He urged, among other suggestions, a special commission to investigate the requirements of humanism as a popular religious movement with its own Bible, hymns and liturgy. To a world outside the rarefied air of academic, scientific circles such beliefs are too often dry and uninspiring. Can any more ironic and fatal accusation be leveled at humanism than the stinging charge that it is not a sufficiently human way of life?

Admittedly it is a value judgment, but it is difficult to avoid the strong suspicion that optimistic humanism gains its high view of man only by quarrying from its Christian cultural heritage. Thomas Huxley is reported to have sung hymns on Sunday nights with his agnostic friends whenever he was feeling his own private melancholy! It is another heavy irony of history that waning Victorian Christianity should have lost the struggle against humanism but succeeded in imposing on its enemies its own smug ethics. Beyond the waning of Christianity's own beliefs these ethics not only lingered but have been elevated into principle.

Borrowing from Christianity a high view of man, optimistic humanism, like idealistic Marxism, is really a Christian heresy. Marxism, whatever it proclaims in propaganda and ideology, betrays the value of man in practice for it elevates the state as an absolute over the individual. Optimistic humanism does the same with its stress on aspirations but silence concerning alienations. But time alone will show whether genuine moral solvency is possible for the humanists or whether they are just living parasitically on past reserves.

If the basis of optimistic humanism is so weak, why wasn't this exposed long ago? The answer to this question lies in the mid-Victorian mood of general self-congratulation into which optimistic humanism was born. A complacent smugness was widely prevalent. This was true of the church; both Roman Catholicism and Protestantism exuded a rare coziness of orthodoxy. It was true also of secular atheism, with its reassuring belief that reason and science were introducing a civilization that would expel all traces of barbarism even from the memory. The twentieth century was anticipated eagerly as the fulfillment of these hopes, and general social stability gave credibility to this myth.

Twentieth-century upheavals have cruelly blown this apart. Hard on the heels of World War I came the Russian Revolution, followed by the Depression and then World War II. With lightning speed the three great European empires of Russia, Germany and Austria disappeared, soon to be followed by the British Empire. With the emergence of communism and the acceleration of modern technology, explosive new forces were unleashed in the modern world. The very fabric of civilization seemed torn apart. It was at times like this, when social eruption forced people to face the logic of their bankrupt base, that people accurately perceived the tenuousness of optimism's brave hold. If they were too optimistic in good times, they tended to be over-pessimistic in dark times, but these latter were the moments of truth.

All of this had been predicted by the Devil's Party. Nietzsche saw modern Europe falling into an abyss, and in the 1880s he prophetically warned of a new Age of Barbarism: "There will be wars such as have never happened on earth."[28] After World War I, a similar point was seized on by Franz Kafka: "The buttresses of human existence are collapsing. Historical development is no longer determined by the individual but by the masses. We are shoved, rushed, swept away. We are the victims of history."[29]

Any powerful social disruption (such as the two world wars) has the effect of tearing away the social fabric and exposing the reality beneath. In the case of Western society, the cancer revealed had already been diagnosed by the pessimistic humanists.

Nonetheless, it has taken this last decade to provide the most sober moment of truth for many optimists. Koestler has described the sixties as the "Age of Climax"[30] and J. R. Platt as the "hinge of history," when momentous issues like the population explosion, the ecological and urban crises, the racial situation and the arms race have been recognized as exponential curves rising sharply. Added to this is the obvious shame arising from the contemptuous dismissal of Western humanism by the Third World. "Leave this Europe where they are never done talking of Man, yet murder men everywhere they find them," Frantz Fanon cries to his fellow Third World revolutionaries, also warning that the United States, "that super-European monstrosity," is a horror in which "the taints, the sickness, and the inhumanity of Europe have grown to appalling dimensions."[31]

If the social disruptions had not come, the stability might have continued longer, but it would have been an Indian summer. They would have come eventually, and there is every indication that disruption is at our elbow daily as this century closes. So the subterranean pessimism, the Devil's Party, surfaces, speaking more prophetically and appealing more popularly in its accurate portrayal of modern anxiety, loneliness, alienation and dread. A description of Thomas Mann could be an epitaph for our era: "He died undecided, hesitating between a desperate optimism and a weary pessimism."[32]

The Striptease of Humanism

This, then, is "the striptease of humanism," a gathering crisis of optimism, an escape from reason, a surfacing of subterranean pessimism. Understanding it as the daily climate of our time, we can now analyze more closely certain features of its arrival and of its permanent residue.

First, there is the strong element of surprise. For any who had read Nietzsche, this should not have been so but in fact it was. In 1929 Freud remarked on this in *Civilization and Its Discontents:* "Man has, as it were, become a prosthetic god. . . . Future ages . . . will increase man's likeness to God still more. But . . . present day man does not feel happy in his Godlike character."[33] In 1951 Camus felt it still more keenly: "During the last century, man cast off the fetters of religion. Hardly was he free, however, when he created new and utterly intolerable chains. . . . The kingdom of grace has been conquered, but the kingdom of justice is crumbling too. Europe is dying of this deception."[34]

The situation is pregnant with irony: There is a crisis of disbelief as well as a crisis of belief. Some religious thinkers may be endlessly reporting the death of God (almost as their contemporary creedal confession), but the fact no longer seems heroic to the perceptive atheist. If the city of God has been razed, who is in need of a home now? Who feels the chill most keenly?

A second feature is the irreversibility of the exposure of humanism. It would be comforting to regard the present pessimism as a cycle, or swing of the pendulum, but there are various reasons why we cannot. For one thing there are new factors which prevent a reversal. Here we come to the difference between Oswald Spengler and Max Weber. Spengler thought the decline of the West was essentially what had happened before. Weber held that what was occurring had never happened before. It was different because, although there were similar symptoms, the "disenchantment of the world" by technology was new. So the situation was irreversible.

Others have pointed beyond these new factors to a certain logical inevitability which flows from the diagnosis of the death of God as a cultural fact. Nietzsche makes this point constantly but especially in his famous parable in *The Gay Science.* A madman enters a market place with a lantern, crying, "I seek God. I seek God."[35] But the busy crowd is unconcerned at his outbursts and laughs at his comical antics. Turning suddenly on them, he demands, "Whither is God? I shall tell you. We have killed him—you and I." But as they ignore the enormity of his announcement, he finally flings his lantern to the ground and cries, "I come too early. My time has not come yet. This tremendous event is still on its way."

The death of God goes far beyond the decline of religious belief. It is as if man has drunk up the sea, sponged away the entire horizon and unchained the earth from the sun. God is dead. God remains dead, and all that for which God was once held responsible must disappear too, and this terrible game is played until the last throw of the dice. In the world without God man is not so much free as overwhelmingly responsible. David Hume had admitted, "I am first affrighted and confounded with that forlorn solitude, in which I am plac'd in my philosophy."[36] Nietzsche's alternative—the will to power—is more appealing, but reality lay nearer to an ominous significance which Sartre later called "total responsibility in total solitude."[37] This was the new definition of man's liberty without God.

The humanists claimed that they could retain Christian values and give them a validity independent of God. But Nietzsche dismissed this as impossible since Christianity was the entire undergirding of all Western civilization, not only of its religious beliefs but also of its social values and its fundamental view of man. He diagnosed, not progress, but a time of decadence whose logic is nihilism. There remains only the void. Man is falling. His dignity is gone. His values are lost. There is no difference between up and down. It has become chilly, and a dark night is closing in. For those who would not face the desperate extremity of the truth now exposed to them, he had nothing but scorn. Nietzsche agreed with Burckhardt in hating the "odious windbags of progressive optimism"[38] and saw only the horror of the abyss. If God is dead and "no new god lies as yet in cradles and swaddling clothes,"[39] there is no alternative except to face the nihilism and then from the ashes of former values and ideals to exercise the will to power which creates the overman.

Some ignore this diagnosis as mere poetry. So perhaps we should look more closely at the issue. Does the death of God really relate, for example, to the rise of totalitarianism? From several different viewpoints it has been cogently argued that modern totalitarianism is closely connected to the death of God and the loss of absolutes.

Nietzsche argued that with God dead and man too weak to live without rules, inevitably the state—The New Idol—will be set up as an arbitrary absolute, forcing men to serve itself rather than God.[40] "God is my word for the ideal," he observed. When equality is confused with conformity and taken to involve the renunciation of initiative, the general levelling leads at best to socialism, and at worst to a totalitarianism perpetuating man's servility in the name of the state instead of God.

Dostoevsky argued only a little differently. In *The Possessed,* his blistering and prophetic exposé of nihilism, Shigalov the revolutionary admits the unfortunate conclusion of his vision of the new society: "I have become entangled in my own data and my conclusions directly contradict my original premises. I started out with the idea of unrestricted freedom and I have arrived at unrestricted despotism."[41] Freedom with no form results in a reaction of form with no freedom. "Shigalov's system" ends up where "one-tenth will be granted individual freedom and full rights over the remaining nine-tenths, who will lose their individuality and become something like a herd of cattle." He would see latter-day twentieth-century socialism, I think, as a secular Tower of Babel held up by strict totalitarian control.

Camus takes a third position, arguing that modern

egalitarianism is the secularization of the soul's original equality before God. "Totality is, in effect, nothing other than the ancient dream of unity common to both believers and rebels, but projected horizontally onto an earth deprived of God."[42]

Despite entirely different premises, these three are each convinced that in the world after the death of God the rise of modern totalitarianism is not accidental or cyclical, but logically inevitable. For Nietzsche, the death of God means that man is disastrously limited. For Dostoevsky, it means that man is disastrously unlimited. For Camus, if God dies so does diversity's place within unity.

Dostoevsky (If God is dead, "everything is permitted")[43] and Nietzsche (". . . the advantage of our times, nothing is true, everything is permitted")[44] were both consistent in seeing the inevitable logic of relativism, but Dostoevsky was the more human. For Nietzsche to be consistent, he needed to become his own superman, but his views were overwhelming even for himself. As he poised over the abyss, he shivered with the horror of being "responsible for everything alive."[45] In the impossibility of this situation, madness perhaps becomes his only possible freedom from the overbearing responsibility. "Alas, grant me madness. . . . By being above the law I am the most outcast of outcasts."[46] All that was left was Nietzsche the exile, branded with the mark of Cain, with "the most painful, the most heartbreaking question, that of the heart which asks itself, where can I feel at home?"[47] From the first step of facing this almost Faustian nihilism he saw no escape and allowed no escape. He scorned Hegel's and Marx's attempts to find some alternative purpose in history and Burckhardt's answer that aesthetics could be the solution. As Erich Heller comments, "Nietzsche to the very end of his insanity spins out the thread of unbelief. In his very spiritual consistency there dwells the madness of desperation."[48]

These elements of surprise and irreversibility were two features of the arrival of the crisis, but of even greater importance are the various symptomatic features of its continuing presence. We shall now examine these. The key to the understanding of each of them is that they stem from the humanist's lack of a basis, the loss of center, the death of absolutes.

Alienation

The first symptom is alienation which occurs when the lack of basis is actually seen, felt or experienced. Whenever a man is not fulfilled by his own view of himself, his society or his environment, then he is at odds with himself and feels estranged, alienated and called in question. Optimistic humanism, lacking sufficient basis for the full range of humanness, also lacks sufficient balance, and alienation is inescapable when this is so. First of all this is true today of metaphysical alienation. Denying the optimistic implications of Darwinism, Nietzsche pointed to man's "ontological predicament": "Man is a rope, tied between beast and overman–a rope over an abyss."[49] Caught between the all-too-human and the superhuman, man, if he is not to despair, must stretch across an unbridgeable chasm to the revalued ideals of the overman. Nietzsche himself felt mocked, even in madness, by this impossible struggle. As all-too-human he knew only anguish, terror, loneliness, desperation, disgust, "the great seasickness" of the world without God.

This last phrase was picked up by Sartre in his first novel *Nausea,* a classic of existentialism. Walking in the city park one day, Roquentin was overcome by the nausea of the meaninglessness of life. Looking around him, he concluded, "Every existent is born without reason, prolongs itself out of weakness and dies by chance."[50] He was forced to the unhappy conclusion that the key to life is its fundamental absurdity. Man as man has to reach towards being God in order to fulfill his aspirations, yet with God dead and the world as it is these aspirations are limitations cast back in his face as an absurdity. Sartre's reluctant conclusion is that "man is a useless passion."[51]

The drastic extremity of this is well portrayed in the drama of Samuel Beckett, whose Parisian home and early research in Marcel Proust's philosophy of time bring him close to the thought world of existentialism. In *Waiting for Godot,* Godot's failure to arrive reduces all of life to the level of irrational absurdity.[52] In *Krapp's Last Tape,* the personality of the old man is completely dessicated by the sequential flow of time shattering his identity into fragments.[53] Beckett's ultimate in economic starkness is *Breath,* thirty seconds in duration, with no actors nor dialogue nor any props on the stage except miscellaneous rubbish; the whole script is the sigh of human life from a baby's cry to a man's last gasp before the grave.

The same metaphysical alienation, expressed in terms of the counter culture, is brilliantly distilled in Yoko Ono's single line poems in *Grapefruit.*[54] All of them are capsules of nihilism, variations on a theme of meaninglessness. "Map Piece" reads, "Draw a map to get lost." Another called "Lighting Piece" runs, "Light a match and watch it till it goes out." These are the poetic counterpoint to *Breath.*

The same sense of alienation can be heard in many expressions of protest chafing at the constricting philosophies and psychologies dominant today. Paul Simon cries out in "Patterns" against the reductionism of determinism that conceives of man as a rat in a cage.[55] Jean Luc Godard says much the same in his film *La Chinoise.*[56] When love is meaningful, to say "I don't love you" is tragic, but when love is reduced to the chemistry of the color of the eye or the preference of the sweater color, to say "I don't love you" is to say almost nothing.

Metaphysical alienation is also seen in the attempt to escape from nihilism through gamesmanship. Whether the games are crass, like the money or success games, or sophisticated and esoteric, like aesthetics or meditation techniques, they are only games created to escape the meaninglessness. Speaking as an artist, Francis Bacon says, "Man now realises that he is an accident, a completely futile being and that he can attempt to beguile himself only for a time. Art has become a game by which man distracts himself."[57]

The heightened tragedy of the contemporary situation is that this is being confirmed, cemented and compounded by a newly felt sociological alienation. This alienation stems partly from the disjointedness of society, but even more from the estrangement induced by a modern technological environment in which men feel unfulfilled, depersonalized, dehumanized and condemned to grow up absurd. Jacques Ellul describes this graphically: "The human being was made to breathe the good air of nature, but what he breathes is an obscure compound of acids and coal tars. He was created for a living environment, but he dwells in a lunar world of stone, cement, asphalt, glass, cast iron and steel. The trees wilt and blanch among sterile and stone facades. Cats and dogs disappear little by little in the city, going the way of the horse. Only rats and men remain to populate a dead world."[58] Man is ill at ease in this environment and the tension demanded of him weighs heavily on his time and nerves, his life and being. If he tries to escape, he is drawn towards an entertainment world of dreams, and if he complies, he falls into a life of crowded, organized routine in which to conform is to feel the malaise of maladjustment.

This alienation, metaphysical and environmental, is an inescapable consequence of humanism and symptomatic of its lack of a basis, making man unfulfillable on the basis of his own views of himself.

Mystification

A second symptom is mystification, the conscious or subconscious masking of the true nature of things. When a man feels his lack of basis, it leads to alienation, and when for all intents and purposes he ignores this and deals with other people on the premise that he has a sufficient basis, it leads to mystification. What is "normal" to him he takes as his "norm," makes it an absolute, judges others who act differently as "abnormal" and treats them accordingly.

Put another way, if there are no universals or absolutes then "normality" is also relative and must be dictated by an arbitrary absolute created either by the state or by the consensus of the population. This is true whether "normality" refers to morality or sanity, badness or madness. One man's "normality" can become an implied or explicit judgment of another man's "abnormality," whether mental or moral. Or, the assertion of one man's "abnormality" may be an assertion of freedom from the other man's "normality." A man's refusal to admit any degree of "abnormality" in himself leads to the process of rationalization required to maintain his "normality" at the expense of the other man's "normality." This process tends to rationalize violence, for men justify their mistreatment of others by considering them as "abnormal" simply because others differ from them.

This has profound implications in our culture. C. S. Lewis warned that in a society where law has objectivity, a man convicted under law can serve his sentence in jail and then demand to be released on the basis of the same law by which he was convicted. But if a man is judged to be "sick," he must serve his time, waiting until the man in a white coat discharges him. Yet, if it was this very man who committed him and "sickness" is not objectively determined, to whom does he appeal?

Lewis's warning is timely in the light of the Soviet custom of placing political prisoners not in a prison but in Ward 7, an asylum. This is dramatically highlighted in the current case of Zhores Medvedev, a brilliant Soviet geneticist, already famous for his book on T. D. Lysenko. (His exposé of the story of the elevation of Lysenko's erroneous genetic theories into unassailable dogma under Stalin is a fascinating example of "mystification" even in objective science.) Fired from his job for this book, Medvedev was unable to find work and so occupied himself writing a book on Russian censorship. For his pains, he found himself hospitalized and later registered as an outpatient with "paranoid delusions of reforming society." In his latest book, *A Question of Madness*,[59] he expresses his fear of a new Soviet repression by means of "psychoadaptation" and concludes, "If things go on like this, it will end with healthy, sane people sitting in madhouses while dangerous mental cases will walk about freely."[60] *Time* magazine reports the recent statement of a leading Soviet forensic expert: "Why bother with political trials when we have psychiatric clinics?"[61]

C. S. Lewis's general warning and the Russian practice are both easy to see, but the problem cannot be held at arm's length. There is no country which is not prone to mystification. An example from the United States is thought-provoking. If there is no mystification, then by what norm or definition of legal "justice" can a man who was openly convicted by his peers for the crime of wiping out almost a whole Asian village, including children, be allowed to live in near freedom with presidential favor, whereas a man of intense religious and moral convictions, convicted only of pouring dove's blood on state papers, was harshly sentenced? Some will consider the contrast between William Calley and Daniel Berrigan too extreme, but it throws searching light on contemporary American definitions of "normality." The United States of 1776 was a revolutionary force in a revolutionary age, whereas the United States of 1972 is a counter-revolutionary force in a revolutionary age. How can this be, when most Americans consider their contemporary concepts of freedom identical to those of the American Revolution? Both the concept and its basis have profoundly changed, but this is not recognized in public statements or by public leaders. "Tell me," Ho Chi Minh would ask American visitors, "Is the Statue of Liberty still standing? Sometimes it seems to me it must be standing on its head."[62]

The reverse side of mystification is the parallel idea that at a certain point "abnormality," whether badness or madness, can be the assertion of freedom from definitions of "normality." Dostoevsky's *The Idiot* could easily be subtitled "the mystification of Myshkin." The prince's saint-like innocence is abnormal in a society of wealth, power and egoism. Society calls him an idiot, but in his innocence he muses, "But can I be an idiot now, when I am able to see for myself that people look upon me as an idiot? As I come in, I think, 'I see they look upon me as an idiot, and yet I am sensible and they don't guess it.' . . . I often have that thought."[63] The prince's tragedy is that he was unable to bear the weight of that maladjusted innocence.

Antonin Artaud of the Theatre of Cruelty wrote to a friend, "I am not entirely myself." But the society of his day would not accept his difference and gave him a drastic series of electrical shock treatments, reducing him to comfortable conformity. Jerzy Grotowski later commented, "Artaud's misfortune is that his sickness, paranoia, differed from the sickness of the times . . . Society couldn't allow Artaud to be ill in a different way."[64] How many thousands who have received such electrical shock treatment are similar victims of mystification? Some, like the early Beats, have responded by holding that lunacy itself may be good therapy. In "The Time of the Geek" Jack Kerouac wrote, "Can't you sense what's going on around you? All the neurosis and the restricted morality and the scatological repressions and the suppressed aggressiveness has finally gained the upper hand on humanity." If what is regarded by previously objective standards as "abnormal" is taken to be normal, then to be "abnormal" by these new standards is to be normal. Erich Fromm, for example, speaks of "the pathology of normalcy,"[65] and R. D. Laing has made this a central feature in his psychology. Examining the rooted alienation evident in personality, family and society, he sees the schizophrenic as the man who is made into a scapegoat. When an alienated man, family or society finds a scapegoat, its treatment of him acts as a lightning rod to alleviate their own abnormality, for that abnormality is projected onto the scapegoat.

The schizophrenic is a man torn between the inner and outer worlds, between his experience and his behavior, between his mind and his body, but this alienation is different from other men's only in degree, not in kind. All are in fact alienated. The difference is that the less alienated are considered sane and the more alienated insane. "The 'normally' alienated person, by reason of the fact that he acts more or less like everyone else, is taken to be sane. Other forms of alienation are those that are labeled by the normal majority as bad or mad."[66] Again we have the rationalized maintenance of a psychological normality that leads on to the mystification of violence, whether in the family situation (where the father can never be wrong) or in international relations. On the basis of relativism, can a "just war" be other than a justified war? Laing concludes, "Normal men have killed perhaps 100,000,000 of their fellow normal men in the last fifty years."[67]

Black comedy majors in the same insight. The world

 is not necessarily metaphysically absurd, but the way men live normally has a fundamental absurdity which is masked from them by their complacent acceptance of the normal. William Burrough's *Naked Lunch,* for example, is a sick joke used as a weapon against society and human existence itself. But John Barth's *Sot Weed Factor* and Joseph Heller's *Catch-22* are parodies whose malicious humor exposes the inner contradictions and paradoxes involved in social normality. The same is true of much of the humor in famous radio programs like the BBC's *The Goon Show.*

What should follow this realization that mystification is so prevalent is "demystification," an honest admission of one's own guilt, a confession and a change of heart. But without genuine catharsis, it is impossible for a man to own up to his guilt. And modern man has nothing to precipitate catharsis. Too often the demystification of violence leads to the rationalization of a newly mystified counter-violence. This is the lesson of many radical speeches, such as those in the celebrated congress on the "Dialectics of Liberation."[68]

Romanticism

The third symptom of the continuing crisis of humanism is romanticism, which begins by aspiring towards an ideal but never reaches it because a sufficient basis is lacking. From its zenith, romanticism spirals downward towards frustration and despair—Icarus encore. This feature should hardly require further illustration. It is the lesson of this chapter and a summary of much of the counter culture. But it is a lesson rarely learned. With his memories of Eden, man is never at rest east of Eden, and he repeatedly throws himself on the flaming, drawn sword of the angel. Illustrations of this can be seen in various periods in this century.

Contemporary society, for example, meets death by escaping into romanticism. It was once a common idea that when the Christian views of death, dying and the afterlife were removed, there could be a new, free, pragmatic, almost casual approach to death, one releasing man from the fear of non-being. The reverse is the case, partially because of the aggravation of twentieth-century social problems and the addition of the Eastern concept of reincarnation, but especially because men cannot escape the fear of non-being. Secular man now has an even greater fear of death and non-being. The gross commercialization of grief and dying is only the flip side of the fear of death; the fear is hiding itself in an extreme romanticism, laying men open to manipulation. Forest Lawn in Los Angeles is its supreme expression; Evelyn Waugh's *The Loved One* is its exposure. The irony is striking: Twentieth-century man has constantly mocked the Victorians for treating sex and the origins of life as taboo; now he himself views death and the end of life as taboo. Death is the twentieth-century pornography which no freedom from censorship can remove!

Various periods of social history also unravel the running thread of romanticism. The United States in the 1920s was the world of F. Scott Fitzgerald's jazz America; youth was prominent, skirts were short, dances were frenzied and everyone lived on an overwhelming sense of unprecedented newness. This romanticism then spiraled dizzily downwards at the Depression.

At the same time, European intellectuals were surpassing this romanticism in their enthusiastic welcome to the new Soviet regime. Early reactions were extravagantly exuberant, as if no lessons had been learned from the betrayal of the French Revolution. From the earlier socialists and liberals to Sartre's refusal to accept the evidence of the Stalinist extermination camps, it was the same story—romanticism. Malcolm Muggeridge described the stream of early Western tourists in Russia: "They were hilarious—clergymen reverently walking through anti-God museums, Quakers smiling radiantly as they were told that in the USSR capital punishment had been abolished, liberals overjoyed to learn that what amounted to proportional representation had been developed."[69] History, of course, has shown where reality lay, and now few would disagree with Muggeridge that it was "a compilation of folly probably unequaled in human history."[70]

England in the fifties and early sixties is a further illustration. Christopher Booker's *The Neophiliacs* diagnoses this period as one suffering from a psychic epidemic, a fantasy syndrome by which men chased a dream which led them further and further from reality; then the dream shattered into a nightmare with "an explosion into reality."[71] The fifties were the dawn of the new Britain, with its New Morality, its New Wave films, its New Theology and its swinging London, classless, vital, superb, professional. But the new Britain was only an image conjured up by the image industry with pop singers, interior decorators, designers, magazine editors and especially the baneful, omnipresent camera. Used by David Bailey or Richard Avedon, the camera was the magic lamp rubbed to produce a genie-like generation chasing "the magic bubble of up-to-dateness."[72] Booker charts this sorry story up to 1963 and the explosion into reality. Behind it all was dust.

The United States in the sixties was the same. The court chronicler of this world was Tom Wolfe, and the romanticism was identical, extravagant, brilliant but hollow. Wolfe captured it in his book *Kandy-Kolored Tangerine-Flake Streamline Baby,* a culture which made Las Vegas its Versailles, where buildings were constructed to fit the neon signs, rather than the signs to fit the buildings. The hollowness was probed by Bob Dylan's rasping early songs (such as "Desolation Row"), sharply persistent like a tongue in a decaying tooth.

History is strewn with the wrecks of romanticism.

Booker explains such romanticism as due to "the dismissal of rational consideration of the realization of the power and nature of evil."[73] Without due regard to man's aberrations (his alienations), the positive aspirations of man are constantly doomed to spiral downward. Based on a half truth, romanticism can achieve no balance.

The Twilight of Western Thought

Rationalism and optimistic humanism have thus turned out badly, and so has the entire Western culture. The striptease of humanism marks the twilight of Western thought which is exposed as a mass of tortuous, twisted tensions, contradictions, oscillations, polarizations–all stemming from the alienations of men who can explain neither themselves nor their universe.

The concept of alienation is often traced from Rousseau in politics, to Hegel in philosophy, to the early Marx in sociology, to the various modern prophets of existentialism. The full story is more complicated than this, of course, but what is interesting is that in the various analyses of alienation (such as Albert Camus' book *The Rebel,* Ernst Fischer's book *The Necessity of Art*[74] or Lewis Feuer's article "What Is Alienation?"[75]) no one achieves a final resolution, either intellectual or practical. One man's answer becomes the next man's problem and the search is thus endless.

The best Christian critiques of alienation have always shown the inevitability of this dis-ease. The first Western man to speak of alienation was not Rousseau, as Fischer claims,[76] nor Hegel, as Fromm suggests.[77] It was Augustine and then Calvin who used the concept of allienation to emphasize that the problem of sin or evil was not just theological but relational–a breach of man's relationship with God entailing a breach of all other relationships. The alienation of evil is theological, between God and man; sociological, between man and other men;

psychological, between man and himself; and ecological, between man and nature. The far-reaching implications of this insight have been developed in two contemporary Christian critiques, both of which center on the presuppositional weakness of humanism which leads to the present impasse.

Hermann Dooyeweerd in Holland surveys philosophy from the pre-Socratic Greeks down through scholasticism to modern humanism.[78] In all these developments of humanism he exposes the essentially religious presuppositions which succeed only by making a particular (such as reason) into a universal or an absolute. If pressed, their dilemma leads to an impossible choice between the tendency towards positivism (the practical acceptance of all perception as substantial because only in this way can perceiving man make sense) and the tendency towards scepticism (the total relativism of radical doubt).

Francis Schaeffer also shows the same impasse as it develops from the incipient humanism of Thomas Aquinas through Hegel, Kant and Kierkegaard to modern man.[79] When reason is made an absolute rather than a tool, rationalism is stretched to the breaking point and is pulled over "the line of despair," creating a basic dichotomy, a two-tiered view of truth, an "escape from reason."

In his preface to Dooyeweerd's *Twilight of Western Thought,* J. R. Rushdoony illustrates the oscillation between positivism and scepticism by citing Metrodorus of Chios, a fourth-century Greek philosopher. Metrodorus affirmed that there were only two things that man could know: "None of us knows anything, not even when we know or do not know, nor do we know whether knowing and not knowing exist, nor in general whether there is anything or not."[80] Yet "everything exists which anyone perceives." The contrast between Professor A. J. Ayer's positivism in *Language, Truth and Logic* in 1936 and the concluding scepticism of his John Dewey Memorial Lectures in 1970 is modern confirmation of the same dilemma.

Camus could not escape it either: "I proclaim that I believe in nothing and that everything is absurd, but I cannot doubt the validity of my own proclamation, and I am compelled to believe, at least in my own protest. . . . Hence it is absolutely necessary that rebellion derives its justifications from itself, since it has nothing else to derive them from."[81] Knowing that as an existentialist he has no base for his values in positivism, he fights against the alternative of scepticism by making rebellion into an absolute.

It is certainly understandable that both optimistic humanism and existentialism rejected the smug Christianity of their day. But humanism is now equally smug and existentialism has elevated despair from a moment to a way of life. There is almost a perverse refusal to reconsider historic Christianity which once produced the answers to these very dilemmas and still offers the sharpest contemporary critique. Nietzsche at least was courageous in facing nihilism squarely. He was impatient with Burckhardt because he felt that Burckhardt knew the desperate truth but constantly avoided it. Writing once of Burckhardt's lectures, he described "their profound thoughts, and their silently abrupt breaks and twists as soon as they touch the danger point."[82]

Modern humanism also refuses to touch the danger points, to face the logic of its own premises. It prefers to live in intellectual inconsistency. In *The Disinherited Mind* Erich Heller says, "In Kafka we have before us the modern mind, seemingly self-sufficient, intelligent, sceptical, ironical, splendidly trained for the great game of pretending that the world it comprehends in sterilized sobriety is the only and ultimate reality there is—yet a mind living in sin with the soul of Abraham. Thus he knows two things at once, and both with equal assurance; that there *is* no God, and that there *must* be God."[83]

Kafka was not unique. Nietzsche himself, for all his scorn, made his leap of faith. He asserts that any attempt to understand the universe is prompted by man's will to power but fails to see that his own conception of the will to power must then be admitted by him to be a creation of his will to power. What to Kafka was a weakness is now a disease of almost epidemic proportions. Erich Fromm ponders, "In the nineteenth century the problem was that God is dead, in the twentieth century the problem is that man is dead,"[84] but Fromm shies away from exploring the connection between the two. R. D. Laing poses the alternative, "Deus absconditus. Or we have absconded,"[85] but his vision of the divine is Eastern, not Christian, and his use of Luther's concept is merely rhetorical.

Thus optimistic humanism is currently in the throes of a gathering crisis. But we dare not let this negate the humanness of its ideals. What is needed is a stronger humanism, not a weaker one. We need a concern for humanness that has a basis for its ideals and the possibility of their substantial realization.

There are several requirements which any contending solution must satisfy. First, it must provide a basis that will define and demonstrate the individuality of man as human. Here the Eastern conceptions of man with their essential negation of the value of man in this life, the communist subordination of the individual to the state, and the post-Christian failure of Western man to resist the trends of dehumanization point to answers which do not satisfy this first requirement.

Second, it must provide a basis for the fulfillment of an individual's aspirations. The Eastern religions, communism and humanism again fall short for similar reasons. So also do determinism and existentialism.

Third, it must provide a basis for the substantial healing of man's alienations in terms of an individual's becoming more fully himself. Many views falter here.

Fourth, it must provide a basis for community, combining social unity and diversity, and it must avoid the chaos of relativism or the swing to control seen in many modern states and intentional communes.

These together must provide a basis for defining and demonstrating a humanness sufficiently robust to be an anchor against the dehumanization coming from social disruption and the fear of global destruction.

A Third Way is obviously required—one which speaks to the basic situation of humanity, both in individuality and in community. It must provide an answer to existentialism and a fulfillment to optimistic humanism. But this is still to run ahead of ourselves.

With the erosion of the Christian culture and the crisis of humanism, the direction of Western culture is uncertain. Will we see a desperate vacuum from which nihilism will rise? Will we lurch on uneasily to a new technological barbarism? Will a novel mysticism turn the West into the East? Or will the slow disintegration of Western culture herald a decline of power, until the egoism of Western culture is judged by the hammer of the Soviets?

Only the future will show. Curiously, the recent preoccupation with "the end of ideology" has given rise to a new ideology—futurology. Here evolutionary optimistic humanism has its last chance. If, searching into his future, man finds grounds for believing in himself and his ability to control his future, then secular humanism may become solvent again. This quest forms the story of our next chapter.

2/Utopia or Oblivion?

"Confident articles on the
future seem to me, intellectually, the most disreputable
of all forms of public
utterance."
Kenneth Clark

"Trust the evolutionary
process. It's all going to work
out all right."
Timothy Leary

"Everything that formerly
made for war now makes for
peace."
Teilhard de Chardin

"Current indications are that
the world is bent on going
to hell in a hand cart, and that
is probably what it will do."
Gordon Rattray Taylor

"You are the orphans in an
age of no tomorrows."
Joan Baez

"Today even the survival
of humanity is a utopian hope."
Norman O. Brown

"The Titanic sails at dawn."
Bob Dylan[1]

"To prophesy is extremely difficult, especially with respect to the future." The exquisite irony of this Chinese proverb is counterbalanced only by the pressing urgency of the question itself: What does the future hold for modern man? Futurology is a fascinating and exploding new study, sometimes called the "foresight saga" or a series of "guesstimates." It is no longer the preserve of dreamers, visionaries, poets and science-fiction writers but the serious concern of government departments, scenario scientists and think-tanks. Soon it will be a new academic industry. Major speeches have a habit of including ritual references to "the challenge of change," and Margaret Mead suggests that soon every university will have its Chair of the Future.

The question of the future is of far more than academic significance. The tangled threads of current problems trail into the future, which alone appears to hold the key or perhaps the confession that there is no key.

The Importance of Futurology

The rise of futurology cannot be seen apart from the end of ideology. Those who have participated in or accepted the death of traditional ideology have elevated futurology into an ideology all on its own. For our purposes in this chapter, futurology is important for three reasons. First, in the wake of the problems represented in the "striptease of humanism," it has become a crucial testing ground for many current philosophies. Often it is only as we examine a man's view of himself in the future that we discover the Achilles heel of an otherwise impregnable opinion. Some, like the old-fashioned optimistic humanists, see no drastic problems now, but as they look into the future the darkening cloud of problems casts shadows over their optimism. Others, like the idealistic anarchists, see desperate problems now but place all their eggs in the basket of tomorrow, pinning their faith on the triumph of human progress. So the question "utopia or oblivion?" is more than an intellectual curiosity. It is finally a life-or-death issue for millions, crucially affecting modern man's view of himself. The question is, which of the two is the more likely? And which side has more evidence and closer reasoning supporting it?

Second, the issue is important in relation to the Christian view of man, society and the course of history, for, if the optimist is correct in predicting an attainable utopia, then the Bible must either be judiciously jettisoned or drastically demythologized. But if in fact history aligns itself with biblical projections, the Bible must be treated more seriously.

A third reason futurology is important is the fact that, whichever way the future goes, there will be areas in which each responsible citizen will be called upon to fight the general dehumanization. For example, it might be necessary for him to stand against the threat of totalitarianism, or to raise specific moral and ethical questions in the name of humanness and freedom. We must understand these issues now in order to take an intelligent and courageous stand later. In a fast-moving society, the man of principle cannot afford to enter the debate thinking out loud.

Despite these reasons there are grave dangers in overemphasizing futurology. The end of any millenium is characteristically charged with the excitement of chiliasm, the idea that Christ will reign on earth for a thousand years. The years before A.D. 2000 are no exception; in fact, peculiar temptations are rife in such a climate. The man whose cherished dreams are unlikely to be adopted this side of the Last Days may be forgiven if he hears with mixed emotions the beating of the apocalyptic hooves. But it is inexcusable if the doomcriers of pop futurism tend only to make otherwise intolerable options more tolerable through the shrill and hasty insistence of their warnings.

Constructing a Scenario

The basic aim of futurology is to ascertain the "futuribles," a word coined by Bertrand de Jouvenel.[2] Using a bottom line representing the "unchangeables" and an upper line representing the "unachievables," Jouvenel sets out to chart a graph of the human possibilities. In this graph there are three areas. The "possible" is the realm of the artist; the "probable" the realm of the scientist; and the "preferable" and "practicable" the realm of the politician.

In *The Year 2000,* Herman Kahn and Anthony Weiner offer as scenarios what they call "surprise-free quantitative projections."[3] But most futurologists would admit that there is a perilous instability to all projections and that there can be no verification for any of them at the present moment. You either believe them or you do not. After all, historians have enough problems attempting to agree about the past—which did happen. So the elusiveness of the future should be no surprise.

Alvin Toffler compares futurology to map-making in the ancient world: There is little final relationship between the initial map and the country discovered. Nonetheless, though the map is usually in error, it is a very useful guide to getting there. Similarly, the future may be entirely different from the scenarios projected today, but the scenarios are useful as intellectual or sociological shoehorns easing us through the problems and into the time they project. Yet Desmond King-Hele is only honest when he admits that living with these projections is "rather like having to balance blindfold on an endless-belt moving tightrope with knots to represent recurrent crises."[4]

One must appreciate the hazardous problems and difficulties of making any scenario and so approach them all with an understanding humility. A word of warning is necessary here: It is vital to examine the presuppositions of any particular forecaster because they often precondition the whole tone and standard of what he writes. Desmond King-Hele's book *The End of the Twentieth Century* is a brilliant example of the beguiling effects of this. He begins by saying we should all be wary of technological forecasters for very often their commercial interests preclude them from predictions that would outrage their backers. He states this warning with commendable strength but then proceeds to supply a parallel example, his own philosophical and psychological preferences taking the place of commercial interests. The definite and obvious presuppositions running through his book condition even his presentation and layout. On the first page he says, "The logical answer to the question 'Has man a future?' is 'Probably not'; or, to be more accurate, 'Man has many possible futures, but the most likely ones are disastrous.' "[5] So he begins with a disarming frankness and unusual honesty, but then goes on to say that he cannot be morbid: "So, in much of this book, I shall display the blind optimism so typical of our species, and assume that, however dismal the omens, we shall somehow avoid the perils ahead and muddle through to the end of the century."[6] Continuing this engaging openness, he confesses that this optimistic attitude will profoundly affect his whole method of treatment. "Disaster is then all too likely, but since most people 'cannot bear very much reality', I have squeezed all the catastrophes into Chapter 2, keeping horrors to a minimum."[7]

Not all futurologists reveal their presuppositions so openly. But if we are not to be misled we need to discover what those presuppositions are. Futurology, like all philosophy, needs to be examined in the light of its premises. All intellectual presuppositions, commercial vested interests and emotional preferences must be unmasked for an objective evaluation of their worth and solidity. Otherwise any optimism may be a fool's paradise and any achievement only a house of cards.

An instructive place to begin is to compare past and present visions of the future. Arthur Clarke has often said that the future can best be imagined today by those most familiar with the visions of the past. A quick survey of many of these former utopias shows a striking difference between them and their counterparts in the twentieth century. In 1516, Thomas More wrote his *Utopia,* depicting an island with fifty-four well designed towns, each with 6,000 households, and communities that were communist in organization, spartan in their ideals and war-hating in their values; there were gardens for every house and euthanasia for the decrepit. In 1872, Samuel Butler wrote *Erewhon,* foreseeing a land where people had risen up against machines and destroyed them. In 1891, William Morris wrote his *News from Nowhere,* the story of a rural paradise set in the year A.D. 2012. These three are representative of the many optimistic utopian projections of past generations.

The difference between them and modern projections can be conveyed in a quick listing of some modern titles: Aldous Huxley's *Brave New World* and *Island*; George Orwell's *1984*; Ray Bradbury's *Fahrenheit 451*; C. S. Lewis's *That Hideous Strength*; Neville Shute's *On the Beach*; William Golding's *Lord of the Flies*; B. F. Skinner's *Walden Two*. Except for *Walden Two*, they are predominantly pessimistic. Technically, they are not utopias so much as dystopias or anti-utopias, and they cut so deeply into the vein of what Arnold Toynbee calls the modern "failure of nerve" that Toffler complains that today we lack the kind of utopian writers whose predictions can be antennae into the future. Thus Toffler advocates the setting up of utopia factories.

The difference between the extremes of optimism and pessimism is increasingly symbolized by two dates. The year 1984 is eloquent in its connotations of apprehensive foreboding, while the year 2000 is fast becoming a shorthand sign for progressive confidence and

printed words. But of them all the most crucial is our lifetime—the 800th. This one lifetime is the center of history with as much happening in it as in all the previous lifetimes put together.[8]

Sir George Thomson, the British physicist and Nobel Prize winner, compares the importance of our age with the invention of agriculture in neolithic times. Herbert Read felt the difference between our age and previous ages is equivalent to the difference between the old and new stone ages.[9] In any case, most agree that time is speeding up and, just as water changes to steam, history is becoming volatile.

These broad contours can be followed through in the four important areas of planetary engineering, global engineering, biological engineering and sociological change.

Planetary, Global and Biological Engineering

Planetary engineering is the first, but for our purposes the least important, of the four. Will there be lunar bases by 1975? Will there be air-conditioned lunar settlements by the year 2000? Will man soon discover an alternative to rocket propulsion, and thus rapidly accelerate space discovery? Will space travelers soon travel in a regulated coma? Could we have cyborg-manned space crews? Is it feasible to make Mars and Venus habitable? Is it possible to dismantle and rebuild Jupiter? Such questions are endless and are far from science-fiction fantasies. They raise questions for the psychology of man as he bores out into space, and demand that we count the cost of such programs in the light of the festering problems still to be tackled on earth. But for our purposes they are less crucial than the more profound human questions in other areas.

The second area is global engineering. How will future communications change and shape the life of man and expand or limit his power? What is predicted is nothing less than the availability of instant, total information. This will depend on each progressive country's possessing a belt of satellites circling the world, a national grid of computer data banks, and within individual homes what could be called the "World Box"—a highly advanced ceiling-to-floor television screen conveying the benefits and amenities now available through television, shopping guides, public libraries, cinemas, newspapers, encyclopedias and university courses. This would convey instant, total information but it would also mean that the state (including the police force) would have available instant, total information on each private citizen. Such progress is thus double-edged!

Further, what will be the results of the coming aquaculture, the exploration of the inner space of the oceans? With two-thirds of the earth under water, we may soon see underwater mining and farming and, perhaps, even whole colonies. Some predict the possibility of "gillhouses" and "gillmen" in the next few years. Immediately this raises the question of who owns the wealth of the oceans. Will it go to the United Nations? Will it go to the nearest nation? Or will there be a Yukon-like underwater gold rush in the near future?

The possibility of increased weather control raises further questions. If man succeeds in seeding clouds and tornadoes, dispersing fogs and using satellite mirrors to concentrate heat, will this bring about ecological imbalance? Doesn't weather control offer new weapons of war? A novel by Theodore Thomas, *The Weathermen,* foresees the world being run by a Weather Council using weather disaster as a political sanction. Even Toffler admits, "Unless wielded with extreme care, however, the gift of weather control can prove man's undoing."[10]

Topographical change is another important aspect of global engineering. Should the Russians be allowed to put into effect their plan to melt the ice cap by damming the Bering Strait? If a dam were built and cold Arctic water pumped out, the warmer Atlantic water would flow back and in three years much of the Arctic ice would melt so that the Arctic temperature would rise eight degrees centigrade. All the present permafrost ground in Russia and Canada could easily become grazing land of immense commercial profit. But would there be unforeseen imbalances? Would Britain be warmer or the United States too hot or the Malaysian rubber industry wiped out because the northern Pacific became colder? What if the sea level rose higher than the projected four inches? Twenty feet would be enough to flood the entire cities of New York and London, and if by chance the Antarctic ice melted completely, the world sea level would rise by 400 feet.[11] Whether each of these sounds probable or improbable, each must be seriously considered because, should they materialize, they would affect large sectors of human society, and the implications would be extremely important.

The third area is biological engineering, which Nigel Calder describes as the "most radical of all technologies."[12] Here we meet a host of questions. Quantitative change is already a feature of modern living, and soon we could have improved self-realization and mood control through drugs or electrodes. Human intelligence will be speeded up through drugs or fetal oxygenation; children already treated this way show precocious ability. Sleep and dreaming too could be controlled, and the human life span possibly lengthened, though even an average extension of fifty years would aggravate the population crisis. Of course, arbitrary limitations as to when life should end smack of authoritarian control.

The real question will not be quantitative change but qualitative change through genetic control. For the first time the human body will no longer be a fixed given. Cloning, the creation of biological carbon copies of human cells and new organisms from the nuclei of adult cells, may be possible within fifteen years. Some prognosticators speak of the possibility of frozen embryos. A woman could buy an embryo free of genetic defect, with guaranteed sex, and choice of eye color, hair color and IQ range. This could then be implanted by her doctor. Others promise the possibility of birth without human pregnancy. The human embryo could be carried within a cow for nine months, thus avoiding the "nuisance" of pregnancy. To most this is still a morally distasteful idea, but to several of the more liberated Women's Lib advocates it is already a cardinal tenet of hope.

What of the possibility of machine-men symbiosis? Will there be cyborgs, disembodied human brains in robot bodies? Or humanoid machines indistinguishable from men? Various suggestions here range from the eminently practical to the bizarre and extraordinary. Dr. E. S. E. Hafez of Washington State University suggests shipping fertilized human eggs to the planets so that a whole city population could be sent in a shoebox. J. B. S. Haldane suggests man should be adapted biologically for extra-territorial conquest. Professor H. D. Block of Cornell University claims that man-machine sex relationships will be practicable and desirable very soon. Gordon Rattray Taylor warns that a paranoid dictator could keep his brain alive in a bulletproof robot body. The projections are a veritable breeding ground of fantasies and fears. Should we propose a breed of smaller men? Will there be sons born a hundred years after their father's death? If we can create carbon copies of an Einstein, a Stravinsky, a Picasso, who is to prevent the duplication of a Hitler or a Stalin?[13] Who is to choose? On what basis will they choose? What is the criterion of "humanness"? Is there a difference to man, and does it make any difference? The answer to these questions is beyond the reach of post-Christian humanism. Even standing on its tiptoes it cannot reach, let alone untie, this suspended Damoclean sword.

Sociological Change

The fourth area is sociological change in which various familiar features of contemporary society will be altered beyond recognition. Work as we now know it will no longer be the basis of society, nor will the service industries hold their present importance. The importance of the transference of information will be supreme. This will mean a shift from the blue collar to white collar workers, the rise of mass leisure and the ascendant importance of education as an industry.

Art and aesthetics are also likely to change. Sir Herbert Read, contributing to *The World in 1984* (Part II), predicted that art and literature as we now know them may have died out by 1984. Sir Herbert may well be right, though others suggest that the trend of aesthetics in the future will be the attempted simulation of human experience by so called "experience makers." Even production will be psychologized. Some initial hints of this trend are already evident. London's Oxford Street is changing its face. On the way out are the old large superstores, and in their place are coming the small boutiques, with an almost medieval intimacy, variety and involvement in color and sound. The traditional decor of many London pubs is changing, for example, to a living simulation of a ship complete with detailed design and authenticity. New York's Cerebrum describes itself as an "electronic studio of participation."[14] Pleasure Palaces of the future, described by Toffler, will simulate human experience and combine the pleasures of Disneyland, a World's Fair, Cape Kennedy, Mayo Clinic and Macao honky-tonk all rolled into one. All this "psychologization" of environments and entertainments will be a new "mood engineering." Its constant simulation of varied experience to ensure human happiness is not only abysmally shortsighted in its crassly materialistic values but also remarkably reminiscent of Brave New World.

The present position of the family will be lost irrevocably. In the past this institution has been a basic transmitter of social values as well as society's giant shock absorber in times of rapid change. Along with the disappearance of the family as we know it will go its beneficial results. If parents can go into a babytorium and select the embryo of their choice, there is bound to be a loss of the mystique of motherhood. And if pregnancy is bypassed, the very strength of motherhood will be sapped. If embryos are conceived by other parents or by multi-parents, parenthood too will be revised. And if embryos are purchased, who are their parents? Could a corporation buy and "own" them?

Furthermore, the family will be streamlined to its most basic components. A Victorian household was often a family with two parents, eight, nine, ten or eleven children, a maiden aunt who helped to care for the children and possibly the grandparents on both sides, all living in the same house. This is described today as a "child-cluttered" family. A family of the future will be down to the basic unit of husband and wife, perhaps with children only after retirement. Professional parents could replace biological parents, the latter becoming scorned as the "greatest single preserve of the amateur."

In place of the family will come communes of all kinds (religious, political, geriatric) and an increase in single unmarried adults' having children, homosexual marriages with children and the legalization of brother-sister marriages. Polygamy too may be practiced again. The essential feature of the marriage relationship will be its impermanence: There will be temporary, serial, trial marriages where the stage in life (and not age) is the vital thing. In his 1946 foreword to *Brave New World* (1932) Aldous Huxley predicted that marriage licenses would be sold like dog licenses, good for twelve months and as many as you like at one time.[15]

The Christian conception of marriage will not just be considered mistaken but dismissed as meaningless. It will become as novel as Christian morality in pagan Rome. Toffler describes with disdain how "the orthodox format presupposes that two young people will 'find' one another and marry. It presupposes that the two will fulfill certain psychological needs in one another, and that the two personalities will develop over the years, more or less in tandem, so that they continue to fulfill each other's needs. It further presupposes that this process will last 'until death do us part.' "[16] This he describes as the "acrobatic feat of matched development."[17] What is this scorn but a criticism of Christian "coupleness?" This may be regrettable for certain humanists who appreciate the morality, but it is also inevitable. No one should suffer from any illusions: Without a genuine Christian reality for its basis, any attempt to maintain the "traditional format" is an exercise in hollow hypocrisy and a losing cause.

The position of religion in society will also change, but here there are conflicting reports as to its final direction. Some predict with certainty the decline and disappearance of religion and the complete envelopment of society by secularism. Desmond King-Hele goes so far as to suggest that Christians should erect only disposable churches which can be dismantled as soon as the supernatural beliefs die out. This fits closely with Bonhoeffer's diagnosis of our age as "religionless" and is a logical extension of C. S. Lewis's "unchristening of the West."

Others, however, see only a change of status for religion. With the final foundering of its hidebound institutionalism, contemporary Christianity, they say, will lose the consensus decisively but will not disappear. Rather, it will take a new lease on life, thriving on the disappearance of former problems (such as science vs. faith) and the emergence of an informal, dynamic faith, shared from home to home. The last ten years have witnessed the most amazing proliferation of thousands of home groups for fellowship, study and worship. This could well be a pattern for things to come.

Others go beyond this and claim that we are beginning to see the end of secularism and the arrival of an increase in religious feeling. Marshall McLuhan says, "We're heading into a profoundly religious age."[18] Correcting an earlier mistake in his analysis, Paul Goodman wrote, "I had imagined that the worldwide student protest had to do with changing political and moral institutions, to which I was sympathetic, but I now saw that we had to do with a religious crisis in the magnitude of the Reformation in the fifteen-hundreds, when not only all institutions but all learning had been corrupted by the Whore of Babylon."[19] Some dismiss this religiosity as a last stirring of religion in its death throes, but the evidence points elsewhere. We must be clear, however, about the essential feature of this new interest: It is not a revival of historic Christianity (with truth, content and objective grounds for faith) but of religious pluralism and perversity where faith may be contentless and experience counterfeit and both vulnerable to manipulation. G. K. Chesterton once remarked that when people cease to believe in God, they do not believe in nothing, they believe in anything. Cheapness and confusion will be the religious climate of the next years. If it is twice as easy for a Christian to speak into such a situation, it is also twice as hard to speak into it intelligibly. Faith that is faddish can be as dangerous as faith that is false.

This is only a selective summary, but it does silhouette some of the broad profiles of the future now being envisaged. As I said, these are important not so much for the accuracy of their predictions as for the range and urgency of the questions and issues that are raised in each of these areas. It is hardly surprising that a closer examination reveals a wide divergence between those who are enthusiastic in their optimism and those who are sober in their pessimism, a polarization we will now examine.

The Optimists

Among the prophets of optimism there are those with a virtually unqualified optimism and those with an optimism that is conditional. The former generally presuppose the achievement (or imminent possibility of achievement) of a qualitative change in human society, or human nature or human consciousness. The attainment of at least one of these three, which will automatically affect the other two, is a fundamental prerequisite for unqualified optimism.

The nineteenth century was rich in such optimists. Ernest Renan predicted in his dialogues (1876) that technological man would create new men who would become gods. August Comte foresaw a utopia led by an elite of managers and scientists. Karl Marx promised a communist utopia, which has become the most powerful social myth in the twentieth century. Nikita Krushchev somewhat conservatively scaled this down to what he called "goulasch and ballet," but, compared with the original hope, this is revisionism in the extreme. Trotsky proclaimed that man had not given up "crawling on all fours"[20] before gods, kings and capitalists only to "submit humbly before the dark laws of heredity and a blind sexual selection." The ultimate goal was to "create a higher social, biologic type, or, if you please, a superman."

More recently the image of the "superman" has been tarnished with fascist connotations, but the same confidence burns as brightly with a wide spectrum of support. B. F. Skinner of Harvard University promises progress through conditioning, both in his scientific writings and his utopian novel *Walden Two*.[21] To disregard conditioning, he maintains, is to endure the present poor results of so-called freedom which is an expensive illusion, the evidence of which weighs heavily on us. If subtle, social conditioning is used through "behavioral technology," man can achieve a society that guarantees survival, common pleasure and universal benevolence. Regardless of whether or not we accept Skinner's determinism, we cannot ignore his central thesis.

Skinner acknowledges the role of freedom in the past but insists that atomic individualism is threatening Western culture with disintegration. Freedom, free will and inner choice are only an illusion anyway. Man is mistaken when he flatters himself that he initiates, originates or creates. The fact is that action is determined by environment, and behavior is conditioned by consequences. That man is autonomous is a superstition which originated only in man's inability to fully understand himself or his world.

Most of Skinner's critics direct their criticism not so much at the technical soundness of his laboratory work on rats and pigeons but at the extension of this into natural philosophy and politics, where the implications are starkly totalitarian. T. E. Frazier, Skinner's alter ego and the founder-director of the utopian community in *Walden Two*, openly admits, "I've had only one idea in my life—a true *idée fixe.* To put it as bluntly as possible —the idea of having my own way. 'Control' expresses it, I think. The control of human behavior. . . . In my early experimental days it was a frenzied, selfish desire to dominate. I remember the rage I used to feel when a prediction went awry. I could have shouted at the subjects of my experiments, 'Behave, damn you! Behave as you ought!' "[22]

In *Beyond Freedom and Dignity* Skinner puts it less dramatically but equally forcefully. "What is being abolished is autonomous man—the inner man. . . . His abolition has long been overdue. Autonomous man is a device used to explain what we cannot explain in any other way."[23] In this book the most crucial question of the end of the twentieth century—Chaos or Control?—is sharpened to its finest point. Skinner's closing words are the cue to utopia, oblivion or the end times: "We have not yet seen what man can make of man."[24]

The drive to play at being God is a tendency to which many classic utopians succumb. From the proto-fascism of Plato's *Republic* to the controlled conditioning of *Walden Two,* there are two salutary lessons which emerge. First, the utopian mentality finds a natural spawning ground in periods of social disintegration. Plato wrote during the cultural chaos which followed the Peloponnesian War, More wrote in a similar period of disorder and violence in the sixteenth century, Skinner wrote just after World War II. For each the utopian concept is a private bridge between the prevalent chaos and his own hoped-for solution. Second, the consequent romanticism of the utopian concept is almost invariably dictatorial. The history of man's utopias is the best anti-utopian argument. Lewis Mumford, for example, wrote a generation before *Walden Two,* "As with the old Greek innkeeper Procrustes, the utopians either stretched the human organism to the arbitrary dimensions of the utopian bed, or they lopped off its limbs."[25] Observing Bolshevism in action the Russian philosopher Nikolai Berdyaev warned, "Utopias seem very much more realizable than we had formerly supposed. Now we find ourselves facing a question which is painful in a new kind of way: how to avoid their actual realization."[26] This fear is shared by many critics of B. F. Skinner. There is menace in the idealistic quest for perfection, for such romanticism is always the womb of the death-wish.

Richard Landers is equally optimistic that this choice will be beneficial. In *Man's Place in the Dybosphere* Landers claims that technology is irresistible and good.[27] Man must adapt himself to technology "as we find it." If there is any man prototypical of the new age, he says, it is the astronaut ("What is true for him today will be true for the rest of us tomorrow")[28] who is totally machine-oriented in his education. If machines are to win, man must learn to live with his conqueror, but this need not be frightening for machines are "morally pure" and we could arrive at the creation of a humanoid without human faults. Landers calls for the rejection of any distinction between the natural and the artificial. Artificial lawns and green concrete will soon be better than real ones. Man can "live and flourish in an asphalt jungle as well as a tree-filled jungle."[29] He also advocates the symbiosis of machines and men (though this could well distort the "moral purity" of machines!) and warns that those most comfortable in the future will be those who are enthusiastic about its arrival. "Darwin's theory of the survival of the fittest is as valid in the dybosphere as it was in the biosphere."[30]

More widely read than either Skinner or Landers is the progressive Roman Catholic theologian, Teilhard de Chardin. In *The Future of Man* Teilhard rightly notes, "The whole future of the Earth, as of religion, seems to me to depend on the awakening of our faith in the future."[31] The question is, on what basis? His own suggested answer is twofold. First, there is change via evolution, which is "nothing else than evolution becoming conscious of itself." Second, there is convergence. Rather than entropy, disintegration and diversification, he sees a process of "enfolding" which contributes to the "planetization of man" or "human unanimization." The final goal of this will be "point omega" or "neogenesis," a stage at which all dualism will have been transcended, spirit will be one with matter, science one with religion, morality one with evolution and salvation universal. This is not the old materialist version of utopia, nor the normal Christian vision of heaven, nor even an Eastern nirvana but the "Noosphere," "a thinking envelope," "a domain of the interwoven consciousness." When this is shaped around our planet, man will have peace, "the ultra human" will emerge and at last there will be "something new under the sun."

Influenced by him but working in a different discipline is Marshall McLuhan, a Roman Catholic convert who since 1951 has been a close reader of Teilhard de Chardin. His hope is not in evolution but in the "electric era" with dawning promise of a new age of pentecostal unity when all mankind will be knit together in a grand global village through the seamless web of electronics.

Many other optimistic views could be cited, ranging from political visions like Marcuse's to scientific scenarios like Arthur Clarke's, but those mentioned are representative.

Almost invariably the optimistic conclusions are weakened, if not betrayed, at one of three points. Some are short on necessary evidence, some are tenuous in their reasoning and others stumble over the inclusion of contradictory evidence which actually militates against their basic thesis. Thus the optimism may be a hope, but it hardly has a fully rational or empirical base. At worst, it is often blind and romantic. Most typical of this is Teilhard de Chardin whose status as a cult hero persists despite his falling short in each of these three ways. This is most striking in two chapters of *The Future of Man.* In chapter eight, "Some Reflections on Spiritual Repercussions of the Atom Bomb," he is almost unique among contemporary prophets in finding the A-bomb a symbol of hope rather than of apocalyptic disaster. But even this pales in comparison with the next chapter, "Faith in Peace." He writes: "Everything that formerly made for war now makes for peace. . . . Mankind is not only capable of living in peace, but by its very structure *cannot fail eventually to achieve peace*. . . . The earth is more likely to stop turning than is Mankind, as a whole, likely to stop organizing itself and unifying itself. . . .

 Peace therefore is certain; it is only a matter of time."[32] To read such statements aloud against a background broadcast of the evening news is to feel the yawning distance between his vision and contemporary reality. His blind romanticism is equaled only by his vague mysticism and his appalling approval of totalitarian control and the loss of individuality.

All these views are ably summarized in the closing passage of F. Scott Fitzgerald's novel *The Great Gatsby*. "Gatsby believed in the green light, the orgiastic future, that year by year recedes before us. It eluded us then, but that's no matter—tomorrow we will run faster, stretch out our arms farther."

Among the conditional optimists, two recent books are the most important, *Technological Man* by Victor Ferkiss, and *Future Shock* by Alvin Toffler. Ferkiss sees humanity "on the threshold of self-transfiguration, of attaining new powers over itself and its environment that can alter its nature as fundamentally as walking upright."[33] If this is attained man can be "finally fully himself."[34] Thus Ferkiss yields to no one in his optimistic view of a future that is possible, but he adds a cautionary warning. Culturally, economically, politically, sociologically, there is no sign of a new man yet. Any toasts of celebration are premature; achievement is lagging far behind prospects. In fact, there is even a serious problem, not the commonly quoted subordination of man to technology but rather the subordination of technology to pre-technological values: "What emerges as the pattern of the future is not technological man so much as neoprimitive man trapped in a technological environment. . . . Technological man does not yet exist. His job is to invent not the future but first of all himself. . . . Bourgeois man is still in the saddle. Or, to put it more accurately, things are in the saddle, since bourgeois man is increasingly unable to cope with his problems."[35] Ferkiss sees the present state of man's development as a curiously unhappy amalgam of forces. He concludes, "The synthesis of postmodern technology and industrial man could produce a new civilization or it could mean the end of the human race."[36] Any final optimism must be sober in its realism and disciplined in its evaluation of evidence. It can be no more than conditional.

Alvin Toffler's *Future Shock* is a brilliant, exciting and optimistic book, although sometimes the exuberant overall confidence is too strong to fit within the cautionary confines of his original thesis. As with Ferkiss, it is not the possibility of a brilliant future which is in question, but the probability of its achievement. The key weakness here is man's adaptive ability, always a crucial factor in evolution: "Unless man quickly learns to control the rate of change in his personal affairs as well as in society at large, we are doomed to a massive adaptational breakdown."[37] Carl Jung warned earlier, "We have plunged down a cataract of progress which sweeps us on into the future with ever wilder violence the further it takes us from our roots."[38] Toffler takes this up in the context of accelerating technology, claiming that too much change in too short a time will lead to "future shock," the "dizzying disorientation"[39] giving rise to a growth of mass irrationalism—a "new cancer in history."[40] He is not speaking of the world which is 70 percent agriculture or even 24 percent industrial but of that 5 percent which is differentiated not by race, religion or ideology but by time. The three factors of transience, novelty and diversity form the triple thrust of future shock, replacing permanence, familiarity and uniformity. His evidence is massive and stimulating, in minute insights as well as wider generalizations, but the overall thesis is cautionary: "When diversity converges with transience and novelty, we rocket the society toward an historical crisis of adaptation. We create an environment so ephemeral, unfamiliar and complex as to threaten millions with adaptive breakdown. This breakdown is future shock."[41]

The Pessimists: Ten Pressure Points

On the other side and increasingly representing a polarized alternative are the prophets of pessimism. The best approach here is to mention leading thinkers of this variety and then to outline the various pointers to pessimism or, as some describe them, the "data of doom." Each of these pressure points is a problem in itself, but it is their aggregate force which is most sobering. Paul Ehrlich, Gordon Rattray Taylor, Isaac Asimov and Bertrand Russell are representative of the wide range of voices on this side. Asimov describes himself as a "doom crier."[42] Rattray Taylor prefaces his *Doomsday Book* with a lengthy quotation from the woes of Revelation 7–9; and Bertrand Russell writes a typically stoic statement, "The man who wishes to preserve sanity in a dangerous world should summon in his own mind a parliament of fears, in which each in turn is voted absurd by all the others."[43] Russell apparently neglects the unfortunate possibility of a unanimous vote.

Even the predictions of the optimists tend to be peppered with premonitions of disaster at some point. Teilhard de Chardin, for all his buoyant blitheness, wrote in December 1953, two and a half years before he died, "Man now sees that the seeds of his ultimate dissolution are at the heart of his being. The *End of the Species* is in the marrow of our bones!"[44] Norman O. Brown, descending momentarily from his rarified romanticism, wrote, "Today even the survival of humanity is a utopian hope."[45] Most sobering of all is the Russell-Einstein Manifesto delivered in 1955 at the Caxton Hall, London, two days before Albert Einstein died. Outlining the risks of thermonuclear warfare, it bluntly warned, "We have found that the men who know most are the most gloomy,"[46] a statement which by its notable pedigree should falsify the myth that all realists are reactionary Jeremiahs. They went on to appeal "as human beings, to human beings; remember your humanity and forget the rest. If you do so, the way lies open to a new Paradise; if you cannot, there lies before you the risk of universal death." The implicit relating of realism and pessimism was prophetic of the present situation. It was captured perhaps more sharply in late photographs of Bertrand Russell in which the strong aquiline features stand out, his whole face a study in bleak bravery.

What are the "data of doom," or the various pressure points? Remembering the double cautions of Ferkiss and Toffler, that there is no sign of the new man yet and that contemporary man is not coping adequately with future shock, we could outline ten further pressure points.

First are the "apocalyptic horsemen," the related problems of war, disease and famine. In regard to war, we have a situation today in which unlimited power to destroy is available and yet the world is still divided into over a hundred competing nations. Few national leaders are conspicuous for their total reasonableness and constant statesmanship. As John Kennedy said to the United Nations on September 18, 1961, "Mankind must put an end to war, or war will put an end to mankind." Speaking of the obvious fear of some monumental error of judgment, King-Hele says, "The logical conclusion is that the weapons are likely to be let loose, probably before the end of the twentieth century."[47] An accident, an error of misinformed judgment or an arrogance of power—each of these threats casts a long shadow over every aspect of meaningful existence. The contemporary expression of this ancient dread of an imminent end is obviously the mushroom cloud of nuclear weapons, although curiously now that the threat is real and not just an anticipated dread, most people seem to have ceased believing in a major nuclear war—a phenomenon that can only be left to psychiatrists or future historians to explain.

Similarly, the spectre of disease and famine needs little elaboration to a generation contemporary with the tragedy of Bangla Desh. Even apart from a war situation, possible "pandemics" are forecast because of overcrowding and malnutrition, including multiplying fears of cholera and bubonic plague. Speaking of famine, Paul Ehrlich sounds an alarm: "The next *nine* years will tell the story."[48] It is thought-provoking to notice that of his three scenarios, only one is cheerful. Some men will be able to survive at a reasonable standard of living only on the basis of two particular premises: (1) that so many billions will die first and (2) that the United States and Russia will both demonstrate maturity and unselfishness. It is hardly necessary to point out that under any circumstances the first premise is tragic and the second is romantic.

A second pressure point is the fear of a population crash as the culmination of the population explosion. Whatever the upper estimates for the ceiling of human population, whether thirty billion or fifty billion, most forecasters agree that there are no sufficient foreseeable solutions. Some dream of creating a breed of micromen, constructing a gigantic building to encircle the earth and house mankind or colonizing outer space. But none of these solutions would be sufficient, and the population explosion cannot go on indefinitely. As the U. S. National Academy of Sciences reported, "Either the birth rate of the world must come down, or the death rate must go back up."[49] Scientists who have studied nature's mechanism to control overcrowding have projected this onto the human situation. In the animal world an initial loss of fertility leads to inadequate mothering, then to extreme neuroses and finally to a stress endangering life itself. This has been witnessed in the world of microbes, rats, deer and lemmings, and it explains why the economists generally remain the more optimistic demographers and the biologists the more pessimistic. Fred Hoyle suggests such a crash in A.D. 2250 when the population is twenty-five billion, involving a crash back down to two billion and the death of twenty-three billion. Another 300 years would repeat the cycle. We must remember that population forecasts have generally been too low, and many demographers predict that twenty-five billion will be reached within the next century.[50] Rattray Taylor thinks it will be before then.

A third pressure point is ecology with possible disasters expected from unforeseen imbalances or pollution. The Nasser dam in Egypt provides a good example of the former. Rattray Taylor describes how the silt is prevented from flowing down so that a consequent lack of nutrients reaches the Mediterranean. In its first operational year, twenty million dollars' worth of fishing was lost and the salinity of the entire Mediterranean was affected. This meant that the lower Nile Valley needed artificial fertilizers which were brought in at enormous extra cost. Then the shallow lake, over 200 miles long, caused such evaporation that there was actually less water. This low-lying water then helped to spread the revolting disease, schistosomiasis, affecting 70 percent of lower Egypt. In lower Egypt, industrial production went down 33 percent, while 22 percent of the Army recruits were rejected, as compared with 3 percent in upper Egypt. So while the dam provided considerable prestige and technological benefits, such as electricity, it also brought a host of unforeseen imbalances in its wake.

The evidence of pollution needs little documentation. Lead, mercury, DDT, junk, radioactive waste, fossil-fuel waste are all poisoning the air, land and sea. Dipping casually into a sample of this week's press on ecology as I am writing, I find the immediate reports no less alarming. French undersea explorer Jacques Cousteau estimates that the vitality of the seas, in terms of fish and plant life, has declined 50 percent in the past twenty years.[51] In the same article, Jacques Piccard warns that if nothing is done, all the oceans will be dead before the end of the century. Most critical of all is the predicted oxygen crisis.[52] It is well known that 70 percent of fresh oxygen is derived from surface sea plants and only 30 percent from land plants. Piccard estimates that up to ten million tons of polluting petroleum float in the sea's sensitive surface every year. A Boeing 747 burns up fifty tons of oxygen every time it crosses the Atlantic. The supply is already so low that the United States produces only 60 percent of what it consumes. Los Angeles is actually 6 percent below the normal human level. The late Dr. Lloyd Berkner reckoned that by the year 2000, the safety margin will be so small that "*we might find ourselves running out of oxygen*."[53] Piccard says equally pointedly, "It's a matter of to be or not to be."[54]

A fourth pressure point is the fear of a genetics race. Already this has been advocated in the Soviet Union by a Dr. Neyfakh, who urges that Russia should gain a decisive lead in the strategic area of biological engineering. His replies to those who rejected his arguments on humanitarian grounds are said to be coldly terrifying, but the discussion makes Fred Hoyle's prediction highly intelligible: "In twenty years' time it is the biologists who will be working behind barbed wires."[55]

A fifth pressure point is the fear of a rising anti-scientism. For many, Hiroshima is the symbol of the forbidden fruit which was eaten and the age of innocence lost. Some charge that science has reached the point of "destructive returns." The superman image of the scientist is disappearing and is being replaced by former images of the dreamer or the mad engineer. This is reflected in popular attitudes, such as the growing preference for non-scientific university disciplines and is evident even among scientists themselves. The metaphor of science as a runaway train is a recurring theme. England's Nigel Calder writes, "The apparent inability of the human species to make discriminating use of science induces a sense of helplessness. The impression is that we are passengers in a runaway train . . . there seems to be no one in the driving cab."[56] From the other side of the Atlantic Ralph Lapp warns, "No one—not even the most brilliant scientist alive today—really knows where science is taking us. We are aboard a train which is gathering speed, racing down a track on which there are an unknown number of switches leading to unknown destinations. No single scientist is in the engine cab and there may be demons at the switch. Most of society is in the caboose looking backward."[57]

A sixth pressure point is the tyranny of technology. We will examine this fully in a later chapter, but its urgency demands attention here. It is not only that the human, aesthetic and moral considerations are being ousted by technological values ("If a thing can be done it must be done"), but that the omnicompetence of technology is now sensed as being infallible. Yet many of its ostensible gains are merely marginal and the interaction of technology with culture is accelerating too fast. Rattray Taylor says, "Technology is what makes the numbers possible; the numbers are what makes [sic] technology so dangerous."[58] Toffler describes technology as "that great, growling engine of change."[59] Do we have the option of halting its effects? Jacques Ellul dismisses this as "a pious hope with no chance whatsoever of influencing technical evolution. The further we advance, the more the purpose of our techniques fades out of sight."[60] Any hope of progress towards a worldwide industrial society is extremely unlikely. The alternative is limited, static, completely controlled societies, bracing themselves economically and politically against mounting pressure from internal discontent and disruption and external jealousy from less developed nations.

A seventh pressure point is the shortage of time. Scientific and technological innovations are introduced faster than ever before, and each decision becomes more far-ranging in its implications, yet political and moral decisions are as slow as ever. H. G. Wells warned that the end of the world would be a race between education and catastrophe. It is one thing to listen to a warning, and quite another to act on it. Rachel Carson's *Silent Spring* was at first scorned as unscientific, and examples like this in the area of ecology add weight to a recent warning, "What makes these thoughts all the more disturbing is the knowledge that our fate could perhaps be sealed twenty or more years before the development of the symptoms."[61] The shortage of time is one more nail in the coffin of humanism. Twenty years ago man generally saw himself controlling his own evolution with millions of years of time at his disposal. Today, the estimates are more pinched; few speak in terms of more than 300 years and some speak only of decades. This is hardly the confident picture of humanist man, arbiter of his own destiny. Man is (or he ought to be) fighting desperately for his very survival.

An eighth pressure point is the moral vacuum. Never has so much responsibility been called for, but the need is mocked by the logic of relativism. Toffler speaks of a "value vertigo," and many apprehensively view the coming ethical discussions as a "biological witch's brew" that is seething in the laboratories. By what values will man choose? Are we creating ourselves like gods? Do we need a new Bill of Rights to safeguard humanness? In this situation science has nothing to say, and those who try to adduce moral values from science or evolution either fail in their attempts or produce an immorality which is even more dangerous. Ferkiss captures this predicament graphically: "Modern man is far from slaying the beast within; why assume that the man of the future will be a completely new creature? What if the new man combines the animal irrationality of primitive man with the calculated greed and power lust of industrial man, while possessing the virtual Godlike powers granted him by technology? This would be the ultimate horror."[62] His prognosis is almost a crossbreeding of Aldous Huxley's earlier *Brave New World* (1932) and his later *Ape and Essence* (1949).

A ninth pressure point is the problem of vested interests, a factor which often becomes the guillotine to effective practical action. Charging that private greed is aggravating the problem of pollution in farming, Barry Commoner says that farmers have been on a nitrogen jag for so long that they have become addicted.[63] What is true of private greed is also true of large industrial corporations, government projects (like nuclear research) and religious attitudes towards birth control. Referring to the Laguna Beach reactor in the United States, Justice Douglas described the government attitude as "a light-hearted approach to the most awesome, the most deadly, the most dangerous process that man has ever conceived." Even among those fighting these interests the ostensible concern there is often a trendy fashion, sometimes hopelessly compromised. One young U. S. Attorney defended a Louisiana industry against genuinely serious pollution charges, while simultaneously working on a government project to end pollution in the Potomac.

The Failure of Nerve

These nine pressure points should be appreciated both in isolation and as an aggregate force. But what gives them a compelling cogency is the tenth and final pressure point, one which is becoming the framework for them all. This point is the increasing lack of purpose in our generation. As George Wald comments, "What we are up against is a generation that is by no means sure it has a future."[64] Some people comfortingly attribute this symptom to the present vacuum of thought and effective action, but the malaise is deeper than this. It is not a temporary tiredness resulting from a short-term setback but a failure of purpose where the current cultural impasse only confirms the dark suspicions of the metaphysical absurdity of history.

Those who inquire about the source of the future orientation which has so marked Western culture are often surprised that its origins are plainly Christian. Looking back at Greek or Eastern thought or the myths of pagan nature worship, we can clearly see why they developed no sense of purpose or progress in history. Their variations on the cyclical theme of time meant that technically time was proceeding nowhere. By contrast, the Judeo-Christian view with its strong teleology and linear view of history gives meaning to man in history and a sense of purpose for the least action or even relaxation. This for centuries has been the backbone of Western culture. Its demise has been gradual, like the striptease of humanism, but its end is equally imminent. At the time of the Enlightenment the Christian sense of purpose was secularized into a humanist doctrine of progress, based not on revelation but on rationalism. Society was seen as progressing towards a humanist utopia rather than towards the consummation of God's plans at the end of history. This idea of secular progress was unknown before the seventeenth century, but its deficiencies, stemming from its parasitical nature, were not immediately obvious. Now, with philosophy divorced from rationalism, science reaching the point of destructive returns, and the current situation ranging itself more and more against optimism, the basis for this future orientation has been severely undermined, philosophically and practically.

The theologian S. G. F. Brandon, relating this deficiency to the world view of modern science, writes: "In this complex, mankind, and its affairs, are dwarfed to an incidental insignificance, being doomed to extinction when the balance of natural conditions, which has permitted the appearance of man, changes as it must undoubtedly do in the course of time. The fundamentally impersonal character of the only *Weltanschauung* which science thus authorizes, and the essential relativity it assigns to mankind and its values is gradually making its chill logic felt. Yet, instinctively Western man still tends to think, with a kind of teleological optimism, in terms of an old-fashioned doctrine of progress, which is still recognizably inspired by the Christian tradition that 'God is working his purpose out.' " He concludes his discussion of "that spiritual milieu that affects our culture and inevitably our personal lives" with these words: "For western thinkers there can be no more urgent task than that of resolving this dilemma."[65]

As he does so often, Rattray Taylor puts the issue candidly: "So the need to believe in man's intellectual purpose and in the certainty that it will provide a better life here on earth has become intensified. The optimists cannot give up this belief without abandoning their optimism, and relapsing into despair. Moreover, no one likes to live in a chaotic system."[66] This predicament is common to all perceptive humanists. Should man be realistic in assessing the situation, even if this pulls him towards an unhealthy pessimism? Or should he maintain a semblance of confidence, even if its basis is rooted only in the need to believe? The latter as a basis for faith is hardly credible after Freud's exposure of wish-fulfillment, but the choice is not enviable. Optimism without sufficient basis? Or realism with despair?

It is in our generation that this despairing logic is most felt. Margaret Mead says that profound aimlessness is a feature of the younger generation. William Kesen, a professor of psychology at Yale University, describes today's young as having "an odd sense of futurelessness —they never seem to want to talk about their own futures at all."[67] Stephen Spender, after his year with the radicals in 1968, says that to them the future is "like a time bomb buried, but ticking away, in the present."[68]

Signs of this are evident in three places. First, our generation generally defines its utopias in terms of the past and rarely the future. The intentional communities, communes and colonies are mostly agrarian, founded on the attempt to return to nature and pre-technological conditions. Rarely does one find members of our generation founding a computer software company, working farsightedly towards some future scenario.

Second, many of the speeches and writings of the radicals betray this premonition of futurelessness. SDS president Todd Gitlin wrote: "An orientation toward the future has been the hallmark of every revolutionary —and, for that matter, liberal—movement of the last century and a half," but the New Left suffers from a "disbelief in the future." He confessed, "We find ourselves incapable of formulating the future."[69] The founding Manifesto of the SDS at Port Huron in 1962 says, "Our work is guided by the sense that we may be the last generation in the experiment with living."[70]

Third, the tone of despair is audible in rock music since 1968, much of which expresses the great divorce from any purposeful future. Joan Baez sang into the disaster area that was the Isle of Wight rock festival, with smoke bombs drifting across the stage, "You are the orphans in an age of no tomorrows."[71] Typical of many others is the album *Chicago III*. One song, "Progress?" is merely initial music drowned out by the sounds of the Industrial Revolution, the groaning climax being the whole business flushed down the toilet. Another song is entitled "Man Versus Man in the End," and the album includes "When All the Laughter Dies in Sorrow," a bleak poem by Kendrew Lascelles in which the poet asks whether, when the universe has come to a "frozen halt in space," will any "greater thinking thing . . . give a damn that man was here?"[72]

The extremity of this despair probably explains why any contrasting utopian optimism is so incredibly romantic and wistful. Joni Mitchell's "Woodstock" is almost mythical in its thematic popularity, but its message is a far cry from reality. So also is John Sebastian's "I Had a Dream."

Even among those who echo the hopefulness of Teilhard de Chardin, McLuhan and Buckminster Fuller there are moments of sober realism more typical of our generation. In *EST: The Steersman Handbook: Charts of the Coming Decade of Conflicts* Clark Stevens champions the "Simulsense Movement" against the "Linear Straights." The former are the "midwives of the transformation"[73] but the stakes are high: "Make no mistake: stoppage of the transformation is the stoppage of life itself."[74] Their rubicon date or "transit zero" is Election Day 1976 in the United States. If there is no change by then optimism is finished. "The stark facts tell us that the tide must soon turn or there will be no future for the peoples of the earth. Ultimate contamination, heat-death, radiation poisoning; it matters little how the biosphere extinguishes. The dead planet will continue to orbit the sun."[75] It used to be that the man who dated his prophecies found that his prophecies had become dated, but the habit is becoming compulsive today.

The wheel has come full circle. If humanism calls for faith in man against the evidence of history, it also calls for faith in the future against much of the evidence of the foreseeable future. The problem is not the future. The problem is man's view of himself as he faces the future. Humanism in its nakedness finds no relief for its acute embarrassment. Arthur Koestler's closing words to *The Ghost in the Machine* aptly ring down the curtain:

"Nature has let us down, God seems to have left the receiver off the hook, and time is running out."[76]

It is hardly surprising that a generation, hotly disdainful of empty cultural memories and boldly impatient with older humanist falterings, should attempt to build its own alternative, a counter culture. Seen as such, it can be understood no better than as "The Great Refusal."

3/The Great Refusal

"Woe unto those who spit on
the Beat generation. The wind'll
blow it back."
Jack Kerouac

"The current generation is
the brightest, holiest, bravest,
and most curious of any
generation in human history.
And, by God, they better be."
Timothy Leary

"If the resistance of the
counter culture fails, I think
there will be nothing in store
for us but what anti-utopians
like Huxley and Orwell
have forecast."
Theodore Roszak

"The dream is over. I'm not
just talking about the Beatles,
I'm talking about the
generation thing. It's over,
and we gotta—I have personally
gotta—get down to so-called
reality."
John Lennon

"Give flowers to the rebels
who failed."
Anarchist poet[1]

Any comprehensive understanding of the counter culture must take into account that its origin is like a series of tributaries joining into the swelling mainstream of a river in flood. It is this whole which alone defines "The Great Refusal" or "The Alternative," a generation's attempt to live counter to anything less than the highest values, principles, ideals and goals of previous generations.

To explore many of the lesser tributaries and to trace their rise would lead to areas beyond our immediate concern. For instance, we could study the origins of international student protest, which stretch back into history but gain momentum specifically from the Cordoba Manifesto in Argentina in 1918. From this came a rising tide which despite contradictory elements succeeded in uniting protest around the world. Usually more powerful in Europe than in the United States and often more powerful in Latin America than in Europe, this tributary suddenly became important in the catalytic events of 1959 and 1960. With the toppling of governments in Cuba, Korea and Turkey, the galvanizing example of international student success was reflected in the dramatic emergence of the New Left in the United States.

A second tributary for possible exploration is the emerging consciousness of the Third World—the world of "the wretched of the earth," the peasants of the poorest areas of the world, the colonies and the former colonies. Championed in the idealistic leadership of Mahatma Gandhi in India, the flaming pragmatism of Fidel Castro in Cuba, the persistent revolutionary nationalism of Ho Chi Minh in North Viet Nam, it finds a voice of articulate rage in the writings of Frantz Fanon, a note of sensitive humanness in the poetry of Aimé Cesar and a symbol of inspiring heroism in the Long March of Mao Tse-tung or the death of Ché Guevara. This convergent influence of the Third World comes largely from the moral capital of Gandhi's *Satyagraha,* or non-violent resistance, from the spectacular success of revolutionary movements in Algeria and Cuba and supremely from the running sore that is Viet Nam.

A third tributary is the rising tide of black nationalism, whose long smoldering origins exploded at the bus boycott in Montgomery, swelled through the Greensboro sit-in and broadened into the Mississippi freedom rides. It includes an understanding of the full significance of Martin Luther King, Elijah Muhammad and Malcolm X, for the abortion of their idealism and the intransigent harshness of reality they faced led inevitably to the world of Stokely Carmichael and Black Power and then to the Black Panthers and the eventual split between Eldridge Cleaver, Bobby Seale and Huey Newton.

This particular influence converges in the counter culture at two critical points: (1) the founding of the Student Non-violent Coordinating Committee (SNCC) in 1960, which was a generating impulse of the New Left and (2) the historic conference in Nashville, Tennessee, in 1966, where the espousal of violence marked a watershed between early principles and eventual pragmatism. If principles without a basis are non-productive, then pragmatism without values is counter-productive. This bitter lesson is the unwelcome legacy divided among the heirs of this event.

Beginning with the Beat

If all this should be included in a full analysis of the rise of the counter culture, any other point of departure is somewhat arbitrary. Nevertheless, perhaps the best place to begin to chart the growth of The Great Refusal is with the Beat Movement, for it was a vital reaction to the world after Hiroshima and a portent of later protest. Most of the early Beats were veterans or non-combatants with experience from World War II. They were shaken and sobered by "free" societies which had exhumed the spectres of barbarism—the Nazi concentration camps, the allied bombing of Cologne and Dresden, the holocaust of Hiroshima—and were settling down uncomfortably to the bleak prospects of continuing cold war. If their reaction to all this was the first breeze in the winds of change in the West, it was not due to any well-reasoned social theory or to any persistent social action. The essential characteristic of the Beat Movement was its total disaffiliation. It bred and cultivated a whole new life style, not as a fad, but as a personal shell of security against the monstrous irrationality of society and life itself. It was a spiritual answer to the problem of survival in a violent age.

"To be Beat was to be at the bottom of your personality looking up,"[2] said Jack Kerouac, or as Norman Mailer wrote later in his famous article "The White Negro," "If the fate of twentieth-century man is to live with death from adolescence to premature senescence, why then, the only life-giving answer is to accept the terms of death, to live with death as immediate danger, to divorce oneself from society, to exist without roots, to set out on that uncharted journey into the rebellious imperative of the self."[3] The Beat philosophy was American body-existentialism.

The founding year was 1948. The scene was New York and the general academic host was Columbia University where several veterans were making gestures at studying, simply hanging around or else dropping out. There were John Clellon Holmes, an aspiring novelist from New England; Allen Ginsberg, a bearded Columbia dropout from Paterson, New Jersey, working in a café but using his spare time to write visionary poetry; Jack Kerouac, a Massachusetts seaman writing a novel and getting ready to take to the road; Gregory Corso, described as the "Shelley of the Mafia"; and Gershon Legman, a highly articulate but bitterly disenchanted eccentric, concentrating on writing the secret sexual history of our times, researched from lavatory graffiti. Overshadowing them all as their magical figure and strong mentor was the dark genius of the well-known adding machine family. From the class of Harvard '36, evidently nervous and hypnotic, reputedly a petty criminal, certainly an artist, junkie and legendary hero, he used many names but his real one William Burroughs. It was from this potpourri of poets, novelists, artists and their friends that a life style was born—and eventually a movement.

"You know this is really a Beat generation," Kerouac said to John Clellon Holmes one day, and there the name was coined. "Beatnik" came later, a plastic media derivative from sputnik. By this time Kerouac was changing his definition. Writing in 1948, he had said, "The word 'beat' originally meant poor, down and out, deadbeat, on the bum, sleeping in subways," but by 1954 he was reinterpreting it as "beatific," born of a vision in which he saw prophetically "the rumblings of a new soul."[4] But whatever the name, it was the style that counted—offbeat, downbeat, antipretentious, cool, man, cool. The years passed, thousands of miles were covered and a whole variety of sensations was experienced and recorded in prose and poem. In 1951, Jack Kerouac typed *On the Road* on a hundred foot roll of shelf paper, the amazing production of an extraordinary mind at high speed, shattering the sound barrier of normal prose. The result was described later by Allen Ginsberg as "a magnificent single paragraph several blocks long."[5] In this form it was predictably refused by all publishers, until eventually mutilated and changed, while Kerouac himself went from bum to seaman, to panhandler, to brakeman, to bum again.

While high on peyote, Ginsberg wrote "Howl," a scathing indictment of Moloch—the social and political system of his day—from the rich experience of a man who hated it. Burroughs traveled like a modern nomad across the country from west to east and from east to west, then to London, Paris and finally Tangiers. There he settled to record what crossed his mind as he struggled to kick the heroin habit. The resulting collage, collected by Ginsberg as scraps from all around the rooms of the house, is his novel *Naked Lunch,* a phrase describing "a frozen moment when everyone sees what is on the end of every fork."[6] A circus of hallucination and satirical insights, it is made devastating by alternating savagery and a painfully beautiful style.

All the while the cult was growing. The emphasis was on sensation, experience, inwardness—all symbolized in the beebop music of Charlie Bird Parker, the compressed immediacy of the canvases of Jackson Pollock, or on screen in the slouching, inarticulate figure of Jimmy Dean. Punctuating the interminable traveling with intermittent pauses for pot, mescaline, sex and booze, the Beats became a loose tribe of experiential nomads who forged an axis from Greenwich Village to Berkeley, with stops between in Denver and Michigan, colonies in North Beach and Venice West and outposts in Mexico, Tangiers and Paris.

For nine years, the Beats were just Bohemians, definitely new, decidedly different but, to most, just Bohemians. Then in 1957 came the breakthrough; Bohemianism itself became Beat and the life style of a few became the image of a movement. Strangely, it was not in hometown New York but in San Francisco with the help of the Californian poets, Kenneth Rexroth, Gary Snyder and Lawrence Ferlinghetti. Large public poetry readings turned enthusiastic city-wide attention into nationwide popularity, and with a landslide of publicity the Beat Movement rose to cultural prominence. Almost at once the City Lights Bookshop published the Pocket Poet Series and Kerouac made repeated appearances on television. He emptied a trunkful of manuscripts onto a public breathlessly prepared and was reported partially drunk during the first weeks his book was a best seller! The *New York Times* rushed in with reviews, *Life* featured them in articles, Ginsberg published "Howl" and almost overnight from San Francisco to Japan he became the best known American poet since Walt Whitman. The rest is history.

Perhaps it is a mistake to credit so much importance to the Beats, though their zany originality has a mesmerizing fascination, but for various reasons they stand like straws in the wind blowing in the direction of the future. This is true of both their surprising differences and their striking similarities. Primarily they were important for the depth of their disaffiliation. One was either hip or square. With a kind of psychopathic brilliance, they felt that all life trembled between victory and defeat. Victories would free them from insanity and defeats would jail them again in the fetid air of an imprisoning system. By itself this disaffiliation was not enough but at least it was a beginning.

Besides this the Beats were creative, especially in novels and poetry. They had inherited something of the New York intellectual world of André Breton and Marcel Duchamps and have now passed it down with integrity to the counter culture.

A feature which made them surprisingly different from later protesters was their apolitical stance; they often elevated incoherence to the point of principle. If the world was phony, politics was a drag. Typical of this was the famous Hunter College debate in November 1958 in which Jack Kerouac, Ashley Montagu, Kingsley Amis and James Wechsler discussed the question "Is there a Beat generation?" Kerouac was palpably less than sober and at times almost incomprehensible. In exasperation Wechsler finally remonstrated, "I think what you are trying to do is to try and destroy anybody's instinct to care about this world."[7] Sometimes their only political statements with any content were expressed in poems against the Bomb, but, as Paul Goodman has pointed out justifiably, they expressed little that exceeded a common-sense anxiety any nuclear-age mother with a family might feel.

Another feature that allied them prophetically with later trends was the religious concern they occasionally betrayed. Their Beat Zen was born of free morals, French existentialism and a casual understanding of the East. Far too hip for square Zen, too loose for purists like Alan Watts, Beat Zen was aptly described by Jeff Nuttall as a "one-is-all-and-all-is-one-so-what-the-hell" religion.[8] Certainly it sat well with their apolitical stance, and, if it had no dogmatic certainty, neither did it have the religiously stuffy pretensions of atheistic secularism. Though radicalism in the West had generally been tied closely to doctrinaire atheism, the Beats thought no more of turning atheism on its head than anything else. Twenty-one years before *Jesus Christ Superstar* or George Harrison's *My Sweet Lord* their novel religious sounds were like seismograph warnings of a trend still unborn—towards the East, the occult and the Jesus Revolution. In 1959, Kerouac mocked, "So you people don't believe in God. So you're all big, smart, know-it-all Marxists and Freudians, hey? Why don't you come back in a million years and tell me all about it, angels?"[9] Or, as he spelled it out more positively, "I want to speak for things, for the crucifix I speak out, for the star of Israel I speak out, for the divinest man who ever lived who was a German (Bach) I speak out, for Mohammed I speak out, for Buddha I speak out, for Lao-tse and Chang-tse I speak out, for D. T. Suzuki I speak out . . . This is Beat! Love your lives out!"[10] Somewhat muddled in its ecumenicity, it was at least prophetic in its eclecticism. Not for another ten years would the counter culture more generally jump on the bandwagon and choose the "mystic" rather than the "mechanistic" fork in the cultural road, thus making religion the "ultimate trip."

Yet another feature was their belief in the therapy of lunacy. In an insane world, the final insanity is the point where insanity becomes sanity because of the respectable aura of its "normality." At such a point the only sanity was to be insane. The only freedom was in madness. This is R. D. Laing before R. D. Laing, and if later radicals are more consistent in their convictions, they have only stumbled onto the same insights which the Beats had already held. After Charlie Parker had spent time in an asylum, he sued a record company for issuing an album which to him was a record of tortured inward experiences. Ginsberg spent eight months in an asylum and dedicated "Howl" to Carl Solomon who was institutionalized at the time. Kerouac was discharged from the Navy as a "schizoid personality," and many others had tensions, neuroses and instabilities.

A final feature linking the Beats to the counter culture was their vulnerability to media. Like others later they demonstrated the "Midas touch" of Madison Avenue, which turns cultural phenomena into commodities marketable to society and manipulable by the system. When Madison Avenue patronized the Beats, the "beatnik" became a stock character in cartoons, *Playboy* magazine ran a "Beat playmate of the month," and, once *Time* and *Life* had touched them, the day of their making was the day of their unmaking. Yet despite this they undoubtedly stand as forerunners of the counter culture with an impressive influence and a strong continuity with later trends. The New Left owes more to the Beats than to the radicals of the previous generation. In the reassuring figure of Allen Ginsberg or the reverberating nasal rasp of Bob Dylan, the image of the Beats moves on and matures into a Movement. The Beat may have been a rebel without a cause, but his was the only rebellion around.

The European Scene

For anyone with concern for radical action, a first glance at the European scene is starkly depressing. A far cry from the Beat world of Greenwich Village pads, California Eldorados or freight trains, we enter the world of the gaslit alley, the juke box, the suburban café and the new-type espresso bar. The mood is at once immature, uncreative, inarticulate; there is no coherent protest, only a chip-on-the-shoulder grudge.

First onto this stage came the Teddy Boys in the early fifties. A teenage generation had broken into a novel self-consciousness for the first time; they had money to spend and no built-in sense of social defeatism. Yet, on breaking through, they found nothing. And out of that vacuum came the Teds—"Edwardians" because of their Edwardian clothes—marked by their drain-pipe jeans, winkle-picker pointed shoes, three-quarter length coats and heavily greased hair. They are hardly worth calling a "protest movement." But across the currents of the south London gangs and the noisy cinema riots over *Blackboard Jungle*, there emerged a distinct subculture, raw, sullen and inarticulate, aggressively non-conformist to all values except its own.

Afterwards came the Mods and Rockers. In the late fifties it was the Rockers with their studded leather jackets, heavy motorbikes and tribal decorations. In Holland their counterparts were the Nozem, and several rungs up the ladder of chromium affluence came the Swedish Raggare, Scandinanvian "Hell's Angels" in cars. Later, in reaction to all this "yobbishness" came the Mods, neat, delicate, affected, supremely self-conscious, riding scooters not motorbikes, chewing gum and hooked chiefly on modish clothes. (Four changes a day—caught in last night's shirt and you were finished—it was the beginning of Carnaby Street.)

The contrast between this and what was happening in the United States is immediately obvious when we remember that in 1964, while the States saw the stirring Free Speech Movement at Berkeley, Europe was condemned to witness the beach battles of the Mods and Rockers, the notorious clash of the "long-haired, mentally unstable, petty little sawdust Caesars," as a Margate magistrate called them.

The Angry Young Men

A more promising source of effective radical action came from the "Angry Young Men," a literary category blown up into a life style. Undoubtedly they appeared more radical at first sight, genuinely creative and infinitely more political. In 1956, John Osborne's *Look Back in Anger* unleashed a strident Jimmy Porter, hotly impatient with tradition, hierarchy and class, angrily demanding immediate action and complaining, "There aren't any good brave causes left." Colin Wilson evoked the aura of French café philosophers and politicans. His *The Outsider* seemed to be the English link with radical continental existentialism. Kingsley Amis openly denied his own connections with any such movement, but the powerful literary influence of Kenneth Tynan built the Angry Young Men into a myth that only time withered to reality. A blunt debunking came from Cyril Wright Mills: "I think Mr. Amis is quite right when he declares that he is no angry young man. . . . He is a young complacent!"[11] Jimmy Porter's anger was a symbol of frustration, not of coherent protest. Mills concluded, "The young complacents are not only spokesmen for this class. They are quite successful members of it, or they are trying to be."[12] History has shown their efforts to have been pathetically successful.

The Campaign for Nuclear Disarmament

Another group to consider is the Campaign for Nuclear Disarmament (CND), the only British movement worthy of more serious treatment. This sprang from the Direct

Action Committee and grew into the CND, supported by an influential group of public figures, including Bertrand Russell, Pat Arrowsmith, Canon Collins, Donald Soper, Spike Milligan and Vanessa Redgrave. Like the Beats, many of the founding members shared a deeply disturbing memory of World War II and a serious disquiet at the complacent course of society. The growth of the movement was phenomenal. In 1958, the Good Friday march from London to Aldermarston and back attracted 20,000 people, and in 1960 it grew to 100,000. But even at its best it was no more than old-fashioned protest with orderly demonstrations, lengthy marches and the accompanying festivity of skiffle and jazz groups, such as Ken Colyer and his fans.

When a split developed over policy, the moderates won the argument and lost the cause. In 1960, the splinter group, the Committee of 100, went on, militant but alone. Their high point was September 17, 1961, when 1,314 people were arrested in Trafalgar Square, the largest mass arrest in British history. But despite everything the Bomb was unmoved, and the CND was exposed as one of the last great causes of the old-line liberals and radicals, now evoking only a nostalgic smile. The innocuous gave way to the banal; only the bearded gave it tradition. Finally it achieved the status of an annual British institution.

By comparison with recent standards, it seems odd to recall that after a boy had stolen a beer mug on the march, the Committee wrote to his mother, complaining of the damage done to the image of the movement and demanding that she repay the cost. Imagine an SDS action committee doing that! But it would be wrong to write it off completely. If it is true that a generation traumatized into apathy by the Cold War was later galvanized into action by the so-called "imperialistic wars," the CND at least represented the first rupture in the silent generation. Long before the anti-Viet Nam movement got under way, the CND questioned the monstrosity of modern war, an issue which became one of the few to pass from Europe to the United States. Moreover, in the CND symbol all radical movements were to find their now familiar peace sign. It would travel far from the muddy fields of Aldermarston and betray many of the ideals of its first users along the way, but basically it symbolized the same deep-rooted disquiet, the same longing for a new order, the same commitment to the radical action of the hour.

The Provos

A last European movement worthy of serious consideration is the Provos (provocateurs, provokers). For any ardent radical, the European scene in the mid-sixties was depressing, a dismal choice between either sullen, immature and irresponsible reaction or old-line liberalism foundering on the harsh realities of strong government and cold-war fears. None of this really qualified to be The Great Refusal.

The one exception was the Provos in Holland, a movement born from the general Dutch disillusionment and the particular deadness of the city of Amsterdam. With its picturesque boutiques in the red-light district, Amsterdam may be a nice "runashore" for sailors, but in 1966 it was considered dead for young people since there was only one teenage dance hall in the entire city. The Provo movement sprang spontaneously from happenings organized in 1965 by young anarchist intellectuals. Held in a public square around Het Lieverdje (the Little Sweetheart statue), they featured a humorous lampoon on the royal family and an anti-smoking song by a well known chain smoker. The entire evening proved a startling success, sparking spontaneous enthusiasm in the following weeks. Crowds increased dramatically and police nervousness heightened. At last, under considerable irritation the police over-reacted and force exploded into violence. With this the Provos were born, their specific aim being to confront authority and make it look ridiculous.

Seen in retrospect, the Provos were not particularly important for their platform of protest or their program of reform which were hardly novel or daring. It was their style which was distinctive. Breaking away from the typically British manner of demonstration with marches, banners and petitions, they were the first to popularize the put-on. Using happenings, community projects, rioting, violence and bitter jokes, they attempted to take social satire out of the television studio and bring it back to the streets. In many ways they were the forerunners of the Yippies and their activities were later reflected in the frolicking Pop Art revolutionary tactics of Jerry Rubin and Abbie Hoffmann.

The zenith of their success came in 1966 when they planned a series of public put-ons to express their social concern-cum-satire. The first was the Orange Committee Anti-Present to be bestowed on the occasion of the wedding of the Royal Princess to Herr Claus van Amsberg of Germany. Touring the country on orange bikes, they collected an "anti-present" for the royal couple, widely advertising free train trips to the wedding in the West German press; the police, in fact, were said to have expected a million Germans to take advantage of their offer. Then, realizing the police would probably ascertain the strength of their support by checking their bank account, they borrowed a cool fortune, deposited it in a bank and baffled experts into suspecting a sinister backing.

After this, they introduced a famous series of "White Plans" (white being the virginal color of the Provos). The first was the White Bike plan, offered out of concern for the city of Amsterdam, snarled and strangled by crawling, polluting traffic. Obtaining 150 bicycles, they painted them white and left them as communal property. Those cooperating were to drive into town, leave their cars and borrow one of the bikes. They hoped eventually to ban cars from the city center altogether. The police predictably overreacted and confiscated them all, claiming they were preventing the risk of theft. A hundred more were promptly provided, this time with locks, but these suffered the same fate.

Next came the White House plan which appealed for houses suitable for old folks' lodgings or student accommodation. Then they introduced the White Chimney plan, suggesting that those in the fight against pollution should paint their chimneys white. Overnight, a forest of white chimneys sprouted in central Amsterdam. After that was the White Chicken plan, issued with the same apparent solemnity, but this time deliberately aimed at the police. The plan suggested that the police disarm, dress in white coats and go around dispensing contraceptives! The reaction, not surprisingly, was furious indignation. They also wrote White Poetry—some political, some private, some poignant. Slapped on walls, lampposts and pavements, it expressed the Provo philosophy in a hundred different ways. By and large it was all an informal anarchism that grew from underground cellars and centered in their famous houseboat headquarters in an Amsterdam canal. Their philosophical ideal was Homo Ludens—diluted culturally from the ideas of Jan Huizinga—sane, creative man, totally at leisure with freedom to play. More often than not the practice failed to fit the theory. Semi-squalid communities with tawdry sex relations and an ignominious resort to begging were often the results.

On the positive side, however, the Provos were successful in electing representatives to the Amsterdam Municipal Council, and many of the issues they introduced are still being pushed by the current Dutch radicals, the Kabouter. But the Provos were eventually betrayed by their own lack of ultimate seriousness. As one of their leaders, Van Duyn, is reported as saying, "Anarchism is a politics of desperation. Of course it won't work totally, but it's a great way of shaking things up."

One further point, shown up in the mirror of hindsight, gives the Provos wider significance. Their treatment by the government authorities was an example of monumental myopia. Perceptively, the *New York Times* described the Provos as "Dada put to political ends,"[13] and the Provo leaders candidly admitted the accuracy of this. They claimed they were only expressing on the streets the logic of the message of the Amsterdam Staedelejk Museum. The authorities who were the proud Patrons of Art in the Museum acted to prosecute the logic of the same message as it worked itself out on the streets. This schizoid stupidity frequently surfaces in the history of the "striptease of humanism."

At their brief best, the Provos showed both logic and integrity. "After the sick capitulation of CND it did look as if we were once again winning," wrote Jeff Nuttall from the English underground.[14] Again the optimism was stillborn; protest ended in posturing. But there were few who cared when a deluge of euphoria descended on Europe and the United States with the advent of the "Hippies" in 1966.

With these European events in mind, we ought to chart all that happened between the sudden prominence of the Beats and the birth of the Hippies. But the significance of this interim period is more easily seen if we first look at the Hippies.

The Hippies

With the Hippies, it was back to California—not North Beach, Venice West or Berkeley, but Haight-Ashbury, where the streets were fabled to be paved with pot and there was woven together an instant tribal community. "Turn on, tune in, drop out" was the text, and Timothy Leary, Allen Ginsberg and Alan Watts were the midwives-cum-High Priests of the new organic community. It was a new society with bells, beads and flowers, peace and love, acid and psychedelia, as if the dream world of the unconscious had suddenly become tangible. This was the zenith of acid rock. The Philmore West was its Mecca, and never have the Grateful Dead, Jefferson Airplane, Doors or Janis Joplin played better. Ken Kesey led the "Merry Pranksters." Tim Leary led the "Family Dog." Across the country in New York there were the Fugs and the Velvet Underground, while in London the early UFO was unlimited freak-out. But all of a sudden the community became a circus, the dream a nightmare, and with the early peace and love fading the romanticism spiraled downwards. The euphoria was terminal.

Ginsberg should have known better. It was one thing for him to complain that the world of Ronald Reagan and LBJ was "a planetary bar room brawl."[15] Certainly, if all is form there can be no freedom, but equally, with no form the stress on freedom leads to anarchy and chaos. Ginsberg's error was only the reverse of his opponents. It was a reaction, never an answer. Actually, with later evidence coming to light, we can now assess his contribution as a somewhat cynical betrayal of his own ostensible idealism, so ardently preached with the best means at his inventive disposal.

Ginsberg attacked the mass media for their manipulating control in a plastic society, but at the same time he shamelessly exploited them to his own advantage. In a letter to Leary at this time he wrote what is almost an adman's memo: "Yesterday got on TV with N. Mailer and Ashley Montagu and gave a big speech . . . recommending everybody get high. . . . Got in touch with all the pro-dope people I know to have . . . [a pro-drug report] publicized and circulated. . . . I wrote a five-page summary of the situation to this friend Kenny Love of the *New York Times* and he said he'd perhaps do a story (newswise) . . . which could then be picked up by UP friend on national wire. Also gave a copy to Al Aronowitz on *New York Post* and Rosalind Constable at *Time* and Bob Silvers on *Harpers*."[16] This is an amazingly honest exercise in the cynical betrayal of the integrity of his protest.

An area where he was only half-heartedly honest was in his assessment of Haight-Ashbury. Despite his claims, Haight-Ashbury was never "Indian" because it was dependent, if not parasitic, and he was finally forced to admit that what he called the "vegetable" culture always needed the "mineral," that is, the backing of technology. Accurately describing the relationship of the Hippies to the technological society, Ellul wrote, "They are a supplement to this same society—the flower on its hat, its song, its garland, its fireworks display, its champagne cork. They reject and indict it—so they think. In reality, they are only the product of its luxuriousness."[17] Actually it was not Ginsberg but the Diggers whose realism matched their concern. Witness their stress on health, their provision of fresh farm food and distribution of medicines. Finally, the media seduced them to succumb to success. Jefferson Airplane sold out to do commercials for Levi's, Ed Sanders made the cover of *Life,* tourists paid four dollars to hear a Leary sermon, and Gray Line sightseeing buses included Haight-Ashbury on their tours. Ultimately there were only the petty criminals, the junkies, the pushers, the boarded-up shops and the broken windows. Icarus encore.

One feature of Haight-Ashbury which survived was its mimeographed magazines and roughly printed papers which mushroomed into the Underground Press. But despite this, the chief significance of the Hippies was their unmistakable failure. Leary's dropout was a cop-out. To leave society changed nothing in society. From then on, only a movement committed to radical political change would be viable. As an editorial in the *Interna-*

 tional Times of London said, "If you can't turn them on, turn on them."[18] Never again would there be such a wide unity and euphoria, such a blending of extremes. By 1967, it was back from psychedelia to politics, and many now find the interval embarrassing for its superficiality.

The New Left

The failure of Haight-Ashbury was the cue for the New Left, not that it began in 1967, but its emergence as a cultural force springs from its exploitation of the mood vacuum created by the failure of the Hippies and the grim escalation of the Viet Nam war.

The "newness" of the New Left must be seen in contrast to two specific areas: the Old Left and the Silent Majority. The Old Left are the communists and radicals following the later Marx, Lenin and Rosa Luxemburg. The Old Left had been betrayed by communism's becoming in practice just one more nationalist elite. Hidebound in its doctrinaire dogmas, it had grown morally loathsome through its intervention in Hungary in 1957 (and later in Czechoslovakia in 1968). All such practitioners were scorned by Cyril Wright Mills as the "Old Futilitarians." Against them the New Left took its stand, stressing ethics rather than economics and psychology as well as politics, and claiming to deal with alienation as well as exploitation. It took pride in its fervent, existential and non-dogmatic humanism.

Second, the New Left stands in contrast with the Silent Generation. Remarkable as it may seem only a decade later, this was a generation when to be radical was considered unpatriotic, when liberalism had almost exhausted its New Deal capital, when McCarthyism was regarded as a vital political movement, and *Mad* magazine was read by nearly two-thirds of the students. There were two major parts to the Silent Generation, both equally scorned by the New Left. The first included former radicals who in middle-aged maturity had preferred to become liberals. The general disillusionment was summarized for many people in Daniel Bell's announcement of "the end of ideology." It was natural in many ways, but there was a danger of its becoming a new ideology, the ideology of complacency. The second part included the younger generation. In 1959, Clark Kerr of the University of California at Berkeley had remarked, "The employers will love this generation. They aren't going to press many grievances. They are going to be easy to handle. There aren't going to be any riots."[19] His words must have later soured in his mouth with a bitter irony, but for the moment what they lacked in prophetic insight they made up for in descriptive accuracy. This was the ungeneration: "They are inactionary, they are out of it," added Mills with corroborative disdain.[20]

So the New Left saw itself as a spearhead comprised of students and intellectuals who would be the vanguard of a new revolution. It was to succeed by reawakening the slumbering proletariat and joining this force to the resurgent Third World. Its role was to be the catalyst, fusing these forces into an effective agency of revolution.

The occasion was a series of momentous events in 1959 and 1960. In the election of John Kennedy to the presidency, it seemed as if youth, action and success were once again hand in hand. The election itself was not directly influential but symbolic and catalytic. If Kennedy founded the Peace Corps that year, then almost by a parallel combustion the New Left began with the founding of the SNCC and the SDS.

More influential still was the successful example of international student revolts. The year 1960 witnessed the overthrow of two regimes, Menderes in Turkey and Syngman Rhee in Korea. In both these events students played strategic roles, just as they did in the Cuban

 Revolution in 1959 and in the widespread unrest in Japan. The lesson of Cuba was that Marxism was alive and well and living only ninety miles from Florida! In September of 1960, the clarion call came from Mills writing in the English *New Left Review*: "The age of complacency is ending. Let the old women complain wisely about 'the end of ideology.' We are beginning to move again."[21]

It is precisely at this point that we see the different tributaries flowing into the mainstream of the counter culture—the International Student Protest, the Third World (via Cuba and Frantz Fanon, then writing in New York), and Black Nationalism—converging to help form the New Left. Here, rather than attempting to survey the kaleidoscopic variety of the New Left, it is easier to take two organizations as representative of the larger movement.

SNCC

The first is the SNCC (The Student Non-violent Coordinating Committee). The slow trend set off by the bus boycott in Montgomery and accentuated by the forced integration in Little Rock had suddenly accelerated after the historic (but at the time unnoticed) Greensboro sit-ins in F. W. Woolworth's in February 1960. In October of the same year 235 students met in Atlanta, Georgia, to found the SNCC. They were described later as "rather square reformers" as they showed a gentleness, an unashamed Christian commitment, an obvious middle-class background and an appeal to the Bible and the Bill of Rights. Their founding manifesto strongly affirmed belief in "non-violence as it grows out of the Judaeo-Christian tradition."[22]

By 1962 and 1963 their members were returning from the South. Some had been beaten, whipped and shot at. Some had been killed. Not surprisingly they showed a toughness that had been through the fires, but bitterness was beginning to tarnish the bravery. One who came through without bitterness, with only incredible bravery and intense human compassion, was Bob Parris. Returning from the heart of Amite County he could only say: "When you're in Mississippi the rest of America doesn't seem real. And when you're in the rest of America, Mississippi doesn't seem real."[23]

It sounds like a line from Peter Fonda, but the courageous dedication of the freedom rider was a long way from the corny drivel of *Easy Rider*. It was no wonder such selfless heroism won Parris a legendary niche in the New Left. For many of the others, bitterness inevitably ousted bravery. The fight against segregation was becoming a total fight against the System, but the word *fight* was still only metaphorical.

The turning point here came in 1966 at the SNCC annual conference in Nashville, Tennessee. Malcolm X had been assassinated, Julian Bond had been denied his rightful seat in the legislature and the killers of Goodman, Charney and Schwerner (lynched and murdered in 1964) were still free. In an atmosphere ugly with frustration and desperate for revolution, the gentle, religious John Lewis was elected chairman, but then, as the debates drained the spirit to the bitter dregs, he was unexpectedly opposed and ousted. In his place was installed the twenty-five-year-old Stokely Carmichael. At one stroke the SNCC of Camus and Baldwin gave way to the SNCC of Carmichael and Frantz Fanon, non-violence gave way to violence, cooperation to separatism, civil rights to black nationalism. Another polarization had been born. Scorning the loss of the shield of liberal approval and the cooperation of white radicals, Black Power and later the Black Panthers set out down their long, lonely road.

SDS

The second organization, equally typical and important

 is the SDS (Students for a Democratic Society). The SNCC and the SDS formed the two most influential early groups in the New Left. Like SNCC, the SDS was also a direct result of 1960. That year, the old League for Industrial Democracy, founded by Jack London and Upton Sinclair, had rechristened its youth department SDS. But no convention could be held since there were so few members. Then in December 1961, thirty-five students met to set up an executive committee and plan a convention for 1962. For this they commissioned Tom Hayden, a young radical from the University of Michigan, to write a manifesto. The convention was held June 11-15, 1962, at Port Huron, Michigan, with fifty-nine people present. From it the SDS was launched.

Two features make the SDS particularly representative. The first is its history, which is a plunging graph of increasing radicalization. Originally the SDS was a liberal-left coalition with a multi-issue perspective and a humane if somewhat verbose manifesto. Few could disagree with certain central statements, such as, "We regard *men* as infinitely precious and possessed of unfulfilled capacities for reason, freedom and love. . . . We oppose the depersonalization that reduces human beings to the status of things. . . . Loneliness, estrangement, isolation describe the vast distance between man and man today. These dominant tendencies cannot be overcome by better personnel management, nor by improved gadgets, but only when a love of man overcomes the idolatrous worship of things by man."[24]

This manifesto also introduced the famous concept of "participatory democracy," and a typical early slogan was "Build, not burn!" Pragmatism, however, has an uncanny way of toying with the loftiest of principles. The SDS very soon fell out with the League for Industrial Democracy over their anti-communism stance and were locked out of their offices by the parent organization. It is surprising that they survived the traumatic birth experiences.

In the elections of 1964, they were still wearing the button "Part of the way with LBJ." That this is unthinkable for them today shows the drastic shift in loyalties; now they are characterized by a total radicalism and a complete, non-cooperative despair about the System.

Tom Hayden's "Open letter to the McCarthyites" written in the *New Left Notes* prior to the Chicago Convention in 1968 expresses this well: "In the beginning, back in the heroic struggle of the civil rights period—say from 1960 to 1964—our assumptions were barely radical at all. Black people should be free, nothing extreme about that. It's the cardinal promise of our country's official morality. Our demands could not have been simpler, 'live up to these promises, America.' And we somehow assumed that somewhere in its mysterious heart America really wanted to do that. You know the end of that particular story—heartbreak and terror."

In 1963, the SDS was the first to copy SNCC in beginning community organizations in the ghettoes. In 1965, they were the first to organize against the draft. Some 20,000 came to the Washington Peace March on April 17, including Berkeley Free Speech veterans, Mississippi freedom riders, disillusioned Peace Corps volunteers and SDS-tutored black teenagers. Within eight weeks they had been manhandled by the media, photographed, publicized, popularized, psychoanalyzed, almost everything but understood. In October they were credited with calling out 80,000 marchers in various cities around the States. By then SDS could claim to be the spearhead of the New Left, but they were heading down the narrow road of radicalization. For the Movement generally there was the increasing trend from frustration towards despair. For the individual, too, there was usually some radical baptism, some moment of truth. The shared danger for the sake of justice was the sacramental baptism of fire. Whether Mississippi 1964, Chicago 1968 or Attica 1971, there was some point of no return. From then on, there was only The Great Refusal.

The second representative feature was their structure. An obvious mark of the SDS was its unusually ecumenical combination of widely diverse groups which have sometimes been murderous rivals. The SDS included anarchists, Marxists, socialists, pacifists, humanists, Bohemians and mystics, and it held them together in autonomous free-form chapters. There was no single national leader, only a council of thirty-five. This was both a feature of strength and a point of weakness. As a strength it had the advantage of creating an effective striking force. By comparison with the elephantine machinery of the Young Republican and Young Democrat organizations, the SDS were a small minority but vocal and highly mobile. Two hundred militants at Columbia could cripple a university of 17,500. So, whether their tactics were blatant as at Morningside Heights or more subtle, their formation was tactically ideal. Basically, the tactics could be summarized in three words—Confrontation! Polarization! Revolution! With such goals, no radical leader hoped to succeed by attracting converts. To attract converts, he made sure he succeeded.

But if this was their advantage, it was also their disadvantage, because these autonomous free-form groups tended towards dissipation if not disintegration. There was no centrally controlled directive, no universally accepted theory, no definitely organized contingency planning. The fear of doctrinaire theory and dictatorial leadership almost became a subtle dogma itself, and frequently this led to appalling anti-intellectualism, romanticism and disorganization. Tom Hayden openly argued that they should rely more on feel than on theory: "We start armed only with questions, believing that the answers can be discovered in action."[25]

There is always a connection between such romanticism and eventual totalitarianism, and the later SDS is no exception. It resulted in wanton destruction. Ironically, it was in the very name of academic freedom that they destroyed research files and burned Ph.D. theses, openly repudiating the entire history of Western academic freedom. Worse still, there was an increasing denial of free speech. Political action at Berkeley in 1964 had focused on free speech, but by 1968 Herbert Marcuse's concept of "discriminating intolerance" contained an open call for an elite. Rhetorically Marcuse inquired, "Is there any alternative other than the dictatorship of an 'elite' over the people?"[26] Only partisan obstinacy can fail to see the extreme dialectical somersault in this doctrinaire denial of free speech.

There was also the dangerous espousal of violence. It seems surprising now to think that in 1966 Jack Newfield cited non-violence as a defining feature of the New Left. Using this, he excluded various parties like the Progressive Labor Party and Black Power as dangerous because of their violence. Even as late as the spring of 1968 Kenneth Kenniston claimed that the general trends were still non-violent. By May such claims had been relegated to history. The tenuous grasp on the principle of non-violence had been shattered by the intractable response of the power elite and the overreaction of the police. On a scale that ranged in real politik from Regis Debray's "To show force is in effect to use it" to Mao's "Power grows out of the barrel of a gun," it was clear that violence was paying and that pragmatism was more productive than principle. Thus, with only relativism or dialectics underlying modern principles, no about-face is unthinkable, no moral somersault impossible. What is anathema today could easily be a firm conviction tomorrow.

Carl Oglesby, President of the SDS had written, "We want to create a world in which love is more possible."[27] but later he said, "Revolutions do not take place in velvet boxes. . . . Nuns will be raped and bureaucrats will be disemboweled."[28] In between, revolution itself had been made an absolute and was steamrolling over earlier human values. Not surprisingly, the Port Huron statement was no longer official policy.

Space precludes discussing other groups, events and leaders, even though they merit serious treatment. For example, we could examine the Berkeley Free Speech Movement (1964), the May revolution (1968), the Chicago Convention (1968), Moratorium Day (1969) and the Kent State shootings (1970). Leading groups would include the Maoists, the Russian Marxists, the Yippies, the Weatherman and the Women's Liberation Front. Powerful personalities would include David Dellinger, Tom Hayden, Carl Oglesby, Paul Booth, Jerry Rubin, Abbie Hoffman, Bobby Seale, Stokely Carmichael, Huey Newton, Alan Geismar, Daniel Cohen-Bendit, Rudi Deutschke and Tariq Ali.

The Failure of the New Left

But beyond the details the question inevitably comes, where are we now? What explains what President Kingman Brewster of Yale University calls the "eerie tranquility" or what *Time* magazine describes as the "cooling of America"?[29] Are we witnessing "the greening of America," as violence reverts to non-violence and a deeper revolution in men's minds makes a revolution on the streets simplistic and superfluous? Are we slowly facing up to a higher level of frustration and the unwelcome reality of the abortion of the counter culture? Or is this merely a period of retrenchment and rethinking?

Two factors cruelly falsify any optimism. The first is the New Left's substantial failure to achieve its goals, and the second is the heightened repression countering the attempt so far.

Plainly, no System in any advanced industrial society has been overthrown. But it would be wrong not to appreciate the influence each national revolutionary movement has had. In mainland China, for example, the Red Guards proved almost too explosive even for their masters. In Spain, the students have been the most successful in cooperating with the working classes. In Germany, the radicals temporarily had the distinction of almost usurping the credible Left Wing political stance. In France, the students were unique in Europe for bringing a government to its knees, if only for a matter of days. And in the United States, the overall failure of the radicals has not prevented the acceptance of many of their ideas. That war is no longer glorious, that pollution is an urgent problem, that the American dream stands far from fulfillment, that the human race is profoundly in trouble—these insights are widely shared on all sides. Also, in the beat of their music, the style of their clothes and their dedication to drugs, the life style of a movement has become the image of a generation. Nevertheless, most of society has remained relatively unchanged. Most of the visible change has been in the radicals themselves—and its terminus is despair.

What are some of the reasons for this failure? Undoubtedly, the central weakness has been the insufficiency of the radicals' program. Both the alternative they offer to the modern technological society and the means they employ to achieve their end are inadequate. This has meant that their critique of the System is both their sharpest insight and their most stubborn failure. This problem deserves a whole chapter by itself.

Passing over this central weakness, we can mention other lesser factors. One is the conspicuous absence of several of the celebrated prerequisites of previous revolutions. No drastic economic crisis has brought any Western country to its knees. There has been no devastating military disaster or extreme national humiliation abroad. No government has seen a mass defection of intellectuals, as happened in France in 1789 or in Russia in 1917. General unrest is hardly the order of the day. Genuine revolutionary attitudes are limited to comparatively small pockets, and the gap between revolution and reality is covered and disguised only by rhetoric.

Another factor is the social isolation of student activists. Their vision of a catalytic role was a stark fiasco, and their true relation to the Third World[1] was more in the order of revolutionary myths and symbols than of practical reality. Often they got little further than pinning Ché Guevara posters to the wall. Their relation to the working class was, if anything, even more distant. Admittedly, not every movement suffered the indignity of the American radicals when workers marched against them, but the masses were generally unmoved and the middle-class origins of the students were cruelly exposed. Only the Spanish students persistently and the French students for a fleeting moment achieved more. The great Paris workers' march on May 13, 1968, was almost unique, with Daniel Cohen-Bendit and the students taking the lead, followed by the trade unions leaders, with the left-wing politicians humbly marching at the rear. But it was all too easy for President de Gaulle to divorce the students' interests from the workers' and to exploit the situation to his advantage. As Herbert Marcuse sadly admitted in an interview on British television, "The students at best can only be called catalysts. A real revolution is unimaginable without the reaction of the masses."

A further factor is the heavy reliance on anarchism. Although understandable as a reaction, the stress on ethics rather than economics and alienation as opposed to exploitation led only to a soft left. Anarchism has always shown two weaknesses inherent in its principles. Without sufficient "force" to seize power or "form" to retain power, its history has become a series of lessons in lost cause. A fuller explanation of this will come later, but the New Left reliance on anarchism was no better than leaning on a broken reed.

A final factor has been their susceptibility to the mass media. Oscar Wilde once joked, "In the United States the President rules for four years and journalism governs forever." The force of this comment in a day prior to television is now sharpened by the abdication of truth for image. The loss of participatory democracy in a day of consensus politics has been a constant cry of the radicals, but ironically they themselves superbly illustrate the Midas touch of the media, as we have seen. What is marketable as an image is manipulable and thereby contained by the System. Jack Newfield complains that "to be a radical in America today is like trying to punch your way out of a cage made of marshmallow. Every thrust at the jugular draws not blood but sweet success."[30] The anger of Leroi Jones or Norman Mailer sounds a little forced after their television fees or their million dollar book royalties. If Haight-Ashbury was "blown up" by the media, the inflation into a myth was also the explosion into reality. Reality had the last laugh on the pun. Woodstock and the Peace Marches each suffered an identical fate. Yippie leader Abbie Hoffman, restyling his own image to more clean-cut lines complained, "Every time I turn on the television I see another movie star with long hair. The counterculture has been co-opted by Warner Bros."[31]

The Parting of the Ways

The failure of the New Left is the occasion of a general parting of the movement. In the increasing diversification, the outline of several specific trends is becoming clearer. These may well provide the direction for the next few years.

The first trend, among those still committed to activism, is a resort to increased violence. An obvious expression of terminal frustration, its mark is the perpetration of more violence but by fewer people. As such, it closely parallels the period in the nineteenth century when anarchists used the slogan, "Propaganda by the deed!" Following a period of general failure, they took to extreme violence as a revolutionary statement against symbols of the Establishment, such as its leaders or government buildings. It was during this earlier period that the image of the quintessential anarchist was born—the sinister slouching figure, hat pulled down over his eyes, smoking bomb in one pocket and home chemistry manual in the other. Romantic at a distance, he was vicious, destructive and nihilist in practice. This is duplicated today in the SDS split and the emergence of the Weatherman faction, and it is exemplified in the bombing of the Wisconsin Math Center. Scorning earlier non-violence with Lenin as "the parson's mode of thought," they are in danger of becoming an underground collective of grimly moralistic Bonnies and Clydes, self-brutalizing in their pretentious principles and counter-productive in their methods.

A second general trend is towards a new-line Marxism closer to Mao. If the softer left or "salon communism" was too weak, there must be a return to the later Marx, with his coldly defined theories, his brutally efficient tactics. It is time to take Guevara off the wall and study the dialectical principles that might turn him loose in the streets.

This has meant a more critical analysis of recent activism. Looking back now, we can see that the New Left was correct in recognizing that Marx's analysis had run aground on the realities of the post-war world. Of all people, the labor unions most needed to be radicalized and were a distinctly counter-revolutionary force. This recognition of a new stage was what gave rise to the New Left and the whole period of marches in the South which had grown into the Movement. The answer, in other words, was to do what any decent human being could do—put his own body on the line. This was sensitive and understandable but not enough in itself. Eventually the rise of the Weatherman warned of the logic of the irrational self-frustrating romanticism inherent in this approach. The new stage, then, is to turn from such a counter-productive conclusion and to strike a new stance as worker-theorists, appealing to Mao as the model. The Maoist intellectual would be a man engaged simultaneously in rigorous theoretical discussion and practical floor-level responsibilities. This worker-theorist-activist is to be the new ideal.

The need for such a new realism is more obvious in the United States than in Europe, for European radicals have always prided themselves on their disciplined grasp of revolutionary theory which Americans match only in the compensating dedication of their large-hearted idealism. Many seem to be returning to Berkeley in particular, almost mystically hoping the revolutionary Phoenix will rise again on Sproul Plaza.

The third general trend is toward completely apolitical areas of involvement. This stems from the failure of political activism and is a return to a climate similar to the romanticism of Haight-Ashbury, but now lent Ivy League respectability by Charles Reich's *Greening of America.* (With this and Erich Segal's *Love Story,* Yale plays the leading role in a momentary swing to romanticism!) Consciousness III salvages the movement's original non-violence, directs it toward a new psychic orientation, combining it with the impulse to withdrawal inherent in drugs and Eastern mysticism. The parting of the ways between mysticism and activism is highlighted in the argument between Norman O. Brown and Herbert Marcuse as to the real focus of revolutionary activity—is it to be internal or external? Commenting on Reich's opting for the internal, Samuel McCracken wrote in

 Commentary, "Reich is the most profoundly counter-revolutionary author of our day, for nothing could be calculated more effectively to dampen revolutionary ardor than the argument that the Bastille will crumble if we will just sit outside it and groove for a while."[32] For committed activists, Consciousness III is the betrayal of serious revolution. In England Jeff Nuttall warns, "It is now necessary to come back from inner space. . . . If we cannot translate the spiritual into terms of constructive physical action . . . then the spiritual is none of our damn business."[33] But to those for whom Reich speaks, the smarting lesson of political failure points in the opposite direction.

A fourth general trend is an accelerating swing toward new communities. Along with the community projects within the cities, these communes, where they are not merely escapist, often demonstrate the highest remaining idealism and integrity of our generation. At its best, this is not the world of the dropout but of a high and sensitive view of freedom, nature, land and soil, in an environment untainted by technological imperative. Growing one's food, making one's clothes, educating one's children—such a return to simplicity and freedom is a natural goal in a world with no more frontiers to the West.

Sadly, this is not the total picture. For every "successful" commune, there are several more reluctantly forced to see the barrenness of their basis for human community. How does one achieve a community with true unity and diversity, with an authority giving "form" but not stifling "freedom," with a way to settle inevitable differences and heal alienations? (Many have discovered that when living in community, it is not so much what someone does that is irritating, as in a city situation, but rather what someone doesn't do.) To found a commune on escapism is to court early disaster, but to build a community only with idealism is little better. Many intentional communities which base themselves on the ideal of total freedom fail within the first year. Their sad dilemma is pinpointed in a poignant letter to the *Modern Utopians*: "If the intentional community hopes to survive, it must be authoritarian, and if it is authoritarian it offers no more freedom than conventional society. I am not pleased with this conclusion but it now seems to me that the only way to be free is to be alone."[34] This is really a cultural footnote to Nietzsche's prophetic insight that in a world without God there is no resolution between form and freedom. To a generation tending to opt universally for freedom without form, it should stand as an epitaph to past efforts and a warning for the future.

The fifth general trend, one that really deserves closer attention, is the Rock Festival phenomenon. Far more than a passing fashion or style of music, the Festivals uniquely express a generation's utopian wistfulness. It all began in Monterey, in June 1967, with Eric Burdon, Janis Joplin, The Who, Ravi Shankar, Otis Redding and Simon and Garfunkel. After three days even the police were wearing flowers, and those not high on grass or acid were high on idealism. If that was the beginning, Woodstock, in August 1969, was the orgasmic climax of love, peace and music. Hailed as an important landmark in the awakening of the collective unconscious, it was later blown up to mythical, cosmic proportions by the film, which broke down distinctions and made all who saw it true participants. (To the press "the Woodstock generation" was at once born!)

But then came an Altamont, the explosion into reality, and 1971 saw a summer of terminal euphoria all over again, with thefts, burnings, delays, violence and cancellations. If "transcendent togetherness" was the peak (*Newsweek*'s description of Woodstock), then *Gimme Shelter* (the filmed record of Altamont) was the cry at the end of the line. "A great spiritual awakening is breaking out," said the disc jockey at the Isle of Wight as the peace signs waved and hundreds of thousands of hands were linked. Bob Dylan should have returned that summer just to sing "When will they ever learn?" Three days later, as violence erupted, the same DJ was cursing. Three weeks later, a trio of the original Monterey stars were dead, all in tragic circumstances under drugs.

Who will forget the pathos of the closing scenes of *Woodstock,* the debris-strewn garbage apocalypse and the haunting improvisations of Jimi Hendrix? "People think I'm free," he once said. "Actually I just have to keep on running." Joni Mitchell notwithstanding, the bombers were still bombers, butterflies were rarely to be seen and the children of God were no nearer to the garden. "I had a dream," sang John Sebastian, but that was as far as it went. Such visions never troubled reality.

Eric Clapton was closer to the truth when he pointed out in an interview in *The Observer* (London), "Their deaths were almost necessary sacrifices. . . . It'll be a long time before I shall feel at peace again. I just wish 1970 would hurry up and go away. It's all been a disaster."

A sixth trend is the quiet compromise of principle and capitulation of action that leads so many radicals back to bourgeois normalcy. For any genuine radical it must be alarming that such a high proportion complete the cycle from idealism to frustration, to despair, to apathy and arrive back again at their point of departure. One wonders how many of today's radicals will be tomorrow's bourgeois? (This is always a problem in the pop world, with its stress on ephemeral images and the induced transience of success. Once you succeed, what do you aspire to during the next fifty years of your life? Those who follow such superficial idols are curiously like them.) If there is no radix of truth for its basis, even radicalism is caught by the relativistic vacuum, and reality bursts through.

The career of the public image of John Osborne illustrates this well: In the mid-fifties he was the Angry Young Man, and in 1961 writing to the British *Tribune* from the south of France, he caustically admits, "This is a letter of hate. It is for you, my countrymen. . . . Damn you England. . . . You're rotting now and quite soon you'll disappear."[35] But in his play of 1964, *Inadmissable Evidence,* he introduces a solicitor, Bill Maitland, who is an older, more disillusioned Jimmy Porter. Maitland attacks the youth of his day as, "all cool, young, dreamy . . . forthright, contemptuous, unimpressed." Five years later, by 1969, Osborne finds himself accused of being right-wing, upper-class, enjoying an expensive Chelsea home. Even he admits his gratitude at being English rather than Russian or American. "Nowadays my instinct is to lower the temperature rather than raise it." Seen from a radical viewpoint this is betrayal; seen another way, it is perhaps acute insight into contemporary reality. This compromise of principle and return to bourgeois morality is one cause of the present vacuum.

Heightened Repression

If the first factor which falsifies any optimism with regard to the New Left is its substantial failure to achieve its goals, the second factor is the ominous suspicion that all unsuccessful activism only hastens the very danger it seeks to overcome, the possibility of increased repression. Here is the cruel irony of The Great Refusal: Having diagnosed correctly the dehumanizing trends in industrial society, the radicals concluded their analysis so hastily that they failed to see the roots of the problem. Building a revolution on an insufficient base, they were inevitably condemned to failure. The betrayal of their idealism and their own pragmatic use of violence has served to accelerate the very forces they were out to combat. It would be reactionary folly to blame the New Left for all recent repression, but it would be equally wrong not to understand their contribution. The principle holds good, for society as well as communes: Without a basis for form and freedom in the post-Christian democracies, the swing toward authoritarian control may be undesirable, but the alternative swing toward anarchic chaos is unthinkable. Recognizing this, a French politician, in May 1968, paced the streets of the Latin Quarter of Paris watching the riots, helplessly wringing his hands and saying, "Every fire lit in the streets is another vote for General de Gaulle." The overwhelming Gaullist majority in the following election proved his point. It would be virtually impossible for the French radicals to bring the current French state to its knees.

The American radicals are learning the same hard lesson. People ought not be deceived about the "law and order" issue. This is no longer an objective law whose "form" guarantees and preserves "freedom." The search rather is for law in the sense of a pragmatic prohibition to curb disorder. It is no longer "right that gives might," but "might that makes right." Truth is the majority law of that group which overpowers all others. The "backlash" tendency in recent elections is evidence of this. John Mitchell is reported to have said, "This country is going so far right you are not even going to recognize it."[36]

In Britain, Peter Buckman, examining the limitations of protest, writes, "Not to over-dramatize, it is possible that the failures of neo-capitalism will be succeeded by a form of neo-fascism."[37]

From Realism to Romanticism

One last descriptive footnote to the present vacuum: It is curious that as the coherence of the counter culture increasingly lacks credibility, the surveys and overviews grow proportionately more romantic and unrealistic. Written in 1966, Jack Newfield's *A Prophetic Minority* is filled with a surging idealism and catches well the early bravery. Theodore Roszak's *The Making of a Counter Culture* written in 1969 gives an incisive critique of technology and a perceptive profile of the movement, but the basis for his own final solution is almost mystical. Charles Reich's *Greening of America,* published in 1970 and instantly a best seller, is a book whose positive solutions can only be described as wistfulness incarnate. Best seller lists reflect campus aspirations more than revolutionary reality. The almost universal sense of failure and the heightening fear of repression tell a different story.

The Great Refusal has unwittingly become The Great Betrayal. This should not drive us to defeatism or despair. It should challenge us to a more exacting critique.

4/One Dimensional Man

"Man becomes, as it were, the sex organs of the machine world."
Marshall McLuhan

"There is a time when the operations of the machine become so odious, make you so sick at heart, that you can't take part, you can't even tacitly take part. And you've got to put your bodies upon the gears and upon the wheels, upon the levers, upon all the apparatus, and you've got to make it stop."
Mario Savio

"Let him believe that he is always in control, though it is always you who really control. There is no subjugation so perfect as that which keeps the appearance of freedom."
Jean Jacques Rousseau

"He is most enslaved when he thinks he is comfortably settled in freedom."
Jacques Ellul

"In the closed room, however, there is only one system of values. That of the rat race itself. This is shared by everybody in the room and held in contempt by everybody in the room."
Paul Goodman

"It is the American Dream that is going to have to give, whatever its more elderly guardians may think. People grow restive with a mythology that is too distant from the way things actually are."
William H. Whyte

"Every revolution has also been a betrayed revolution."
Herbert Marcuse[1]

Vital to an understanding of the counter culture is the fact that their critique of society is not peripheral but central. It is simultaneously a point of strength, indicating the razor sharpness of their insights, and also a point of weakness, since here their lack of a basis and failure to provide an alternative are most conspicuous. My aim is first to discuss their critique of society and then to show where their inconsistency in thought and action (especially where inconsistency in thought led to weakness in action) eventually precipitated frustration and final failure.

The Critique of Technocracy

But first we should note the folly of attempting to understand the counter culture apart from the centrality of its critique of the technological society.

One common mistake is the attempt to explain the counter culture in terms of comparatively isolated factors such as the generation gap or the cold war. These have their place, but such theories eventually dismiss the counter culture as a reaction and never appreciate its significant action. Such critiques may be good readings in determinism, with its sociological mechanisms of stimulus and response, but they aptly illustrate the one-dimensional mentality which the counter culture so strongly opposes.

A second common mistake is the attempt to explain the counter culture in terms of "pancultural" theories. Three analysts immediately come to mind. Marshall McLuhan, for one, explains the pattern of recent events in terms of a clash between the Gutenberg Galaxy and the Electric Era. He claims that the two generations caught between these modes exhibit two different reactions. The older generation indulges in backward looking, "an orgy of rear view mirrorism,"[2] but the younger generation, feeling its crisis of identity and having no roots in the past, takes to violence as an involuntary quest for identity. He explains both Student Power and Black Power in this way. But such an explanation is desperately oversimplified and actually explains away more than it explains. Sometimes, reading a shorter article by McLuhan, one has the uncomfortable suspicion that it is not so much a review of the work of another man as it is a way to castrate a theory to fit McLuhan's own thesis. Such an article usually expounds McLuhan more than the subject under review.

Alvin Toffler is a second analyst. He sees men divided, not by nation, race or ideology but by their pace of life and position in time. He believes that many in our generation are unable to face the adaptive change required. As particular examples he cites the "hippie" colony at Matala Beach in Crete: "These young people, and millions of others—the confused, the violent, and the apathetic—already evince the symptoms of future shock. They are its earliest victims."[3] Again, his tendency is to explain away too much. Even if this applies to small pockets of the counter culture, it is hardly fair as a description of the whole.

The third critic is Jeff Nuttall. Despite his own radical affiliation, he makes the same kind of mistake in his thesis in *Bomb Culture.* Speaking from the heart of involvement with the London underground, he says, "What has happened is that the pressure of restriction preceding nuclear suicide has precipitated a biological reflex compelling the leftist element in the young middle class to join with the delinquent element in the young working class for the reaffirmation of life by orgy and violence. What is happening is an evolutionary convulsion rather than a reformation."[4] Again the counter culture is seen more as reaction than as action. As a descriptive explanation of subcurrents like the Mods and Rockers, it is valid, but it does no justice to the greater part of the Movement or to its products such as the *New Left Review* or the poetry Nuttall himself writes. All these analyses include sweeping generalizations and are vastly oversimplified. Attempting to explain the whole in terms of only one point, they only explain it away.

The System

The crux of the New Left's critique has been the reverse: To explain a small point in relation to the larger whole gives clear insight into the nature of the whole. The New Left has discovered that a penetrating critique of one point leads automatically to a critique of the whole. The issue of the Bomb is a good example. Nuttall claims that our generation has reacted to the Bomb as if it were simply an event that has occurred in history. This does not probe deeply enough. A better approach is to examine the Bomb in terms of its relation to the nature of society. It is not so important as an "event" which influences particulars as it is as an "ethos" which informs the whole. War comes to be seen as part of a whole life style. This insight is often an integral part of the process of radicalization. Tentative, limited criticisms inevitably lead to an involved, systematic critique.

Probing further into the issue of the Bomb, for instance, one might examine the nature of modern warfare and its relation to a technological society. For the first time, the "necessity" of warfare is so stalemated by the "absurdity" of warfare that the traditional resort to war as a solution to international problems is no longer viable. Certain tirades against the Bomb reveal a petulant annoyance at the removal of society's ultimate recourse. But rather than meaning the end of war, the Bomb merely forces violence further down the strata of society. In fact it means guerilla warfare and increasing limited wars. Moreover, violence erupts at the more penetrating and deeper levels of communications and advertising. Further issues—like the means of modern warfare, the involvement of citizens in war, the methods of training participating armies, the use of propaganda by governments, the gearing of economy and education towards war effort—all throw light on the modern nation as a "Welfare-Through-Warfare State" (Marcuse).[5]

It is this "whole" of any advanced, industrial society, with its intricate web of highly complex interlocking relationships, which is the System, a convenient, all-purpose word for the political, economic and social mechanisms of technological society. Of course it should not be necessary to stress that the word *system* in itself is not derogatory but descriptive, though it can be used with connotations on either extreme, as a witch word or as a panegyric. Marshall McLuhan describes the System in the Electric Era as the "seamless web" or the "global village,"[6] which to him has only positive and optimistic connotations in line with his hope for a new pentecostal unity. But for a radical *System* carries connotations of capitalism or fascism and immediately summons up feelings of strong disapproval. For him *System* is used as a witch word spewed out as the ultimate epithet.

Since this is an area in which words are often strong in connotation and weak in definition, we will approach it, not through the heated rhetoric of student radicals nor the ideological criticisms of Marxists, but through the critiques within the West. What is evident is a growing consciousness that Western technological development is increasingly militating against human fulfillment. Of these critiques not all are radical by any means, but curiously they provide ammunition for the radical salvo even if their premises and conclusions ultimately put the author on the other side.

The work of Max Weber is of fundamental importance, for he was the first to define bureaucracy and relate its rise to the growth of modern industrialism. For Weber bureaucracy has three essential features: It is characterized horizontally by a division of labor and specialization of roles, vertically by the nature of its hierarchy and overall by its permanence as a structure.

Probably it is best portrayed in the novels of Franz Kafka, especially *The Castle* and *The Trial.* Kafka's vision is more than sociological, but the sociological absurdity certainly compounds the metaphysical. The world of *The Castle* is the domain of power and authority; telephone exchanges produce more muddles than connections; bureaucracy drowns in a deluge of files and forms; a stifling hierarchy makes it impossible to find the man above; countless petty officials work endless overtime and get nowhere; innumerable interviews are held, and all of it comes to no purpose. In *The Castle* man is reduced to a file and in *The Trial* to a case. Kafka once said, "The conveyor-belt of life carries you on, no one knows where. One is more of an object, a thing, than a living creature."[7]

Kafka was describing the world of the late Hapsburg Empire, but already he observed the deeply-etched human effects of the rise of bureaucracy as delineated by Weber. Several decades later some, like Hannah Arendt, see bureaucratic power as the main factor unifying otherwise contradictory streams of protest in East and West.

From this early work, we can pass on quickly to social critics nearer our own time, and first of all to the critics of the fifties.

Critical Voices of the Fifties: Riesman, Whyte, Goodman and Mills

David Riesman advances Weber's thesis with his idea of society as the "lonely crowd." Writing in 1956, Riesman, studying the "iron cage" of Weber's latter-day capitalistic bureaucracy, noted that morality had been reduced to morale, that parental influence had been usurped by peer groups and that all around us is the "whip of the word,"[8] the pervasive influence of the mass media. In this atmosphere society has become the "lonely crowd." This is characterized by a polarization between old-fashioned individualists ("the inner directed") and a new majority who are conformist ("the other directed"). Both have problems. The first group is archaic, appealing to values that are no longer valid, and the second group is dangerous in its complacent conformity. Sadly, few people represent his own alternative–responsible, autonomous individuality.

William H. Whyte took this further in *The Organization Man* in 1956. Under his analysis, gone was the Protestant ethic, the American dream and even the Weberian bureaucracy. In its place Whyte saw the rise of a smoother social ethic for which men left their homes, spiritually and physically, to take the vows of a new organizational life. The "organization man" was not necessarily an executive for a recognized corporation; he could just as easily be a medical student for a corporate clinic, an engineer in the Boeing complex, a seminary student training for the established church hierarchy, a physics Ph.D. aiming for a government research lab, or an apprentice with a Wall Street law firm. He was a man who believed in the group as his source of creativity, took belongingness as a goal of individuality and affirmed the omnicompetence of science to achieve his social goals. Whyte pictured him as the "well-rounded man" emerging through the "pipeline" of his education and living in his classless suburban situation.[9]

Of particular importance was Whyte's originality in stressing the "fatal friendliness" of the system. This is a point Marcuse was later to develop even more forcefully and one that Aldous Huxley had already predicted. Whyte wrote, "It is not the evils of organization life that puzzle him, but its very beneficence. . . . In seeking an ethic that offers a spurious peace of mind, thus does he tyrannize himself."[10] Following Aldous Huxley, Whyte was the first to define sociologically the caress of what Marcuse has called "technological rationality." He also saw that this changes the ground rules for revolutionary thinking, for we will find no rebels with the heroic cast necessary for revolutionary action. "Hell is no less hell for being antiseptic. In the 1984 of Big Brother one would at least know who the enemy was."[11]

A third critic of the fifties is Paul Goodman whose general position is well expressed in *Growing Up Absurd.* Surveying society he arrived at the blunt conclusion that " 'man' . . . is what suits a particular type of society in a particular historical stage."[12] Society is not created to suit man and his humanness, but man is socialized and educated to conform to society. In fact, it is not that man is educated to conform but that education itself is culture-conforming. In the light of this, Goodman presumed the Beats and the Angry Young Men could simply be described as "inadequately socialized."[13] But then the question comes, socialized to what? Whole men come from wholly fulfilling environments with real opportunities for the development of human aspirations. Analyzing society to see if this was currently feasible, Goodman examined such areas as jobs, individual significance, class structures and patriotism, and he finally concluded that it was society, not men, which was to blame for the dehumanizing of man. "Our abundant society is at present simply deficient in many of the most elementary objective opportunities and worthwhile goals that could make growing up possible. It is lacking in enough man's work. It is lacking in honest public speech, and people are not taken seriously. It is lacking in the opportunity to be useful. It thwarts aptitude and creates stupidity. It corrupts ingenuous patriotism. It corrupts the fine arts. It shackles science. It dampens animal ardor. It discourages the religious convictions of Justification and Vocation and it dims the sense that there is a Creation. It has no Honor. It has no Community."[14]

Such a society wants men only on its own arbitrary terms. "Conform or Die!" read a sign at Hunter College in the fifties, aptly satirizing the choice of technological man. Goodman predicted that those who were misfits would just "grow up absurd," out of joint, out of line with the mainstream of social conditioning: "Where now there are thousands of these young men, there will be hundreds of thousands. The organized system is the breeding ground of a Beat Generation."[15]

Although he wrote out of the context of the Silent Generation, Goodman was already relating the rise of protest to the depersonalizing System. While one might debate several of Goodman's ideas, such as his strange stress that boys and not girls have the real problem (made even more curious by the rise of Women's Liberation), his analysis was undoubtedly prophetic. He strikes a modern chord in his delineation of the features of the System when he says that society is "an apparently closed room in which there is a large rat race as the dominant center of attention."[16] Here he comes close to the world of Sartre's *No Exit,* where hell is other people. The particular hellishness of the modern system is its reduction of all values and countervalues to the level of pseudovalues. "In the closed room, however, there is only one system of values, that of the rat race itself. This is shared by everybody in the room and held in contempt by everybody in the room."[17]

A fourth important social critic in the fifties, one who also examines the idea of the "closed room," was Cyril Wright Mills, the Texan sociologist and Columbia University professor who became the father of the New Left. In 1951 Mills published *White Collar,* his analysis of a particular group which he saw as vital because of its falsification of Marx. Because in the United States the capitalist entrepreneur and the proletarian workers had united, twentieth-century American history had run counter to Marx's prediction of their polarization leading to revolution. This marriage not only characterized modern America but was in fact "more typically American than the frontier character probably ever was."[18] Nonetheless, Mills argued, man was not rewarded deservingly, for he was no longer free, as the American dream had promised: "He is always somebody's man, the corporation's, the government's, the army's."[19] Five years before William Whyte, Mills revealed the dilemma of the small man, the Willie Lomans of society. The nineteenth-century workers had faced material hardship, but the twentieth-century white collar workers, "the new little people,"[20] faced a new psychological hardship. Having lost their beliefs, they were morally defenseless and politically impotent; and, having lost hope, they had no grounds for action. Again, the reason for this was the nature of the System, their final environment: "What must be grasped is the picture of society as a great salesroom, an enormous file, an incorporated brain, a new universe of management and manipulation."[21]

By 1956, Mills' critique was more scathing, his indictment more stinging. In *The Power Elite,* he analyzed the structure of American society and was forced to conclude that the country was dominated by an economic, political and military elite that formed a powerful trinity of immorality and irresponsibility.

Its first pillar was the economy. Once it had been run by genuinely private enterprises made up of small production units, but now the situation had developed to the point where 300 corporations were in control, many of them with annual budgets larger than the Gross National Product of smaller nations. The second pillar was politics. Where once several dozen states had federal government only as a loose spinal cord, they now passed over more and more power to a strongly centralized executive. The third pillar was the military. Once there had been small state militia with frequent distrust towards central command. Now the "Military Industrial Complex" (Eisenhower) had become the largest feature of government, almost a government within the government. Thus, "As decisions tend to become total in their consequence, the leading men in each of the three domains of power—the warlords, the corporation chieftains, the political directorate, tend to come together, to form the power elite of America."[22] Any remaining institutions, such as families, schools and churches were important only as means to greater ends and so were forced to adapt themselves to modern life. It was the government, the army and the corporations who truly controlled the System.

There are obvious weaknesses and omissions in Mills. Strangely he says nothing about the situation of the blacks, little about the poor and almost nothing about American involvement overseas, all of which have become salient issues among later radicals. Yet his studies are incisive in analysis, if almost pamphleteering in style. He attacks the "commanders of power unequaled in human history,"[23] condemning them for their "higher immorality," their "organized irresponsibility." In several places his work is strangely prophetic of many of the charges leveled against America in the sixties, especially in its involvement in Viet Nam. "America . . . appears now before the world a naked and arbitrary power, as, in the name of realism, its men of decision enforce their often crackpot definitions upon world reality."[24] With equal accuracy he also predicted a sorry level of national debate, when "in the liberal rhetoric, vagueness, and in the conservative mood, irrationality, are raised to principle."

Many accuse Mills of inaccuracy, charging that his descriptions are caricatures. But a careful look shows that many cut close to the bone and are far more accurate than some would like to admit. Poking fun in imaginary advice to an executive, he counsels, "Speak in the rich, round voice and do not confuse your superiors with details. . . . Execute the ceremony of forming a judgment. Delay recognizing the choice you have already made, so as to make the truism sound like the deeply pondered notion. . . . Speak to the well-blunted point. . . . Caricature what you are supposed to be but never become aware of it much less amused by it. And never let your brain show."[25]

Much that Mills once attacked as outrageous is today accepted, if not advocated. Speaking of public leadership, Daniel Boorstin regretfully said, "The qualities which now commonly make a man or a woman into a 'nationally advertized' brand are in fact a new category of human emptiness."[26] An example of how this works out in practice is provided by a memo of R. K. Price, a speech writer for Richard Nixon in the 1968 election: "*We have to be very clear on this point that the response is to the image not to the man.* . . . It's not what's *there* that counts, it's what's projected–and carrying it one step further, it's not what *he* projects but rather what the voter receives. It's not the man we have to change, but rather the *received* impression. And this impression often depends more on the medium and its use than it does on the candidate himself."[27] Mills' imaginary caricature of the selling of an executive is far less disquieting than McGinnis's description in the *Selling of the President.*

A third source of critiques is one that is distinctly non-radical. For this reason it is all the more intriguing to find that even from those who are humanists, liberals or even optimists, there is material which, despite the premises and conclusions, supports the radical critique. John Kenneth Galbraith's *The Affluent Society,* replete with its famous aphorisms like "the bland leading the bland," fits comfortably with the radical's charges against the inherent selfishness of capitalist society. Galbraith's *New Industrial State,* with its striking outline of the techno-structure and its call for a leadership from an academic scientific elite, is based on a critique of the

 System that mirrors that of more radical thinkers and heightens the fear of a swing toward the right which the New Left so earnestly resists.

Lewis Mumford both as a scholar and a man is representative of the highest humanism, yet his mammoth studies are more and more forcing him to the reluctant conclusion that modern man is depersonalizing "himself so effectively that he is no longer man enough to stand up to machines."[28]

Perhaps the clearest example of all is Marshall McLuhan, a man of highest hope whose material is often the perverse contradiction of his general thesis and underlying cheerfulness. On the one hand, his notion of the Electric Era and its convergence with Teilhard de Chardin's "Noosphere" is nothing short of supreme optimism for mankind generally. On the other hand, a countering argument from his evidence is seen in the light of two questions. What is the relationship of the media to men? Can the effects of the media be contained or controlled?

In answer to the first question, McLuhan suggests four roles which media have in relation to man. The first is "extension"; the media take the things a man can do with a part of or with the whole of his body and project them out into the world of technology (a wheel replacing a foot). The second role is "exchange"; once the media are extended, they provide a store or exchange of ability which other men can use (a book storing the wisdom of a brain). These first two roles are valuable and positive. But the last two roles relate to damaging side effects of this positive advance. The third role is "entrancement" or "exclusion"; each new extension magnifies one sense at the expense of the others, so that "when these ratios change, men change."[29] Consequently "all media work us over completely."[30] If a car is the extension of a foot, a car culture can eliminate the foot to the point where continual drivers might as well be amputees with no legs who have invented the car to get themselves around! The last role, and perhaps the most damaging is "evolution"; man, who once modified his machines for his own progress, is ultimately modified by them. "Man becomes, as it were, the sex organs of the machine world."[31] Or again, "Since the new information environments are direct extensions of our own nervous systems, they have a much more profound relation to our human condition than the old 'natural' environment. . . . Quite naturally they take over the evolutionary work that Darwin had seen in the spontaneities of biology."[32] The initial relationship is reversed. Man no longer modifies and develops. He is himself modified, and his very sense of himself is undermined.

The second troubling question is whether the effects of the media can be controlled. McLuhan's comments here are not uniform; in fact, he gives three contradictory replies. The first, which holds out real hope for a successful answer, I have found only once in all his books and interviews. This is when he describes "the antidote of related media like print."[33] If this remark is to be taken seriously, it is extraordinary, partly because it is unique in his books but mainly because it runs counter to his basic thesis that the perceptions natural to "hot" media (such as print) cannot withstand the "cool" (TV, for example). McLuhan's more normal answers take one of two directions. For the most part, he strongly suggests that "there is . . . no way of refusing to comply with the new sense ratios,"[34] a view which tends to leave us with a weary helplessness. At other times, however, he partially relieves this gloom by suggesting that in the person of the artist society has an "early warning system" against "media fallout." But, if the artist with his more acute sense perceptions is one step ahead of society, he is still one step behind the real position of the culture. If McLuhan were less excited by the inflated optimism of Teilhard de Chardin, the underlying vein of pessimism in much of his material might well show through.

The Critical Voice of the Sixties: Marcuse

Coming to the critiques of the sixties, we can do no better than take Herbert Marcuse as the best example. The well-known banner carried by radicals in Rome—"Marx, Mao and Marcuse"—coincided with the peak of his popularity in the counter culture, and for many his writings gave sociological depth and philosophical integrity to an American movement otherwise heavily majoring on action rather than theory. All his books are a crushing argument to prove the necessity of revolution. In *Reason and Revolution* he uses Hegel to argue that it is philosophically necessary; in *Eros and Civilization* he uses Freud to prove the psychological necessity; but it is supremely in *One Dimensional Man* that his arguments are given compelling force by sociological evidence. In many ways, this is his least Marxian book, yet it explains the failure of Marx's prediction that in the twentieth century the bourgeois and the proletariat would polarize to the point of revolution. Marcuse admits the almost total collusion between the two and explains it in terms of the nature of modern society, especially its "technological rationality." The centrifugal forces of society foreseen by Marx have been conquered not by terror but by techonology, "on the dual basis of overwhelming efficiency and an increased standard of living."[35]

So the technological society is marked by the integration of opposites, the decline of pluralism, the blurring of ideologies and the paralysis of criticism. This, in a word, is containment. To the degree that it is able to "deliver the goods" an established society is able to control man, "using the scientific conquest of nature for the scientific conquest of man."[36] Thus society is stabilized: "In the medium of technology, culture, politics and the economy merge into an omnipresent system, which swallows up or repulses all alternatives."[37] The result, as Marcuse sees it, is One Dimensional Man, flattened out by "a comfortable, smooth, reasonable, democratic unfreedom."[38]

This grave charge Marcuse attempts to substantiate in the twin areas of society and thought, both of which are said to be only one-dimensional. His section on "one-dimensional thought" is weakest. Here he argues that the shift from metaphysical idealism to methodological empiricism has meant the triumph of one-dimensional thinking and the defeat of dialectics. Thus, "the explosive historical dimension of meaning is silenced."[39] Empiricism he denounces as "philosophic behaviorism,"[40] but his arguments are more ideological than philosophical, and his accusation that empiricists were inevitably closer to fascism is quite contrary to the facts. Far from being conformists, the truth is that almost to a man empiricists such as those in the Vienna Circle (Carnap, Schlick and Wittgenstein, etc.) were socialists, radicals and anti-Nazis; on the other hand, the connection between Hegel and Fascism, or between his dialectics and his eventual elitism, is too close for Marcuse's own comfort.

But in the first half of *One Dimensional Man,* when he deals with one-dimensional society, Marcuse is at his best. His main target is the dictatorial power of the mass media and the monolithic mentality of "telenewsmagspeak," which Theodore White has called "the opinionated Mafia." Analyzing its effects, he claims it builds totalitarian truth: "The unified, functional language is an irreconcilably anti-critical and anti-dialectical language."[41] Television turns all culture into a commodity; art, politics, religion and philosophy become marketable and lose their aesthetic sensitivity and their critical quality.

Mass media are also the creators of "hypnotic definitions"; connotations become definitions and judgment is silenced. (Two examples of this are the fate of the word *free* on different sides of the ideological divide, and the differing interpretations of the equation: insurgency = terrorism = war of national liberation!) Another side effect of the mass media is its stimulation of the illusion of classlessness. The working-class girl and the millionaire's wife both aspire to similar values via the same advertising, and this serves only to anesthetize the pain of the unbridgeable gap between them. Marcuse illustrates well the inherent depersonalization and anti-critical tendency latent in the very style of magazines like *Time.* The resulting reduction is One Dimensional Man. The creation of "the Happy Consciousness–the belief that the real is rational and that the system delivers the goods–reflects the new conformism."[42]

Written in 1964, his thesis found a loudly amplified echo in the Free Speech Movement that same year. The famous speech of Mario Savio on the steps of the Administration Building at the University of California (Berkeley) centered on the same features of society as a System. "There is a time when the operations of the machine become so odious, make you so sick at heart, that you can't take part, you can't even tacitly take part. And you've got to put your bodies upon the gears and upon the wheels, upon the levers, upon all the apparatus, and you've got to make it stop. And you've got to indicate to the people who run it, to the people who own it, that unless you're free the machine will be prevented from working at all."[43]

Marcuse himself rather sadly admits, "There are very few students who have really read me." There would be still fewer in the Third World who have ever heard of him. Yet whether he was right or even read, he was *in*, and thus for many of the radicals of the sixties Herbert Marcuse was the angel of the apocalypse, just as Cyril

Wright Mills had been for the fifties.

The Critical Voice of the Seventies: Ellul

At this stage, it is too soon to say whose voice will be the most prominent in the seventies. Possibly it will be Noam Chomsky, now speaking with increasing cogency. Some point to Charles Reich, but his alternatives for the future are too vague to be more than merely fashionable. Perhaps it will be some of the more thoughtful activists of the sixties, Stoughton Lynd or Tom Hayden, for example, writing with a maturity fired by direct experience. But my own suggestion is that this will be a period of increasing prominence for Jacques Ellul, who, although he wrote his books much earlier (*The Technological Society* was published a decade before Marcuse's *One Dimensional Man*), is only now coming to the attention of a wider English-speaking audience.

Ellul was the first to use the phrase "technological society," and his analyses have always been prophetic, but to read his opponents, one might easily imagine that he is a severely reactionary "machinoclast." Even Theodore Roszak, who admits that his books are the best global picture of technocracy in action, charges that his *Technological Society* is "an outrageously pessimistic book."[44] But this is unjust. Ellul has a fine record as a World War II resistance fighter and as a professor of law in the University of Bordeaux. Neither by nature nor by conviction is he a pessimist. His concern is merely "whether things are so or not." Judgments that he is a habitual pessimist derive from those whose disgruntled humanism is based on such premises as "man is free," "man is good" or "progress is inevitable." Ellul does not wish to compare modern society with a romantic and fictional freedom of the past. Maybe we have only changed the "taboos" of the past for the "technics" of today, but both operate at the inevitable expense of freedom. If Ellul gives no remedy, it is because he believes that searching diagnosis must come first. If the technological society can make art innocuous and mysticism an escape, if it can turn principles into propaganda, then technical solutions will only tighten the screw and spurious solutions will only delay a more realistic remedy.

Aldous Huxley, who virtually "discovered" Ellul for American readers, praised his book for having "really made the case" that he had tried to make in *Brave New World.* Admitting he was "jealous of the author's penetration," he repeatedly compared Ellul's work with Spengler's magnum opus and predicted that *The Technological Society* would become one of the twentieth century's most authentic documents of social criticism.[45]

For Jacques Ellul the essence of "technique" is not that it is "mechanical"; rather "technique" is the more subtle "mentality" that grew from the "mechanical." The "mechanical" is merely the crude clockwork of machinery; "technique" is the consciousness of a mechanism applying itself to all man's life and finally to man himself. It is a principle made out of a process, a mentality made out of a machine, whereby one uses an ensemble of procedures, practices and resources to achieve certain ends. The total aggregate of the best possible means in every field will together produce a technical civilization, covering all man's acts, from shaving to landing on the moon. "Today no human activity escapes this technical imperative,"[46] he writes. "Our civilisation is first and foremost a civilisation of means."[47] This technique will be increasingly applied to man in medicine, genetics, education, vocational guidance, advertising and psychology until finally "here man himself becomes the object of technique."[48] This development is not ideological, and therefore it is not restricted to one side of the Iron Curtain. Capitalism may be the bourgeoisie's conscious realization of technique, but communism should equally be seen as the proletariat's conscious realization of technique.

His thesis can best be grasped by understanding certain features basic to technique. First is the fact that technology is the blood brother of rationalism. Technique is the translation into action of man's concern to master things by means of reason alone, to account for the subconscious, to make quantitative what is qualitative, to clarify and make precise the outlines of nature, to take hold of chaos and put order into it. Technique is the calculus of efficiency, the reduction of facts, figures, forces and even men to procedures in the service of the tyranny of objective rationalism.

A second feature is the element of artificiality. Technique rapidly approaches the point where the natural environment will be replaced by the technological. Some, like Richard Landers, may applaud and welcome this, but most are ill at ease with the plastic unnaturalness of such a world.

A third feature is the "automatism" of technique. The Holy Grail of the technologist is the consuming search for the "one best way." When this is found, the process immediately becomes self-directing. Everything that can be done must be done or the result is poor technology. At once human, moral and aesthetic values are either ousted or relegated to a lower position. Then only the technical is left to fight the technical. The debate over the Bomb illustrates this. During the national discussion in France in 1966, Jacques Soustelle expressed this view bluntly: "Since it was possible it was necessary."[49] More telling still is the story of Robert Oppenheimer, widely known for his lack of zeal for the H-Bomb. What is not generally known is that he later changed his mind in favor of this super bomb because of the improved design he had been shown. Studying it, he exclaimed that it must be tried, because it was so "sweet and lovely and beautiful."[50] So when the one best way is found, the procedure is automatic. Ellul claims that this means "there is no place for an individual today unless he is a technician. . . . To be in the possession of the lightning thrust of technique is a matter of life and death for individuals alike; no power on earth can withstand its pressures."[51]

Another related feature is technique's "self-augmentation." The self-directing process of "the one best way" slowly subsumes more and more to itself. "In the future, man will apparently be confined to the role of a recording device."[52] As technology progresses, technique "modifies whatever it touches, but is itself untouchable."[53]

One last feature worthy of mention is the related tendency of monism. The Technological Society becomes a System, a unified whole subsuming all within it to the point of containment. If this is in fact so, the problem of technology at a certain stage is not the question of its use or abuse but of its nature. This explains the radicalizing insight that to attack one point is to be led on to attack the whole, for it is this whole which most persistently contains all change. "The infusion of some more or less vague sentiment of human welfare cannot alter it. Not even the moral conversion of the technicians could make a difference. At best, they would cease to be good technicians."[54] Think through the implications of this in terms of the police forces of the future. McLuhan, cheerful in his moral neutrality, predicts the possibility of "womb-to-tomb surveillance,"[55] with total, instant information on each citizen available to the government. But it is not difficult to see the more sinister dangers of this. If the notion of a technically perfect police force is in line with the required availability of instant, total information, then such technological perfection is hardly distinguishable from the harshest fears of a police state or a totalitarian regime. Ellul cannot agree with McLuhan's facile optimism. "The techniques of the police . . . have as their necessary end the transformation of the entire nation into a concentration camp."[56] Aldous Huxley in his customary farsighted way had long foreseen this in his 1946 foreword to *Brave New World*; he wryly remarked, "Government by clubs and firing squads . . . is not merely inhumane (nobody much cares about that nowadays); it is demonstrably inefficient—and in an age of advanced technology, inefficiency is the sin against the Holy Ghost."[57] With such evidence Ellul concludes, "Technique cannot be otherwise than totalitarian."[58]

These are just some of his outlined features of "technique." Perhaps the most vivid summary is his picture of technology as a tyrant, in which "technique" is the psychology of the tyrant, the state is its circulatory apparatus, the economy is its digestive system, and man is reduced to being its cellular tissue.

Such a level of technology poses its greatest threat in the present context of a mounting series of problems and the fear of social chaos, for the hasty application of technological solutions could lead to a powerful marriage between government and technology. They would become "the most important forces in the modern world; they buttress and reinforce each other in their aim to produce an apparently indestructible, total civilisation."[59] If Ellul's verbal pictures (such as his image of the tyrant) were not backed by such clear analysis and patient documentation, his charges would look like radical rhetoric and would make ideal ammunition for radical cartoonists. The fact is, however, that Ellul is marked by a high honesty in his determined refusal to reduce protest to posturing or radical truth to rhetoric.

Sometimes, in fact, he is openly scornful of the image and status some have achieved in the wake of the revolutionary vogue. Writing of Henry Miller, he says, "It is harmless to attack a crumbling middle-class morality.

 True, persecutions, seizures and law suits have been directed against the 'black' authors. But I would like to point to the tidy profits that such minor scandals have brought them. I am somehow unable to believe in the revolutionary value of an act which makes the cash register jingle so merrily."[60]

As we glance back over these critiques from Max Weber to Jacques Ellul, two general features become prominent, both constantly stressed by the New Left. The first is the "totality" of the System, whether panegyrically used of the "seamless web" and the "global village" or thrown as an insult at the System seen as the "closed sales room." By now this point should be obvious. From war to education, all facets of society are merely integral parts of an interlocking whole.

The second feature, until now more implied than obvious, is the latent hypocrisy of the System. The erosion of the Christian basis to Western culture removes the grounding of traditional morality, and secular humanism has not replaced it. But with a perverse refusal to face reality, the American dream and the British sense of "tradition" are still self-justifying, still tacitly assuming they rest on valid principles. The gap between principles and practices is increasingly difficult to conceal and becomes, as we have seen, the spawning ground for mystification. Goodman speaks of the "sense of hollow-rightness" and of "the missed revolutions of modern times—the falling-short and the compromises."[61] William Whyte points out, "It is the American dream that is going to have to give, whatever its more elderly guardians may think. People grow restive with a mythology that is too distant from the way things actually are."[62] Kenneth Kenniston, speaking of the lack of credibility in modern society, refers to the "institutionalization of hypocrisy."[63]

Whether it issues in outright lies, devious deceptions,

or sincerely held delusions, either way the totality of the System and its intrinsic hypocrisy are common themes in a growing number of analyses of society. Slowly but inevitably, by its refusal to admit the true nature of contemporary reality, modern society is forcing a generation to the position of noncommittal doubt or open cynicism. R. D. Laing states, "Unfortunately we are forced by the cynical lies, multifarious deceptions, and sincerely held delusions to which we are now subjected through all media–even the organs of scholarship and science–to a position of almost total social scepticism."[64]

Technophobia or Clarity of Vision?

Now we come to a vital question. Are these critiques accurate on the whole? Do they describe things "as they really are," as Ellul says? Or do they represent the archaic "politics of nostalgia" blown up into a dangerous technophobia? Alvin Toffler, for example, describes such critics as latter-day Luddites and technophobes. Such counter charges must be taken into account. The integrity of the counter culture's critique of society is at stake.

A good example of such a counter charge is Alasdair MacIntyre's critique of Marcuse with its basic contention that Marcuse's analysis can be dismissed as "fairly crude technological determinism."[65] He correctly sees that Marcuse's analysis is often so elevated that it could apply equally well to any advanced industrial society. This only blurs the still real differences between the United States and Russia or the United States and Britain–distinctions vital to any debate. But even so this does not alter the basic thesis, against which MacIntyre's otherwise brilliant arguments have an ironic result. Marcuse suggests that most men are impotent because some men (an elite) have control. MacIntyre counters by arguing that most men seem to be impotent because of the fundamental lack of control: "The most impressive political fact is the accidental character of our policies."[66] But surely, if things are beyond human control, man is impotent. MacIntyre's answer is actually worse than Marcuse's problem. It is bad enough to have to fight against a specific elite, but a situation where policies are not humanly controlled because they are uncontrollable is far more gloomy.

That modern policies are accidental and uncontrollable is the main thrust of a thesis developed by Michael Harrington in *The Accidental Century.* Originally, he says, as history stumbled into new social systems, the revolutionists of the past consciously proposed visions which outstripped reality. Today revolutionists unconsciously create realities which outstrip their vision. This makes for an ironic situation: The most rational, scientific century of all has become the most accidental. So MacIntyre's answer, far from alleviating Marcuse's problem, actually points out more explicitly yet another area where the effect of technology serves only to aggravate the problem. David Riesman had seen this earlier: "Who really runs things? What people fail to see is that, while it may take leadership to start things running, or to stop them, very little leadership is needed once things are under way—that, indeed, things can get terribly snarled up and still keep running."[67]

Alvin Toffler likewise provides a spirited defense of technology and an indignant blast at technophobia. Such pessimism, he says, is outdated, kept alive only by "a generation of future-haters and technophobes" with their "ironclad consensus," "belatedly hurling their rusty javelins."[68] Toffler sees two grounds for a new hope that dehumanization will be halted. First, bureaucracy, he says, is now being replaced by "adhocracy." Transience has outmoded permanence in all human relations, and this is reflected in the working world by the rise of small task forces created for specific purposes.

Thus bureaucracy's three features of permanence, hierarchy and division of labor are being broken down. With the "adhocracy," "the fast-moving, information-rich, kinetic organization of the future, filled with transient cells and extremely mobile individuals"[69] will transcend the constricting structures of Weberian bureaucracy.

Second, uniformity is being replaced by diversity and this is giving rise to greater freedom of choice. Complaints against mass standardization were genuine, but this represented only stage one of industrialization. A second stage achieved in the super-industrial society leads to the possibility of diversity. "It is only primitive technology that imposes standardization. Automation, in contrast, frees the pattern to endless, blinding, mind-numbing diversity."[70] So whether we wish to design our own Mustang or enjoy the possibility of joining a surfeit of subcults, the option now is not one-dimensional uniformity but multi-dimensional overchoice. The evidence for his arguments is more substantial than MacIntyre's and it would be wrong not to recognize a new stage.

Nonetheless, in his reformulation of the contours of technology there are still two things which militate against the freedom of man—the complexity of the technocracy and the increasing impotence of the individual within such a society. Neither of these is altered by Toffler's arguments. In a society of baffling complexity the increasing diversity will not mean increasing freedom and participation but rather a tendency towards withdrawal. Herman Kahn, hardly guilty of radical rage, predicts that because most political decisions will be so far beyond the average citizen, he will be tempted to leave his decision making to elites, experts and committees. As the Party Secretary says in Alexander Solzhenitsyn's novel *For the Good of the Cause,* "You can just tell them that this is a State institute and the why's and wherefore's of the matter are none of our business."[71]

 The average man will then lapse further into apathy, demanding from his government only a charade of justification of its policies and a good standard of living. So while the complexity will bring diversity and pluralism, the result could well become a new smile from Marcuse's Happy Consciousness beaming down on Mills' "cheerful robots." Rome was no less totalitarian for having a pluralistic wealth of societies, cults, clubs, mystery religions and esoteric cliques. It just meant that citizens were better adapted to totalitarian control and did not give vent to their grievances.

Much of Toffler's evidence actually points in a different direction than the optimism which is its keynote. He admits that "choice may become overchoice and freedom unfreedom"[72] (almost as if to curb his optimism, and remind us of his original thesis which concerned the bad effects of Future Shock!). At another point, he even describes technology as a "great, growling engine of change" and sees its danger in a passage reminiscent of Michael Harrington: "Many social ills are less the consequence of oppressive control than of oppressive lack of control. The horrifying truth is that, so far as much technology is concerned, no one is in charge."[73] The wheel comes full circle; with his super-contemporary evidence Toffler strengthens rather than weakens the arguments against technology.

The Weakness of the New Left—Not Its Critique But Its Alternative

All this is of central importance to the counter culture. It shows that the case against the New Left is not so much that its critique of society is faulty, but that its alternative is inadequate, and, on closer examination, we see that this is the result of its sharing many of the same humanist premises it pretends to reject. Ironically, their very change became their own containment. Their revolutionary alternative was one-dimensional too. Let me point out certain facets of this in some random areas.

First, by way of a backdrop, it should be obvious that the ideal of a "successful" revolution is on the order of myth. The Revolutions of 1789 and 1917 are the twin pillars of this myth, the former especially so since for the first time in modern history a successful revolution, social in content, was carried out in the streets. Yet, quite above the immediate facts of history, a legend was created which gained historical and ideological momentum after 1917 and still operates. This legend firmly imprints the idea that revolutions are dialectically inevitable and successful and that revolutionaries are only the midwives of history. So much for the legend. Historical evidence points elsewhere. History seems callous to such inevitability and cynical of such success. Yet movements still feed on the myth. The anarchists take 1789 as prototypical, despite its open betrayal of many of their basic principles, the decentralization of government and abolition of property, for example. The anarchist revolutionaries are thus forced to use historical blinkers and selectively commend only the period prior to Robespierre's Reign of Terror in 1793.

Revolutions are too often the graveyards of revolutionary ideals. Twentieth-century realists have long predicted the betrayal of idealism in modern revolutions. Oswald Spengler warned that, although socialism was anti-imperialist in his day, "One day it will become arch-expansionist with all the vehemence of destiny."[74] Albert Camus gave a similar cautionary comment: "The prophetic dream of Marx and the over-inspired predictions of Hegel or of Nietzsche ended by conjuring up, after the city of God had been razed to the ground, either a rational or an irrational State, but one which in both cases was founded on terror."[75] However, this is not a call to opt for conservatism but rather to examine more closely the inner contradictions which have so often betrayed humanism in its attempt to realize idealism in revolution. These inner contradictions have inevitably brought about the failure of the New Left particularly and the counter culture generally, and hence deserve more specific attention. The reliance on anarchism and the philosophy of Herbert Marcuse will be our examples, for each shows the inner contradictions that make success impossible.

Anarchism has two weaknesses. First, the basic elements of modern anarchism are totally contradictory; it has become the uneasy alliance of two incongruous sources. The initial source was religious, growing from the medieval revolutions which were millenarian and apocalyptic, stressing the necessity for sudden change and drastic purges. The second source was the Enlightenment and the rationalist belief in the inevitability of progress and the perfectibility of man. Anarchism thus oscillates between drastic realism and utopian romanticism. This explains its ecumenical inclusion of such diverse temperaments as Thomas Godwin (1756-1836) who believed wholeheartedly in the perfectibility of man and Michael Bakunin (1814-76) who admitted that his own turbulent temperament came from "a passion for destruction."[76] But the inner contradictions are seen even more sharply in the classical debate with the Marxists, Bakunin representing the anarchists and Marx and Engels the communists. The questions at issue were these: How does one succeed in revolution? and How does one preserve freedom after the revolution? The dilemma was that both sides were half right and half wrong. Each was betrayed by a weak premise at a vital place.

Over the question of gaining control in revolution, the Marxists were correct in their insistence that revolutions, to be successful, must be authoritarian. Engels argued, "Anarchists demand that the first act of the social revolution shall be the abolition of authority. Have these gentlemen ever seen a revolution? A revolution is certainly the most authoritarian thing there is; it is the art whereby one part of the population imposes its will on the other part by means of rifles, bayonets and cannons—authoritarian means if such there be at all."[77] Without authoritarian means no revolution would be successful: Society has amply confirmed this argument. Any anarchist hope to succeed through autonomous free-form groups is utopian and is doomed to failure.

On the second question, How does one maintain control? the anarchists were correct. They warned that revolutionary methods inexorably impose their character on the end result. Bakunin insisted that the organization of the revolution should resemble the desired goal. A Swiss anarchist supported him: "How can you expect an egalitarian and a free society to emerge from an authoritarian organization? It is impossible. . . . The International, embryo of future human society must be from this moment the faithful image of our principles of liberty and federation, and reject from its midst any principle leading to authority and dictatorship."[78] But this leaves the anarchist in a real dilemma. Without either the force necessary to seize power or the form necessary to retain power, the history of anarchism can only become a lesson in a lost cause. Their revolutions are sometimes disastrous, sometimes quixotic, but always abortive, the sorry victims of fatal inner contradictions.

A second place where we can see the weakness of the humanist premises in revolutionary thinking is in Herbert Marcuse. His reasoning founders on its own inescapable tensions. His treatment of Hegel is a first example. Regardless of whether his reading of Hegel is fair or not, Marcuse is correct that the dialectical principle, "what is, cannot be true," is potentially revolutionary. By their very nature all philosophies and political systems carry the seeds of their own dissolution.

 Revolution is not accidental. As the status quo turns into its opposite (thesis to antithesis) it is only expressing the essence of the dialectic. He is also candid in admitting that Hegel himself was more than a little reactionary in practice. But what he fails to see is that the same dialectical principles has repressive tendencies; it subordinates right to might, makes the individual subject to the state and postulates history as deterministic. The seeds of totalitarianism later to erupt nakedly in Marcuse's *Critique of Pure Tolerance* are already latent in his *Reason and Revolution.*

His treatment of Freud gives an even clearer example and is even more extraordinary. Most Marxists tend to disapprove of Freud; if they are favorable it is usually only towards his practical therapy not his metaphysical theory. But Marcuse takes Freud with all his open pessimism, his basic determinism and his personal political conformism, and tries to use him to justify revolution. The task is too great. Almost like some Hegelian Houdini Marcuse offers to shut himself into the box of Freudian repression and then demonstrate his escape. The former he manages admirably with a perverse masochistic honesty, but he fails to make good his intended escape by any rational argument. He does produce rare passages of lyricism which temporarily escape the cage of his normally turgid prose, but eleven years later he rescinds them in the bleak admission that his *Eros and Civilisation* was "an optimistic, euphemistic, even positive thought"[79] which was soon to give way to the bleak realism of *One Dimensional Man* in 1964. This by contrast was described by Julius Gould as "dialectics of despair" and by a reviewer in *Dissent* as "One Dimensional Pessimism." Like so many others Marcuse finds himself caught in the constant oscillation between optimism and pessimism. Where his arguments are at their strongest empirically (as in *One Dimensional Man*) the overtones of his work are strongly pessimistic, and where his arguments are weakest empirically (as in *Eros and Civilisation* or *An Essay on Liberation*) his optimism is unbounded. He is held in a vice by this impasse. Does he choose the empirical facts? Then he is pessimistic. Does he choose the romantic hope? Then he finds himself short of evidence. The transformation of society is objectively necessary, but the agency for transformation is conspicuously absent. As he admits in his article "The End of Utopia," he is caught in this vicious circle and all there is to show for it practically is little better than what Lenin dismissed as "infantile disorder" or Raymond Aaron described as "eternal nostalgia for a salvationist upheaval." Despite himself and his goals he ultimately ends nearer to Freud's realistic sobriety: "From the slave revolts in the ancient world to the socialist revolution, the struggle of the oppressed has ended in a new, 'better' system of domination. . . . An element of *self-defeat* seems to be involved in this dynamic. . . . In this sense, every revolution has also been a betrayed revolution."[80]

If in Marcuse's own writings The Great Refusal ends in The Grand Betrayal, the chance of improvement by those who make anti-intellectualism into a principle is slender.

Marcuse's dilemma is also practically shown in his differences with Norman O. Brown. Marcuse brings together in his theories Hegel, Freud and Marx, but raises this question: While the dialectic goes with either Freud or Marx, which of the latter is the basis for revolution? Is the social reality the true one (as Marx said) and psychic reality its shadow? Or is the psychic reality the true one (as Freud said) and social reality the shadow? In his excellent discussion of this, Roszak shows that while both Brown and Marcuse come to Freud, Marcuse brings his Marxist background and will not follow the implications so far as Brown, the non-Marxist, liberal Freudian maverick. So Marcuse offers only marginal gains in removing surplus repression and adjusting to life's basic repression. "Basic repression" for Marcuse is biological and inescapable, whereas "surplus repression" is the current historical or sociological domination unnecessarily added to this. Brown plunges further to promise the removal of almost all repression (including death) from the world of man. *Love's Body* runs out in symbolic, fiery, visionary terms which quarry heavily from Blake, Nietzsche and Boehme. The book closes, promising "the antinomy between mind and body, word and deed, speech and silence overcome. Everything is only a metaphor; there is only poetry."

Marcuse's reply was instant, sharp and practical, hotly defending revolution as real, pragmatic, of the here and the now. A revolution that is not this empirically real, he said, will tail off into mystical, imaginary rhetoric and be socially useless: "Brown obliterates the decisive difference between the real and the artificial."[81] One could almost gasp at the significance of this. Here, the "real" is not the dialectical negation of "what is" but rather the empirical reality of one-dimensional positivism which he had so bitterly rejected! Roszak rightly shows that where Marcuse draws up, Brown goes on and much of the counter culture with him.

Thus, both the anarchists and the followers of Marcuse are caught in one-dimensional thought systems. Their premises are either the same as or similar to the vitiated premises they seek to root out, and they lack any clear agency to bring about change. Without a basis and balance for a true alternative, they oscillate between the logic of Marxism which achieves too much and the logic of mysticism which achieves nothing. If it takes a Marxist to make a revolution, it also takes a Marxist to appreciate the revolution he has made. The first is a tribute to his clear thinking; the second is a tragedy because of his inner contradictions. Ironically, the greatest victory of the nineteenth-century bourgeoisie occurred when its Marxist opponents took over the task of perpetuating in the twentieth century the shallow reductionist view of man of nineteenth-century mechanistic science.

Tragedy, Irony, Absurdity

In conclusion, certain lessons stand out sharply. The first is the necessary understanding of the tragedy in all this. However it arrives, one by-product of modern technology is a mounting mood of alienation, depersonalization and dehumanization. Whether it comes through technological evolution as McLuhan suggests, or through totalitarian control or conditioning, or just through the disruption caused by those in revolution against such a system who bring down further repression, alienation is only compounded for more and more people.

A second lesson is the irony in all this. Describing the media, McLuhan quotes the psalmist who speaks of the idol worshippers and their idols and remarks that "their makers grow to be like them, and so do all who trust them."[82] The pagan in the psalmist's time had his own view of ultimate reality, so he extended his presuppositions about the nature of this reality into the external world by creating idols. These in turn became his environmental presuppositions and conditioned him to be less than he really was. Finally, they stifled his human aspirations until he, like his idols, was deaf, dumb and immobile. It is this way also with media and man when technology is the logic of his rationalistic reductionism without a compensating basis for his aspirations and humanness. Soon it changes from being the extension of his presuppositions to being the conditioner of his environment and finally of his nature. The technological society is not so much suffering a crisis of humanism as a crisis of Man. Ginsberg's modern Moloch is merely the consequence of modern man's settled choice. Perhaps soon, like the primitive animist, modern man will endow his idols with spirits and worship them.

The third lesson is the patent absurdity of searching for answers where there are none. The Munich comedian Karl Vallentin, a rare humorist and metaphysical clown, was famous for a skit which illustrates the folly of the contemporary revolutionary. Coming onto the stage in almost total darkness, with one solitary circle of light provided by a street lamp, he paced round and round with a long, worried face, searching for something. Soon a policeman crossed the stage and asked him what he had lost. Vallentin answered that it was the key to his house. The policeman joined in the hunt, but after a while the search appeared fruitless. "Are you sure you lost it here?" asked the policeman. "Oh no!" said Vallentin, pointing to the dark corner, "It was over there." "Then why on earth are you looking here?" asked the policeman. "There's no light over there!" replied Vallentin.

Contemporary man, with his self-drawn picture of society as the "closed room" with No Exit, is caught metaphysically and sociologically. In the darkness of the room evidently without windows, perhaps without doors, he gropes round and round the edges. Can one hope that someone will dare to wonder whether there is any light other than the feeble sparks of his own making? Or will he stubbornly persist in treading the barren circle of poor premises?

5/Violence: Crisis or Catharsis?

"Violence is a cleansing force."
Frantz Fanon

"I cannot see why man should not be just as cruel as nature."
Adolf Hitler

"Political power comes out of the barrel of a gun."
Chairman Mao Tse-tung

"Violence has no place in America! Anyone who preaches violence should be shot like a dog!"
Heard on KGO Radio, San Francisco

"There is a beastliness in the marrow of the century."
Norman Mailer

"Nature has let us down, God seems to have left the receiver off the hook, and time is running out."
Arthur Koestler[1]

From the National Conference of the SNCC in May 1966 through the Weatherman bombing incidents, it is clear that a defining feature of part of the New Left has been its open espousal of violence, justified both pragmatically and philosophically. This is part of the newness of the New Left in student radicalism. Even when they throw bombs and not just rocks (usually after warning people to escape), their action is still qualitatively and quantitatively different from the violence of bombing in Viet Nam or the slow corrosive violence to the poor in America. In fact, it hardly equals the violence of early labor union struggles. But it is still violence. Some would point out that violence of the New Left is more in theory and emotion than in practice—that it is rhetorically justified rather than realistically pursued—but the justification of violence remains. Perhaps only in a climate where romanticism is rarely far away could radicals fail to see the inconsistency between extreme rhetoric and the fortunate moderation of their general practice, but the problem still remains.

The early Marx had rejected violence only to change his mind and regret that it was inevitable in industrial societies where any other means of revolution was impracticable and non-violence was scorned as "the parson's mode of thought." Earlier socialists, like Georges Sorel who made a virtue of violence, were dismissed as fascists. But the New Left has been radical, anti-fascist and at times openly violent. Their resort to violence deserves understanding on its own account, but raises the larger question of violence in modern society.

If we remember J. R. Platt's "The world has now become too dangerous for anything less than Utopia,"[2] we realize that violence is one of the explosive issues which both delays utopia and demands it. It is perhaps surprising that until recently little has been written on violence. Now a flood of studies is rising—presidential commissions, the findings of psychology departments, the theories of philosophers and the statistics of sociologists. This is also reflected at the general level of culture in books and especially in subject matter and style in films. In *Weekend,* Jean Luc Godard pictures society as a social slaughterhouse, and in *If,* Lindsay Anderson uses the story of violence in a boarding school as a metaphor of society in England and of life in general. His film poses the issue in almost the exact form raised by much modern discussion. Is violence to be understood as crisis or catharsis? On one level *If* is just a strong caricature of the nineteenth-century boarding school, representing an authoritative establishment. Violence is seen in terms of a crisis which results in the breakdown of the school's authority, discipline, law and order. But on a deeper level are the subtler overtones which many have missed because they were so intrigued by the story or outraged by the caricature. Like Thoreau, the boys return from their vacation, having spent some time in the forest. The record player plays the Congo Mass. On the walls they have a picture of the Simba Rebels; a typical statement of their philosophy was "War and violence are the only pure acts left."

Here the school authority does not represent order so much as repression, since it is a system where the boys are taught to "fight" at the levels of sports, Army training or the Chapel religion ("Fight the good fight with all your might"). Thus their eventual violence is justified. It is not crisis but catharsis, an assertion and discovery of freedom from repression. Significantly, it is the liberal headmaster, standing out on the lawn and calling for reasonable discussion, who is cut down by the first bullets spattering from the machine gun.

Is violence crisis or catharsis? This is the polarization which many modern theorists, both those opposing and those advocating violence, seem to offer. Like all polarizations, this one is an unsatisfactory formulation of the problem and this prevents the finding of a genuine solution. A closer study could demonstrate that even in those who suggest that violence is either crisis or catharsis, there is also a conscious or unconscious expression of the opposite pole. Thus the radical strongly affirms violence as catharsis, but it is in fact only catharsis because of the intolerable nature of the crisis. Likewise though the establishment speaks of violence as crisis when it represses dissent, in fact only the mystification of its own violence prevents it from seeing violence as an inherent affirmation of catharsis. Take, for example, the subtle equation of violence, masculinity and patriotism. (Nately remarks in *Catch-22*: "Anything worth living for is worth dying for.")[3] How are courage and manliness proved in America? Why were the Chicago police in 1968 making bets as to who could crack the most heads of "those God-damned Yippies"? The elements of crisis and catharsis are psychologically inseparable, so that the polarization is finally fruitless. However, it is worth examining as it is so often the manner in which violence is seen.

In the light of the present struggle for means of change and renewal, the way we view violence is crucial. But before we analyze the current situation, it is important to understand the emergence of the theory of violence, particularly as it relates to this modern dilemma. Beyond the immediate interest of the widely divergent theories, one essential point must be grasped. Common to all of them is the idea that violence in human society has a certain "normality." Here is the Achilles heel. In these theories violence, beginning as "normal," soon slides to "necessary" and then to "legitimate."

Violence in Political Theory

Let us consider first how the notion of the necessity of violence has emerged in political theory. Rousseau's conception of the Noble Savage is basic: "Man was born free but is everywhere in chains." The Noble Savage was the primitive man, unrepressed by culture, education or social conditioning. When this freedom is replaced by repression or restriction, violence has a liberating value. This theory has been developed especially by the anarchists to justify violence, not only as pragmatically effective but also as morally valuable. Bakunin said, "The will to destroy is a creative will," and he ardently practiced his own truth.[4] Georges Sorel took this still further in *Reflections on Violence* in 1906. For him the violent destruction of a decadent society was not just politically revolutionary but, as an expression of the life-force, morally purifying: "It is to violence that socialism owes its high moral values, through which it brings salvation to the modern world."[5] Few leftists quote Sorel very warmly because he later progressed from supporting Lenin to enthusiasm for Mussolini, yet his tone was prophetic of contemporary radicals. The essential point is clear: Violence is first considered "normal" and then soon seen to be necessary and legitimate as catharsis.

Violence in Evolutionary Theory

Second, we should examine the emergence of the necessity of violence in evolutionary theory. Charles Darwin's concept of natural selection, especially as interpreted by T. H. Huxley, appeared to justify the value of survival by means of violence, for life was viewed as a continuous free fight. Three examples show the implications of this for modern behavioral theory.

The first is Desmond Morris in *The Naked Ape,* considered here only because of its extraordinary popularity. Like other behavioral scientists, Morris interprets human violence in the light of its animal origins, observing that whereas animals only want defeat or domination man goes on to murder. Morris's explanation focuses on the development of armed conflict. With unarmed conflict there was no danger of violence; aggression was conventionalized, channelled into contests and sports, such as judo, athletics, wrestling, boxing. But armed conflict in making two decisive extensions has created the horror of violence. The first is an extension of the hands—clubs, spears, guns, bombs and missiles, each with a greater potential destructive force. The second is the extension of the space between the antagonists. During a fist fight men see each other eye to eye, but, when they use clubs, spears, guns, bombs and missiles, the gap between them widens and the opponents become impersonal, blurred by distance. Morris concludes, "We are, to put it mildly, in a mess, and there is a strong chance we shall have exterminated ourselves by the end of the century. Our only consolation will have to be that, as a species, we have had an exciting term of office." [6] If somewhat facile in his glib carelessness about the possibility of human extinction, he does at least emphasize the normality of violence in the present human situation.

A second example, more serious and yet more optimistic, is that of Konrad Lorenz in *On Aggression.* As a humanist, he rejects both morals and metaphysics as possible avenues for understanding violence: "We shall not improve our chances of counteracting it if we accept it as something metaphysical and inevitable, but on the other hand we shall perhaps succeed in finding remedies if we investigate the chain of its natural causation."[7] Lorenz progresses from the animal world ("what I know") to the present human world ("what is probable") to his own solutions for humanity ("what I believe"). The very progression from empirical certainty to hypothetical faith is instructive. In the animal world aggression has four valuable functions relating to survival: spatial distribution, selection of the strongest by rival fights, defense of the young and contribution to the complex of drives within the animal psyche. For animals aggression is not destructive and diabolical, but essential and life-preserving; in fact, with their aggressive instincts animals also have built-in inhibitions which prevent aggression from becoming violence.

Man, however, is in an evolutionary crisis. He has all the aggressive instincts of animals but not the sufficient inhibitions. This is because the progress of man's culture has outpaced the progress of his social inhibitions, and man's rationality, morality and love are too weak. "All the great dangers threatening humanity with extinction are direct consequences of conceptual thought and verbal speech."[8]

Lorenz's solution ("what I believe") is possible only through controlled behavior, and his discussion of this leads him to optimistic conclusions. The last chapter is titled "An Avowal of Optimism," but it is his basis for optimism that is fascinating: "The obvious conclusion is that love and friendship should embrace all humanity, that we should love all our human brothers indiscriminately. This commandment is not new. Our reason is quite able to understand its necessity as our feeling is able to appreciate its beauty, but nevertheless, made as we are we are unable to obey it, and the utmost exertion of will power cannot alter this fact. But the great constructors can and I believe they will. I believe in the power of human reason, as I believe in the power of natural selection."[9] The immensity of this is breathtaking! Having spent so much of his book (and the first half of this paragraph) emphasizing man's dilemma as the result of an evolutionary crisis and man's deficient inhibitions in reason, morality and love, he then grounds his optimism in the Great Constructors (evolution personified) and human reason!

A third example, essentially pessimistic, is in *The Ghost in the Machine* by Arthur Koestler. He, too, sees an evolutionary crisis: "It appears highly probably that *Homo sapiens* is a biological freak, the result of some remarkable mistake in the evolutionary process."[10] But

Koestler explains it as a pathological condition resulting from a lack of integration between the archicortex (the old brain) and the neocortex (the new brain): "It is entirely unprecedented that evolution should provide a species with an organ *which it does not know how to use*."[11] This leads Koestler to an unremitting pessimism as he surveys the world, and the last third of his book reads remarkably like a prophecy of apocalyptic doom. His only answer is the hope of discovering a pill to join the two brains, but his closing words are closer to the tenor of the whole book: "Nature has let us down. God seems to have left the receiver off the hook, and time is running out."[12]

Thus in behavioral science we have an extraordinary paradox: The very feature which distinguishes man becomes the feature which damns him (for Lorenz, culture; for Koestler, the upper brain). Through it all there is still the fact of the "normality" of violence in human society.

Violence in Psychoanalytic Theory

Third, we will examine the notion of violence as a necessity in psychoanalytic theory. The key here is the idea of repression which, as Freud said, is "the pillar on which the whole edifice of psychoanalysis rests." Psychoanalytic theory deals with the conflict resulting from the clash between the "pleasure principle" and the "reality principle," meaning that either by nature (his ontogenesis) or by social organization (his phylogenesis) man is a neurotic animal. No adult is free from conflict and repression, the dualistic tension between the basic instincts of *eros* and *thanatos*. Because of this clash, violence is inextricably rooted into man's nature. It is not caused by his environment, his ignorance or his poor education but is much more radical. Freud bluntly dismissed communism as too shallow in its diagnosis. Aggression was never prompted simply by the desire for property, but rather "forms the basis of every relation."[13] Wherever civilization may develop, "One thing we can expect, and that is that this indestructible feature of human nature will follow it there." This is a harshly realistic analysis of violence in human nature.

Expounding Freud, Norman O. Brown pins this down in three places. "Freud's fundamental perspective is that the evil in man is not to be explained away as a superficial excrescence on a basically good human nature, but is rooted in a deep conflict in human nature itself."[14] So while external, circumstantial factors may be aggravating, they are never the root cause of human violence. This means that "Freud has so formulated the conflict between eros and the aggressive instinct as to preclude the possibility of salvation or cure. . . . With an innate tendency to aggression mankind's only alternative is to turn it outward and destroy others or turn it inward and destroy himself."[15] This in turn progresses to the third implication: "It still remains true that if aggressiveness is innate and accumulates with the growth of civilization, then psychoanalysis may, like Freud, hope for a rebirth of Eros, but rationally it can only predict the self-destruction of the human race."[16]

It should be obvious that if this is so, violence is inextricably rooted in the human psyche and is inevitable as an outburst of the subterranean conflict. Thus again violence has a certain normality and necessity to it. Nonetheless, while violence may release repressed instincts temporarily, it is no final resolution of the dualism.

These ideas are echoed in modern sociology and politics. Paul Goodman, for example, from his psychoanalytic background felt that face-to-face violence (like a fist fight) is natural, so it's better to have the fight out. But as soon as violence becomes organized, then to exert violence turns a man into a thing because violence exerts too much of him to be able to do it at somebody else's direction. This distinction between involuntary and organized violence he draws from the premises of psychoanalysis.

An example of the justification of involuntary violence is the statement of Malcolm X: "I'm non-violent with those who are non-violent with me. But when you drop that violence on me, then you've made me go insane, and I'm not responsible for what I do."[17]

Violence in Cultural Theory

Finally, we will examine the emergence of violence as a necessity in cultural theories. Here we unearth the old idea that violence is a symptom of an individual or society under extreme stress. So whether it is a slum boy cornered against a wall or a nation threatened economically, both lash out in violence. As Engels remarked, "Violence is the accelerator of economic development."[18]

Marshall McLuhan's is perhaps the most striking modern expression of this, with his claim that new technologies change the sense-ratios, causing psychic friction, "cultural blues," or a "collidescope." Thus violence is the birth pangs of any new technology that gives rise to the quest for a new identity. In *War and Peace in the Global Village* he says, "When one has been hurt by a new technology, when the private person or corporate body finds its entire identity endangered by physical or psychic change, it lashes back in a fury of self defense."[19] Thus, "Violence is an involuntary quest for identity."[20] This analysis is applied in his understanding of the violence of the New Left or Black Power and could be illustrated by such writings as Eldridge Cleaver's *Soul on Ice* ("We shall have our manhood. We shall have it or the earth will be leveled by our attempts to gain it").[21] All these analyses and many others are important for various reasons, but here I am concerned with them only as variations on one essential theme—the understanding of the normality of violence. To appreciate this in the present climax of moral relativism and the value vertigo is to see the writing on the wall with ever more clarity. With no moral framework "normality" slides easily towards "necessity" and necessity towards "legitimacy." Without any moral reference point, violence will be increasingly prevalent in the power struggle created by relativism.

This is the lesson of our times. "Men of action when they are without faith have never believed in anything else but action," warned Camus.[22] "All politics is a struggle for power; the ultimate kind of power is violence," warned Cyril Wright Mills.[23] Hitler's comment, "I cannot see why man should not be just as cruel as nature,"[24] finds its contemporary counterpart in Chairman Mao Tse-tung's "Political power comes out of the barrel of a gun. . . . The gun must never slip from the grasp of the Communist party."[25]

Right no longer gives might; might makes right. Law is what a man can get away with; lawlessness is what he will not allow the other man to get away with. Truth becomes the majority law of the group or nation which can impose its view (i.e., values) on all others. Clausewitz issued his famous dictum, "War is the continuation of politics by other means," but the modern dilemma is more excruciating. Since violence is now internalized, Hannah Arendt says, "Peace is the continuation of war by other means."[26]

With the death of absolutes the prospects are grim for any lover of justice, freedom and order. Western culture will lurch drunkenly between chaotic lawlessness and countering authoritarianism, which in some particularly abysmal vacuum of confidence could finally issue in a supreme dictatorship, mocking the Western aspirations for democracy as ineffective and demonstrating the strong alliance between technology and the state. Until then, violence, blood brother of such a totalitarianism, will play its fateful part, naked or disguised, in an inevitable power struggle on all levels.

A by-product of the death of absolutes has been the failure to be able to hold any balanced middle ground. The polarity between violence seen as extreme crisis and as necessary catharsis is typical of this, and we will now examine two expressions of these extremes in the form of a radical demanding violence because it is catharsis and a liberal decrying violence because it is crisis. The extremity of the polarization is pointed up in the comparative unpopularity of non-violence, which has slipped in status from the high respect it held ten years ago. Even the two great heroes of non-violence, Gandhi and Martin Luther King, are being explained away in terms formerly inconceivable. Some point out, for instance, that Gandhi had other factors in his favor. If the Indians had lain down in front of Russian tanks, they would have met the fate of the Hungarians or Czechs. Gandhi's success says something for the remaining Christian morality of the British in India, however enfeebled. Others are even whispering that Martin Luther King died "just in time" not to see the logic of his failure and the swing to a pragmatic violence so opposed to his own spirit. However unfair, this critique is definitely part of the present climate and has come in the wake of the polarization of violence as crisis or catharsis.

Violence as Catharsis

First, let us consider a radical who demands violence because it is catharsis. The best example here is Frantz Fanon in *The Wretched of the Earth.* Fanon was born in Martinique in 1925 and died of leukemia in New York in 1961 at the age of thirty-six. He studied medicine and psychiatry and became before his premature death a spokesman for the Algerian revolution and the Third World. He was proud to call himself the "champion of the poorest men on earth." Basic to his vision of the

Third World was the warning that it must never be a third Europe ("Have we not other work to do than to create a third Europe?").[27] Europe had ostensibly been humanist yet had denied this by constant inhumanity. "For centuries they have stifled almost the whole of humanity in the name of a so-called spiritual experience," or "She has only shown herself parsimonious and niggardly where men are concerned."[28] The second Europe was North America, "that super-European monstrosity."[29]

It is out of this hatred of "European" inhumanity that Fanon's call to violence comes, for he sees colonialism as inextricably bound up with violence that takes shape in three stages. The first stage is oppression when foreign invasions, military or economic, enter and oppress the people in any country. The second stage is repression. With the colonist too powerful to be overthrown, the natives are forced to turn their natural aggression against themselves; thus results a period of chronic tribalism, magic, and fratricidal murders and in-fighting. Western psychologists may describe this as "congenital aggression," but Fanon denies this, suggesting rather that natives, unable to fight back against the colonist, take their aggression out on themselves. The third stage is revolution or, as Sartre terms it in his Preface, "the moment of the boomerang, the third phase of violence."[30] Fanon himself puts it, "He of whom *they* have never stopped saying that the only language he understands is that of force, decides to give utterance by force."[31]

In such a situation violence is not only indispensable as a pragmatic tool to overthrow the colonial government; such violence is cathartic and re-humanizing. His book is punctuated with this constant reiteration: "The colonized man finds his freedom in and through violence."[32] "This violence, because it constitutes their work, invests their characters with positive and creative qualities."[33] "Violence is a cleansing force. It frees the native from his inferiority complex and from his despair and inaction; it makes him fearless and restores his self respect."[34] Fanon dreams of the workless, the prostitutes, the hopeless dregs of humanity being reawakened to rediscover themselves through violence, taking their place to march proudly in a great procession of liberated nations and men.

Sartre's Preface drives this home with equal emphasis. Writing of the revolutionary, he says, "This irrepressible violence is neither sound nor fury, nor the resurrection of savage instincts, nor even the effect of resentment: it is man re-creating himself."[35] Or again, "When his rage boils over, he recovers his lost innocence and comes to know himself in that he himself creates his self. . . . To shoot down a European is to kill two birds with one stone, to destroy an oppressor and the man he oppressed at the same time."[36] Writing of the colonial powers, he adds, "We [the French] have sown the wind; he [the revolutionary] is the whirlwind. The child of violence, at every moment he draws it from his humanity. We were men at his expense, he makes himself man at ours: a different man; of higher quality."[37]

Echoes of this can be heard in many such as Herbert Marcuse, Eldridge Cleaver, Stokely Carmichael and R. D. Laing. What they are all clearly saying is that in a situation of repression violence invests the revolutionary with new life, new hope, new ideals and a new humanity. In short it is cathartic. A full critique is irrelevant at this point, but, as a footnote, there are two elements in Fanon which make the ardor of this violent propaganda very surprising.

The first is his earlier moderation. In *Black Skin, White Masks* he wrote in a different vein: "I do not trust fervor. Every time it has burst out somewhere, it has brought fire, famine, misery . . . and contempt for man."[38] This earlier moderation is swept aside by later propaganda. The second surprise is that when he writes *The Wretched of the Earth* Fanon the heady propagandist is totally contradicted by Fanon the practicing psychiatrist. His case histories include studies of many perpetrators of violence who suffered later from acute anxiety, insomnia, suicidal obsessions and other psychological problems.[39]

Violence as Crisis

Second, let us consider a liberal who decries violence because he sees it as crisis. Here we will cite Arthur Schlesinger, Jr.'s *Violence: America in the Sixties.* This is vital not only for what it says but for what it shows of the troubled conscience and soul-searching disquiet of a liberal in 1968, following the assassinations of his close friends the Kennedys. A running survey of the chapters is enough to tell the story. He begins with "A Sick Society?" quoting everyone from LBJ, Lord Harlech and *The Times* of London to Yevtushenko and Breschnev, and he suggests that because of their violence the world's verdict on Americans will be that they are "the most frightening people on this planet."[40] Then he delves back into history and shows the common theme —a resort to violence as the American way of life. From the killing of the red men and the enslaving of the black men down to the current assassinations, such violence is a recurrent theme. The only time when this was absent was the fifty-year period after the Civil War, the period which he says created the image of the normal America.

Another chapter examines shooting—the American Dream. The cause of violence could not be that America is a frontier nation, because so also are Canada and Australia whose crime rates are only a quarter of that of the States. Nor is the trouble that America is industrial because so are Great Britain, Japan and West Germany, and they with their combined population of 214 million have only 135 gun murders a year, whereas America with a population of 200 million has 6,500. (Philadelphia alone has a higher gun murder rate than the whole of Britain.) Nor is it even that America is capitalist, because despite its capitalist problems its record is still better than the Nazi's or even Stalin's Russia. The only explanation is the resort to the gun—the American phallic symbol.

Another chapter goes into "televiolence" and is mainly a catalogue of TV programming around the time of the assassinations. (By the way, the average American watches television nearly nine years of his life; on TV he sees violence on an average of once every fourteen minutes and a killing once every forty-five minutes.)[41] The book is hardly up to Schlesinger's own normal standard and does not compare with more weighty tomes on violence, but it is representative of an attitude which is common from the liberal left to the conservative right, including much of the Silent Majority. To all such, violence generally including that of the radicals is seen as a crisis tearing at the fabric of society itself.

In an essay on the psychology of murder, Virginia Adams speaks of the United States' "murderous preeminence" with its "unhappy distinction of leading advanced Western nations in the rate at which its citizens destroy one another."[42] This has led some behavioral scientists to speak of a national "crisis of violence." The rediscovery by America of its violent past is one of the most important intellectual legacies of the sixties, with implications which will reverberate far beyond the United States.

Writing in 1968 in the afterglow of the Chicago Convention, Norman Mailer pictured America "roaring like a bull in its wounds," ending with this gloomy prediction: "There is a beastliness in the marrow of the century. . . . We will be fighting for forty years."[43]

It would be possible to examine other theorists, strategists or analysts of violence, or even to analyze the landmark incidents of violence from Sharpville to Pinkville. But the same polarized alternative is showing through them all. One side sees violence as a crisis which breaks down the order and values they stand for; the other side sees it as catharsis, the re-creation of people repressed by cultures and governments.

Any evaluation of the present position can be seen only in terms of the Striptease of Humanism, one more tightening of the screw towards dehumanization. The sting is felt at two places. First, whether open or masked, violence is socially destructive. Because of the containing effect of technology violence today can rarely deliver its promise of change. Whatever the theory, the effect is increasingly the same. Whether it is the Viet Cong massacres, the Kent State shootings, the Kennedy assassinations, the bombing of an Israeli school bus or the Wisconsin Math Center, it is men who are being killed, homes that are being destroyed and society which is being disrupted. Reason and morality falter, power becomes a principle, might equals right. There can be no prospects for humanity except havoc and hurt.

Second, violence is a focal point of alienation. What view of man is brought to light, when the very thing which distinguishes man from the animals and machines becomes the thing which damns him? The examples of Koestler and Lorenz are far from unique and point again to modern man's low view of himself. Distinguished, but damned—a fateful modern tribute to man. Or what grounds of substantial hope are offered, if, with Freud, rationally we can only predict destruction and the desire for love and eros is a hope against hope with no basis? Increasingly violence is being recognized as a point of alienation. It is an aspect of the present system that prevents the full realization of humanness. Yet if such realization can come about only by violence against the present system, what guarantee is there that any system can survive the present violence? It becomes like a game of Russian roulette with ever mounting stakes.

Up to this point most of my comments have been an analytical commentary on the cultural situation. But as we look at some of the broad contours of the counter culture, I will begin to introduce more of the answers of Christianity, what I have earlier referred to as the Third Way. I will, however, leave the vital and fundamental question of the truth-claims and evidence for the Third Way until the last two chapters. In each area it should be obvious that the Christian answer provides the basis and balance for a third alternative, which is never a compromising middle position. The present discussion of violence as crisis or catharsis illustrates this well.

Christianity and Violence: Traditional Views

First, let us attempt to gain a perspective by understanding the traditional views which have been held by Christians through the centuries. The first and often majority view has been the belief that force is justified. Basing their arguments on Paul's letter to the Roman Christians where he asserts that the state has a certain God-given validity and making a decisive distinction between force and violence, these theorists have supported the possibility of just warfare, as expounded in the Council of Arles in A.D. 314. Representations of this view can be found in the writings on many theologians of different persuasions through the centuries. Such giants as Augustine, Aquinas, John Calvin and Karl Barth are among them. Most who hold a just war theory would say that a coup d'état, rebellion or revolution is wrong because it is revolt against the divinely ordained state and is, therefore, violence. A wide variety of differences in interpretation is still possible. Some would obey the state only if and when the state is not opposed to the higher law of God; others, for example those in the Church in Germany who remained silent regarding

 Hitler, tend to obey the state rather more blindly than this.

The second position, also widely held, is that of non-violence. Many claim that very probably this was the general position up to the fourth century. No text before the second century shows Christians in the army, and in the first to do so, Tertullian condemns army involvement, explaining that it was happening only because soldiers were under duress. Many of the famous martyrs in the early church were those who abstained or resigned from the army because of their Christian conversion. In the third century Maximilian said, "I cannot be a soldier. I cannot do evil. I am a Christian." But gradually this was relaxed. It was first qualified when Christians were allowed to join the peace-keeping force (*militare*) but not a fighting army (*bellare*). But the watershed was the "conversion" of Constantine when the Roman Empire became ostensibly Christian. Since then and the theological justification in the Council of Arles, non-violence has not been the majority view, though of course it emerged again, for example, with Francis of Assisi and among the Waldensians. It was also in vogue after the 1914-18 war.

The third group are those who have justified violence. I would stress that this has very much been a minority view down through the centuries. Typical of this are the third-century Nile anchorites who descended on Alexandria, beating and clubbing the citizens in an attempt to "purify" the city as Christ had purified the temple, seeing themselves as human instruments of divine judgment.

The same attitude appeared like a rash in medieval times under disintegrating social conditions. The rising of Fra Dolcino in 1507, the famous peasant revolt under Thomas Munzer and the seige of Munster in 1535 by John of Leyden are illustrations. Similar tendencies could also be found in the writings of the Levellers, a

Puritan group more extreme than Oliver Cromwell. In 1653, for example, John Lilburne wrote *Legitimate Defense* which in some ways is one of the first theologies of revolution against tyrants. "The most authentic servants of Christ have always been the worst enemies of tyranny and the oppressor."[44]

But it is in our own time that such a view has flowered most fully, especially among the extremes of liberal Protestantism and progressive Roman Catholicism. A Roman Catholic priest, Father Cardonnel, has said, "God is not the dominator but the awakener of guerillas among oppressed peoples."[45] A Black Power spokesman in Detroit, Pastor Albert Cleage, also claims that violence is *redemptive.* Once again violence is justified, for God is at work in the zones of revolution. It is in the essence of revolution that we witness the contemporary irruption of God's sovereignty. The crisis of new birth is exchanged for the crisis of revolution. But I would again stress that this is very much a minority view.

Jacques Ellul, whose book on violence gives such a clear survey of these positions, especially the last, makes two comments which show why so often the shameful extremes of the first and the third positions are a far cry from Christianity "rightly understood." First, Ellul comments that often the differences between them are more temperamental than theological. The first tends to appeal to the man who is conformist, institutional, reasonable and somewhat moderate in his character. The second tends to appeal to the man who sees himself as a sufferer in the sacrificial, heroic mold. The third position tends to appeal to the man who is apocalyptic, immoderate and simplistic. Where such views are backed up with theology, they tend to be monistic and simplistic, using the Bible selectively, more as a source for proof texts than as a base for true principles.

Ellul shows secondly that when changes are made between these two positions, all too often they are made according to the spirit of the times rather than Christian principles, and therefore they lack specific Christian witness. The nineteenth-century spirit was mainly nationalistic, so it was normal for the bishops to bless the cannons. The twentieth-century spirit is mainly revolutionary, and today the bishops are blessing the guerillas. In 1933 Hitler accused the German Christians of being weak, beggarly, introverted and effeminate (a critique close to Nietzsche's scorn). In response, the German Christians sadly espoused courage, virility and violence and found their position totally compromised. Ellul charts the same dangers today. Since 1950 the World Council of Churches has more and more espoused the cause of the poor until it is almost in danger of deifying the poor in the place of God who is dead. A French priest expressed this honestly when he said that if Christ is God it is only because he is the poorest of men.[46]

I would add a third comment. Just as a balanced non-violence is held to be historically passé in the secular world, so is this also sadly true of much contemporary Christianity. The emotional reactions of many people reflect their general political position rather than carefully thought through Christian principles.

Christianity and Violence: A Radical Understanding

The crux of the problem is the Christian view of the nature of violence. It is here that Christianity is both most radical and most realistic for it begins by diagnosing the character and inexorable logic of violence. Biblical teaching and human history seen in the light of biblical principles illuminate five facets of the essential nature of violence.

First, the identity of violence. The first recorded murder in biblical history is the murder of Abel by his brother Cain. But this account in Genesis 4 cannot be understood in isolation from the preceding story in Genesis 3, the story of man's Fall. When man chose to stand against God, he set himself up as his own integration point and violated the vertical relationship between himself and God. This was not the end. After the vertical relationship was disrupted, the horizontal relationship between man and man, between man and himself and between man and nature was also impaired by alienation. Cain's violation of Abel's life was only the outflowing of what was already incipient in the Fall. Genesis 3–4 and 9 clearly teach that violence is the violation of who a man is before God. Although finite like the rest of God's creation, man has a distinctive difference in that he alone is made in the image of God. Because he is made in the image of God, man is inviolable. This inviolability is fundamental. Violence, therefore, is to be seen in terms of all that which violates man as he is before God and as he is in himself. At the lowest level this inviolability includes his essential property, his belongings, his clothes, his food. More importantly it includes his territory, the sphere of his work, his leisure, his home. More crucially still it includes his personality, his reputation, his image, his security, his drives, his aspirations, his character. Supremely it involves his life.

This understanding of man's inviolability in itself makes the Bible's the most radical of all views of violence, but Jesus sharpens it still further in refusing to make a total distinction between external assault and internal attitudes, that is, between murder and the motive which can lead to it. The assault is only the anger spelled out in action.

Jesus said, "You have learned that our forefathers were told 'Do not commit murder; anyone who commits murder must be brought to judgement.' But what I tell you is this: Anyone who nurses anger against his brother must be brought to judgement."[47] Jesus thus placed the guilt due to violence back in the area of psychology. This means that for the Christian violence is far more than physical wounding or killing. It can be physical, economic or psychological, applied with a velvet glove or an iron fist. It is spelled out in terms of the violation of humanness. It comes from all sides and at all levels, from the Viet Cong or from the GI's, from a president or a parent, from the dehumanization involved in Army training or the dishonest manipulation in advertising from Madison Avenue. Any refusal to see this becomes mystification all over again. The extraordinary reactions to the Calley verdict show that if Calley was on trial for the generals, the generals were on trial for men at large. As R. D. Laing says, "We are all murderers and prostitutes–no matter to what culture, society, class, nation one belongs; no matter how normal, moral or mature one takes oneself to be."[48] Jesus was saying the same thing in a far more profound way. Any man who knows the nature of his own heart realizes that violence is not another man's problem. It is everyone's problem. It is my problem. "There but for the grace of God go I." Unlike R. D. Laing's demystification that leads to counterviolence, for the Christian demystification must lead to penitence. This first facet means that the justification of violence is never legitimate and its calculus is never possible. One human life, seen before God, is priceless.

The second facet is the correct understanding of the necessity of violence. All the theories outlined earlier showed the psychological, cultural and political normality if not necessity of violence. The Christian view of the nature of man as he is now also stresses that, understood in God's framework, violence is normal in a certain sense. Man, alienated from God as a sinner, when he acts according to his fallen nature, is not totally free to choose his action but is forced to react according to who he is. Thus the "necessity" of violence is seen as an inevitable expression of man's fallen nature. The Christian, knowing his own nature, is never surprised by violence in himself or others. Sometimes shock at such violence simply betrays a romantic view of man. Violence is normal in a fallen world, although we will see later how important the phrase "in a fallen world" is to the concept of normality.

The third facet of violence that Christianity reveals is its reciprocity. In the Garden of Gethsemane Jesus said, "All who take the sword will die by the sword."[49] This is not a quaint homily but an assessment of the reciprocal nature of violence made realistically under the shadow of his arrest when everything in his disciples called for violent resistance. Ever since Cain's club killed Abel, violence has not so much begun as continued. This reciprocal nature of violence is written all over the face of history. The Corsican, Arab or Mafia blood feuds are classic examples of this principle. But it can come home to our own society in many more subtle ways. Ellul cites the French atrocities to the Nazis in return for all they had done to them prior to 1944. In the United States this principle operates in every violent incident, as, for example, in the Judge Haley shooting at the Soledad Brothers' trial. After such an event every judge, every prisoner, every juryman goes into every future court in California knowing the screw has been turned once more, heightening the bitterness, heightening the fear, heightening the hatred. Violence is reciprocal.

The fourth important facet of violence in a biblical perspective is its continuity. Violence may be pragmatically "successful" in overturning an existing order that is corrupt, but it is utopian to imagine that the next order will be free of all such problems. The continuity of fallen nature in the most idealistic revolutionaries makes sport of pre-revolution promises. All men are fallen. *We,* as well as *they*; *I,* as well as *you.* The Bible's emphasis on the continuity of fallen nature is amply corroborated by the story of modern revolution. Camus concluded sadly, "All modern revolutions have ended in a reinforcement of the power of the State."[50] Marcuse speaks gloomily of the "continuum of repression." Violence still rides in the saddle. Only the name changes. Left may oust right, or right depose left, but the violence is continuous.

Many of the same men who resisted the Nazis in France in 1944 massacred thousands of blacks in Algeria in 1945 and in Madagascar in 1947. No one can fail to sympathize with Camus' doctor as he valiantly fights "the plague," knowing that it may break out elsewhere, but later the native Algerians see Camus himself and the white settlers as part of that great plague. Even as he wrote, the plague was in his own heart too. Tolstoy hammered this home bluntly: "The difference between repressive violence and revolutionary violence is only the difference between cat shit and dog shit."[51] Similarly, Karl Popper, looking around the scene after the Second World War, made the comment, "The spirit of Hitlerism won its greatest victory over us when, after its defeat, we used the weapons which the threat of Nazism had induced us to develop."[52] History is strewn with such examples. Oliver Cromwell fought against Charles I on the grounds of his authoritarian tyranny, developing in the process an approach equally authoritarian. Liberation armies have a disquieting habit of brutalizing themselves and so perpetuating what they attack. (See the story of the Red Army, the N.L.F. in Vietnam or the Black Panthers.) Nineteenth-century humanism fought against Victorian Christianity, only to perpetuate its smug optimism; early Marxism fought against Western bourgeois capitalism, only to perpetrate capitalism's shallow reductionist view of man. The list is endless, but the lesson is rarely learned.

The fifth facet of the nature of violence is it duplicity. This is not so much a biblical principle as an observation made from the study of human history. Violence is always introduced by propaganda in terms of idealism, but generally this idealistic justification is either false or simplistic or utopian. Revolution without reconciliation never brings the promised change in depth, yet the unjustifiable is always justified. Pure, abstract, bloodless violence is only a myth: Fear and hatred are always close behind. The propaganda of a Hitler or a Rap Brown is frank in its honesty about the hatred they wish to stir up. But such violence can never be justified. For the Christian, a single human being made in the image of God is unique, and therefore violence can never be justified. Its pragmatic usefulness cannot be calculated in terms of individual human lives, whether by a murder or by scenario scientists plotting the strategies of future wars in terms of mega-deaths. Violence has a dark record. It corrupts the best of ends and brutalizes the bravest of ideals. Its nature is to be exaggerated; it has nothing in common with moderation and cautious means. And yet despite these contradictions, men always try to justify violence with ideological constructions. Such justification is deceitful.

It is hardly surprising that, with the preceding view of the nature of violence, the ethic of Jesus was uncompromisingly non-violent. Whenever his disciples showed the slightest inclination towards a violent solution, Jesus emphatically countered it. James and John wanted to call down fire on an offending village, but Jesus firmly said no. Peter seized his sword and began to defend Jesus in the Garden of Gethsemane, but Jesus said, "Put up your sword!"[53] thus disarming the church for all time, some say. This resolute veto on violence can be seen both in the life of Christ and in his teaching, as in the parable of the tares and the wheat. But this raises the question: With such an ethic how can a Christian live realistically in a world where the violence of power without principle is the order of the day?

Non-Violence and Christian Realism

Non-violence as a conscious ethic would be superfluous

in a perfect world, but in the world that is and because of the violence in it, the practice of non-violence is an imperative that is inescapable however difficult. As such it is possible only for the man with a sufficient basis and with no illusions, and then only with an attitude of conscious and constant realism.

Perhaps this is the place to ask the question again: Does a Christian see violence as crisis or catharsis? Obviously the answer is neither, for neither the situation nor the solution is that simple. For one thing, to live in a fallen world, abnormal from the point of view of God's original creation, means not only that there is good as well as evil but that that which on the surface is good can mask the evil and that that which is potentially totally evil can be used towards a higher good. Furthermore, while a Christian believes in absolutes, no one should imagine that a tailor-made code of ethics drops from the sky each time there is a moral crisis. The absolute is the immutable character of God before whom the Christian lives. Where God has spoken absolutely there are absolutes and norms, but where he has not the Christian has the freedom and responsibility to make an existential judgment of the situation within the ultimate framework of God's revelation and under the immediate leadership of the Holy Spirit. This in some ways is the highest form of situational ethics; for a Christian, while he is not open to a vacuum of complete relativism, has a responsible freedom to follow the leading of the Holy Spirit within the norms of revealed Christian morality. I would suggest, therefore, that the realistic practice of non-violence for the Christian is a question of pursuing the governing mentality of non-violence within the guidelines of two boundary principles which make it substantially practicable if never perfect in a fallen world.

These two principles concern the *use* of force and the *understanding* of violence.

Non-Violence and the "Use" of Force

Provided that there is a legitimate basis for its use and a vigilant precaution against its overreaction in practice, a qualified use *of force is not only necessary but justifiable.* Within the Christian framework there is the possibility of truth, justice and authority which are not arbitrary, relativistic or mystifying. Thus an important distinction between force and violence is possible. Force, on the one hand, is the controlling discipline of truth, justice and authority in action. Violence, on the other hand, can come from one of three directions—from the maintenance of authority without a legitimate basis, from the contravention of a legitimate authority or from the injustice of a legitimate authority overreacting as it deals with opposition or violation. Overreaction in the name of truth too easily becomes the ugly horror of violence once again.

This distinction between force and violence is crucial. Jacques Ellul's deliberate refusal to make it in *Violence: Reflections from a Christian Perspective* is a weakness in an otherwise brilliant book. One must add, however, that speaking as he does as a penetrating critic of the post-Christian world and writing from a country which has never had a basis of Reformation influence, it is certainly understandable. Violence is not force merely by being state-exercised. Moreover, outside the Christian framework no such distinction can be better than arbitrary, but this is part of the logic of relativism that we now face. Either all force is unmasked as violence (with the consequent chaos of disrespect for all law), or else all violence is masked as force (and there is no redress except by recourse to greater force). The ideal of justice within law can only be pursued with this distinction between force and violence kept carefully in mind.

Without such a distinction there can be no legitimate justification for authority or discipline of any kind, whether on a parental or on a presidential level. In a fallen world the ideal of legal justice without the exercise of force is naive. Societies need a police force; a man has the right to defend his wife from assault. A feature of any society which can achieve a measure of freedom within form is that responsibility implies discipline. This is true at the various structural levels of society—in the spheres of the state, business, the community, the school, respectively.

Without this distinction much pacifism becomes a sensitive reaction to violence but a poor replacement to the structures which perpetrated the violence. Many pacifists who are rightly urgent in their warnings against state violence today and who would reject this distinction between force and violence as a mystifying camouflage for establishment violence quietly presuppose the very same distinction at other levels of their relationships (such as with their own children).

Of course the mere statement of the ideal of force without violence does not mean that it can be easily or constantly attained. Far from it. But this should not lead to a dilution of the ideal. It should mean that on the one hand we make it our aim to substantially approximate the ideal, while on the other hand we attempt this in an attitude of realistic humility. It is not that we succeed for a period of time and then fail. Rather we succeed only as we attempt it in the light of our constant proneness to failure. Even as we aim for the ideal, we must realize and remember that at the very same existential moments we are always aware of our falling short, always aware of our being sorry for our falling short, and always equally aware of God's forgiveness of our falling short (Martin Luther's *semper peccator, semper penitens, semper justus*).

Some force, then, is necessary, but here an emphatic reminder of the two provisos to the principle is required. There must be a legitimate basis and a legitimate exercise of force. No force that does not issue from justice and that is not restrained by justice can achieve justice. Outside this there is only violence. As we have seen, this is the problem of the post-Christian era. There is no modern justification for governments except that of power. Governments simply are, and not surprisingly their maintenance is based on violence at many levels. It is in this context that Ellul speaks with such clarity of the omnipresence of contemporary violence. Moreover, even where there is a legitimate authority, with some aspiration towards the maintenance of principle, the second proviso holds good: Any overreaction, even in the name of truth, crosses the line from force to violence again.

If the Inquisition stands as the starkest example of the overkill of an authority with no legitimate basis, Martin Luther's attitude toward the peasants is an example of overreaction in the name of truth. The same lack of legitimate basis and tendency toward overreaction is around us today, represented by the overkill of law and authority, whether in governments, police forces, college administrations or families. Some force is necessary, but it is imperative to exercise it within the norms of Christian values and with a due recognition of man's nature (i.e., ours!). The only man responsible enough to exercise true force is the man who is most realistic about its corrupting and brutalizing effects on his own nature if he overreacts to the slightest degree. This warning—that the end does not justify the means—is especially urgent in a technological civilization like our own. Today technical means are almost our only ends, usurping human, moral and aesthetic principles and goals. When technical means masquerade as ends, the ends society uses to justify its means are doubly illusory. The Christian must see that society does not manipulate Christian values, relying on their emotive memory to provide an "end" that seems to justify technological means which are far from Christian. This could well be a danger as increasingly Christian principles are recited only out of society's conventional politeness to the past.

Non-Violence and the "Understanding" of Violence

Provided that there is no compliance with the violent and no condoning of the violence, a qualified understanding *of violence is both necessary and justifiable.* To a limited extent violence is effective in unmasking hypocrisy, liberating the oppressed and judging the oppressor. Violence is thus an integral part of both the human and divine weaving of judgment, and at times can be understood correctly from this viewpoint. This understanding will lead to a prophetic grasp of the situation and to an informed compassion and outrage which are prerequisties for social comment and action.

In stating this second principle the qualifing proviso should perhaps be emphasized first. There must be no compliance with the violent nor the slightest condoning of their violence. And we must not use this understanding to smuggle a Christian justification of violence through the back door. The principle of non-violence must not be contradicted. There is no justification for "Christian" violence, nor in fact for any violence at all. The identity of violence is still the same. Its reciprocity and continuity are still characteristic. The resort to violence always breeds further violence. This is a call for the *understanding* of violence, not its *use.* Often it will help us to feel a human sympathy towards the victims of an oppression so inhuman that its victims can resort only to violence. Sometimes it will help us to catch a glimpse of the weaving strands of divine judgment in history.

A biblical example of the latter is Israel's entry into the promised land. Anyone with sensitivity is bound to query the justice of God's giving his people a "promised land." Is this not a violation of the rights of the Canaanites who lived in the land and were about to lose it? This is a valid question but one God foresaw. When God first promised Abraham that his descendants would enjoy the promised land, he also added in Genesis 15 that it would be a considerable time before the Israelis would gain the land; the Canaanites were in rightful possession and would lose it only when their evil was so great that they were ripe for punishment.[54] So Israel's entry was the Canaanites' exit; his gift of the land to Israel was the reverse side of his punishment of the inhabitants who had forfeited it.

A later example involves a naked violence against Israel that is used by God as judgment. God delivered Israel into the hands of foreign invaders because they rejected him and had even outdone the evil of the original Canaanites.[55] No one should delude himself by imagining that the Assyrians, who overran Israel in judgment, maintained a distinction between force and violence! Assyria was probably the most brutal power of any generation in history with the possible exception of our own. But it was the Assyrians' violence, gross in its extremity, which God used as judgment. Then, at the very point when the Assyrians overreached themselves, arrogating to themselves too much power and pride, God used the Babylonians to judge Assyria. This means that, while violence breeds further violence, the result is not "sound and fury signifying nothing" but a situation pregnant with lessons for the perceptive watcher. No concerned Christian today can fail to have a deep-felt sympathy for the poor and the oppressed and a gut understanding of the radicals who come to their aid. If a man watches and learns, there is value; but if he ignores the lesson and resorts to violence, thinking himself an instrument of divine or human judgment, then he sets the brutalizing and reciprocal principle in motion again.

The problem with these two guiding principles is that few people hold them in the balance of a fruitful tension. Instead they rely instinctually on one or the other without prior consideration of their importance as principles or the necessary balance that each needs. Someone of an Establishment mentality, for example, will probably react in a violent situation by invoking the first principle (*using* force), little realizing that he is stretching it to cover a post-Christian "force" which is nothing other than violence. Similarly, someone of a general radical persuasion will probably react in a violent situation by invoking the second principle (*understanding* violence), little realizing that he is stretching it until it covers the justification of revolutionary violence. Both are instinctual political reactions and not Christian responses.

It is in this sense that it is best to regard the two principles partly as boundaries and partly as two aspects of a balanced tension. As principles they are outer limits, defining the boundaries of a realistic non-violence which should achieve a discipline without authoritarianism and a compassion without compliance. Only when the two are held together in this balance can there be the operation of the inner principle of non-violence which each is designed to guard.

This was a mistake the Jews had made about the law. Jesus said, "You have learned that they were told, 'Eye for eye, tooth for tooth.' But what I tell you is this: Do not set yourself against the man who wrongs you. If someone slaps you on the right cheek, turn and offer him your left. If a man wants to sue you for your shirt, let him have your coat as well."[56] Then he added, "Love your enemies and pray for your persecutors." Looking back at the law and their interpretation of "an eye for an eye," we can see, in the light of what Christ said, that the Jews had made a mistake in considering this a norm and a right instead of a boundary limitation.

In the context of a situation very similar to a Corsican blood feud, the principle of an eye for an eye was a limitation on an interminable, mindless blood-letting. But what had been instituted as a limitation, designed to guard the principle of mercy, had become a norm and even a right so that if one man's eye was taken by the other man, the second man's eye could be taken by the first, and so on. But if this latter is so, then what Jesus was doing was upsetting the law. Yet Jesus reiterated strongly that he had come to fulfill the law, not abolish it. Therefore, Jesus was saying, I believe, that this was a *limit,* not a *norm.* The inner principle it guarded was the turning of the other cheek and the love for one's enemies. The Jews, however, had made the principle harsh because they were living out on the boundary limits all the time. The limits had become their norms, their rights.

This is a common mistake of many within the church today. In a violent situation they react instinctively and rarely in a Christian way. If they are right-wing by political persuasion or sociological background, they think automatically in a violent situation of resorting to "law and order." All too often this is not a Christian concept of force, but an instinctive resort to law to curb disorder. The opposite extreme is true of people living closer to the left, who in a violent situation instinctively favor a resort to revolutionary violence which they see as catharsis.

If these are the two guiding principles, one last question arises: How can the essential non-violent mentality be practiced in the present situation? How practically does one follow a positive non-violence that is neither utopian pacifism nor lethargic passivism? How does one assert truth, discipline, force or justice without becoming authoritarian, violent, reactionary and a source of mystification? How does one "understand" violence without condoning it or joining it? How does one affirm the inviolability of man without being soft? Or the prerogative of God to judge, without becoming hard? What does it mean in daily life to love our neighbor, to forgive the man who has wronged us, to seek change by a reconciliation and not violent revolution? How, in fact, do we follow the non-violence to which Christ called us and still recognize that God can overrule in the use of violence and that some force is necessary?

The raising of these questions leads us into two areas of problems—those which arise from situations where we are likely to be tempted to *resort* to violence and those which arise from situations where we are forced to *respond* to violence from others.

Non-Violence the Only Resort

How should one act when tempted to resort to violence as an individual or as a member of a group? Since (as a Christian realizes) violence in the fallen world is necessary in a certain sense, every man will be prone to use violence. When he is "merely" angry with his brother or uses a weapon to kill, the Christian knows before God that he violates the image of God in his fellow man. But here is a crucial difference. For the Christian, while violence is "necessary" by virtue of our fallen nature, it is never legitimate. First, man does not stand in a vacuum of moral relativism but before a God who judges violence as wrong, and, second, for the Christian, although his old nature helps to make violence "necessary," his new nature frees him from this very necessity. To be violent is to fall back on the order of necessity, of fallen nature. It is to react and not to act. All violence is therefore sin, and as such it calls for penitence.

Merely to say this, however, does not remove the Christian from violent situations in which he is aware of his own volatile nature, highly vulnerable to the constant tendency towards violence. Certain practical points are a help here. The first is a simple test. In any potentially violent situation often the best way of knowing whether one should be there or not is to ask the question, What does the resort to violence signify at this moment? and to answer this question biblically, historically and psychologically.

A friend of mine was very close to certain black radicals with whom involvement often led to the precipice of violent action. But as he asked the question, What does the resort to violence signify? and as he looked at it biblically and psychologically, he saw that it often signified a terminal despair of method in the black psyche. The situation was understandable but, for the Christian, the violent solution would be wrong. Therefore, as a Christian he could say, "I too stand for human justice. I too am outraged by all that oppresses and dehumanizes you. But at this particular point, knowing the nature of violence and my calling as a Christian, I cannot go with you, although I understand why you are driven to it."

The same question points up many motives which for the Christian would be totally unacceptable. If the violence of the blacks often signifies a raging terminal despair, the violence of the Weatherman faction is closer to a terminal frustration of immaturity, and the violence of the anarchist implies a romantically utopian belief in change which to the Christian is unrealistic. On the other side of the political spectrum, when one hears an Establishment speaker calling for law and order, and, even if one can appreciate his concern for a particular problem, one must often refuse to join him, knowing that his concept of force has no curb to prevent the overreaction into violence. Such a cry for law and order does not signify a Christian view of form and freedom, but is much closer to the American mentality that habitually resorts to the gun. In each case I suggest that the Christian can and should fully appreciate the causes, the reasons and the motives for violence. But on the verge of violence he stands back and affirms a higher way.

A second practical point arises concerning a Christian's participation in a movement of mass redress. A Christian must be, and be seen to be, a co-belligerent with the movement for redress but never its ally. His specific witness must be made clear in action and in words. A man's presence is often taken as a moral guarantee that he approves of all that goes on, and in a mass movement it is too easy to slide down the slope towards violence, arson and murder. With his higher morality, his unalterable convictions about the nature of man, the Christian should be a conscience in his group. His presence must never be used to provide a Christian justification for evil. To stand as a co-belligerent and not an ally will be to rally the middle ground for a genuine Third Way without mediocre compromise.

The Third Way will not be easy. It will be lonely. Sometimes the Christian must have the courage to stand with the Establishment, speaking boldly to the radicals and pointing out the destructive and counterproductive nature of their violence. At other times he will stand as a co-belligerent with the radicals in their outrage and just demands for redress. The Christian is co-belligerent with either or both when either or both are right, but he is also fearless in his opposition to either or both when they are wrong.

A third practical point must be remembered. If a movement of redress achieves success, then the boot is often on the other foot. The former "have nots" become the "haves," and the former "haves" are "have nots," for with the continuity of violence the oppressed all too easily become the oppressors. This old lesson was given an unmistakably savage and public demonstration in the aftermath of the Bangla Desh victory. The continuum of violence switched sides from the Pakistanis to the Bengalis. When this happens the Christian radical must be prepared to fight for the newly oppressed against those who were perhaps his former co-belligerents. The Christian is not a partisan, nor must he be prone to propaganda. His struggle is for universal human justice under God. As so often, Jacques Ellul demonstrates this best. Having fought the Nazis on the side of the French resistance, he was the first to stand against the resistance when they treated the Nazis brutally in return. Many of the current liberal or radical causes are heavily blinkered in their selective outrage. South African apartheid can always be relied on to raise a banner, but other issues and incidents on an outrageous scale are ignored with blithe indifference because of gross political myopia. The Christian with social concern must champion all those who need champions, not just those whose championing is currently popular.

Forgiveness Our Only Response

The second main area of questions deals with the problem of response to violence as it flares up. What are the practical implications of Christianity here? First, with his radically realistic horror of violence, it is the Christian's task to unmask the false claims for violence on either side. Raw violence is rarely primary. The fuel for rage is provided by propaganda poured onto a highly combustible situation. The Christian must constantly expose and undermine this false propaganda, with its spurious moral, psychological and political claims. Underneath, the naked nature of violence is the same, so he must lay bare all justifications and must himself stubbornly refuse to provide one. This general negative role will serve to de-fuse hostility, and it will be valuable if at the same time the decreasing tension is used as a chance to tackle the genuine root grievances.

Second, what if violence erupts against the Christian? It will be no use to start thinking when that day arrives. A Christian's reaction must be the settled behavior of long-held convictions. These convictions must arise from the central principle that it is forgiveness and not violence that is cathartic. This is not to be confused with a woolly permissiveness, for it is balanced at times by the just and compassionate use of discipline. As a private individual no Christian is responsible to God for what another man does to him. The other man is himself responsible to God and the law for that. But the Christian is responsible to God for his own reaction to what the other man has done to him. Here forgiveness is his only response. Even if he must act elsewhere with a delegated authority (such as that of a judge), his disciplinary role in administering justice must be balanced by a personal attitude of forgiveness. The exercise of force without this forgiveness is violence once more.

Deep and long-lasting change is not brought about by revolution but by reconciliation and reconstruction. Too many make the lamentable mistake of thinking that turning the other cheek is only a monumental stoicism, with the Christian submitting until he is punch-drunk and beyond personal pride or caring. Non-violence is not "passivism." Christians are to be active peace *makers.* The Stoic view completely misses the point of Christ's teaching on forgiveness.

The key is to be found in the parable of the unforgiving debtor.[57] Jesus tells the story of the king with a servant who is millions of dollars in debt. Threatened with imprisonment, confiscation of property and the loss of his family, the servent is amazed when his king freely forgives him the entire debt. But as the man comes out of the palace, he meets another man who owes him a few dollars. The man who has just been forgiven refuses to forgive the minute debt owed him and drags the debtor off to jail until he can pay. The king, hearing the news, revokes his original pardon and the servent ends up in jail. Jesus turns solemnly to those around him and says, "And that is how my heavenly Father will deal with you unless you each forgive your brother from your hearts."[58] In the Christian perspective, nothing that any man will do to us in life will ever

 (without overreaction) and "understanding violence" (without compliance) Christianity calls for the practice of non-violence not only as a negation of violence but as an affirmation of the Christian view of the nature of God and man and as an offering of a non-humanist forgiveness made possible by the redemption of Jesus Christ. In this practice of the Third Way, Christians together should be seen as a reconciling community, healing divisions, de-fusing hostility, bridging communication gaps. Sadly, most Western Christianity demonstrates the polarizations and not the healing. A better example is the story told me of how the Ceylonese Christians acted during racial riots, when the situation was impossibly polarized between the Hindu Tamils and the Buddhist Singhalese. In the bitter clashes between the two, it was often the Christians who came together as a third group to prevent civil war. At the end of the riots, the prime minister publicly thanked the Christian church for being a healing community. Knowing themselves to be One in Christ, although coming from Hindu and Buddhist backgrounds, they were neither one nor the other but One in Christ and so a Third Way. At the risks of their own lives, they were a healing community.

One final word of warning. Often as I have spoken or written about this, it has been rightly recognized as a strong critique of violence. But then it has been used, not to support a Christian affirmation of non-violence but rather as a critical weapon to attack any radical who advocates violence. So it ends as a support for the Establishment position. Such a response lacks integrity and becomes cheap propaganda all over again. I am writing to the man who knows his own nature well but is so urgently concerned to see change in modern society that he is led inevitably to the brink of using violence as the only means to effect change. It is only at that point, shivering on the edge of violence with an intense desire for change, that the Third Way can begin, born of an understanding of the character of God, the inviolability of man and the difference that Jesus Christ makes.

Modern thinking in rejecting this Third Way has created its own insoluable dilemmas. The polarization between "crisis" and "catharsis" only covers the situation in which man responds to the logic of relativism by elevating power into a principle. The ugly violence which is the ethic of death unleashed on all levels he then disguises behind spurious values or shining technological super-means. There is no breaking of this deadlock except by increased violence—or a return to the Third Way.

The counter culture has certainly found no resolution to the problem. Swinging from the idealism of early non-violence (which became romantic) to the pragmatism of later violence (which became counter-productive), many are settling down into a limbo of lethargy. Such a person is ripe for the appeal of the East.

6/The East, No Exit

"East is East and West is West,
and never the twain shall meet."
Rudyard Kipling

"Orientation means to know
where the orient is."
R. D. Laing

"Elementary ecology
leads straight to elementary
Buddhism."
Aldous Huxley

"If you want to get the plain
truth, be not concerned
with right and wrong. Conflict
between right and wrong is
the sickness of the mind."
Yun-Men, Zen Master

"If God is One, what is bad?"
Charles Manson

"I am nowhere a somewhatness
for anyone."
Buddhagosa[1]

A second defining feature of the counter culture, and a strong movement within it, is the swing to Eastern religions. Parallel to the political, social and moral revolutions, another revolution is in the making—a revolution of consciousness equally critical of the system and society but dramatically different in its solution. This swing to the East has changed the tidal flow of three hundred years of Western radicalism (which had closely related revolution and atheism), yet it has come about almost overnight and with extraordinarily little debate. If we had been living a century ago and had listened to Kipling's famous line, "East is East and West is West and never the twain shall meet,"[2] we would probably have considered it well justified. The British Raj was at the height of its power; as late as 1830 the Indians were still practicing suttee, slavery and sacrifice. In fact, the peoples of India had been servile for centuries, not only under the European rule but also under the Moughals and Turks. But suddenly the whole balance is changed, the status quo is upset and the swing to the East to find philosophic and religious answers is an important trend. If Western culture fails to find the answers to its problems in either Christianity or humanism, is it possible that it can find such answers in the East?

East Meets West in San Francisco

The East made its first entry into the counter culture in San Francisco through the Early Beats. Although Ginsberg in his early poetry showed a real quest for God, Eastern meditation was introduced to the Beats by Gary Snyder who had just returned from two years under a Zen master in Japan. Jack Kerouac's *The Dharma Bum* seems to be a disguised history of this entry through Snyder. But as it spread in the early fifties, the leading figure was Alan Watts. Having written seven books on Zen before he was thirty-five, this one-time Anglican counsellor is a leading popularizer of the Eastern religions in the West. For many years he taught at San Francisco's School of Asian Studies, and he has become the foremost spokesman for the East in America. Some scornfully dismiss him as the "Norman Vincent Peale of Buddhism," but his wide knowledge, sensitive appreciation and clear writing are beyond this reproach.

Zen was obviously appealing in the climate of the Beat existentialism and antinomianism. The saying of the ancient T'ang master Lin-Chi ideally suited the philosophy of the early Beats: "In Buddhism there is no place for using effort. Just be ordinary and nothing special. Eat your food, move your bowels, pass water, and when you're tired go and lie down."[3] The text of Zen soon became the pretext for Beat Zen laziness. At least the atmosphere was congenial.

The rapid acceleration of interest in the East hardly needs documentation, for today the influence is everywhere in a rich profusion, if not confusion. For some it is a matter of the utmost seriousness; for others with minimal understanding and an amazing susceptibility to commercialism it is only a passing fad or a shallow commitment. The meditation centers, the practice of vegetarianism, the Eastern communes, the belief in reincarnation, the wearing of Indian clothes, the enjoyment of sitar music—all are as familiar now as blue jeans, beards and rock music. Accompanying these is the vogue for Eastern scriptures. For many the Bhagavad Gita, the Rig Veda, the Ramayana, the Pali Canon, the Tibetan Book of the Dead are known and read as widely as the Bible. In New York I have met blacks learning to read Mandarin Chinese in order to study I-Ching, the Book of Changes, in the original.

Another parallel is the popularity of the novels touching on the Eastern trend: *Siddartha* and the *Glass Bead Game* by Herman Hesse and *Island* by Aldous Huxley, for example. The last few years have seen the proliferation of the sects, Baha'i, Sokagakai (the true sect of

Nichiren) growing rapidly in many parts of the United States and Europe.

But above all, there are the thousands of young people on the road to the East either spiritually or physically. Some with intense dedication are working in the village communities in India; others, searching seriously, have been initiated under gurus and are studying in ashrams; many are delighted to find Kabul or Kathmandu a heaven for dropouts, with food, drugs and leisure in celestial proportions.

All this has turned Kipling on his head, but the trend was foreseen by others. James Joyce prophesied, "The west shall shake the east awake."[4] Marshall McLuhan wrote, "Soon, in order to Westernize our kids properly, we will be sending them all to the East,"[5] and R. D. Laing, changing the original meaning somewhat, has said, "Orientation means to know where the orient is. For inner space, to know the east, the origin or source of our experience."[6] The point is this: The East is still the East, but the West is no longer the West. Western answers no longer seem to fit the questions. With Christian culture disintegrating and humanism failing to provide an alternative, many are searching the ancient East. No one can understand this trend without first appreciating the underlying factors behind the movement.

Stirrings in the East and West

The first factor I would describe as "stirrings in the West." Many signs show that Western thought is somewhat played out, anemic and lifeless. With the failure of Western Christianity and secular humanism modern thinking has reached a terminus. Hendrik Kraemer writes, "There is evident in the fields of pictorial arts, of novels, of thinking and of depth psychology, a kind of premonition. They manifest a spontaneous openness, a readiness to be invaded, to be 'spiritually colonised' by the Orient. There are open 'gates' for an eastern invasion."[7] The Western escape from reason has produced a twin reaction, first, to more imagination generally and, second, to more imagination particularly through the East. Schopenhauer warmly appreciated Buddhism and was influenced by the Upanishads. Goethe showed great interest in the East. The papers of Wagner evidence the study of Buddhism, and an opera like *Tristan and Isolde* is heavy with Eastern pessimism. In Sir Edwin Arnold's poem "The Light of Asia" (the story of Gautama Buddha in poetic tract form), we see Western intellectuals looking towards the East because of the bankruptcy of Western thought. Much more could be said about this feature, but this is sufficient to show its background importance.

A second, more important feature is the stirring in the East itself. What we have seen in the last hundred years is nothing short of a rediscovery of Eastern culture, especially in the richness of the heritage of India. The India of the British Raj was no more the real India than the Britain of the 1970s is the Britain of the British Empire. As more knowledge of India's history comes to light, two features are of paramount importance. The first is that India's culture has a historic continuity from her pre-historic origin to the present, and no foreign conquest or invasion has ever severed that continuity. The philosophy of Shankara in the ninth century is as sophisticated and diverse as any in the West. Some even put him on a par with Plato and Aquinas combined. Psychology, although primitive, was developed in the East thousands of years before the West invented the term, and the same could be said of astronomy and commerce. The caves of Ellora and Ajanta have frescoes, some of which rival those in Florence, while the sculptures of the temples at Konarak and Khajuraho are alive with form and grace. And in Mahabilipuram we have the ruins of an early trading center whose commerce perhaps reached as far as Rome and China.

The second point transcends this historical, archeological interest. Through the origins of Aryanism, Hinduism has a direct relationship with pre-Christian European culture. As modern Europe is "de-Christened," losing its Christian foundations, it feels itself in danger of losing its soul. Yet as it searches for its pre-Christian roots, it is strangely finding itself closer to the origins of India than to its former Judeo-Christian tradition. It may be that this reflects the fact that the ancestors of the Aryans lived in close proximity to the ancestors of the Greeks. Scholars are becoming increasingly convinced that the impulses leading to Greek philosophy were closer to the Indian than to the Judeo-Christian world view.

The question of time is an important case in point. Both the Greeks and the Hindus viewed time as cyclical and limitless; men in the Judeo-Christian tradition view time as linear, teleological and limited. Another point of contrast is the question of reality. The Greeks viewed the physical universe as a world of shadow, less true or less real than the transcendent ideal which was beyond knowledge; for the Hindus the physical universe is a world of "maya," or illusion, while the true reality is Brahman or the God beyond. This is in total contrast to the Christian and Jewish view of God's creating a real universe which is not an extension of his essence but is distinct from himself. It is well known that Pythagoras was a teacher of reincarnation, and even Plato taught an Eastern type of asceticism and recognized the need for an illumination somewhat similar to the more developed Hindu meditation.

In this renaissance of Indian study there have been three avenues of rediscovery. The first but the least important was the patient work of scholarly research and government-sponsored investigation. When the British arrived in India, many of the caves were lost, many of the temples were ruined, certain rituals were no longer in practice, and even the Taj Mahal had been used as a stable. Much of the greatness of the past, such as the vast Buddhist empire of Emperor Asoka, had been forgotten. It was only towards the end of the eighteenth century, after the founding of the Royal Asiatic Society by Sir William Jones, the founding of various other Oriental and Sanskrit societies, the restoration of the temples, the renovation and maintenance of the rituals, the rediscovery of the caves, the finding of Asoka's rock edicts and their deciphering by Prinsep that for the first time Indians began to realize the richness of their heritage.

A more important avenue of rediscovery was the translation of the various sacred texts. Max Müller founded and edited the famous *Sacred Books of the East.* In England, Professor and Mrs. Rhys Davids worked on the Pali Canon. Through these and earlier great orientalists such as Sir William Jones (who had been brought to India by Warren Hastings), Western scholars for the first time had the Eastern writings in their own native languages. In this way came an awareness of the Rig Veda (the early Hindu poems of creation), the Vedanta (the great body of Hindu literature), the Bhagavad Gita (the crowning portion of the Vedanta), the Ramayana (a book of religious myths) and the Pali Canon (the Buddhist scriptures).

The third avenue of rediscovery, and by far the most important, was the patient work of the various apologists from the East.[8] Raja Ram Mohan Roy was the first (1772-1833) and has been popularly called the Father of modern India. Interestingly, his work, like that of many others, was in direct reaction to evangelical Christians such as William Carey. Carey had been instrumental in bringing education, the printing press and a new status for women and in introducing medicine to his part of India. Ram Mohan Roy was at first attracted to Christianity and Western education and studied the

Bible under the Serampore missionaries. He even felt that Christian truths were "more conducive to moral principles and better adapted for the use of rational beings than any other."[9] But he also saw that if Hinduism did not reform itself, it would be outflanked by Christianity. He therefore founded the Brahmo Samaj, a Hindu reform movement, and led the attack on suttee (widow burning, declared illegal in 1829), child marriages and other abuses. He died in Great Britain fighting for India's rights.

After him came Ramakrishna (1836-1886), a man devoted supremely to Kali (the mother goddess and patron of Calcutta) but also claiming visions of Mohammed and Christ. He was important because he saw that Hinduism, until then almost synonymous with India, was wider than this and could be claimed as the crown of the world's religions. His work was grounded and spread by his disciple, the Swami Vivekenanda (1863-1902). Educated at the Mission College in Calcutta, Vivekenanda was the spiritual heir to Ramakrishna and founded the Ramakrishna Mission, combining preaching with social action. In 1893, he became world famous when, unknown, unnoticed and poor, he came to the first Parliament on World Religions in Chicago. Speaking there unscheduled, he captivated the audience and through it gained the wider ear of the United States. Developing the commitment of Ramakrishna, Vivekenanda breathed fire into Shankara's monism. Claiming Hinduism as the "mother of all religions," he said, "We accept all religions as true."[10] This was the neo-vedantism which later impressed Aldous Huxley and at certain times has deeply influenced the United States. A reporter for the *New York Herald* wrote, "After hearing him we feel how foolish it is to send missionaries to this learned nation." Traveling widely in the United States and Europe, he achieved great popularity, and his death at thirty-nine was mourned as a national calamity in

 India.

Another great influence in the nineteenth century was the founding of the Theosophical Society. If Vivekenanda gave Hinduism self-consciousness, the Theosophical Society gave it pride, although the founders' zeal often outran their discretion and few Indians would agree with the strange amalgam of Hinduism, Buddhism and the occult that theosophy has become. Also important was Sri Aurobindo (1872-1950). With the benefits of an education in England, including classics at Cambridge, Aurobindo strenuously entered into politics as a young man, becoming a leader of the Nationalist Party. But after a vision in 1910, he retired to his ashram in Pondicherry to write *The Life Divine.* Remaining there the rest of his life, he suffered a measure of disillusionment in his closing years as his vision was little nearer to fulfillment. The ashram is now led by a French woman.

In our own century several leaders stand out. Rabindranath Tagore (1861-1941) was the Leonardo of the Bengal renaissance–poet, dramatist, actor, composer, painter, philosopher and prophet. The names of Mahatma Gandhi and Dr. Sarvepalli Radakrishnan, the Philosopher President, hardly need mentioning. But perhaps the point of influence for most has been the work of the various gurus–Krishnamurti, the "intellectual's guru," the Maharishi Mahesh Yogi, Meher Baba, Yogananda and, supremely important on the Buddhist side, D. T. Suzuki of Kyoto, Japan, a follower of the Rinzai school of Zen, stressing sudden enlightenment without Buddha or the scriptures. With all these, ostensible disciples range from shallow commitment to a deeply serious understanding. Among those who have followed Suzuki closely are John Cage, Erich Fromm and Martin Heidegger.

The East and Post-Christian West

The third great factor and the most important of all has

been the convergent coincidence of Eastern thought with post-Christian Western thought. There has been a dovetailing in so many areas as to form an almost inescapable climate. The East has not directly influenced the West at all these points, but the process is a growing series of "parallelisms," as Alan Watts describes them.[11] In a panorama of areas—from man's origin in the past to his utopian hope in the future—there is a coincidence of Eastern and post-Christian thought. In some areas the coincidence is real, in some it is only apparent (and in fact unfortunate) and in others it is completely mistaken. Examples could be given from each of these areas.

The Silence of God

In philosophy, for example, there is the question of whether or not there is a God and, if so, whether he can speak. The East and the post-Christian West converge in saying there are two alternatives, either "sheer silence" or a "mere symbolism" of mysticism. It is perhaps surprising that the concept of God lasted so long in Western philosophy, for, although many philosophers believed vaguely in a personal God or used the concept in their philosophical arguments, very few had an adequate view of revelation. The steps to the present position followed each other quickly. Emmanuel Kant made a complete dichotomy between the "noumenal" and the "phenomenal," between things as they are in themselves and things as they are toward us. Only the phenomenal is knowable; the noumenal is in the world of the philosophical "other" or "beyond." Wittgenstein developed this with his notion that the sphere of language only circumscribed the area of the phenomenal, that which is open to sense verification. So, although we speak of the noumenal, we must beware of being hexed by the "bewitching nature" of language. Verbalization cannot penetrate the unknown and unknowable noumenal. His conclusion was: "Whereof one cannot speak, thereof one must be silent." If this relegates God to the world of the noumenal and reduces theology to silence, for Wittgenstein this was a mystical silence and not an atheistic silence. There was a failure of language, not a failure of God. This quotation is a crucial step in modern thinking. Alan Watts, for example, cites these words from the *Tractatus,* regretting that Western philosophy did not take the chance to explore mysticism but went on to the third step, atheism. As Wittgenstein's mystic silence has come down to A. J. Ayer and linguistic analysis, it has become the sheer silence of atheism. It is impossible for a sentence to be significant and be about God. It isn't that the sentence is not true, but that it is meaningless.

This leaves the Western discussion of God with only two possibilities—the sheer silence of the atheist or the mere symbolism of the mystic. The latter is the virtual conclusion of much liberal theology. Theological language is not what God means about himself to man, but rather what man has made of meaning about God. It is symbolic truth, "silence qualified by parables" (T. R. Miles) or non-rational "disclosure situations" (Bishop Ian Ramsey). History is explained as myth, and faith has little continuity with facts or reason. Some may emphasize the immanence of God as the ground of being while others stress his transcendence as the God behind God, but it is always one or the other; there is no clear link of revelation between the two or between God and us. The theological use of religious connotation words to disguise the fact of the death of God is a compromise that many modern atheists recognize as lacking integrity. For them, there is only silence, however hard or unwelcome.

For Ingmar Bergman the dilemma is expressed by Tomas, the doubting priest in *Winter Light* (1961). After a barren counseling session in which he has ministered not human comfort but despair, Tomas gazes up at the qrotesque wooden crucifix in the deserted church and moans, "God, my God, Why have you abandoned me?" But there is only "God's silence, Christ's twisted face, the blood on the brow and the hands, the soundless shriek behind the bared teeth" (Bergman's scene description in the script). Eventually he gasps, "No. God does not exist anymore." For Bergman from then on there is only "the echo-god," "the lie-god," the "spider-god."[12] God no longer speaks, and soon without divine revelation there is no human relationship. This Bergman explored next in his film, *The Silence* (1962). John Cage has called his autobiography *Silence,* and a recent play by Harold Pinter has the same title.

This is strikingly close to what the East has always said, and it has not gone unnoticed in the West. Martin Heidegger remarked that if he understood D. T. Suzuki correctly, his own existential philosophy was saying the same thing. John Robinson's *Honest to God* and Paul Tillich's books are widely read in India and can be seen in the libraries of many ashrams. One swami in Rishikesh pointed to *Honest to God* and said to me, "But surely your Western theologians are saying what we have been saying all along." Tillich, asked at the end of his life by a student at Santa Barbara, "Sir, do you pray?" replied, "No, I meditate." The reason is obvious. Liberal theology has no propositional content, no verbal revelation; theological meaning is only what *man* means about God. This view can only inspire meditation, not verbalized prayer. R. D. Laing from his own experience of philosophy and psychology writes, "At the point of non-being we are at the outer reaches of what language can state. . . . In using a word, a letter, a sound, OM, one cannot put a sound to soundlessness, or name the unnameable."[13] This leads us to where the East has always been, and if Hinduism is closer to liberal theology's stress on "mere symbolism," then Buddhism is the parallel to Western atheism's stress on "sheer silence."

In Hinduism, Shankara's monism is typical of one main stream of thought. Constantly he stressed that the final characterization of God could only be "neti neti," that is, that God is "not this" and he is "not that." God is always beyond, unknowable in his pure essence; any description we give him in terms of words or pictures is only a reduction for our human understanding. God cannot be known through rational, conceptual, verbalized thought of any kind. He is to be known only through intuition or meditation, both of which stress the non-rational or the super-rational. Shankara used to tell the story of a pupil who kept asking his master about the nature of Brahman or God or the Absolute Self. Each time the question came the teacher would turn a deaf ear, until finally he turned impatiently on his pupil and said, "I am teaching you but you do not follow. The Self is silence."[14] A well-known saying in the Upanishads is, "The gods love the obscure and hate the obvious."

A parallel witness to this is the role in Indian philosophy of the Bhakti movement. In the twelfth century A.D. the philosopher Ramanuja led a reaction against the idealistic monism of Shankara. Particularly he felt it was too lofty and impersonal to provide a deity viable for worship, devotion and prayer. The Bhaktis by contrast strongly stress a personal God, but, although this has a necessary appeal to pietists, it is untenable philosophically within the premises of Hindu thought. The Bhaktis are still a vitally strong movement, keeping alive the warmth and devotion of Indian religions, but their emotional commitment has always been stronger than their philosophical basis.

D. S. Sharma, a modern Indian philosopher, points out the reason behind this failure: "The particular name and form of any deity are limitations which we in our weakness impose on the all-pervading Spirit which is really nameless and formless. The Supreme Being is a person only in relation to ourselves and our needs. . . . The highest theism is only a sort of glorified anthropomorphism but *we cannot do without it.*"[15] The last five words clearly show the Freudian nature of Indian symbolism about God. It is not that "God is there" defined in the high verbal symbolism of a philosopher or the rude stone symbolism of a villager sacrificing to his idol in the temple. Rather, God is there for them only because each "needs" this representation. Shankara had already expressed it caustically: "Such a *Jiva,* that is, the aspirant betaking itself to devotion, inasmuch as it knows only a partial aspect of Brahman, is called of narrow or poor intellect by those who regard Brahman as eternal and unchanging."[16]

On the side of sheer silence Buddhism provides the parallel to Western atheism. It is said that whenever he was asked about God, Gautama Buddha always answered in terms of "resolute" or "roaring silence." "And why, monks, have I not declared it? Because it is not profitable. . . ." The Buddha is normally considered an atheist, though some now say that perhaps he was a mystic with an acute insight into the problems of language thousands of years before the intricate subtleties of Wittgenstein. It is said that when Lord Buddha was about to enter Final Nirvana he assembled his followers upon the Vulture Peak for a farewell. For a long while he sat before them in silence. Finally, picking a flower, he held it out in front of his disciples and watched for some sign of comprehension. After several minutes of silence, all except one were bemused and puzzled. Only Mahakasyapa smiled comprehendingly. Buddha congratulated him as the only one who had understood what he was talking about, or, more literally, why he wasn't talking at all. Final truth is only in being; this knowledge is beyond words.

Many of the sayings now enjoying vogue on the

campuses also illustrate this silence. One is Lao-tse's "Those who know do not speak. Those who speak do not know." Zen is much concerned with the subtle paradoxes of language, and the Zen Koan is a deliberate intellectual teaser designed to jolt the mind into freeing itself from rationality, escaping into the non-rational by intuition, where alone the true self lies. "What is the sound of one hand clapping?" "What is your original face before you were born?" Rationality stumbles in its earnestness, but it is only when it falls that the higher levels of super-rational knowledge can be reached.

I have spent almost too long on this first example of coincidence, but the picture should be plain. Intellectually both East and post-Christian West have arrived at the silence of atheism or mysticism. Any view of revelation is out of the question in this situation. We might also add that emotionally such commitment to an intriguing silence contrasts well with the garrulous preachiness of Christianity, and so the East becomes a natural harbor for the inward and inarticulate moodiness of many from the Beats onward.

Ecology and the Nature of Nature

A second example of this current dovetailing of East and post-Christian West is in the area of ecology and the question of the basis for a proper treatment of nature. Here is an ostensible parallel which is actually mistaken. Few would deny that Western industrial society has been conspicuous for its failure to treat nature well. Through ignorance, haste and ghastly economic greed in every field, the rape of nature is a vivid reality. Why is this? Lynn White, Jr. is typical of many who are now blaming Christianity for this disaster, claiming that Christianity taught man to think himself so distinctively different from nature that he went on to dominate nature to its ruin.[17] Others have suggested that the only answer to this exploitation is pantheism, a view that bases the respectful treatment of nature on man's basic unity with nature.

Aldous Huxley in *Island* (1962), his sequel to *Brave New World* (1932), depicts a utopian community based on scientific humanism and Buddhism. The community is betrayed in the closing pages, but as the ideal is worked out earlier, both ecology and Buddhism are basic to his solutions. The Palanese school children begin their primary school lessons with ecology. "Elementary ecology leads straight to elementary Buddhism."[18] That is, when man understands that he and nature stand in unity on a physical or natural level, man then comes to see that he and nature itself are really one on a more basic level.

Such arguments are common currency in many circles and in campus discussions today. They will undoubtedly increase. Nonetheless, this argument has no more than surface plausibility. A little study will show that, although Christians must admit their share of guilt for complacency and silence, this complacency is a gross caricature of the true Christian position. The real situation is precisely the reverse.

Historic Christianity sees man as distinct, but not divorced, from nature. On the level of his personality man is distinct from the rest of finite creation, finding complete fulfillment for his aspirations only in God. But on the level of his finiteness man is one within nature as part of the wider finite creation. Thus, despite real differences, man has a relationship to nature that is the source of his responsibility to it and his respect for it.

Pantheism does not have this balance. As Francis Schaeffer has shown, far from raising the lower (nature) to the level of the higher (man), pantheism tends to lower the higher (man) to the level of the lower (nature).[19] Paradoxically, in India the cow, though sacred, is often treated worse, short of being killed, than cows in most other countries. While there is a great differentiation in treatment according to size and quality (and some are pampered as pets), there are far too many cows in India. They not only take food needed for humans but are themselves close to starvation. They wander the streets, eat garbage from the public bins and stand on their hind legs to tear off paper from the advertisements to feed themselves.

The same point is even clearer in the attitude towards vermin. Several times in New Delhi I saw people putting rats into their neighbor's garden, refusing to kill them themselves because of the doctrine of Ahimsa. A United Nations expert told me that every year in India vermin eat enough food to feed the entire population of Canada, but nothing can be done about this because of the religious taboos. This would mean sufficient food to solve the dire problem in a major famine area like Rajastan where millions are at subsistence level.

The fact is, then, that a pantheistic view of man and nature may do at least as much ecological damage as the "Western" view. The fully Christian view of man and nature, on the other hand, leads to ecological responsibility.

Other areas also tell the same story of coincidence between the East and post-Christian West: the question of evolution, the space-time scale, parapyschology and the hopes for utopia centering around a future cosmic consciousness. These too are creating a climate in which it is entirely natural for Western man to look for intellectual stimulus from the East. Space, however, does not permit examining them in detail.

The point, I think, is already clear: Taken as a whole, the defeatism in Western thought, the stirrings in the East and the coincidence in so many areas of thought are pushing the West further and further towards the East. Nonetheless, at the risk of being tedious, I would like to stress just once more the importance of seeing how "understandable" this swing is. Some further factors will therefore be considered here.

The Weakness of Western Christianity

The swing to the East has come at a time when Christianity is weak at just those points where it would need to be strong to withstand the East. Without this strength, the Eastern religions will be to Christianity a new, dangerous gnosticism, but this time much of the fight will be lost before many see the nature of the danger. Modern Christianity is crucially weak at three vital points. The first is its compromised, deficient understanding of revelation. Without biblical historicity and veracity behind the Word of God, theology can only grow closer to Hinduism. Second, the modern Christian is drastically weak in an unmediated, personal, experiential knowledge of God. Often what passes for religious experience is a communal emotion felt in church services, in meetings, in singing or contrived fellowship. Few Christians would know God on their own. Third, the modern church is often pathetically feeble in the expression of its focal principle of community. It has become the local social club, preaching shop or minister-dominated group. With these weaknesses, modern Christianity cannot hope to understand why people have turned to the East, let alone stand against the trend and offer an alternative.

Even within the church itself many have an understanding of their faith extremely blurred at the edges. This is particularly so in places like California where Eastern ideas are so prevalent. While in an ashram in India, I lived in a room next door to a Canadian Roman Catholic who spent long hours each day telling me how his new understanding of Hinduism was a shot-in-the-arm for his Christian faith. He was due to return to Canada to continue as a professor in a Roman Catholic seminary.

It is important to stress, however, that in the East

 there is much that is valid and good, much that we must acknowledge as true. The general emphasis on the spiritual is a welcome contrast to gross materialism; the stress on quiet and stillness is a relief from hectic rush. More particularly, there are valuable benefits from such practices as physical exercises, concentration, mind control, the ability to determine the blood pressure or the heart-rate.

Why, then, does the East so strongly appeal to the West? From traveling widely in the East and from many conversations with those going East (physically or spiritually), I think the basic appeal is the force of contrast with what people have experienced in the West. The East stresses experience not theory and thus is a welcome relief from the sterile memory of preachers and pulpits, six feet above contradiction and life. For the East, verification is via participation. The Tat Tvam Asi ("Thou art that") is not a metaphysical proposition but a psychological experience. As a guru said to me with a fair measure of accuracy, "To the Christian, talk of God is rather like the great bulk of an iceberg, whereas his experience of God is only the tiny tip of the iceberg; but for the Easterner the experience of God is the bulk of the iceberg, whereas his talk about God is only the tip."

Furthermore, the East stresses integration and not isolated individuality. This insight into a oneness with nature often brings a sense of flooding release, relief, peace and joy. This is all the more real by force of contrast with the individualism and alienation which are so often the experience of the sensitive person in a materialistic, industrial society or an inadequate church situation. Aldous Huxley claimed that "the urge to escape from selfhood and the environment is in almost everyone almost all the time."[20] This is too strong a generalization, though it is true that the urge is commonly found today in those who are introspective, sensitive and perhaps over-intellectual. For all such the

East is a natural harbor. One has much sympathy for Alan Watts when he speaks generally of modern Christianity's "sheer genius for drabness," its "constipation of the bright emotions,"[21] or when he describes an average service: "Participants sit in rows looking at the backs of each other's necks, and are in communication only with the leader."[22]

Monism: An Eastern Presupposition

I have much sympathy for anyone going East. I understand, I think, why it appeals and what it holds in promise. Nonetheless, the East is ultimately wrong and the hope it holds is spurious. So I would like to turn to a critique of it, at least of its central conceptions. I will not look so much at its practices (like the caste system) or the full range of its beliefs (such as reincarnation), but rather at the basic premises—the presuppositions, the prior theoretical commitments—and the overall results of these in the culture. Put another way, we will see how their view of the nature of ultimate reality works out practically as it washes down in the rain of normal living. Here the critique will focus mainly on one stream of Hinduism, making only occasional references to the other streams or to Buddhism.

There is a great range in Hindu theology. Seen one way there are as many gods as there are Indians. But, although the early stage showed a strong polytheism and the Bhaktis still provide a reaction of a personal theism, the highest and most influential stage (and certainly the most intellectually consistent) is the concept of monism. From the ninth-century philosophy of Shankara through the nineteenth-century vision of Vivekenanda to the twentieth century and the Maharishi and Radakrishnan, the mainstream of Indian thought has been Advaita, or non-dualist, Vedanta, a pure monism. This is still the most vital school in modern India. It is certainly true that other varieties of Hinduism, not to speak of Buddhism, have vastly differing epistemologies or ontologies. But when stripped of their philosophic backgrounds, all the paths of yoga amount to much the same thing in practice. Their common aim is the liberation of the self (however that is understood) from all that which is non-self, until the latter (whether external world, human body or temporal psyche) ceases to exist.

As a key to monism we can see how it tackles the problem of unity and diversity, answering it in terms of unity. Monism is one answer to the problem of the one and the many. For example, in trying to see which is more important, the unity of the universal or the diversity of the particulars, one might ask, "Which is more real–a particular dog (a German shepherd, poodle, terrier, dachshund) or the concept of dogginess?" Looked at one way, the particular dog is much more real; it can be seen, heard, felt, even smelled. But looked at another way, the concept of dogginess, although not open to the five senses, is actually what makes any dog a dog and not a cat. Long after the particular dog has died the concept of dogginess persists.

In answer to this question, the early Greek Cynics and the modern existentialists reply that there can be no universal, no final unity; man is left only with diversity. In the resulting alienation of this position there is only the authentication of individualism against a universe incapable of providing wider meaning. Both the Indians and many of the Greeks (such as Plato), on the other hand, would say that the unity is real and the diversity can be explained only in terms of that unity. Plato spoke of the phenomenal as a shadow of the real world and the Indians say that only the absolute self is real and the world of diversity is maya or illusion. As the Bhagavad Gita says, "Weapons cannot hurt the Spirit and fire can never burn him. Untouched is he by drenching waters, untouched is he by parching winds. Beyond the power of sword and fire, beyond the power of waters and winds, the Spirit is everlasting, omnipresent, never-changing, never moving, ever One."[23] Some may wonder if this is significant, whether, in fact, in discussing monism we are being enmeshed in obscure problems of philosophical complexity with no apparent relevance. In fact, the question of the One and the many is more than a philosophic problem; it is basic to every area of life. Modern philosophy may have grown camera-shy in facing the question, because the likelihood of its finding an answer is small, but modern society is an attempted answer nevertheless. These basic premises of monism relate to the final forms of the culture; to understand the latter one must grasp the former. We will, therefore, examine Indian monism and relate it to the three crucial areas—the monist understanding of reality, personality and morality.

Monism and Reality

First, what is the relation of monism to reality? If unity alone is real, then what is the world of diversity or the phenomenal external universe as we know it? Early Vendantism, which was polytheistic, explained this in the picture of a spider spinning its web or of a fire throwing out sparks. But as monism developed, the relation of God to his world was described in terms of a dreamer (who alone was real) and his dream (which was unreal). The phenomenal world as we know it is *maya,* whose root meaning in Sanskrit is to measure or classify. Thus, maya, the world of scientific phenomena, is illusion, ignorance and shadow, a world where individuality and diversity are thought to be real but are not. God as the original unity plays hide-and-seek with himself, "freaks out" at the end of his cosmic dance or forgets himself temporally. "This is the magic power of God by which He is Himself deluded," says Shankara.[24] The trend from polytheism to monism has led increasingly to the stress on the unreality of the universe as we know it. Shankara, for example, says that the world is maya but is taken for real in the way a man mistakes a rope for a snake or mother-of-pearl for silver. The world is considered real only because of our ignorance. "Brahman alone is real, the phenomenal world is unreal, or mere illusion."[25]

The importance of this view of reality can be traced in two practical directions. The first is the Hindu view of science. Both A. N. Whitehead and Robert Oppenheimer paid tribute to the Reformation in openly admitting that only in the Christian milieu could modern science have arisen. Perhaps it is because of its views of maya that India did not progress beyond a certain stage in science and technology. The question comes: Will Hinduism and Buddhism be able to withstand the pressures of twentieth-century science and technology? Professor Zaehner of Oxford University predicts that just as Islam, Taoism and Confucianism all failed, so too will Zen and Hinduism, reminding us that "it was within a Western Christian setting that our technological civilisation came to birth, and this was no accident, for Christianity is both this-worldly and other-worldly."[26] The East could never have given birth to modern science as we now know it.

The second practical direction is the problem of the distinction between fantasy and reality. If the world that we know as reality is actually illusion, what then is the difference between fantasy and reality? As Lao-tse puts it, "If, when I was asleep I was a man dreaming I was a butterfly, how do I know when I am awake I am not a butterfly dreaming I am a man?" As we sit reading in comfort this has little philosophical menace. But to any who have lost the ordinary reality through carelessly applied mental techniques or through repeated acid "bummers," the inability to distinguish fantasy and reality can become a living hell. So here is the first problem: Monism as related to reality does not give a sufficient basis on which to ground continuing scientific investigation or to distinguish between fantasy and reality.

Monism and Personality

The second area is the relation of monism to personality. Here we examine the Hindu view of man's being. If the unity, God or Brahman, alone is all-important and the world of diversity is maya, then what is man? Who are you? Who am I?

Shankara's answer is simple: "Who are you? Who am I? Whence have I come? Who is my mother? Who is my father? Think of all this as having no substance, leave it all as the stuff of dreams."[27]

Within this framework man is the extension of God's essence into the world of diversity in the sense of the dream, the dance or hide-and-seek. Radakrishnan says, man is "God's temporary self-forgetfulness." Alan Watts explains it: "God entranced himself and forgot the way back, so that now he feels himself to be man, playing—guiltily—at being God."[28] The "true self" is God, and the "I" which I consider myself to be is really the "not-self" caught in the world of illusion, bondage and ignorance. Thus, yoga (which is related to the root meaning of yoke or union) is the liberation of the "not-self" and its assimilation back to the "true self," whereby that part in man which is the divine spark becomes one again with God. By the self-realization that it is in fact God it remerges with the Absolute. As the River Ganges flows ceaselessly down to the sea and the Bay of Bengal, so the individual soul achieves a final unity with God, merging with him as the Absolute. The Upanishads contain many illustrations and parables explaining this. Just as pollen merges with honey, just as salt loses itself in sea water, just as the river flows into the ocean, so the divine spark in man is freed by its merging with the

 Absolute. The liberation of the not-self is the extinction of the illusion of individuality, which itself is a mere by-product of maya or illusion. All these parables stress that individuality must be lost in a larger whole; this alone is freedom. But it is important to see that such freedom (Mukti or Moksha) is freedom "from" individuality as we now know it and not freedom "to be" the individuals we know or want ourselves to be. Individuality is never more than the mistaken not-self; only God is the true self.

The implied retreat from individuality is openly expressed in the Hindu ideals in life. A normal man after marriage and a life in business is expected in the closing years of his life to come aside to pursue spiritual goals. Exceptional men like the gurus, rishis, seers or men like Gautama Buddha leave life much earlier, often totally abandoning wife, family and business. In the Bhagavad Gita Lord Krishna says man must be cut from "the dark forest of delusion."[29] D. T. Suzuki has said, the goal of Zen is not incarnation but "excarnation." Alan Watts often hints that the Eastern answer for personality is not so much solution as dissolution.

This view of personality—in essence an excessive attachment to detachment—inevitably leads to a radically pessimistic view of the value of individuality in this life. This, by the way, is also true of Buddhism which sees man as a stream of consciousness, unified as personality only by the momentum of selfish desire. The man who perceives his true self, Buddhagosa says, "grasps the fourfold emptiness disclosed in the words: 'I am nowhere a somewhatness for anyone.' "[30] Western thinkers who reflect Eastern ideas generally have the same disparaging view of man as he knows himself to be in this life. Alan Watts describes man as the "ego-mask" or the "skin-encapsulated ego."[31] R. D. Laing describes him as "this identity-anchored, space- and time-bound experience."[32]

Monism does not see man's dilemma as moral (in terms of what he has done) but as metaphysical (in terms of who he is). Monism thus leads to the notion that a man cannot be helped as an individual because his individuality is the essential problem. He must be helped *from* his individuality; he must merge with the Absolute. Meher Baba says, "A real merging of the limited in the ocean of universal life involves complete surrender of separative existence in all its forms."[33] This cannot but lead to a radical negation of any positive aspiration towards individuality in this life.

Lewis Carroll expressed this playfully in *Through the Looking Glass.* Speaking of the dream, Tweedledee says,

> "And if he left off dreaming about you, where do you suppose you'd be?"
>
> "Where I am now, of course," said Alice.
>
> "Not you!" Tweedledee retorted contemptuously. "You'd be nowhere. Why, you're only a sort of thing in his dream!"
>
> "If that there King was to wake," added Tweedledum, "you'd go out–bang!–just like a candle!"[34]

Such epistemological uncertainty has the further twist of leading people to realize that life is not only lived in illusion but on the wheel of samsara or suffering. Many parables in the Upanishads are pessimistic; they show the human predicament that results from the misery of samsara. One depicts samsara as a well without water where man is struggling frantically and hopelessly in the mud. Another describes man as dangling head-down in a pit; snakes threaten him from below, elephants from above; he is kept alive only by the creeper on which he is hanging, and this is being slowly gnawed by a black rat and a white rat, symbolizing the shortening of his life throughout both night and day. Western man must consider this situation soberly. Is such metaphysical depersonalization a true answer to man's search for significance? Or is it only an escape?

Is it not plain why both communism and secular humanism are "Christian heresies"? From nowhere in the East could one quarry a sufficient basis for such high views of man. Communism may have betrayed its humanism in practice, making an arbitrary absolute of the state and so overriding the individual. Secular humanism may have so shown itself deficient in providing a basis for its optimistic view of man that it is foundering in the swift currents of technological dehumanization. But the East has never had a high view of man. In both philosophy and practice it exhibits a dangerous carelessness about the higher reaches of man's aspirations of humanness. If we were to examine Buddhism, with its slightly different premises, the conclusion would be, if anything, even more radically pessimistic and life-negating.

This should also make us wary and critical of such cult heroes as Pierre Teilhard de Chardin, who, despite a certain disdain for the East as escapist and dated, comes perilously close to the same negation of individuality. As Teilhard sees it, there are only four options open to mankind: "to cease to act, by some form of suicide; to withdraw through a mystique of separation; to fulfil ourselves individually by egoistically segregating ourselves from the mass; or to plunge resolutely into the stream of the whole in order to become part of it."[35] These are the answers, respectively, of "the pessimist," "the Buddhist," "the pluralist" and "the monist."

Teilhard's own choice, the "Grand Option" is the last one, and he specifically disassociates this from Hindu monism, attacking as unfounded prejudice "the widespread idea that *any* destiny on 'monist' lines would exact the sacrifice and bring about the destruction of all personal values in the Universe."[36] On the contrary he says, "socialisation, whose hour seems to have sounded for Mankind, does not by any means signify the ending of the Era of the Individual upon earth, but far more its beginning."[37]

But what is it in Teilhard's vision that will ward off the totalitarian principle inherent in monism and allow unity to fulfill diversity and not swallow it? His answer is in terms of a " 'conspiracy' informed with love . . . the one natural medium in which the rising course of evolution can proceed. With love omitted there is truly nothing ahead of us except the forbidding prospect of standardisation and enslavement–the doom of ants and termites."[38]

Interestingly, mention of his final goal gives rise to talk of "mystical 'annihilation' "[39] (reminiscent of Nirvana) and "the Absolute"[40] (reminiscent of the divine absolute of Hinduism). Despite its distinct vagueness his goal is not unattractive, but this vagueness in fact turns out to be chronic. Who would bet on so fuzzy a concept of love being able to solve so effortlessly the perennial problems of unity and diversity, and form and freedom on which optimism has so often foundered? But if love does not win, we face the unwelcome logic of monism again, only this time the negation of individuality condemns man to "the doom of ants and termites." If both roads lead to the pessimism of negation, better the frank realism of the East than the fuzzy romanticism of Teilhard. How paradoxical that so many clergy are still uncritically lauding what finally denies what both Christian and humanist traditions have seen as man's special glory.

Arnold Toynbee catches something of the essential negation and alienation of individuality in all world views which are ultimately non-personal when he says that "we might think of a human person . . . as being a wave that rises and falls, or a bubble that forms and bursts, on the 'immortal sea's' surface. . . . But, if that is what we are, we have to live and die without ever knowing in what relation we stand to the Ultimate Reality that is the source and destination of our being in our ephemeral human life on earth. Are we accidents that have no meaning in terms of this reality from which, as persons, we are temporarily differentiated? Or are we truants, who have alienated ourselves from the source of our being by a perverse *tour de force* that we cannot sustain beyond the brief span of a human life's trajectory?"[41] The question is not a light one for Western man.

Monism and Morality

The third important area is the relation of monism to morality. If man's dilemma is metaphysical and not moral, what is left of morality? Monism says that good and evil are only distinct because of maya. There are no moral absolutes; moral values are only relatively true or sociologically useful and the question of ethics is only the question of optimal game rules. Alan Watts likens the moral situation to a play. On stage, you see the "good man" fighting the "bad man," although you know that backstage the actors are the best of friends. Only in this life do you believe in good and evil as real and distinct. Backstage, God and Satan are the best of friends. Within the framework of monism God contains both good and evil and is beyond good and evil. Zen is close to Hinduism here too. The master Yun-Men said,

> If you want to get the plain truth,
> Be not concerned with right and wrong.
> The conflict between right and wrong
> Is the sickness of the mind.[42]

Anyone who achieves transcendence, who is "immersed in Itness," as Bernard Berenson described it, has an insight into the universe that soars beyond good and evil, sees behind moral distinctions and categories and knows things just as they are, self-evident and self-sufficient. Alan Watts puts it this way: "Each thing, each event, each experience in its inescapable nowness and in all its own particular indiviuality was precisely what it should be, and so much so that it acquires a divine authority . . . the conviction that this entire unspeakable world is 'right,' so right."[43] A superbly funny caricature of this was the brilliant Zen sermon by Donald Sutherland in the film *Little Murders.* Dostoevsky likewise foreshadowed the implications of nihilism beyond morals in *The Possessed.* Kirilov argues with Stavrogin,

> "Everything is good."
>
> "Everything?"
>
> "Everything. Man is unhappy because he doesn't know he's happy. That's the only reason. The man who discovers that will become happy that very minute. That stepdaughter will die, the little girl will remain–and everything is good. I suddenly discovered that."
>
> "So it's good, too, that people die of hunger and also that someone may abuse or rape that little girl?"
>
> "It's good. And if someone breaks open that man's skull for the girl, that's good too. And if someone doesn't break his skull, it's equally good. Everything's good."[44]

Thus the ideal is to attain to the level of bliss where one is so transcendent in consciousness that he is beyond the distinctions of good and evil. This has even given rise to the bizarre idea that a true test would be to do some deed of total evil, then check to see if there is any pang of conscience or feeling of remorse. In *Crime and Punishment* Dostoevsky pursues precisely this motif.

Why and how, then, do I fight social injustice or moral evil? Once more the answers are radically pessimistic. Since life on earth is the metaphysical hassle of samsara, suffering is the norm of life on the wheel. My suffering is the result of my karma, the just deserts from my previous incarnation. As this works out in practice, there are two general tendencies.

The first is the tendency towards personal resignation, fatalism. After all, action to relieve suffering is the abortion of karma. What makes much in India so profoundly sad is not just its staggering problems but the glazed pride and the terminal resignation so deeply sunk into the eyes of the common man. Yet many tourists don't see this. American travelers would often say to me, "Why speak to Indians when you can surely see how happy they are? Compared with their contemporaries back in Berkeley, or Columbia, or Kent State, surely you can see that they are happy." For me, this remark was sadder still. It demonstrates that their lack of compassion derived from their failure to understand what they saw. I would watch them after their initial exposure, traveling a class higher on the trains, sleeping in better hotels or eating in more expensive restaurants. Few can look this suffering in the eye.

Much closer to the truth was the angry frustration of several communist agitators whom I met. In a culture without a developed consciousness of the worth of individuality, these activists were unable to find a lever on which to press for revolution. Some say that perhaps few other countries in the world are so ripe for revolution, yet the communists make surprisingly little headway. With the numbing prospect of interminable reincarnation on the wheel where the raw unsatisfactoriness of life is basic and where there are no grounds for any positive affirmation of individuality, can men be other than pessimistic and mutely resigned?

The problem is not that Hinduism and Buddhism are not water-tight systems but that in their admitted internal consistency they do not fit well with what man feels himself to be. There is always a tension at some point between what a man says he is and who he is. The most poignant example of this comes from the Japanese poet, Issa (1762-1826), perhaps the best loved of all Haiku poets because of the humanness of his writing. His own life was very sad. All five of his children died before he was thirty, and then his young wife died. After one of those deaths he went to a Zen master and asked him for an explanation for such suffering. The master reminded him that the world was dew. Just as the sun rises and the dew evaporates, so on the wheel of suffering sorrow is transient, life is transient, man is transient. Involvement in the passion of grief and mourning speaks of a failure to transcend the momentum of selfish egoism. Here was his religious philosophical answer, but on returning home Issa wrote a poem which translated literally runs:

> This Dewdrop World–
> a dewdrop world it is, and still,
> although it is . . .[45]

Or more simply,

> The world is dew–
> The world is dew–
> And yet,
> And yet . . .

Here is a truth which should make Eastbound Western man stand still in his tracks, but, it is expressed in such distilled beauty that the fragrance of its pathos and poignancy becomes such a jewel of poetry that its lesson is easily lost. Issa the orthodox Zen believer must say, "The world is dew, the world is dew," but Issa the father, the husband, the human being, with his agonized grief and tortured love can only cry into the unfulfilled darkness where Zen sheds no light, "And yet, and yet." He feels the inescapable tension between the logic of what he believes and the logic of who he is.

The second tendency is towards a general communal detachment. If the only solution for individuality is dissolution by merging with the Absolute, obviously the answer is not to be found in the run and ruck of human life but in mental or physical withdrawal. Shankara points the way: "By ceasing to do good to one's friends or evil to one's enemies [one] attains to the eternal Brahman by the yoga of meditation."[46] Gurus, asked what they were doing for the man in the street, have smilingly replied that they were sending down their vibrations. But political radicals, when asked what they felt the gurus' vibrations contributed, frequently answered by vehemently spitting on the ground. R. C. Zaehner, who has followed President Radakrishnan in the Spalding Chair of Eastern Religions and Ethics at Oxford University, underlines this strongly when he writes of Hinduism and Buddhism, "In practice it means that neither religion in its classical formulation pays the slightest attention to what goes on in the world today."[47]

Some may immediately object that this is unfair, that it ignores the constant emphasis on Karuna or compassion which is a real feature of Buddhism, from Gautama and the Boddhisattvas to Huxley's Palanese island. But this emphasis and practice of apparent unselfishness is deceptive, a far cry from Christian compassion. For the Buddhist the practice of unselfishness is simply part of the overall technique of divesting oneself of the illusion of self. Zaehner writes, "Compassion is recommended not as being intrinsically good but as being empirically efficient in ridding the mind of the erroneous idea of individual personality."[48] Thus, Karuna is not technically compassion, but "right-mindfulness," a further stage on Gautama's Noble Eight-fold Path.

From this examination of the monistic premises of Hinduism and their relation to reality, personality and morality (allowing for both the real differences and the essential similarities between Hinduism and Buddhism), it should be evident that monism is not only deficient but dangerous–deficient within the cultural situation of the East, but, more important for this discussion, dangerous in our Western situation.

Can we afford a view which rejects the reality of the physical universe? Western philosophy, torn between unfounded positivism and unwelcome scepticism, no longer provides a basis for understanding that reality. So as we witness the rising fear of anti-scientism in popular attitudes, the engine of technology is allowed to thunder alone down its runaway track. The Eastern contribution is dangerously deficient at this point.

Can we afford a view which contains so radical a negation of individual personality and which fails to support or give credence to human community? Already suffering from the internal problems of the "striptease of humanism," Western man is struggling against the dehumanizing forces in society and technology. Here too the East fails to provide a genuine alternative.

Can we afford a view of morality that is relative at its best and at its worst produces resignation and withdrawal, both tendencies tantamount to cultural suicide for Western man in his present impasse? Already reeling from value vertigo and dreading the ethical questions he must soon answer, Western man may think the East offers a welcome escape. But the concerned searcher will be forced to look elsewhere for a true basis to morality and a firm motivation for social action against injustice. A sign should be blazoned across the pathway of our times–The East, No Exit!

A Christian Alternative

Here we can ask whether Christianity is really a "metaphysical filibuster"[49] as Alan Watts charges, or whether the lemming-like, suicidal rush from the truth of historic Christianity has drowned its meaning and message. It is a perverse fact that what people scornfully reject in Christianity (such as a non-material supernatural), they welcome with open arms in Eastern mysticism. This despite the fact that Christianity is strong at just those points where the East is critically weak. All these strengths stem from the conception of God as revealed in Jesus Christ. If pre-Christian Western deities failed because, although they were personal, they were finite (were the Greek gods behind the fates or the fates behind the gods?), the Eastern gods now fail because, although they are infinite (and so sufficient to carry philosophical unity as a universal), they are impersonal and thus offer no basis for the value of human personality.

But God, as he reveals himself in Jesus Christ is personal (thereby avoiding the dilemma of the East) and also infinite (thereby avoiding the futile irrelevance of the pre-Christian Western gods). From this conception of the difference of God and the difference it makes flows a full and systematic understanding of man in this world. It answers the very points of Eastern weakness and provides a higher but different humanism.

Within the Christian conception of God there is no problem of unity and diversity. The Christian is not forced to choose between unity and diversity, to join the monist or the existentialist. A balance is struck, relatively in this world and absolutely in God himself, for God reveals himself as already three-in-one in his trinitarian unity. In Christianity, God is not just three-in-one in a symbolic, modal expression, but back of all things, as he is in his own mystery of Being; he is there and to himself still three-in-one. At the heart of God's own Being there is diversity within unity and unity around diversity. This means that when God creates the world, it is not an extension of his essence with unity temporarily disguising itself under the mantle of diversity; it is distinct and yet not divorced from himself. There is a balance between unity and diversity derived from God himself but now, after the Fall, temporarily and partially out of joint because of alienation. This makes for a view of the universe that has both reality and rationality. As Christians like Francis Bacon and Isaac Newton saw, this calls for the practice of art and science as necessary roles for man as a guest in God's universe.

It also means that Christianity strongly affirms personality. God, being personal in himself, has created man in his own image with the high aspirations of personality. If on the level of finiteness man is related to all other finite creatures, on the level of personality he is related upwards to God, before whom alone are his aspirations totally fulfilled and his being explained. For the Christian, freedom for the individual is never freedom from individuality, but rather freedom to be finally fully himself. Man's alienation is moral, not metaphysical; therefore with the redemption made possible in Christ, man is liberated to enter into the growing freedom of the new birth.

Morality too is meaningful in the Christian framework. The Christian God is not beyond good and evil, nor does he contain both. The immutability of his holy character is itself the Absolute and the final court of morality. When God says he is good, this is resolutely and implacably opposed to his being non-good; the call for distinct moral categories and dynamic social commitment is an imperative for all who know him in this flaming reality.

These for the moment are still sketchy hints. I will discuss these issues in more detail in later chapters and deal with the question of their verification in chapter nine. For the present I am simply interested in showing that at just those points where the East is weak today, a Christianity rightly understood carries answers of titanic significance. These answers do not float in an intellectual vacuum but are based on a unique historical disclosure. Hinduism believes in only shadowy avatars as revealers of God, but Krishna is worshipped warmly; Gautama Buddha said that there was no God, but he has been deified by many of this followers; Mohammed held that it was blasphemy to call any man God, but Islam has made him into a quasi-deity. Thus, these men have achieved deity against the explicit statements of their teachings and their claims simply on the grounds of their followers' needs (the Freudian basis again). But Jesus is the only one who lived and died and claimed to be the Son of God—all in the open arena of history.

Tolerance: East and West

One final point of importance is the apparent contrast between the "tolerance" of Hinduism and Buddhism and the "intolerance" of Christianity. The real nature of the contrast does not lie where it is often supposed, but in the relativistic climate following the death of absolutes; there is a marked reluctance to think beyond the surface appearances. It is not surprising that in such a mood the tolerance of the East has strong appeal and the ecumenicity of Baha'i is popular.

Alan Watts, for example, illustrates the relationship of Judaism, Christianity and Hinduism by comparing them to Chinese boxes, the smaller being contained by the larger, and the larger by the even larger. So Christianity contains Judaism but is itself contained by Hinduism. In this vein, several gurus have written on "The Blessed Lord Jesus Christ," claiming that Christ's teaching fits in admirably with Hinduism. For example, Jesus' sayings, "The Kingdom of God is within you" or "In my Father's house are many mansions," are cited as other versions of the Tat Tvam Asi of Hinduism. Such scholarship lacks integrity; it selects what is suitable by arrogantly ignoring the contexts of the statements. Christianity is pressed through the grid of the premises of Hinduism, and such claims as "I am the way, I am the truth, and I am life. No man comes to the Father except by me" are ignored. Christianity is not taken seriously on its own premises.

If Jesus had spoken as he did to Indians and not Jews, everyone would have smiled, tossed him some flowers or a garland and passed on down the street. His claims to deity would not have been unique. In fact, one more avatar might have been welcomed. But Jesus spoke deliberately and plainly to the Jews, the one nation on earth which was historically and theologically predisposed to reject categorically any idea of God becoming incarnate in human flesh. There was no misunderstanding. In fact the Jews understood so well that their reply was the logic of crucifixion. Jesus was no misunderstood Mahatma nor an avatar unaware.

It is quite plain that, if treated fairly on its own premises, Christianity excludes the full truth and final validity of other religions. If Christianity is true, Hinduism cannot be true in the sense it claims. Even though on the surface it appears that Hinduism is more tolerant, both finally demand an ultimate choice. Many Indians admit this. Some speak of the subtlety of Hindu toleration as "the kiss of death." Radakrishnan has described it as "being strangled by the fraternal embrace." The initial tolerance disguises an encroaching framework of truth which finally overpowers all other presuppositions. The best way for Hinduism to contain the rampant reform movement of Buddhism in India was to declare that the Buddha was only a further avatar of Krishna. Buddhism's uniqueness was thus "strangled by the fraternal embrace." Probably the same approach will be made openly to Christian theology in the next few years. Liberalism is already showing signs of response before the overtures are made.

The difference between the ultimate intolerance of the East and the intolerance of Christianity can be illustrated as follows: Christianity stands across a man's path like a soldier with a drawn sword saying, "choose or refuse," "life or death," "yes or no"; the choice and the consequences are extremely obvious. The subtlety of Eastern religion is that it enters like an odorless poison gas, seeping under the door, through the keyhole, in through the open window, so that the man in the room is overcome without his ever realizing there was any danger at all. In Rishikesh I shared a room at the ashram with a friend of Federico Fellini. This man reminded me ad nauseam that he was still very much an atheist and an Italian and not a Hindu. But after only a week with him, I could see that all his views of man, morality and life were thoroughly Hindu in timbre, though not in name.

The Hindu circle of tolerance does not include the contradictory premise of other views. Alan Watts, who had previously attempted a synthesis, eventually admitted, "Any attempt to marry the Vedanta to Christianity must take full account of the fact that Christianity is a contentious faith which requires an all-or-nothing commitment. . . . My previous discussions did not take proper account of that whole aspect of Christianity which is uncompromising, ornery, militant, rigorous, imperious, and invincibly self-righteous."[50] Of course, a Christian must remember that such "intolerance" must be an intolerance of principle; it must never become an intolerance against the people who hold the alternate views.

We should be able now to understand why a generation disillusioned with the West has searched for alternatives in the East. We should note, however, that their euphoric enthusiasm has been generated more by the contrast offered by the East than by any real resolution of the dilemmas. Many of those most heavily "into the East" are now returning disappointed and disillusioned. Others have remained there, claiming to have found spiritual fulfillment, but only rarely are such people still involved in the social, racial and political struggles left behind. If the present fashion becomes a cultural way of life, the Brave New World will be that much nearer to realizing the full development of its soma. And if the East can shed its lumbering cultural baggage of backwardness and be translated into a consciousness easier and more appealing to the Western mind, then the process can be dramatically accelerated.

This is the promise of the psychedelics.

7/The Counterfeit Infinity

"Euphoric, narcotic, pleasantly hallucinant—All the advantages of Christianity and alcohol; none of their defects."
Aldous Huxley

"Don't give me your occupation-game labels! We are Beautiful People, ascendent from your robot junkyard! . . . For a year we've been in the Garden of Eden. Acid opened the door to it. It was the Garden of Eden and Innocence and a ball."
Ken Kesey

"My crime is the ancient and familiar one of corrupting the minds of the youth. This charge is a valid one."
Timothy Leary

"Alas! Man's vices, horrible as they are supposed to be, contain the positive proof of his taste for the infinite."
Baudelaire

"The man wanted the dream, now the dream will govern the man."
Baudelaire[1]

A third defining feature of the counter culture is its resort to drugs, particularly the psychedelics, to achieve a transcendental consciousness and a true infinity. For those within the movement, drugs have attained an almost sacramental importance, virtually the bread and wine of the new community, while for many outside the movement they are a spectral horror, a phobia almost on a par with communism. Some describe them as "cortical vitamins"[2] or "the honey of the spirit,"[3] lauding "the fifth freedom, the right to get high"[4] and praising the "molecular revolution." Others damn them as "instant insanity," describing their advocates as "laxative salesmen" with "delusions of grandeur," a new breed of "holy rollers" living in "a spiritual Disneyland."[5] This polarization of opinion with its irrational emotionalism on either side hardly allows any objective consideration of their real significance. But the psychedelic movement deserves serious attention, both as a feature of the counter culture and as the combination of two important trends—the perennial "taste for infinity" (as Baudelaire described it)[6] and the urgent modern search for a new consciousness as a short-cut solution to the problems of man.

Paradise Now

Speaking of the perennial taste for infinity, Pascal observed, "Most of man's troubles come from his not being able to sit quietly in his chamber." More recently, Aldous Huxley noted that the urge to transcend self-consciousness and selfhood is one of the principal appetites of the soul.[7] For centuries there has been the search for the attainment of that ideal which the Greeks called ataraxia, the ideal of quiet calm, of deep inner contentment, beyond the restlessness, frustrations and tensions of normal living. Many searched for this via philosophy and religion, but always there has been the parallel search for short cuts, for "paradise in a single swoop," as Baudelaire put it.[8] It is little wonder that these short cuts, once discovered, were given the halo of neo-divinity. Thus, peyote was divine to the Aztecs, coca to the Incas, soma to the Vedas, and ambrosia to the Greeks. Probably they were discovered accidentally; certainly the details are lost in pre-history, but their use became intertwined in the blurry realms of religion, magic and illumination.

Through chemistry modern man is heir to this age-old search and has added to its urgency his own quest for a new consciousness as a solution to the problems of man in the post-Christian era. Here, the psychedelics supply a limited chemical means towards a greater psychic end, which, it is hoped, will lead to a reformulation of man, by which technology will be counterbalanced and a utopian society made possible. Nothing short of this is promised by certain prophets of the psychedelic movement.

Charles Reich, writing of Consciousness III, with mind-expanding drugs integral to his vision, claims, "Only Consciousness III can make possible the continued survival of man as a species in this age of technology."[9] Timothy Leary is no less extravagant in his appraisal: "Human beings born after the year 1943 belong to a different species from their progenitors. . . . Our favorite concepts are standing in the way of a flood tide two billion years building up. The verbal dam is collapsing. Head for the hills, or prepare your intellectual craft to flow with the current."[10]

What we are being promised is a "Paradise now" through cosmic consciousness, a new answer to the problem of man's inability to live with his normal consciousness. East of Eden, man's desire returns longingly to the "recherche du temps perdu." He dreams of life as play (à la Huizinga), love as "pregenital polymorphous perversity" (à la Freud), history as timelessness (à la Marcuse) and nature mysticism as prenatal bliss (à la

Jung). Parallel to these themes and others such as naturism and unisexuality is the perennial taste for infinity.

We will attempt to analyze the story and the claims surrounding the psychedelics, trying to delve beneath the unrestrained euphoria on the one hand and the reactionary ignorance on the other. I have no interest here in their medical or pharmacological implications, but will examine them for their philosophic and religious significance and for their place within the counter culture.

Two preliminary qualifications must be made. First, we are concerned with the psychedelics and not the depressants or stimulants. Many of our generation have taken speed, heroin and opium; others have resorted to nutmeg or airplane glue. These drugs range from the trivial to the terminal; the former are hardly worthy of attention, and the horrors of the latter are well documented. The psychedelic movement, on the contrary, shows the resort to drugs at its highest and is close to the nerve of the counter culture. We are not using their former names, *hallucinogenics* or *psychotomimetics,* but rather *psychedelics,* a word coined in 1957 by Humphrey Osmond to describe their mind-expanding qualities. The common feature of all these drugs is well known: Their effect appears to trigger a release which slips the leash of the normal, rational, waking mind. That which reasons logically, separates the self from the external world and quantifies reality into colors, shapes, smells and sounds is disinhibited. A "transcending" consciousness is achieved whereby identity is often submerged into a feeling of oceanic unity, linear thinking gives way to a flooding awareness and patterns, colors and sounds often take on an existence for themselves, highly intensified. Sometimes this produces synesthesia or the crossover of sensations.

The explosive possibilities of this transcendence were

glimpsed early by William Blake: "If the doors of perception were cleansed everything would appear to man as it is, infinite."[11] But it was much nearer our own time that a more accurate understanding of its scientific possibility was first shown. William James, after experimenting with nitrous oxide, wrote in 1902 a passage which has since become classic: "One conclusion was forced upon my mind at that time, and my impression of its truth has ever since remained unshaken. It is that our normal waking consciousness, rational consciousness as we call it, is but one special type of consciousness, whilst all about it, parted from it by the filmiest of screens, there lie potential forms of consciousness entirely different. We may go through life without suspecting their existence; but apply the requisite stimulus, and at a touch they are there in all their completeness. . . . No account of the universe in its totality can be final which leaves these other forms of consciousness quite disregarded. . . . Looking back on my own experiences, they all converge towards a kind of insight to which I cannot help ascribing some metaphysical significance."[12]

With the doors of perception not just glimpsed but blasted open with chemicals, more recent writers are hotly impatient with normal perceptions. Colin McGlashan writes about dreams as "a file smuggled into the space-time cell where man lies captive; a cell whose walls and ceilings are our five senses, and whose warders are the inflexible concepts of logic."[13] But in all these understandings the psychedelic drugs are related to the mind as the microscope is to the eye; both expand the powers of apprehension, vision and awareness.

A second preliminary qualification is that any general principles or experiences must be interpreted in the light of the set and the setting of the user, his character and the circumstances under which he takes the drug. One must expect widely differing reactions to the same drug.

A paid research volunteer experiences one thing, a curious artist quite another, a status seeker still another, while the man using drugs to search for God may have quite a different experience again.

Kenneth Kenniston cites three basic categories of drug takers—the "tasters," who use them only occasionally, usually experimenting; the "seekers," who use them regularly, but not with any life style built around them, apart from a general search for relevance; and the "heads," that small but highly vocal minority who have a totally "turned-on" ideology and for whom drugs are the passport to their subculture.

The History of Marijuana

History is valuable as a background to any objective discussion.[14] But with the psychedelics, and marijuana in particular, it is difficult to know what to leave out and what to include. For the benefit of those whose knowledge is limited, I will try to be inclusive. Those familiar with the topic may wish to pick up the argument at page 249.

Generally speaking there are three distinct periods in the discovery of psychedelics. The first stage is the pre-Western history, the second the period of serious but limited research in the West and the third the era of popularization.

First, let us examine marijuana. The marijuana plant is *cannabis sativa,* so named by Linnaeus in 1753, but as Indian hemp it is one of the oldest domestic plants known to man. A tall, weedy, annual herb, first cousin to the fig tree or the hop, it has the male and female flowers on separate plants. The stems of the male plant go into making the rope hemp, while the stems of the female plant give off a resinous exudation, golden yellow in color and minty in smell. In India this is made into one of three things. The first is bhang, a decoction of smoking mixture, derived from the cut tops of uncultivated female plants with a resin content decidedly low. This is scorned by all but the poorest Indians, yet interestingly it is most popular in the West. The second is ganja, a specially cultivated and harvested grade of hemp; the tops are cut and used for smoking mixtures, beverages, sweetmeats, but the resin is not extracted. This was once a licensed agricultural industry in India. The third is charas, a pure unadulterated resin from the best cultivated plants, extracted from flowers; it is known in the West as hashish.

The known history of marijuana begins in China, where there is evidence that in the year 2737 B.C. the Emperor Shen Nung, writing a book on pharmacy, knew more details about hemp than most of us today. Already it was troubling the Chinese moralists, criticized by some as a "liberator of sin" but commended by others as "the delight giver." Shen Nung prescribed it as medicine for "female weakness, gout, rheumatism, malaria, beriberi, constipation and absent-mindedness."

From China it came further west to India, and there it came into its own. Probably known prior to 800 B.C., it is certain that since then it has become intertwined in the religion and philosophy of India as recorded both in the Vedas and the Bazaar: "Bhang is the joy giver, the sky flier, the heavenly guide, the poor man's heaven, the soother of grief. . . . No god or man is as good as the religious drinker of bhang."

Gordon Wasson of Harvard, a mycologist and a scholar, argues that the Rig Veda devoted at least one-tenth of over a thousand psalms to celebrating the plant god, Soma.[15] Some even argue that Yoga arose in India only as a means of altering consciousness after the legendary soma was no longer available. It is commonly believed that Lord Shiva himself smoked marijuana and on his birthday marijuana paste with almond milk is drunk as an offering. Some gurus consider ganja a beginning to Saddhana, the Yogic part of discipline, using it to still the distractions of the world. Undoubtedly its relationship to alcohol in India is exactly the opposite of that in the United States. For the Indian it is alcohol that is related to passion and aggression; marijuana leads to calm and detachment.

From India marijuana came further west, into the Middle East, where the early stories are strangely bizarre. Herodotus described Scythians who, before a battle, threw hemp seeds on hot stones and inhaled the vapors. There is evidence of a strange Tibetan custom in which hempbrew was emulsified in warm human fat and served as a drink in a chalice of human skulls. But the most colorful story centers around the legendary Hassan-i-Sabah, the so-called "Old Man of the Mountain." He lived around A.D. 1090 (just prior to the first Crusade) in a strong mountain fortress near Baghdad, straddling the caravan route to Mecca. A fanatical Muslim, he saw it his sacred duty to purge the world of false prophets and did this by implementing a new secret weapon—political assassination. His disciples and devotees were a dreaded group called the assassins. Their reign of terror was long and notorious, until 12,000 of his followers were wiped out at one time by Genghis Khan in the thirteenth century. His full name, Hashishin, was linked with hashish and assassin, but his secret was curious. He held his followers in a grip of fanatical devotion because he controlled the hashish. Those who died in battle went straight to heaven. Those who survived got more hash!

From the Middle East marijuana spread slowly to other countries, especially in the Muslim world where, unlike alcohol, it was never prohibited. Kif, as it is called, was introduced to Morocco by the Arab conquerors in the seventh century and flourished despite opposition until declared illegal under American pressure in 1954. It is also widespread in Africa and parts of Latin America. Jamaica knows it as the "wisdom weed" and a modern protest movement uses Ganja as its political symbol.

The second historical stage involves serious Western interest and limited research. Much of this centered on the Club de les Hachichins in Paris in the 1840s. On the left bank of the Seine, in the old neo-gothic Hotel Pimodan, a group of French intellectuals clubbed together and among their other activities they took marijuana. Among them was Charles Baudelaire, the celebrated French art historian who joined the club in 1844 and lodged in an attic in the hotel. In 1860, he described his experiences in *Artificial Paradise* and deplored hemp's undermining of the structures of morality. In words foreshadowing the modern-day "trip," he described his experiences: "You now have enough ballast for a long and singular voyage. The steam-whistle has blown, the sails are set, and you have a curious advantage over ordinary travelers—that of not knowing whither you are going. You have made your choice: hurrah for destiny!"[16] Some think it was hash that drove him to an asylum, but more probably he suffered from a disease.

Theophile Gautier was another member of the club who experienced fantastic hallucinations on his initiatory trip, probably heightened by the melodramatic setting. His description of the death of time under the experience is very close to the descriptions of many modern acid trips. He experienced a great panic when he saw, "Time is dead!" But as the drug wore off, he cried, "Hallelujah! Time has risen from the dead!"

In the United States in 1860, Fitzhugh Ludlow, a friend of Mark Twain, bought some marijuana in an apothecary shop in Poughkeepsie, New York, for a few cents. He used it for years but later wrote of it as a "lullaby of hell," a reversal of his early enthusiasm, under which he had written, "For the humble sum of six cents I might purchase an excursion ticket all over the world."[17]

The third stage is the recent one of popularization. United Nations statistics in 1951 estimated that there were over 200,000,000 marijuana users in the world. But it was in the mid-thirties that the first wave came to the United States and Europe, followed by a second wave in the sixties. The first reaction was instant popularity and the second was an immediate polarization which has plagued the situation ever since. The Establishment panic against the drug was met by a counterbalancing paranoia in those taking it. Typical of the panic was the extreme campaign by Harry J. Anslinger, chief of the Federal Bureau of Narcotics, who claimed that the use of marijuana was related to crime, violence, rape and insanity: "Its continuous use leads direct to the insane asylum."[18] This irrational panic is still reflected in many circles.

The paranoia, too, is equally evident if understandable and is a common trait of many in the counter culture. Even Allen Ginsberg admitted, "It is no wonder then that most people who have smoked marijuana in America often experience a state of anxiety, of threat, of paranoia in fact, which may lead to trembling or hysteria. . . . I myself experience this form of paranoia when I smoke marijuana."[19]

The alleged dangers of marijuana are said to include insanity, sexual perversion, violence and a dependence link with heroin. Two famous reports, however, need to be read to put the present situation in perspective. The first is the report of the Indian Hemp Drug Commission in Simla, British India, in 1894. Running to 3,000 pages and seven volumes, this is a classic on the subject; the report took two years to research and some 800 doctors were involved in analyzing the evidence gleaned from informants ranging from coolies to yogis. The report emphatically concludes that there was no evidence of mental, moral or physical harm; that moderation never led on to dependence; and that when there was excess, it was only with the idle or dissipated. As a result, Ganja palaces were taxed and growers were licensed.

The second report is Mayor La Guardia's in New York in 1938. It is all the more significant for coming at a time when much of the country was seized by a theatrical panic. La Guardia asked the New York Academy of Sciences to provide impartial scientists to study the problem. Their findings, published in 1944, flatly contradicted the panic then current. Although assailed by the Federal Bureau of Narcotics, the researchers came to the same conclusions as the British: "There was found no direct relationship between the commission of crimes of violence and marihuana."[20] In his foreword, Mayor La Guardia said, "I am glad that the sociological, psychological, and medical ills commonly attributed to marihuana have been found to be exaggerated *insofar as* the City of New York is concerned." The British Wootton Report in 1969 confirmed the same general conclusions.

But even if this restores some balance to the discussion, there is increasing evidence of one criticism of marijuana. The effect of its frequent heavy use is to undermine motivation. In 1858, Baudelaire had warned, "Later on, perhaps, a too frequent consultation of the oracle will diminish your strength of will; perhaps you will be less of a man than you are today."[21] This is true, not of occasional users but of regular users. This may be partly a rub-off from the atmosphere and attitudes of the groups and situations in which it is taken, but, because of the explicit nature of the drug, it has internal causes too. I have frequently noticed this decline of motivation among habitual users who are political activists or artists.

If I have taken too much time on the history of marijuana it has only been to set the whole subject in a balanced perspective and to prepare the ground for a rational discussion of the present postion.

Mescaline

It would be interesting to spend time on a second psychedelic drug, psilocybin, developed from the sacred mushroom. Early seals from Byblos, around 3000 B.C., show a priest giving two mushrooms to a supplicant, and many now believe that the Eleusinian mysteries were mushroom-induced mysticism. Soma was perhaps a mushroom and some wonder why Hieronymus Bosch has a gigantic mushroom at the door of hell in his triptych, "The Hay-wain."[22] That John Allegro considers that Jesus was only a mushroom is well known! But we will spend more time on mescaline, because its introduction to the counter culture has had greater significance.

Mescaline comes from peyote, an insignificant-looking pin cushion cactus with a fleshy top. It was a plant sacred to the Aztecs and Mexicans, both of whom proclaimed it the flesh of the gods, believing that maize was for the body, peyote for the soul. Around its use there has developed a series of elaborate rituals; preparations before the harvesting, for example, involve prayer, fasting, sexual abstinence and penance. This ritual reached its highest development in the Native American Church, whose peyote night was similar to the "agape" or love feast of the early church. Mescaline entered the realm of serious research in the West when it was discovered at the end of the nineteenth century, and the news crossed to Havelock Ellis in London. Taking a mescaline button, he experienced a good trip and said it "may be described as chiefly a saturnalia for the specific senses, and, above all, an orgy of vision. It reveals an optical fairyland. . . ."[23] An artist friend who also took some, however, had a "bummer" and was violently sick. William James experimented with it too, but experienced only a severe stomach ache. He wrote to his brother, "I ate one bud three days ago, was violently sick for twenty-four hours, and had no other symptoms whatever. . . . I will take the visions on trust."[24]

The watershed for mescaline was May 1953, when Humphrey Osmond introduced it to Aldous Huxley in Hollywood. Osmond passed a very troubled night before he did so, of which later he wrote, "He was uneasy: he would be disappointed if nothing happened, but what if the mescaline worked too well? . . . He did not relish the possibility, however remote, of finding a small, but discreditable niche in literary history as the man who drove Aldous Huxley mad."[25] But far from driving Huxley insane, the trip made him ecstatic. "I was seeing what Adam had seen on the morning of his creation—the miracle, moment by moment, of naked existence."[26] He recorded his experiences glowingly in *Doors of Perception* and *Heaven and Hell* in 1954, and advocated its use in the article at the end of *The Humanist Frame* in 1961, as a means to higher human potentialities. Reading these early hopes and claims for first-order experience, we find them remarkable for their timidity by contemporary standards. Later, however, Huxley felt strongly that biochemical mysticism could be the key to his "philosophia perennis." Struck by the similarity of thought and expression which he found in all the mystics, whether Hindu, Buddhist, Taoist or Muslim, he came to the conclusion that behind all the world religions there could be discerned an ultimate truth of which each religion was only a partial expression.

LSD

The fourth psychedelic drug, LSD, is a synthetic chemical, so not unnaturally it has no prehistory, although for centuries there was a purple parasitic fungus called ergot which caused chaos whenever found in cultivated fields of rye. The aberrations and visual disturbances were called St. Anthony's fire. One active substance of this fungus was lysergic acid, although this in itself is not hallucinogenic. The accidental discovery of LSD came in April 1943, when Dr. Albert Hofmann was working in the Sandoz laboratories overlooking the river Rhine in Switzerland. Researching a painkiller for migraine, he added a diethylamide to the lysergic acid to make lysergic acid diethylamide. After he took 250 micrograms of this new substance, his lab notebook tails off humorously and incoherently, and there is a comic description of his cycling home through Basel, heavily under the influence of the first known acid trip. The period of scientific research which followed this was cut short by the premature popularity of LSD. The "miracle drug" of the early days was soon to become the "nightmare drug." But in between was the brightest and most glorious hour for the psychedelics, when no ideal seemed unachievable and no frontier beyond discovery.

Among the incidents which stand out now was the so-called "Miracle of Marsh Chapel" which occurred on Good Friday, 1963. Dr. Walter Pahnke, who held both an M.D. and B.D. and was in the process of a doctoral study at Harvard, was convinced that the basic experience underlying all mysticism was identical and could be duplicated by psychedelic drugs. To prove this, he gave psilocybin to twenty of his fellow graduates, all theological students. All who took it reported that they had felt the most profound "religious" experience of their lives.

A famous group which caught the public eye was the Church of the Awakening, incorporated in October 1963. The group had originated in Sorocco, New Mexico, gathering around a disgruntled Presbyterian, John Aiken. In 1959, they had contacted the psychedelics through Dr. Osmond, and many atheists had been "converted" in their sessions. There was no doctrine, but there was a sacrament—a drug-induced psychedelic experience—dispensed to all members no more than once every three months. The Neo-American Church was similar, but took an even more militant stand on the legality of using peyote as a sacrament.

Such incidents and groups helped to put the psychedelics on the map, but the charismatic influence of two men, Timothy Leary and Ken Kesey, was far more significant. Leary was the movement's high priest, its messiah and martyr, virtually summing up in himself all the aspirations and ideals of the psychedelic movement. Described by Humphrey Osmond as "Irish and revolutionary and to a good degree reckless"[27] and by his wife as "the sanest, funniest, wisest man I've ever met,"[28] Leary was virtually "converted" under the influence of psychedelics. Previously he had rejected his Roman Catholic background and dropped out of West Point, offending both his Roman Catholic mother and his military father. After receiving his Ph.D. from the University of California (Berkeley), he lectured at Harvard on chemical psychology, later describing himself as "a forty-year-old smart-aleck atheist Harvard Professor."[29] The turning point came in 1960 in Cuernavaca, Mexico, where the thirty-nine-year-old Leary ate one of the mushrooms and was swept over the edge of a "Niagara of sensory input."[30] He returned to Harvard and from then on was in the forefront of developing and popularizing the psychedelics. In early work in Concord State Reformatory, he was allowed to give psilocybin to thirty-five inmates. Most of these, he claimed, experienced profound religious experiences and character changes.

His work gained immediate popularity and instant notoriety when his became the first Harvard firing in history, "regretfully" dismissed because of avid undergraduate interest. The facts, as reported at the time, can be read in the *Harvard Crimson* of November 26, 1962, but the interpretations are even now in the process of a super-rationalization.

Undeterred by his expulsion, Leary went on to found the International Federation for Internal Freedom (IFIF) in 1963; it was comprised of an informal group of theologians, ministers and research psychologists. Under Leary IFIF conducted independent research into the psychedelics. Their work included research projects, the editing of the *Psychedelic Review* and the running of communities in Mexico, Massachusetts and Millbrook. All the time they aimed for a grand "turn on," tirelessly proselytizing through records, movies, prayer books, public discussions and sermons. The same year Leary founded the Castalia Foundation which derived its name from the sacred order described by Hermann Hesse in *Magister Ludi.* Millbrook was prototypical in all this.

Leary's tangle with the Harvard authorities was nothing in comparison with his confrontation with the government. On April 16, 1966, a squad of Dutchess County police descended on Millbrook, searched it, found a minute quantity of grass and arrested the four there. Leary at this time was already appealing a conviction from December 1965, when he was found en route to Mexico with half an ounce of marijuana. This had led to a fine of $30,000 and a thirty-year prison sentence from a Texas judge. The stiffness of the sentence only added to Leary's lustre as he made his defense, arguing that chemical agents were food (cerebral vitamins) and that the new transcendence was manifestly superior and preferable for people of all classes.

This was the period when he began to promote psychedelics as the new evolutionary religion. Turning on was not just a childish rebellion for kicks but a sacred rite: "The LSD kick is a spiritual ecstasy. The LSD trip is a religious pilgrimage"[31] —the way "to groove to the music of God's great song."[32] He encouraged people, "Start your own religion," "Write your own Bible," "Write your own ten commandments."[33] For Leary there were two absolutes. First, Thou shalt not alter the consciousness of thy fellow man; second, Thou shalt not prevent thy fellow man from altering his own consciousness.

As a religion it was a kind of bizarre psychic-Darwinism, where the tripper is the new man and LSD is the "sacrament which will put you in touch with the ancient two-million-year-old wisdom inside you," freeing you "to go on to the next stage which is the evolutionary timelessness, the ancient reincarnation theory that we always carry inside."[34] At many of his public meetings, Leary appeared as the prophet replete with white cotton pajamas, incense and four-dollar admission prices.

The second important man was Ken Kesey, and who knows whether he or Leary turned on more people? But the difference between them was vast. After visiting Leary at Millbrook, Kesey described it as the "Crypt Trip," and his reception a "freaking frostiness. . . . It was unbelievable—this was Millbrook, one big piece of uptight constipation."[35]

If Leary was the professor, Kesey was the novelist, working not from Harvard but from Stanford's Perry Lane. But his great days came later as the "Chief" of the Merry Pranksters. With him there were Faye (his beatific pioneer wife), Neal Cassaday (hero of Kerouac's *On the Road*), Babbs, Hagan, Mountain Girl, all together following out their "fantasy," watching their own "movie" with their psychedelic music, day-glo paint and acid. Buying an old 1939 bus, they marked its destination FUURTHER and set out on a crazy trip across the United States. The great heyday was January 1966 with the Trips Festival, the Acid Test and the Electric Kool-Aid Acid Test. Following that, Kesey became the Californian day-glo pimpernel, and LSD was served to an intoxicating background of acid rock, strobe lights and freaked-out dancing. The heroes were the Grateful Dead and the "Owsley Blues" (a 500-microgram capsule of acid sold with a picture of Batman).

Others influential in the psychedelic movement include Hermann Hesse, whose *Steppenwolf* was the bible for the first celebration of Leary's group; Leary describes him as the "poet of the interior journey."[36] Leary also applauds the English as "the original hippies,"[37] showing a pedigree of psychedelics coming down through Humphrey Osmond, Aldous Huxley, Alan Watts, R. D. Laing and Paul McCartney. Somewhat fancifully he says, "The spiritual cord that holds our civilisation from suicide can be traced from the Himalayan forests where Vedic philosophers drank soma, down the Ganja, through the Suez by P. and O. and over to Liverpool."[38]

In the early days, acid taking was by no means limited to the counter culture. Among well-known celebrities who it is claimed also tripped were Cary Grant ("I will have enjoyed more living in the latter part of my life than most people ever know"), Herman Kahn and Henry Luce.[39]

Objections to Psychedelics

What, then, are the normal objections to these drugs? Are these objections valid? Generally there are two: that they are dangerous and that they are an escape.

The question of their danger throws light on the present position of psychedelics in the movement; this is best illustrated by a discussion of LSD. In 1961, on the basis of an investigation into 20,000 trips taken by over 5,000 people using either LSD or mescaline, Sidney Cohen concluded that they gave rise to no serious physical complications, although there were slight side effects including physical discomfort, nausea, vomiting, aches and pains, panic, paranoia and occasional later undesirable effects.[40] If the user was unstable, there might be serious depression or psychosis. There were no instances of physical addiction. But four years later, in 1965, he was forced to conclude that the incidence of "bummers" and bad trips had risen sharply. There was an alarming number of panic states with acute paranoia, notions of omnipotence, schizophrenic responses and marked character alteration. As well as possible nerve cell damage, there was the fear of chromosomal alteration. Much of this Cohen attributed to the rise of the black market, the sale of impure drugs and their improper use.

This may have had some effect on the eventual swing away from psychedelics, but the main reason for their decline is their inadequacy. Alan Watts even goes so far as to defend them despite the dangers: "Every worthwhile exploration is dangerous. . . . It was hardly hygienic for Jesus to get himself crucified, but these are risks taken in the course of spiritual adventures."[41] So the swing from LSD is not so much a swing away as a swing beyond. The psychedelics are unable to take one to the high areas of transcendental consciousness which can be reached by more subtle meditative techniques. Robert de Ropp, in *The Master Game: Beyond the Drug Experience,* claims that drugs lead only to mental and physical exhaustion, a form of "spiritual burglary."[42] His warning is echoed by many Eastern gurus and Western psychologists: "*He who misuses psychedelics sacrifices his capacity to develop by persistently squandering those inner resources upon which growth depends.* He commits himself to a descending spiral and the further he travels down this path, the more difficult it becomes for him to reascend."[43]

If only a comparative few fall foul of the dangers of these drugs (though this in itself covers many tragedies), the proportion who succumb to the escape they offer is dramatically high. Baudelaire called marijuana an escape from "the hopeless darkness of ordinary daily existence."[44] Even Leary admits, "The age-old appeal of the psychedelic experience is its solution to the problem of escape. The visionary revelation answers the escape question. There is no death. Ecstatic, mirthful relief. . . . It is of interest that the heroin addict and the illuminated Buddha end up at the same place. The void."[45]

Furthermore, it is a constant complaint of activists and radicals that those regularly using the psychedelics aim for the goals of Consciousness III but end where dropout becomes cop-out. Thus the resort to psychedelics is parallel to the "happiness" supplied in *Brave New World* by soma and illustrates Marcuse's repressive desublimation. Many who turn on regularly or indulge in a periodic freak-out are just flirting with answers and escaping the real issues. Whether as an intentional motive or the end result, escapism figures heavily in our generation's use of psychedelics.

Two years ago, passing a café in Kathmandu, I was amazed to hear Dylan music coming out the door. When I looked in, I saw about twenty-five young Americans and Europeans, sitting at long, trestle tables, with heads on their arms. As I opened the door, all of them looked up with dull, unseeing, heavy eyes and slowly looked down again. Constantly stoned, many were twenty-four-hour zombies who had come to Nepal only to die.

Charting the Psychedelic Experience

The next important issue is the nature of the psychedelic experience. As the psychedelics disinhibit the normal, rational, waking mind, they appear to act like a series of optical lenses, raising the level of conscious awareness.

According to Timothy Leary there are six levels of consciousness.[46] His analysis is disputed, but it is typical of the type of claims made by many avid users of the psychedelics.

The first level is minimal or anaesthetic, the consciousness of sleep, coma or stupor; here only sharp external stimuli are noticed. This is often induced by alcohol, barbiturates or narcotics. The second level is symbolic consciousness, the normal consciousness of our waking minds; here external objects are seen as external objects. The third level is external sensory awareness; here consciousness seems to focus on the sensory nerve endings that receive information for us from outside—the retina, the ear drum or the taste buds. The fourth level is the internal sensory awareness; here our consciousness seems to focus on the nerve endings which receive impulses from the visceral organs—the sexual, digestive, eliminative, cardiac, respiratory and cortical—the *cakras* of Eastern thought. The fifth level is the cellular; here, Leary claims, consciousness focuses on life in the cells themselves. The sixth level is the atomic pre-cellular consciousness; here one is conscious of the ultimate state of being, pure energy, very close to what the mystics describe as the "void" or the "white light" or the "flame." Only in this last category does Leary appear at all hesitant. "Can such experiences be mapped and made available for subsequent observations? I do not know. I present this sixth level of consciousness hesitantly, knowing that I risk losing even the least skeptical of my readers."[47]

Also he admits that there is a vast variation in the effectiveness with which various drugs "expand the optical lenses" and take one to greater depths of awareness. Marijuana will reach the internal sensory awareness level only if one is mentally disciplined and other external stimuli are excluded. At the fifth level, moderate doses of LSD and mescaline are successful only if the external stimuli are shut out; marijuana or mild doses of LSD are insufficient here. At the sixth level, he says, only large doses of LSD are finally effective.

But then the vital questions come. What is this world of transcendental consciousness? And how is the drug-induced consciousness related to other forms of consciousness? These questions are still a puzzle—inevitably so because of the imprecise nature of mysticism—and any attempt to answer them is bound to be tentative. One way to describe the normal, rational, waking consciousness is to see it as a highly limited scanning beam of concentrated awareness focused on a small area of reality and deliberately excluding unnecessary peripheral awareness (unnecessary, that is, for normal living, a somewhat relative norm with cultural variations). Beyond this small area is the ec-static world of un-usual perceptions, those which are paranormal and transcendental. The boundaries of this ec-static world, however hazy their delineation, include those areas described as "the subliminal or transmarginal region" (William James), "the cosmic consciousness" (R. M. Bucke), "the collective unconscious" (Carl Jung) and the "Mind at Large" (Aldous Huxley).

Normal, rational consciousness thus functions like a scanning beam mounted on a carriage which is itself able to move only slightly on a railway track whose terminals are sanity and insanity. But the track is not straight. It is bent into the shape of a horseshoe; there is still a narrow gap where the two terminals almost meet. Since this meeting point is beyond the range of the scanning beam of normal consciousness, it would be wise to distinguish it from the sanity of normal consciousness. Following Sidney Cohen, we could describe the normal consciousness as *sanity* and the two terminals (in the world beyond usual perceptions) as *insanity* and *unsanity* respectively. By this definition both insanity and unsanity are paranormal, but insanity is considered unhealthy while unsanity is considered healthy.

On the side of unsanity various mystical experiences might be charted in the geography of the transcendental.[48] These include peak experiences (rare, sudden moments of insight, rapture and bliss), integration experiences (mystical experiences where there is neither enlargement of personality beyond its natural bounds nor merging with nature, but only self-awareness or self-realization which transcends the space-time awareness of individuality), pan-naturalist experiences (an awareness of nature in all things and of all things as being one, but without necessary reference to any idea of God), pantheistic experiences (identical with the pan-naturalist experiences but this time related to the idea of a God who is one with nature), isolationist experiences (such as the goal of Yoga and Zen, in which the self is isolated from all that which moves and has being in space and time, but in which, when the soul is isolated from all higher than itself, it reaches a ceiling beyond which there is nothing), and theistic mystical experiences (such as those of the Sufis and Bhaktis with direct reference to personal deities). Many of these positive experiences have some form of negative counterpart in the area approaching the opposite terminal of insanity.

An adequate account of the phenomena must do justice to two obvious and counterbalancing facts. First, prior conceptions condition perception, so the variety of actual experiences objectively considered many not in fact be so great. That is, two men may look at one situation but see it in two ways because of their differing backgrounds. Second, the data is of such variety that it cannot all be explained as issuing from an identical experience (such as the view that all experiences are only variations on the *philosophia perennis*). It is true that the common factor in all these experiences is that in some sense they are unitive; they are experiences of being *one* with something or someone other than oneself. But this leaves unanswered the question as to what one is united with. It is here that the variety begins, and the evidence must be carefully sifted. Among obvious factors affecting variety in mystical experiences are the differences of means (such as drugs or mental techniques), a priori conceptions (such as pantheism or psychoanalysis) and objects of mysticism (such as nature or the demonic).

Thus the psychedelic drugs are but one means, among many, of altering the consciousness. Other suggested analogues to the psychedelic experience include meditation and hypnosis, and among the many well-practiced means to achieve a transcendental state are the various breathing techniques and the use of chants, oscillating body movements and self-flagellation. All these are only means; they can be either directed toward the transcendental world of unsanity or misdirected toward depression and distortion in the world approaching insanity.

Hindu meditation, for example, is a highly developed technique designed to eliminate the external stimuli by zeroing in on one of the senses, such as the eye, via a mandala; the ear, via a mantra; or the taste, touch and smell via a tantra, to the point where the mind is disinhibited and achieves the transcendental consciousness which is the bliss of yoga. The Maharishi often explains it simply like this: In a glass of water, rising bubbles start small at the bottom, getting larger as they break surface near the top. The bottom would represent our subconscious minds and the top our conscious minds where thoughts and ideas break surface and are expressed and appreciated.[49] Normally, when we are listening to a conversation or a concerto or reading a book, sounds, words and thoughts pass across the surface of our minds (in one ear and out the other!) and have no permanence in our minds. But the effect of a mantra, a symbolic sound representing the name and nature of the deity, is to form a continuous circle of thought within the mind. When this is done, the thought stays within the conscious mind, then, as it were, it proceeds down the bubble stream backwards. This means that thought is not just appreciated at its conscious levels but at all the subtler levels too, finally bringing the subconscious mind within the range of consciousness. The power of the conscious mind is thereby increased manyfold.

Some suggest that forms of sensory deprivation are also related to this.[50] The normal mind requires constant feedback of external stimuli. If these are lacking, one may suffer deprivation to the point of hallucinations or transcendental consciousness. Occasionally this happens to cave explorers, solitary shipwrecked sailors, drivers crossing vast stretches of glaring desert or elderly hospital patients with bandaged eyes and restricted movements. It can happen easily to a normal person in a soundless, lightless room. This is a possible explanation of some mysticism in the past. The Egyptian temple rites, for example, involved sensory deprivation, fasting and social isolation. The Sioux Indians have a sun ritual of heat and thirst, which leads them to crude delirium. The Sufis practice long breath retention and vigils of abstinence which achieve the same thing. Possibly this was behind the Delphic oracle: The Pythoness, an old woman, used to sit over a fissure in a rock from which carbon dioxide was emitted; this led her into a trance-like state of divination. If no gas came from the rock, one alternative was to burn sacred laurel leaves in a copper bowl and to inhale the carbon dioxide fumes which they gave off. Once her consciousness changed, she would make her inarticulate utterances which the cynically political committee of priests would translate into a prophecy for the worshippers, always with extreme ambiguity and a canny eye to the appropriate fee.

Thus psychedelics, Zen meditation, yoga meditation, nature mysticism and aesthetic mysticism may very well be analogues, different routes to the transcendental world. Of course, the experiences are all different, and not all trips arrive at precisely the same destination. But, then, even within the range of psychedelics, marijuana is less powerful than acid.

On this point, I have heard long discussions between gurus and acid heads. The guru would argue that without the ethics and discipline of Yoga true transcendental consciousness or bliss is impossible. But the acid head would reply that he had tried both meditation and drugs and the difference was only one of degree, and not of kind. A close friend of mine is a seasoned Alpine climber of considerable experience. I suspect that he would be more than a little scornful if he climbed the Matterhorn again only to discover at the peak someone lowered there by a helicopter. Their routes to the top would be very different in terms of the discipline, skill and strength demanded, and the sense of satisfaction at having arrived would be accordingly different, but the view from the top would be much the same. Listening to the gurus debating with the acid heads, I often had the feeling of a similar situation.

I re-emphasize that this attempt to chart the geography of the transcendental is speculative and no more than tentative. Yet if it contains any truth at all, it is important to examine the implications of the psychedelic drugs in still further areas.

Death and Evolution

The first area is their relation to the problem of death. Death for twentieth-century man, as we noted earlier, is the new pornography. The fear of non-being is a constant fear in man. Dr. Eric Kast, the expert in relating death and LSD, observes that there is no animal that experiences "the disease of conceptualizing death."[51] For man, as he knows himself as an individual personality, death has two stings: The first is the loss of individuality and the second is the loss of his future orientation, both of which are basic to the human psyche. Now if the effect of LSD is to disinhibit the sense of individuality and replace it with oceanic unity and to disinhibit the sense of future orientation and replace this with timelessness, then in both areas LSD will be removing the sting of the fear of death or non-being.

Psychiatrists like Dr. Kast have done serious research into the relationship between LSD and dying, for LSD seems to offer a panacea to the ultimate fear. Aldous Huxley in his novel *Island* describes the death of Lakshmi on psychedelics. The night Huxley himself lay dying (November 22, 1963) his wife administered LSD to him. None of this is surprising.

The second area is their relationship to evolution. Many LSD subjects claim that in their trips they experience previous forms of racial and subhuman species and that this is scientific evidence for evolution. Leary says, "The psychedelic experience is the Hindu-Buddha reincarnation theory experimentally confirmed in your own nervous system. You re-experience your human forebears, shuttle down the chain of DNA remembrance. It's all there in your cellular diaries. You are all the men and women who fought and fed and met and mated. . . . Where LSD subjects report retrogression and reincarnation visions, this is not mysterious or supernatural. It's simply modern biogenetics."[52] If true this would be evidence for the validity of the theories and hypotheses of evolution.

But two objections immediately arise. First, the evolutionary trees so described are often contradictory; no biologist could subscribe to their accuracy. Second, it is almost certain that the psychedelics tell us more about our feelings of reality than they tell us about the nature of reality itself. They draw from our subconscious minds and make explicit what are already our deepest presuppositions, our world view. Thus they are evidence of the reality of our beliefs but not of their validity.

Communication

The third area is their relation to communication. It is

the constant contention of the psychedelic prophets that communication has broken down on the symbolic level and has been reduced to dry, arid, dusty, rationalistic, mechanistic verbalization—words, words, words. Alan Watts describes this as "a specialization in differences, in noticing, and nothing is definable, classifiable, or noticeable except by contrast with something else."[53] Leary says, with equally derogatory implications, "Our current reliance upon substantive and closing off concepts will be the amused wonder of coming generations. We must entertain non-verbal methods of communication if we are to free our nervous system from the tyranny of the shifting simplicity of words."[54] Watts and Leary see the psychedelic drugs as a means to communicate above communication.

But we must ask if this is really communication with depth, content and meaning or only a deepened experience of sensory awareness. It is obvious that an immediate problem of such "meaningfulness" is that it is impossible to communicate it to the normal world because there are no categories. Of course, this is a problem inherent in all mysticism and not necessarily invalidating. But it is a specially crucial problem with the psychedelics, as William James recognized, "Depth beyond depth of truth seems revealed to the inhaler. This truth fades out, however, or escapes, at the moment of coming to; and if any words remain over in which it seemed to clothe itself, they prove to be the veriest nonsense."[55] This was written almost seventy years ago, yet it still stands as the best comment on many of the pretentious claims which end as vacuous.

With a poignant personalness, Timothy Leary illustrates what William James is saying, and, by the way, thereby substantially falsifies his own claims. In an interview with Paul Krassner, editor of the *Realist,* Leary claimed for the psychedelics extraordinary powers of communication on various levels, one being nature and another being sexual intercourse. In both these areas Leary's extravagant claims were reduced to rhetorical vagueness by probing questions from Krassner. Speaking of nature, Krassner said, "You've gone on record as saying that you talk to trees; what I want to know is, do the trees hear what you're saying to them?" Leary replied, "Well, I hear what the trees are telling *me.* I *listen* to trees. Whether they hear me, I don't know. You'd have to ask a tree. I think they do."[56] This is hardly communication in the sense he was claiming. Much more sensitive is "Voice" by Zbigniew Herbert, describing his search for a true voice from nature, but concluding,

my experience takes on
the shape of an alternative
either the world is dumb
or I am deaf[57]

The questions about sexual intercourse were even sadder. In another interview Leary had claimed, "There is no question that LSD is the most powerful aphrodisiac ever discovered by man. . . . Let me put it this way: compared with sex under LSD, the way you've been making love—no matter how ecstatic the pleasure you think you get from it—is like making love to a department-store-window dummy."[58] He even cautions against taking it with anyone but the person one knows well and loves deeply—a kind of psychedelic monogamy. "It's almost inevitable that a woman will fall in love with a man who shares her LSD experience."[59] But when Krassner gently asked him to explain why his second marriage, despite the use of LSD, broke up on the honeymoon, Leary refused to comment. The refusal was understandable, but what is strange is his failure to see the inconsistency of his claims.

Utopian Dreams

A fourth area is the relation of psychedelic drugs to the

utopian claims made for them. The disarray of the present situation must be contrasted with the extravagant claims for the new stage of evolution of which they were to be chemical midwives. Leary explicitly tied them to Teilhard de Chardin's prospects of the *Noosphere,* asking, "Can you see any hope for this homicidal, neurologically crippled species other than a mass religious ecstatic convulsion?"[60] Following the psychedelic revolution he predicted, "Grass will grow in Times Square within ten years. . . . The third generation from now will not need LSD. The fourth generation from now will be in such perfect harmony with every form of molecular, cellular, seed and sensory energy that LSD will be unnecessary."[61]

Such enthusiasm was also reflected in the more sober hope of psychiatrists like Humphrey Osmond: "These agents have a part to play in our survival as a species. . . . I believe that the psychedelics provide a chance, perhaps only a slender one, for homo faber, the cunning, ruthless, foolhardy, pleasure-greedy toolmaker, to merge into that other creature whose presence we have so rashly assumed, homo sapiens."[62]

The evidence of the success in terms of individual enlightenment or communal achievement is slender. The attempt to inflate psychedelics to cultural proportions is an inglorious fiasco.

Charles Reich claimed for Consciousness III that, "Beside it, a mere revolution, such as the French or the Russian, seems inconsequential. . . . What is coming is nothing less than a new way of life and a new man."[63] Rousseau rides again, but empirical reality reduces the claim to the ludicrous. Roszak saw it as an obsession typical of the worst of American commercialism: "Start with a gimmick; and you end with a *Weltanschauung.*"[64]

The Psychedelics and God

The fifth area is their relation to religious experience.

 How do we evaluate the evidence of those who claim to have experienced God under psychedelic drugs? Many from differing religious traditions—Hindu, Jewish, Christian—as well as agnostics and atheists have made this claim. Alan Watts is a one-time Anglican, Walter Pahnke a liberal theologian, Timothy Leary an atheist, but all have described their psychedelic experiences as a deep religious awareness. After his first mescaline trip Aldous Huxley pronounced that the Beatific Vision, the Bliss of the Hindus and the Dharma-Body of the Buddha were "as evident as Euclid."[65] Many are "converted" under LSD. Paul McCartney described on British television that through acid "God is in everything. . . ," and Theodore Gill, President of San Francisco's Presbyterian Theological Seminary, remarked, "The drugs make an end run around Christ and go straight to the Holy Spirit."[66]

The question is inescapable. If by the psychedelics we can be in immediate touch with God, does this not nullify Christian ideas of the necessary norms of revelation? How does this psychedelic "god" relate to the Christian conception of a personal God known only through Jesus Christ? To understand, we must examine exactly what it is they are claiming. Several comments on this come to mind at once.

First, the definitions of their experiences are those which any atheist or humanist could accept and still remain an atheist or humanist, as many in fact do. The Buddhist has a similar experience and does not interpret it as "god," and, of those who take acid and have the same experience, only a proportion interpret it as religious. Others have cried with Rimbaud, "I wait on God like a glutton"[67] but like him have had to admit that an altered consciousness has brought them no nearer to God. The description of psychic transcendence is one common to both religious and secular feelings.[68] Walter Houston Clark defines religion as "the inner experience of an individual when he senses a Beyond." But this is no more "religious" than the modern physicists' understanding of the deeper sources of created energy. In fact, Professor U. A. Asrami of Benares, himself a mystic, is attempting to show the relationship between modern physics and mysticism. "The modern techniques of scientific research," he writes, "could be helpful in determining the limitations, the after effects and the utility of the mystical experience. . . . If mysticism and mystical experience can be freed of their 'supernatural' connotations, there is no reason why modern science cannot acknowledge and even absorb them into its domain."[69] Both the Christian and the atheist would agree to this.

Leary candidly writes, "To talk to God yourself, you are going to have to throw away all your definitions and just surrender to this process. . . . God is the DNA code, because the DNA code, as biochemists describe it, is all the attributes that we have attributed to God: the all-powerful, ever-changing intelligence far greater than man's mind which is continually manifesting itself in different forms."[70]

The evidence is totally inconclusive. It could be interpreted in either a religious or an atheistic framework. Thus searching questions are raised for the man who takes transcendental consciousness as a definitive experience of God. William James counseled, "We have no right . . . to invoke its prestige as distinctively in favor of any special belief."[71]

If this is so, it prompts a second question: Why is it called God? After much wrestling with this, my conclusion is that the experience is called God and given religious connotations because of the impelling force of its contrast with previous awareness. Either for Gautama Buddha in his strenuous search or for many Westerners today, the experiencing of oneself as individual is the focal point of a marked degree of isolation and alienation. Aldous Huxley was described as a man who "had, it seems, not been a happy man; and because he was both unhappy and introspective, he needed a philosophy or a religion that would deliver him from both his unhappiness and himself."[72] Being an intelligent man he realized that unhappiness and the self are not unconnected, and this is the beginning of Eastern religion. But it is this very individuality which is evaded when the psychedelics disinhibit the normal rational mind. The sense of being a "skin-encapsulated ego" is shattered, and the contrasting sense of overwhelming oceanic unity brings flooding relief and release. This easily results in an interpretation of the experience of unity with the ground of being as having religious connotations. This is my own conclusion after listening to the testimonies of hundreds of acid takers who claimed to have experienced God.

Recently I was interested to come across a passage in Martin Buber which indicates that he was thinking in the same direction. He argued that the soul is "bound to imagine" that this is God. "Nevertheless, in the honest and sober account of the responsible understanding this unity is nothing but the unity of this soul of mine, whose 'ground' I have reached, so much so, beneath all formations and contents, that my spirit has no choice but to understand it as the groundless."[73] Buber, too, saw the impelling force of contrast as the explanation for the religious interpretation. This is the old error of confusing natural and supernatural mysticism. A clearer distinction is possible within a Christian framework.

Psychedelics and the East

The sixth area, and one which easily follows, is the relationship of psychedelics to the Eastern religions. The definition of the experience as a sense of the beyond aligns well with Eastern metaphysics. Not surprisingly, Leary the atheist is now close to Hinduism and Watts the Anglican is a champion of Zen. Although some disagree, most would interpret the psychedelic experience as being in the same direction as the East. Gurus who flatly deny this are indignant at the thought of "bottled samadhis" or "encapsulated satoris." There is an Indian saying, "If heaven can be obtained for a penny why should you be so envious?" Or as Meher Baba says, "If God can be found through the medium of any drug, God is not worthy of being God."[74] But today this reflects more on the validity of his notions of God than on the psychedelic experience.

Far closer was Thomas de Quincey's comment on taking tincture of opium, "Happiness might now be bought for a penny, and peace of mind could be sent down by mail." Devaluation and the black market have put prices exorbitantly beyond a penny, but the mail is still a vital carrier of illicit drugs!

The clearest way to show this relationship to Eastern thought is to recall the three areas—reality, personality and morality—in which Hinduism and Buddhism are deficient and to see that these are equally a dilemma for the regular users of psychedelics. The deficiency in regard to reality is obvious. On the practical side, many acid heads suffer terribly from their inability and failure to distinguish fantasy from reality. But there is a theoretical weakness too. Leary downgrades what we call reality: "Sensory conditioning has forced us to accept a 'reality' which is a comic-tragic farce illusion."[75] Alan Watts refers to it as "the master illusion, whereby we appear to be different" or as "a measly trickle of consciousness."[76] This comes very close to the epistemological scepticism of the East and its view of maya.

Psychedelics lead to an equally low view of personality. Watts, describing his "skin-encapsulated ego," says, "What we call self-consciousness is thus the sensation of the organism obstructing itself, of not being with itself, of driving so to say with accelerator and brake on at once"[77] —an apt description of alienation but hardly the basis for any high view of man. Little wonder that the sole solution is via dissolution. Leary expands on the same theme of alienation but relates it to communication: "Each human being is a galaxy spinning lonely in space, and the only contacts we have with other galaxies (light years away, really), are the flimsy flickerings on our sense organs."[78] This is almost identical with the Eastern view of the self as "not-self" caught in a web of maya.

The deficiency in morality is also obvious. Like yoga, the drug experience is beyond good and evil. On achieving this state, one simply says, "This is it," and then it is possible to see through the distinctions, divisions and categories under which normal differences between good and evil are alone possible. Watts says, "For in this world nothing is wrong, nothing is even stupid. The sense of wrong is simply failure to see where something fits into a pattern. . . . Each one of you is quite perfect as you are, even if you don't know it."[79] In support Leary writes, "That intermediate manifestation of the divine process which we call the DNA code has spent the last 2 billion years making this planet a Garden of Eden. . . . Into this Garden of Eden each human being is born perfect."[80] To see this is to see a "Joyous Cosmology" or to indulge in "The Magnificent Frolic," but for any who have glimpsed the horror of great darkness in Nietzsche's abyss or who have looked resolutely at the state of man in his world, this is either a romantic blindness or a moral holiday.

In the past mystics have been few and far between, even in India, and little harm has been done by any who had, or who thought they had, transcended good and evil. The arrival of psychedelics in commercial quantities has changed all that. Taken one way it leads to the perverted logic of a Manson (using psychedelics, seeing himself as both God and Satan, and so beyond good and evil); taken another way it adds to the paralysis of motivation, so much a part of the counter culture.

Having briefly mentioned marijuana's effects in undermining motivation in frequent heavy users, we now see that this is partly due to the nature of the drug and not just the setting. The same would apply even more strongly to the more powerful psychedelics. If the drug experience transcends individuality and moral distinctions, then it bypasses both man's initiative and his critical judgment, both fundamental to an understanding of motivation.[81] Watts and Leary openly admit this. Watts writes, "Decision can be completely paralyzed by the sudden realization that there is no way of having good without evil, or that it is impossible to act upon reliable authority without choosing, from your own inexperience, to do so. If sanity implies madness and faith doubt, am I basically a psychotic pretending to be sane, a blithering terrified idiot who manages, temporarily, to put on an act of being self possessed? I begin to see my whole life as a masterpiece of duplicity."[82] Slowly, like a centipede wondering how on earth it coordinates all its hundred legs, this sort of reflection becomes a creeping paralysis. Leary is more blunt: "Render unto Caesar everything external" (that is, "society, politics, rules"). Thus, as with the East the end is the loss of moral categories, followed by the tendency to withdrawal. Many of the regular users of psychedelics, let alone the extreme acid heads, are living examples of this cultural lack of guts.

The Psychedelics and Alienation

The last area of importance is the relation of psychedelics to a sense of alienation. Many take drugs to escape alienation, only to find that these drugs tighten the screw further. For one thing, the very drive to transcend implies a degree of alienation. Man is the only known species who experiences the urge to escape his ordinary range of consciousness which is obviously unsatisfying to him; this urge gives him a sense of being at odds with himself, feeling other than he is. It is no accident that psychedelics and Eastern religions, ending as they do with conceptions that are basically impersonal, finally negate the individuality of man.

Second, if such transcendance is achieved, it is never more than transient. "The problem with LSD is not enduring change. The problem is that it doesn't last long enough," admits Timothy Leary.[83] Coming down from his first trip, Carlos Castaneda wrote, "The awakening to serious, sober consciousness was genuinely shocking. I had forgotten I was a man! The sadness of such an irreconcilable situation was so intense that I wept."[84]

Moreover, it implies the reduction of life to a game. If life has no meaning, then all that is left, as Nietzsche foresaw, is the game plan. Gamesmanship is becoming a common theme in contemporary thinking. Stephen Potter could write about it humorously; Eric Berne is far more serious in his *Games People Play,* but we are beyond these now to the point where there is no meaning to life; all that is left is the game to disguise the lack of meaning. Robert de Ropp, recommending his meditation as a higher game beyond drugs, advises, "Seek, above all, a game worth playing. . . . Though nothing means anything and all roads are marked 'NO EXIT' yet move as if your movements had some purpose. If life does not seem to offer a game worth playing, then *invent one*. . . . Any game is better than no game."[85] Watts steels himself to look into life and say, "Come off it, Shiva, you old rascal. It's a great act, but it doesn't fool me."[86] Hermann Hesse depicts the subtlest and most developed extreme in the esoteric mysteries of *The Glass Bead Game.* Leary was once asked if he would drop out of the drug scene and go to something else. His reply was in the same vein, "I'm ready. And do *what*? You've got to name me a *better* game. . . . I'm ready to give up LSD at a moment's notice if someone will suggest to me a game which is more exciting, more promising, more expansive, more ecstatic. Tell me. . . . I'll take off my shoes and follow you."[87] Rimbaud had already seen where this game led. He wanted God but could not find him through mysticism. He was forced to conclude: "Life is a farce that all must go through."[88]

A final point of exacerbation is the idea of life being reduced to a "movie." Ken Kesey's psychedelic pilgrimage shows this. Instead of achieving elevation to a timeless world, the Pranksters saw it not so much as timelessness but as condemnation to spend their lives watching a movie of themselves, for, with the sensory lag between action and the senses, real life always happened one-thirtieth of a second ago. This was the frustration of the Merry Pranksters: to desire the "eternal now" but to see its tantalizing impossibility. Tom Wolfe described it as a "man forever watching his own movie and never being able to get to the paradise beyond the screen."[89]

The Psychedelics and Christian experience

The last important issue is to relate the psychedelic experience to Christian experience and to see whether one can understand other forms of mysticism within the Christian framework. If Christianity is true, this does not automatically mean that other experiences are unreal or necessarily wrong, and yet many interpretations can be seen as unacceptable in the light of the fuller understanding of Christian truth.

In fact, what was implied in the tentative mapping of a geography of the transcendental accords well with the Christian understanding of man and his world. Man, to the Christian, has relationships on two different levels. First, he knows himself as a distinct personal entity (by virtue of his being in the image of God), and in this he is distinct from all the rest of finite creation. It so happens that man is especially, but not exclusively, aware of this personal level in the decisions, emotions and thinking of his normal waking consciousness. But, second, man also knows himself to be finite, and in this he shares a relationship with the rest of finite creation, whether animal, plant or machine.

Seen this way the psychedelics *prove* nothing at all. As they transcend the normal waking consciousness, they attain a transcendental consciousness which is nothing more (or less!) than a measure of unity possible on the level of finite creation. There is in nature a deeper and more intimate unity than is normally perceptible, and the barrier between the individual and his environment is far from absolute. This level man shares with the rest of creation, in the sense that the energy which is the dance of life in man dances also in all nature. This means that within the Christian framework such consciousness may be transcendental and paranormal but is not supernatural, because it is still only an awareness of unity with finite creation.

By contrast with this, there are for the Christian two supernatural areas. The first is a genuine experience of God and the second is an experience of the occult powers, the devil and evil spirits. While both are real and supernatural, only the former is legitimate; the latter is real but wrong. Understanding this, we can see that for the Christian there are still two legitimate mystical experiences. The first is natural mysticism including nature mysticism and aesthetic mysticism; the second is supernatural mysticism, a genuine experience of God. Both are legitimate forms of mysticism, but it is a common error to mistake the natural mysticism for the supernatural and to give it connotations that are spiritual. This probably explains some medieval Roman Catholic mysticism; the reason for suspecting this is their use of techniques of deprivation, such as extreme fasting and flagellation, which, as we saw earlier, can bring about mystical experiences.

It cannot be stressed too strongly, especially in the climate of a growing and dangerous vogue for contentless religious experience, that the mystical experience is only a part of the Christian's total experience. Spiritual reality is also a result of diligent study, disciplined understanding, daily obedience to God and growth in character. But the mystical experience is a part, and certain Christians are denying it to their own poverty.

This raises the final question: What is the difference between the transcendental consciousness involved in the various forms of natural mysticism and the genuine supernatural experience of God which can also be mystical? There are two areas of difference. In the first are those differences which provide a marked contrast in degree but not in kind. Usually in an experience of natural mysticism, the awareness is non-personal. Personal "revelations" are also rare with psychedelic drugs. Often where visionary figures are revealed, these have more to do with the occult than with genuine personal relationships. *The Teaching of Don Juan: A Yaqui Way of Knowledge* by Carlos Castaneda illustrates this. But the Christian's mystical experience is always intensely personal.

A second marked difference is that natural mysticism is rarely rooted in a specific life-historical context. The context is usually incidental, the experience being ahistorical and its inducement often mechanical, as by a drug. A Christian's experience of God always comes in his life-historical context, often relating to it very specifically.

Another marked difference is that natural mysticism can be explained in terms of a trip ("Every religion in world history was founded on the basis of some flipped-out visionary trip," said Leary),[90] but the Christian's supernatural experience of God is always in terms of truth. This judgment runs counter to much current theology let alone mysticism, so let me use the classic account of Paul's conversion in Acts 9 to explain what I mean. Paul's conversion is often taken as a prime example of a mystical experience of God which Paul later "rationalized" in terms of his own theology. But a close study of the evidence contradicts this interpretation. For one thing, Paul was actually converted; there was a change in his life and convictions. There was content to his experience. Paul did an about-face and headed in a direction totally antithetical to that in which he had been traveling before. Clearly his was no undefined experience which he later rationalized in the light of previous premises. Where was that content? Two strands are evident. The first was the clear and courageous speech of Stephen. Hearing this as a Pharisee with strong anti-Christian prejudice, Paul rejected it and was an accomplice in Stephen's stoning. But as he saw the ascended Lord in all his glory, whom as a Jew he would know as JHWH, Paul was forced to ask, "Lord, who are you?"[91] Back came the answer with its content which completely changed him: "I am Jesus, whom you are persecuting."[92] This Jesus, whom Stephen had preached and Paul had rejected, the peasant carpenter from Galilee, crucified in Jerusalem as a petty criminal, was the Lord, JHWH. It was the conjunction of the two truths, the Lordship of God and the humanity of Jesus, that was the essential content prompting the turning point in Paul's conversion.

A further detail drives this home forcibly. In recounting the story later, Paul mentions with fascinating attention to detail that Jesus had spoken to him "in the Jewish language,"[93] that is, the very language, logic, grammar and syntax of Paul's cultural heritage—not Greek, not Latin, not Aramaic, but Hebrew. Taken as a whole, the biblical account clearly indicates an experience that was mystical; much of it was beyond words. But it was also personal and propositional.

The second area of differences includes differences of kind and not merely of degree, that is, differences of quality, not of quantity. Illustrative examples of such supernatural experiences of God are recorded in the Bible and can be seen in the lives of Moses (Exodus 3), Isaiah (Isaiah 6), Ezekiel (Ezekiel 1), Paul (Acts 9), and John (Revelation 1). These and other experiences from Christians outside the biblical record show that there is an area of total difference. This area has three distinct but related aspects. In his experience of God, a Christian has a strong sense of his individuality, never of his unity with God. Expressed more sharply, he has a strong sense of the Creator-creature distinction, never of merging or absorption. Or, to put it more sharply still, a Christian has a sense of his moral sin and not just of his metaphysical smallness in the face of the beyond. The dilemma for man is not who he is but what he has done. His predicament is not that he is small but that he is sinful.

Consequently, for a Christian psychedelic drugs are not morally wrong in the sense that any specific biblical absolute vetoes them. Rather, in the context of Christian truth and life, drugs are, first, totally unnecessary, either as a way to gain meaning or as an escape and, second, in the context of an increasingly drug-dependent culture, they are unhelpful.

Some Christians who read this may understand the critique but wonder why they are still not satisfied in the quiet of their rooms. Hours of critique are no alternative to seconds of the genuine existential reality of knowing God that is possible through the Spirit of Jesus Christ.

The psychedelic movement has become one more spiral within the counter culture. From the surging enthusiasm of the early sixties, we have come almost full circle. The psychedelics have proved to be only an illusory, counterfeit infinity, but many of those who

8/Encircling Eyes

"The current interest of youth in astrology, clairvoyance and the occult is no coincidence. . . Mysticism is just tomorrow's science dreamed today."
Marshall McLuhan

"This void may not be empty. It may be peopled by visions and voices, ghosts, strange shapes and apparitions."
R. D. Laing

"I got to know them after they already had too much power. I now had the world of spirits I had wanted to see. The demons came up from the abyss."
Karl Jaspers

"Spiritual warfare is just as brutal as human warfare."
Rimbaud

"The kingdom of God is not a matter of talk, but of power."
Paul of Tarsus[1]

"There are two equal and opposite errors into which our race can fall about the devils. One is to disbelieve in their existence. The other is to believe and then feel an excessive and unhealthy interest in them."
C. S. Lewis

It should be apparent by now that it is a mistake to think of the counter culture as a monolithic unity. Compelling in its comprehensiveness but also contradictory in its complexity, it rolls on like a relentless river of amorphous people, trends, fashions, ideals and aspirations. At any moment there are a hundred eddies, cross-currents and whirlpools, and it is easy to be preoccupied with the inconsequential. But developing alongside the psychedelic movement and related to the logic of its failure is a further trend we shall consider. It is a recent but already real defining feature of the movement; it may, in fact, envelop the counter culture and go far beyond to be a profound influence in the closing years of the twentieth century. I am speaking here of the resurgent trend towards the occult.

The Fire Burns Low

Early hunters on safari in Africa used to build their fires high at night in order to keep away the animals in the bush. But when the fires burned low in the early hours of the morning, they would see all around them the approaching outlined shapes of animals and a ring of encircling eyes in the darkness. When the fire was high they were far off, but when the fire was low they approached again.

As we have witnessed the erosion and breakdown of the Christian culture of the West, so we have seen the vacuum filled by an upsurge of ideas that would have been unthinkable when the fires of the Christian culture were high. But of them all, this last trend is the most sinister. It is far more than another compulsive spiral, down which many have plunged, caught by the current of fascination with the weird and the wonderful. The trend is difficult to chart except for the points that are spectacular, silly or sinister and thus basically irrelevant to its deeper reality. At this deeper level the occult needs to be felt to be understood. So far as its future is concerned, only the gray outlines are emerging. But these are enough to quicken an appreciation of the horror of great darkness which is sweeping over the West, inexorably rolling inwards like a swelling black tide or looming larger in the darkness with its encircling eyes.

In many ways this trend is the most surprising of all. Only a short time back any belief in such a world as the astral, the supernatural or the occult would have been relegated to the ridiculous. Such spine-tingling stories, like horror films, were modern man's surrogates for his loss of belief in hell. They were anything but real. Perhaps stories of the occult were to be expected as part of the Middle Ages or the missionary world, but certainly they had little to do with the twentieth-century West and still less to do with the avant garde and the young. But the occult can no longer be relegated in time or distance. Yesterday's sceptics are some of today's firmest believers.

Yet generally speaking there is still a patronizing disregard for, if not outright disbelief in, any such talk. Probably it would still be virtually impossible to publish an article expressing belief in the reality of this world in any respectable journal of psychiatry in Britain or the United States, dominated heavily as they still are by a naturalistic framework. The long overdue "Anti-materialists' Liberation" may be about to break, but the same disdain is still found in most recent books.[2] Pennethorne Hughes, a British authority, writing as late as 1965, pronounced with finality that witchcraft is "dying rapidly before the popular Press, popular education, a national education, a national health scheme, and the American way of life."[3] He concluded emphatically, "Witchcraft, as a cult belief in Europe, is dead. As a degenerate form of a primitive fertility belief, incorporating the earliest instructive wisdom, the practice is over."[4]

This is not atypical nor is it surprising, for even in much theology, where one would expect to find a measure of belief, there is little acknowledgement of the supernatural, either positive or negative. The writings of Paul Tillich or Reinhold Niebuhr may use the word *demonic,* but not to refer to an objective demonic world. The word *demonic* is rather used as a symbol of man's bias toward evil. That a man like Archbishop William Temple should actually have believed in a personal devil was regarded as extraordinary in so prestigious an archbishop and so profound a scholar.

But now it is in the West and among the young and avant garde that we are seeing an unmistakable resurgence in the belief and practice of the occult, ranging from the harmless to the horrifying.

For the sake of any who read this chapter lightly, we can do no better than begin with the warning of C. S. Lewis: "There are two equal and opposite errors into which our race can fall about the devils. One is to disbelieve in their existence. The other is to believe and then feel an excessive and unhealthy interest in them."[5] His *Screwtape Letters* was written to a generation caught in unbelief by a mechanistic world view which appeared to castrate the supernatural or unseen. Lewis reminded them brilliantly of the subtlety and reality of such things. Perhaps today, he would be writing a sequel in the opposite direction.

At the risk of blurring real differences and seeming to be selective at several points, I would like to examine the resurgence under the three main categories where it is visible: superstition, spiritism and Satanism, although these distinctions will obviously be arbitrary in certain areas. Different individuals and groups involved in the occult have widely differing impulses behind them. Some people, from a jaded experience of life, are in it for kicks; some are seriously pursuing higher psychic ends; some have an almost antiquarian interest in the revival of pagan nature worship; some are openly selling their souls to the devil; and others demonstrate a weird amalgam of semi-beliefs and practices, involving themselves in the esoteric world in a totally eccentric way. Nevertheless these three general categories offer a helpful outline.

Back to the Occult—Why?

What cultural factors lie behind this swing to the occult? What makes this resurgence intelligible? The first factor is the death of rationalism. Before and during the Reformation witchcraft was persecuted relentlessly by the witch hunters. Their efforts, however, often served to keep it alive. It was actually killed by the development and cultural adoption of Reformation theology and later yet by rationalism. The Reformation held that witches were real but wrong. Rationalism went deeper still and scorned them as non-existent; witchcraft was simply meaningless. The rise of rationalism in the eighteenth century coincided with the disappearance of witchcraft. Witch hunts were eventually abolished in 1737. But now in the twentieth century rationalism has stumbled, its wings severely clipped by psychoanalysis and modern philosophy. The door to the non-rational, the irrational and super-rational is wide open. One of the many previous "unthinkables" which has squeezed through the door is the occult.

A second factor is the scepticism towards the supernatural in liberal theology. Ever since D. F. Strauss, Ernest Renan and the rise of Higher Criticism, there has been a persistent infiltration from the secular premises of naturalistic philosophy. One constant sign of this has been the exorcism of any lingering supernatural ideas. The old and new quests for the historical Jesus and the movement to demythologize the gospel have both foundered on the intrinsic impossibility of dividing the human from the supernatural. But the legacy of their scepticism has had two results. In a period when liberal theology appeared to speak for intelligent Christianity, it looked as if Christianity as a whole had succumbed to naturalism disguised by semantic symbolism. Christianity (no longer affirming the occult as real but wrong) lost its balanced position between the sceptics who denied it all and those who accepted it completely. So anyone who searched for spiritual reality and did not find it in the church was forced towards the occult. Ironically, the last people to believe in these things today are often churchmen, lulled complacently to sleep by the smug rationalism of their theology.

The second result of liberalism is that biblical revelation's critical control has been lost. The Bible affirms the reality of the occult but denies its validity, and in doing so it gives critical norms by which a Christian can judge between true spirituality and its counterfeit. Without these biblical norms as a critical control, experience itself becomes normative. This loss of critical control explains why so many who once totally disbelieved now uncritically accept all such phenomena. The second position, equally foolish and doubly dangerous, is the result of taking experience as normative.

A third factor is the influence of Eastern religions. We have already noted the perverse fact that what people reject in Christianity they welcome with open arms from the East. It is evident in all Eastern religions that, however high the ethics or sophisticated the philosophy, at grass-roots level there is open idolatry, animism and spiritism. Whatever Shankara, Gautama or Mohammed may have said, the average Tibetan priest or Malaysian Bomo is a firm believer in the practice of the occult. Not surprisingly, belief in the occult often follows as an accepted part of the world view of those who are into the Eastern trend, especially those familiar with the various Books of the Dead.

The fourth factor is the chaos and complexity of

modern culture. Just as anxiety is a symptom of existence in a bottleneck, so the upsurge of belief in the occult is symptomatic of short-cut thinking motivated by the baffling complexity of modern life. At the time of the decline and fall of Rome, superstition flourished among the refugees from the various religions which were failing. Today, astrologers recognize similarly that their popularity results partly from the failure of modern convictions, the general uncertainty and the lack of alternative props. "We're afraid to say no, no, no to the bearded man upstairs before we have a substitute,"[6] says an American astrologer. Modern man, insecure in his crisis of identity and his loss of center, finds occult participation one answer, an answer so popular that a psychic epidemic seems to be sweeping the post-Christian world.

A fifth factor is the present state of psychic and parapsychological research. Not so long ago, all transcendental experiences were denied as invalid, mistaken, deviant or mad. Now they are merely regarded as different, paranormal or mystical. The Society for Psychical Research was founded in England in 1882. But it was the pioneer work of William James which for many opened the door to a serious appreciation. In 1903, he wrote: "In delusional insanity . . . we may have a *diabolical* mysticism, a sort of religious mysticism turned upside down . . . ; only this time the emotion is pessimistic . . . ; the meanings are dreadful; and the powers are enemies to life. . . . [These] spring from the same mental level, from that great subliminal or transmarginal region of which science is beginning to admit the existence, but of which so little is really known."[7]

Since then, the work of Dr. J. B. Rhine of Duke University on ESP and the theories of Carl Jung on synchronicity also point towards a similar end and suggest a paranormal state which closely parallels what was once held to be the astral plane of the occult. Synchronicity is the idea that all in the universe at any given moment participates at that moment with all else sharing that particular moment. Jung often referred to astrology as "scientia intuitiva," even casting horoscopes for his patients. He looked into the crystal ball of these horoscopes, not to foretell the future but to unearth elements of a patient's personality.

More recently R. D. Laing, writing of the present state of psychology, has said that we may be back to "a world long lost. This void may not be empty. It may be peopled by visions and voices, ghosts, strange shapes and apparitions."[8] Exploring the paranormal and its relation to sanity and "unsanity," Laing says, "Madness need not be all breakdown. It may also be break-through." In his usual inimitable style, McLuhan captures this feature of the present mood: "The current interest of youth in astrology, clairvoyance and the occult is no coincidence. . . . Mysticism is just tomorrow's science dreamed today."[9]

The sixth factor, but one with more relevance to the Christian and anyone who shares a similar world view, is that the supernatural really does exist. Within the Christian framework there is not so much a natural and supernatural world, as if the natural were the real and the supernatural the less real; rather there is a seen and unseen world, and both have equal reality.

These are just some of the factors which contribute to the movement towards the occult. The movement is part of a larger trend towards the perverse religiosity which is characteristic of our times. This larger phenomenon is in turn a reaction to the failure of atheism; it exhibits what McLuhan describes as the reversal of the overheated medium. Atheism, with its termini in mechanistic science, rationalistic philosophy and technological objectivity, has suddenly rebounded into producing an entirely new and profoundly religious era, an era whose central hallmarks are the mystical and the subjective and whose by-products are the contentless, the counterfeit and the confused. This was prefigured earlier by the religious stance of the Beats, the swing to Eastern religions in the early fifties and the heralding of psychedelic mysticism in 1963; the occult is the fourth wave; and the recent Jesus Movement is very much a later wave still. The sixties was the decade marking dramatic growth in the occult. In fact, 1966 can be taken as the year in which the movement surfaced into popularity. Several of the more famous Satan Churches and Magic Circles and Witches' Covens were founded that year.

Before we examine the story of the resurgence, two further points need to be added. First, it is important to understand the various levels at which this subject could be studied on its own account. This chapter is emphatically not an apologetic for the reality of the supernatural world or the devil. I write presupposing the reality of these things from both personal experience and strong convictions. We have seen coming to our community at L'Abri many for whom it is far too real. Curious dabbling and casual involvement have led them out of their depth until tragically they confront a reality beyond their control. But were there time to treat the subject adequately on all possible levels, one would need to look at the physical, medical, psychological, parapsychological and pastoral implications of the phenomena. I would merely say here that, as a Christian, I always attempt to avoid an over-sceptical rationalism on one hand or any premature escape into a magical explanation on the other.

A good illustration of the necessary balance can be seen in the relation of herbalism to modern medicine. Moldy cheese was once applied as a cure for festering sores. Whether men believed this was supernatural magic or whether it was merely a superstition, we now know that they were simply stumbling on a primitive application of penicillin. Foxgloves were once used for heart ailments, but modern medicine has isolated digitalis from the foxglove and uses it as a stimulant in modern heart drugs. Indians once used the rauwolfia root to cast out strange spirits, and pharmacology now uses some of the substance from this root in the manufacture of tranquilizers. This underlines the necessity of examining each phenomenon in the light of all the various implications and avoiding extreme interpretations on either side.

A second point is that the three main categories—superstition, spiritism and Satanism—are arbitrary in the sense that they do not speak to the question of the reality of the phenomena or to the validity of their practice. These are later questions which need to be asked of any of the categories. Broadly speaking all the phenomena can be divided into two general classes: those which are hoax and those which are genuine. But even of those which are genuine, in the sense that they succeed in some way that is objectively verifiable, there are three possible sources for their success: purely psychological power and knowledge, supernatural influence from the occult and supernatural influence from God. Thus there are always four possible interpretations (fraudulent, psychological, demonic, divine), and sometimes the line between them is not easy to draw. Critical discernment is of prime importance.

Superstition

The first general area where we can begin to see this resurgence is in the increase of superstition. *Superstitere* is the Latin word meaning to stand still over; it describes man's dread of baffling forces beyond his control, especially his fears, desires and hopes before an unknown future. Much of the evidence in this area is casual to the point of being inconsequential, but it indicates a far deeper groundswell, and at its more serious level it takes on personal, political and even criminal implications.

The origins of astrology are lost in the dim mists of antiquity, but certainly by 3000 B.C. the Chaldeans and Babylonians had developed an astrological system of immense sophistication. Centered around the construction of the ziggurats and structured on the priestly class, their astrology had two basic premises. One was the belief in the determined conformity of the macrocosm (the universe) to the microcosm (man); the other was the belief in the identification of stars with active deities. From the Middle East astrology spread further east to India and China, south to Egypt, west to Rome and finally to Europe. It is important to recognize how pervasive and all-embracing its influence was, not just among the common people but in the highest circles of court and politics, influencing decisions on every level.

The poet Ennius said, "Horoscopes cost one drachma and are one drachma too expensive." But such scepticism was extremely rare, and we are apt to forget today how recent widespread scepticism is. Scepticism grew first from the powerful scorn of the Christian church in the West. Where astrology still flourished it was closely allied to Roman Catholic corruption at its worst. Augustine called astrology the most stupid delusion of mankind ("This dog is chained"). Savanarola strongly attacked it in Florence, and Martin Luther described it as a "shabby art." But despite this, even a reformer like Philip Melancthon held a chair of astrology and the celebrated scientist Johannes Kepler did also, although with considerable reluctance.

When we ignore how short-lived historical disbelief is, we smile in a superior way at all superstition. When we hear of Burmese who refuse to wash their hair on holy days or of Zambians who think that the eating of eggs causes sterility or of Chinese travelers who never turn their fish on a plate lest the junk also capsize or tribes who do not boil milk over fires for fear the cow too will suffer, we smile at such benighted ignorance. Is not this the twilight zone of the undereducated or the over-anxious? Yet the first evidence of today's occult is in this area, a resurgence prophesied by astrologers and recognized by both psychologists and sociologists, but amazingly still taken up seriously and semi-seriously by the most scientifically sophisticated generation of young adults in history.

The astrologers are saying that after two thousand years of Pisces (the era of disillusionment and scepticism following the death of Christ), we are now entering the age of Aquarius (an era of faith and aspiration in which astrology comes into its own):

> When the Moon is in the seventh House
> And Jupiter aligns with Mars,
> Then peace will guide the planets
> And love will steer the stars.

So say the well-known lines from *Hair.* This is a new heyday for superstitions.

The hallmark of this new wave of superstition is its hedging of the bets. Nothing is believed totally. Each superstition is characterized by a half acceptance and a half denial which gives superstitious modern man the best of both worlds. On the one hand, there is a resurgence of the "old" superstitions, many of which have become ritual reactions whose meaning no longer explicitly relates to magic and spiritism. "Touch wood" or "knock on wood" was probably originally related to belief in a primeval forest god. Not walking under a ladder indicated respect for the Egyptian sacred numerology in which the mystical three was the sacred triangle which could not be broken. Throwing salt over one's shoulder was thought to bring good luck because it was cast in the face of the evil spirit who walked behind the left shoulder. Sneezing was always followed by a blessing—"God bless you!" "Salute!" "Gesundheit!"—because the sneezer had made himself vulnerable to the evil spirits. These ritualized reactions are now almost instinctive and subconscious, but the increase in superstition by a growing number of people is reflected in the semi-denial and semi-belief accorded even to those. The scrupulous persistence in practicing them points to some sort of belief, while the self-deprecating mockery in which they are practiced is the counterbalancing denial.

On the other hand, there are a mounting number of new superstitions. In this category some psychologists place belief in flying saucers and the notion that H-bomb tests cause rain or that test bans cause drought. But it is intriguing that many of these new superstitions are to be observed among the scientifically and technologically sophisticated. *Time* reports that airline pilots spit on a wheel after their preflight inspection and that a famous European Grand-Prix driver refuses to drive if a single peanut is found in his pits.[10] Many computer experts, faced with the "intelligence" and complexity of their machines, are tending to anthropomorphize them in a way that is superstitious. The manager at a research corporation near Boston was quoted as saying, "I hired everyone building the computer by the zodiac signs under which they were born." But he was a Leo and was prejudiced. "I hired two Cancer men and they both ended up with ulcers."[11]

This form of superstition is not a general feature of the counter culture, but with the boom in astrology the story comes nearer home. At the moment, this boom is the most spectacular indication of recent interest in the supernatural. In 1969, *Time* estimated that there were 10,000 full-time astrologers in the United States. The evidence is too obvious to need recounting—the rash of horoscopes (some computerized) in magazines and newspapers, the vogue for hostesses casting "I-Ching" for dinner dates and sending their invitations on astro-notes, the smorgasbord of courses on astrology at the free universities, the astrological credits in pop records, and the respectability of leading seers like Carroll Righter, Jeane Dixon, Maurice Woodruff and Arthur Ford. The whole question of a man's individual significance is overshadowed with uncertainty, and the process of decision making is relegated to the zone of astrology, cartomancy, palmistry, crystal gazing and the ouija board. The ouija board is particularly important, both because it is widely used and also because for many it is the doorway to a much more serious occult involvement. The word *ouija* comes from the French and German words for "yes" combined. Thousands of boards are sold commercially, most, of course, being used quite harmlessly as a game. But with a small percentage the game backfires and several have found themselves out of their depth as a spirit has taken control of the board. For some this experience has been their initiation into a continued practice of contacting spirits and developing mediumistic powers. Thus the ouija board is typical because, although most would merely laugh at such a suggestion, those who have seen it work appreciate the reality of the supernatural realm.

This first area—superstition—provides a good example of the necessity for critical discernment. Nothing here comes in any way from God. We can divide the phenomena into three basic types. The first and by far the largest of the categories includes all the evidence which can be described only as fraud, hoax and swindle. This is the greater part of those superstitions which cash in on the credulity of modern man. Perhaps ninety-five percent or more of modern astrology is of this type and can be seen reflected in the astrology vogue in merchandizing and show business. Examples of this are legion. Kurt Koch tells the story of a student in Paris who did his research thesis on the psychology of superstition.[12] Placing an ad in a newspaper as an astrologer, he promised detailed horoscopes for all who would pay twenty French francs. Casting one horoscope for all 400 clients with complete disregard for the zodiac signs, he found that if he included enough positive encouragement and negative warnings (based on a psychological understanding of the influence of fear and wishful thinking), all his horoscopes were greatly appreciated. Through these, he financed his studies and gained an honors degree!

Parallel to this is Koch's story of a conference in Germany where a newspaper editor told how one weekend the horoscope had not arrived so he inserted a previous one, totally incorrect because of his ignorance of the zodiac signs.[13] Despite the wide circulation of hundreds of thousands, no one noticed the error. Saving his astrologer's fees he repeated this deception twenty-two times, concluding, "During the time of the incorrect horoscopes everything went well. It does not depend on the horoscope, but on what the people believe." Modern astrology has no scientific basis; its fraudulence becomes successful not because of what people "read" but because of what they "read into" their horoscopes. At best such astrology is only constructive counseling, always with a classic Delphic ambiguity. The widely divergent predictions by astrologers concerning the same event illustrate the same point; for every horoscope which is correct, many more predict completely falsely. Jeane Dixon is remembered for prophesying the assassination of President Kennedy; all those prophesying his re-election, his divorce and many other events contingent on his continued life are completely forgotten. It is exactly because this category covers the greater part of modern astrology and superstition that many believe all of it to be fraud and swindle, successful only with a strong degree of psychological rationalization, or sheer luck. But this is not so.

Two other groups deserve more serious attention. The second category is that group of powers which do succeed but only because of the natural powers of telepathy or suggestion. Neither psychological knowledge nor psychological power are supernatural; both are entirely naturalistic. Koch gives an example of this.[14] A girl once met a Gypsy woman who tried to sell her household goods at the front door. When she refused to buy the goods the Gypsy snatcher her hand and said, "Oh, that's interesting. You will marry within two years." Naturally intrigued, the girl left her hand there and the Gypsy continued, "Several men will ask you to marry them. You will marry the tallest one. In the first year of your marriage you will become a mother. But I see your life line stops quite suddenly. You will die during the birth of your first child!" Dropping her hand the Gypsy hurried off. As prophesied, the girl (who was highly marriageable in age and appearance) was married, but, before the birth of her first child, a paralyzing fear gripped her, creeping over every part of her life. It was a fear which no psychologist's analysis nor any assurance from her husband could calm. The child was eventually born and the birth itself was uncomplicated. But a fever broke out for no apparent organic reason, the girl became mentally deranged and died three weeks later. The doctors were forced to conclude that she had been subject to thanatomania or the death wish.

In several countries the fear of spells, curses, witch doctors and voodoo probably relates to this, not that a genuine occult power is never used but that sometimes the subject of the curse of magic succumbs to a total paralysis of life because of fear. Much of the evidence in this second category is not so ghastly or criminal, but the point is that, even when it is as serious as this, it need not imply any more than the power of telepathy or suggestion.

The third category includes those powers or prophecies which succeed because of genuine occult influence, and there are many examples of this today in healing and fortunetelling. Both are effected successfully in the sense that the cure is made or the prophecy comes true. But this is not the end of the matter. The successful conclusion is usually accompanied by one of two things: either a hardening against spiritual things or what comes later and is often called "compensation" or the "devil's bargain." Following such a mediumistic healing there may come severe depressions, spiritual heaviness, an obsession, a strong addiction to alcohol or cigarettes, some psychological instability or a terror of people. This is one sign that the successful healing was from a medium with occult power. Among several biblical examples, Paul's exorcism of the divining girl at Philippi, whose mediumistic powers were being exploited commercially, could be given many modern parallels.

If most of the current phenomena can be put into one of these three categories, it should be obvious that the fraudulent is superficial, the psychological possibly more serious and only the mediumistic in any way sinister. But it should also be clear that experience alone can never be normative. We need a true understanding of the source and nature of the experience. The last category, that of genuine occult power, should more properly come under spiritism or Satanism and not under superstition, but the lines between the categories are here more than a little blurred. This section on superstition is primarily important for showing the first hints of what is coming and for indicating the credulity and uncertainty of modern man in the area of rational consideration and decision making.

It is no compliment to Western man's view of himself that he leans heavily on the fragile crutch of astrology. Nor is it any cause for confidence when Western leaders and public figures are swayed by mediums and metaphysicians, genuine or bogus. The resort to superstition is the lengthening shadow of the eyelid of night closing over Western culture.

Spiritism

The second general area in the resurgence of the occult is spiritism, a large part of which involves the increasing belief in animism and the practice of witchcraft. The word *witch* comes from the Middle English word *Wicca,* meaning wise and is related also to the word *wicked* and *wick,* meaning alive. Witchcraft is "The Old Religion," the cult of Wicca, the power, the craft, the left-hand game; it is said to be the true religion of Europe which was usurped by Christianity. Very probably three sources contribute to witchcraft as we know it. The first is the ancient fertility-cult beliefs indigenous to Europe prior to Christianity and common to most pagan nature worship. The second is the heritage of magical practices derived circuitously from the priests of Egypt. The third is the series of parodies directed at the major religions contemporary with the various phases of witchcraft. It was particularly the latter which was bound to make witchcraft controversial, and for this reason the objective facts of its history are beyond discovery. The records of witch hunts come only from the witch hunters, and few of these were known for their impartial, unbiased objectivity! Their methods of identifying witches were totally arbitrary and monstrous. A wart, for instance, was taken to be a third nipple and a sure sign that the woman was a witch. So it is not surprising that persecutions were barbarous. The Dominican monks saw themselves as the "Domini Canes," the hounds of the Lord, and the Middle Ages witnessed a ghastly series of burnings, hangings and drownings. In Strasbourg alone in a twenty-year period over 5,000 were reckoned to have been burnt and whole villages were wiped out. The echoes of many notorious stories still ring down to our own time.

Because of this, interpretations of witchcraft are radically split. The orthodox Roman Catholic view, powerfully represented before World War II by The Rev.

Dr. Montague Summers, was that witchcraft is the work of the anti-Christ.[15] Since the witches were in league with the devil himself against Christendom, any persecution could be justified if it rooted out this vile heresy. This is probably a grossly simplistic view of the original situation; in no way does it justify such monstrous ecclesiastical violence.

The second and opposite view is that witchcraft was entirely an invention of its enemies. In the clear light of later reason the evidence of the witch trials was laughed out of court or explained as extracted under torture. This is the opinion of liberal historians, such as Trevor-Roper, who blame the excesses of witch hunting on Roman Catholic inquisitors and torturers. According to this view, these churchmen invented witchcraft as a public phobia so that they could suppress their political enemies. The horror of the Inquisition's suppression of its enemies by accusing them of occultism could be portrayed no more graphically than by director Ken Russell in his film *The Devils.* But again the idea that witchcraft was only an invention of its enemies is a simplification of the whole evidence and the present resurgence is somewhat embarrassing to this view. Probably far closer to the truth is the view of Margaret Murray, that witchcraft was an outgrowth of pre-Christian fertility cults, demonstrating different phases but combining them all within a continuing tradition coming down to our own day.[16] Related to this is the view of Aldous Huxley and Gerald Heard who see witchcraft as the continuation of the ancient search for rediscovering a higher consciousness long lost but open now through magic and the astral plane. Huxley and Heard were sympathetic to the world of the yogi, the shaman and the witch doctor. For them, the Sabbat is the joyful festival of escapists from a predominantly penitential medieval age. Theodore Roszak with many in the counter culture is also enthusiastic about such a mysticism.[17] He calls for a new brand of radicalism which turns to shamanistic precedents for its inspiration. As a reaction to the "Myth of Objective Consciousness" this is understandable, but as a way of life Roszak's suggestion suffers from vagueness, and it opens the door to phenomena which may be more than psychological.

Whichever impulses one sees behind medieval witchcraft, what is important is that what has lain dormant for centuries is again breaking surface today. In 1951, the Witch Act was repealed in England and replaced by the Fraudulent Medium Act. Since then there has been a mushrooming of witches and covens across Europe and the United States. Estimates of the numbers in England range from the hundreds to the tens of thousands; most of the known general involvement is among lower-middle-class groups, fairly conservative and generally non-proselytizing. The preoccupation with sex and violence in most of these groups is a media-created myth, vastly overstressed and rarely present. In fact, the commitment is often studiously serious, even boring.

The involvement of our generation has been far more flamboyant and fashionable. It is this which is well reflected in news articles, the interest in occult bookstores, the reading of cabalistic dictionaries, the fascination with encyclopedias of demonology, occult books like the *Sixth and Seventh Book of Moses* and the various guides, amulets and talismans. Circles and covens are common in the most surprising places, prevalent in school from junior high to Ivy League colleges. During the last three years I have come across male and female witches on many English and American campuses, and increasingly their characteristic views are viable alternatives proffered in student discussions. Between the extremes of black magic and white magic are a whole medley of new witches whose search for religious experience has brought them to the occult; many are openly dabbling in rites, ritual healings, ceremonies and practices once punishable by death.

Celebrated witches of the recent past include Aleister Crowley and Gerald Gardner. Crowley, described by many as "The Great Beast," made himself out to be a great magician but was later exposed as an amoral charlatan. Gerald Gardner, who died in 1964 off Africa, was the self-styled "King of the British Witches." After a strange childhood and a long fascination with the East, he wrote many occult books and founded a witchcraft museum on the Isle of Man. In 1959, he wrote, "I do not think that anyone . . . dared hint that there might be anything in witchcraft today without being laughed at." But within a decade his successors had become cult heroes with the power of the media to give them maximum exposure to the public.

Among the rival claimants jockeying for position in the witches' hierarchy and popular esteem is a middle-aged English woman, Sybil Leek, who left England in 1967 after trouble with her neighbors at Ringwood, Hampshire, and settled in the United States. Her jackdaw, Hotfoot Jackson, sits on her shoulder, and, through her frequent radio and television appearances and her columns in the *Ladies Home Journal,* she has become quite a national celebrity. Following a burglary in her house, she warned the thieves, "All hellishness will break loose." Under pressure of this threat, the goods were promptly returned.

In Los Angeles there is a woman living sumptuously in a high-class suburb who claims she is a reincarnation of an Egyptian queen and entertains her followers with a black swan on her nude body. With ludicrous egocentricity she rules an assorted collection of addicts, homosexuals and psychopaths.

In England Alex Sanders is the new King of the Witches. Probably the most flamboyant of them all, he claims he will soon make Aleister Crowley look like a Boy Scout. He has achieved almost pop star status with his books, films, interviews and shows.

Critical discernment is again needed, for the ostensible distinction between white and black magic sometimes only blurs the issue. White magicians claim their influence is only benign and that it is black magic which brings witchcraft a bad reputation. Black magic, they say, explicitly uses demonic power for the evil influence; white magic only uses benign, if not divine, help. Where the witchcraft is only hoax or empty ritual, the difference is negligible, but all too often the white magic is "successful" in healing. Such healing is not a hoax. The ritual repetition of numbers and names, such as the divine names three times or the sign of the cross three times, is one indication that the success was due not to divine intervention but to occult power. Furthermore, "compensation" follows from white magic where it is successful and thus shows that it is neither a hoax nor merely psychological.

Overlapping with this is the area of spiritism (such phenomena as voices, visions, levitation, telekinesis, light forms and mediumistic healings where they are definitely not hoax or merely psychological power and knowledge) which extends into cultic Spiritualism. Two factors explain the particular increase in this area. First, there is the difficulty of discernment because of the experiential, contentless nature of modern religion. By merely looking inward or calling on subjective criteria, it is impossible to distinguish false spirituality from true spirituality, the genuine from the counterfeit. The fact is that religious phenomena such as prophecy, healing and speaking in tongues can have one of three sources—psychological, demonic or divine. The appeal is wider than the legitimacy. But in a day of contentless religious experience, few ask where the phenomena come from. Experience itself is self-authenticating, and the result is perverse confusion. We are now in an era in which the counterfeit flourishes alongside the genuine and the spiritistic passes for the spiritual.

The second factor is modern man's uncertain view of death, dying and grief which is often reflected in a recourse to necromancy and Spiritualism. Bereaved relatives find themselves inconsolable through the loss of the one they love, and necromancy provides a short-cut solution to this grief. During World War I a famous example of this was Sir Arthur Conan Doyle (the creator of Sherlock Holmes) who became a spiritualist; in our own time we have the testimony of Bishop Pike.

What is the mediumistic gift? How does it become available? In general religious terms, it is obvious that certain individuals have a greater sensitivity to the spiritual or mystical due sometimes to their temperament, heredity or cultural background. In a more acute way, the same is true of mediumistic gifts. Some people have this gift as an inherited family sensibility, whether they are aware of it or not; others gain it by persistent mental training and practice, and still others stumble onto it by opening their minds until they find themselves in turn open to a greater mind. Many who take acid regularly or who practice yoga or Zen meditation have found they have opened their minds to blackness and spiritism, seeing themselves as mediums and describing themselves as possessed. This has happened to several people listening to a musical group like Quintessence, and it has happened at rock festivals such as Glastonbury. Several times when I have been lecturing recently on the occult, I have been intrigued to find among the questioners those who claimed to have discovered that they had this gift. Mostly they had been unaware of it until some medium had pointed it out, or else they had been led into it by a persistent series of psychic phenomena, such as déjà vu. Sometimes when I asked them to check their family histories, they wrote later to tell me they were surprised to find that, though their parents had kept this dark from them, their families had a long tradition of mediumistic abilities. Gerald Gardner wrote that his own witchcraft involvement was by this linear descent. Occultists approached him and said, "You belonged to us in the past. You are of the blood. Come back to where you belong."

Speaking once at Essex University, I saw sitting in the front row a strange-looking girl with an odd expression on her face. Remembering an incident the previous night when a radical had tried to disrupt the lecture, I spoke on but also prayed silently that she would create no trouble. She remained quiet the whole evening but came up as soon as it was finished with a very troubled look and asked me what spell I had cast to keep her quiet. She told me she was part of a spiritist circle in the South of England and that the spirits had ordered her to travel to Essex, where she had never been before, to disrupt a series of lectures beginning that week. The curious sequel to this was that when I arrived back in Switzerland someone else in the community, far from a fanciful visionary, asked me what had happened in the Essex lectures. Praying for them one morning, she had seen in a vision, as real as waking reality, the lecture hall and the strange girl about to disrupt the meeting. Having prayed for her, she was convinced that nothing had happened, but she wondered if it was just her imagination. The presence of a Christian praying in the power of the Holy Spirit is always enough to render the occult inoperable.

Kurt Koch tells the story of a German farmer's wife who had what she thought was a strong rheumatic pain.[18] To her surprise, she made the discovery one day that the pain would subside if she wrote whenever it came. So whenever the pain became unbearable, she would take a pen, sit down, begin to write and the pain would subside. Soon this developed into a real writing compulsion. Eventually she found herself writing beyond the experience of her own life and far deeper than the intellectual levels of her own mind. Finally, what she was writing became essentially religious; occasionally the name Felix would appear. Felix claimed to be a spirit and said that he wanted to use her as his prophetess. In this way the simple farmer's wife became a spirit medium.

For those of our generation who stumble on the spirit world accidentally, the two most common paths are LSD and misapplied meditation techniques. The last three years have seen a growing number who opened their minds by these means only to find themselves open to heady forces and vibrations beyond their control, until finally they developed mediumistic powers and knowledge rivaling the most practiced mediums. Sometimes to empty the consciousness of all content is to invite in seven devils from the unconscious. A student who had been heavily involved in this scene recently told me, "In the beginning we must be seduced to yield ourselves to it, but as our mutual familiarity increases, so does our psychological dependence. Our identity becomes increasingly the identity of the force we are dealing with. Our point of view becomes its point of view, and we are kept in line by threats of its leaving us if we fail to comply."

Of more casual significance but reflecting the same fascination is the perennial popularity of such television programs as *Bewitched* or *Dark Shadows,* or the fact that a magazine like *Man, Myth, and Magic* sold over a million copies in its first edition. This involvement should not be ignored as being limited to a general superstitious public or to a few young people with insatiable if odd curiosity. Karl Jaspers, reflecting on a time of almost self-induced illness when "the personal self had grown porous because of my dimmed consciousness" wrote, "I had forced untimely access to the 'source of life.' . . . I recognized too late that murky elements had taken a hand. I got to know them after they already had too much power. There was no way back. I now had the world of spirits I had wanted to see. The demons came up from the abyss."[19] Probably Jaspers did not believe that these demons issued from the supernatural realm but from the morbid depths of his own psyche. In any case, his description, if heard by one who had experienced the reality of the occult, might easily be understood in a different way.

In a stimulating English interview with Lewis Freedman on film, the Swedish director Ingmar Bergman discussed the genesis and evolution of his philosophy as reflected in his films. He had always been fascinated by the function of demons and the voices inside, but in *The Hour of the Wolf* he tried to make them visible. Struggling over the writing of his script in the long northern Swedish night hours, he could not sleep for demons in the room. Suddenly he exclaimed, his voice cracking, "They were there! All of them. And I had difficulty to select them. They would come, all of them, about fifty or sixty of them. . . . I couldn't sleep there because they were there. . . . Yes, they wouldn't get out!" Once again, as with Jaspers, the demons pressed up from the abyss. It is hardly surprising today that so many are coming to know God out of a background of firsthand acquaintance with the reality of the occult. Philosophical arguments are unnecessary. *That* God is, is no problem. It is *Who* God is that is the crux of their conversion.

The highest form of spiritism is cultic Spiritualism. This was founded in 1848 by Margaret and Kate Fox, two sisters in New York state, following a bizarre series of psychic events in their own lives. It is not generally known that both sisters died of alcoholism but not before both had openly renounced their own Spiritualist cult. In 1888, Margaret Fox in the presence of her sister Kate said, "I am here tonight, as one of the founders of Spiritualism, to denounce it as absolute falsehood . . .

 the most wicked blasphemy the world has ever known."[20] Personally I wonder if the extreme bondage in which their alcoholism involved them was not what the occultists call the "devil's compensation." Despite this disavowal, the Spiritualist churches flourish today, scornful of all lower forms of spiritism and certainly in their practice both intellectually and ethically more lofty. They use songs, prayers and even sermons very similar to those of the Christian church. They even use the Bible, although they have changed references to "the dead" to "living spirits" and rule out the prohibitions against necromancy. Christ's resurrection is viewed as psychic and spiritual, not physical, while Christ is not so much God incarnate as a super medium.

Hardly distinguishable from this is the later theology of Bishop Pike, whose story dramatically highlights the dilemma of the liberal theologian involved with the occult. Bishop Pike once said that after leaving Union Seminary his view of the Bible was no better than "a handful of pebbles." Through Higher Criticism any rational content as a basis for his faith had been so stripped away that biblical revelation was no longer normative. After his son's tragic suicide in New York, Bishop Pike went to Cambridge, England, where there occurred a series of curious phenomena involving post cards, the hands of a clock, the fringes of his secretary's hair and cuts under her fingernails. Through these incidents he felt that his son, Jim, was attempting to get in touch with him. This led him to mediums and seances, even conducted publicly on televison, through which he claimed to be in contact with his son.

He spent his last years re-examining his entire theology, interpreting Christ's resurrection, for example, as a psychic phenomenon. His dilemma was the lack of critical norms to judge the phenomena he was experiencing. With his view of the Bible as a handful of pebbles, he somersaulted from critical disbelief in the supernatural to an uncritical acceptance of its validity solely on the basis of experience. Once he was asked if he had considered the possibility that he might be experiencing the world of evil spirits. The questioner then related some stories of spirit worship in China. Bishop Pike replied that the thought had crossed his mind but that it was too disturbing and had been buried. The manner of Bishop Pike's death was the final tragedy, for he became lost in the wilderness both literally and metaphorically. To compound the tragedy, even the mediums failed to provide more than contradictory predictions as to where he was.

Satanism

The third and last general area is Satanism. Some reject even the talk of this as mere sensationalism and a love for the lurid, but this is precisely where a part of the counter culture is most heavily involved. Satanism should not be confused with witchcraft. The latter is almost as old as man, but the history of Satanism begins in France in the thirteenth century, where the Black Mass was devised as a parody of the Roman Catholic Mass. The Black Mass was a Requiem Mass for the living, its specific purpose being to cause harm and to propagate evil influence. Instead of bread and wine, a toad, a turnip or a filthy mixture of blood, urine and feces was used, being consecrated in the name of the victim.

In seventeenth-century France, Madame le Voisin was executed as an innovator of this rite. The alleged evidence against her included the sacrifice of babies and the blackmail of high court officials. Madame de Montespan, the mistress of Louis XIV, is said to have offered herself sexually as a living sacrifice to retain the king's love.

The eighteenth century witnessed a riot of such orgies with sacrifice, sex and extreme hedonism. The particular popularity of it focused on the Hell Fire Clubs located all over Europe, especially attracting aristocrats. One of the most celebrated of these was an infamous club at Medmenham Abbey in England; the so-called Medmenham Monks included many aristocrats, several earls and even the Chancellor of the Exchequer. Probably the most notorious was the Eagle Tavern in Dublin, a club which was used as a cover for several of the aristocratic English to scandalize the Irish poor and the Roman Catholic hierarchy. Some have claimed that cannibalism was among their rites. Fortunately such revolting abandon died out at the end of the eighteenth century, largely on account of the Evangelical Awakening and the subsequent profound change in the moral climate and social concern of Britain.

Surprisingly, it is in this area that we are seeing the resurgence today and, interestingly enough, it parallels the main divisions in modern theology. On the one hand are those who are virtually "conservatives"; they believe explicitly in the objective reality of a devil. On the other hand are the "liberals"; they have demythologized the devil and turned the whole "religion" into a semantic Satanism, a psychological reality with the connations of magic.

Notorious in itself and typical of others who have demythologized the devil is the Church of Satan in San Francisco. Founded by Anton Szandor LaVey, in April 1966, it now claims over 10,000 members. LaVey, a bizarre extrovert, published his Satanic Bible in 1968. He has also become famous for keeping a pet lion, for hosting a satanic wedding in 1967 and for claiming to have prayed down demons on Haight-Ashbury. Such sensational events attracted a huge press, who played up with lurid interest such ceremonies as a nude girl on an altar. Set among the attractive whitewashed San Francisco houses, the church is not difficult to find; it is a black house with black windows, black curtains and black cats playing on the steps. Inside are coffins, skeletons, stuffed owls, whips, a star of David and various ghoulish pictures and ritual instruments. When you enter, LaVey himself meets you, wearing a black cowl, a horned balaclava and a priest's huge ring. To his great delight he has been called America's "Black Pope," and, as he gives his weekly lectures, the listeners include many under thirty and several who have tasted and tried other cults and trends, and found satisfaction only in the Church of Satan.

It is the content of his belief that is most interesting. Satan, for LaVey, is only the symbol of man's natural and vital evil forces: "There is a demon inside man. It must be exercised, not exorcised." Selfishness is sacred. ("Have you seen the devil?" someone asked him. "Yes, every time I shave!") If the devil is demythologized, the only reality is in the ritual. "Yesterday's ritual is today's psychodrama." When the members enter the ritual chamber, the ceremonial psychodramas, which use the emotional involvement and symbolic magic words, recreate all the powerful effects of magic without affirming its true reality. The ritual chamber becomes an "intellectual decompression chamber." LaVey openly admits, "We hang our intellects at the door." The underlying similarity between this and much liberal theology in its approach to the creed or liturgy is striking. Asked about this, LaVey answered, "I admit this. The only difference between the liberals and ourselves is that we've been honest about what we've done." LaVey's cult has been described as Ayn Rand with black robes, or an illustration of Comte's theme that men freed of superstition must still have rituals.

The ceremonies practiced include the ritual of the Black Mass where a girl is the altar and many ancient rituals stretching back to the times of the Knights Templars in Malta. The fetishes destroyed are no longer Christian symbols which he considers outdated but marijuana flushed down the toilet, a picture of Timothy

 Leary hung upside down or an LSD cube crushed to pieces.

The other half of the movement, that portraying a true Satanism with belief in an objective devil, is the more sinister. It is represented by various Satan Churches and the Church of the Anti-Christ, now spread through different parts of Europe and the United States. Branches can be found in Rome, Paris, Geneva, London, New York and Los Angeles. This is the world suggested in *Rosemary's Baby,* described in Dennis Wheatley's novels (*The Satanist,* for example) and forecast in the dire predictions of Aldous Huxley in *Ape and Essence.* Few realize the terror and nausea that is characteristic of these circles. Any satisfaction or amusement that some apparently find from the widely spreading high-school Satan circles quickly evaporates upon close involvement. Often the devotees use a ruined or deserted church, sometimes an overgrown cemetery. Their ritual begins at eleven o'clock at night, aiming to finish at twelve. Central to the ceremony is an altar with a black cloth, six black candles, a chalice and a crucifix turned upside down. The altar is a naked woman lying on a table and holding black candles in her hands. The priest consecrates the host on her bare stomach. The Black Mass is the Roman Catholic Mass repeated verbatim, with the word *Satan* substituted for *Christ.* The Roman Catholic host is often stolen from a real Mass in a handkerchief. The high point of the ritual comes when the priest has intercourse with the girl on the altar, an act often accompanied by crude sadism. Many such evenings end with drunken dancing, drug taking and a general sex orgy; often the next day there are found skinned cats, beheaded chickens or ritual bags containing drugs, potions, animal bones and occasionally human fingers. The latter is a grim reminder that Satanism is often related to other problems. It is a menace, as macabre and repulsive as any in the notorious past of the occult.

First, this sort of Satanism is often related to heroin. A tragically high proportion of those involved in the Satan groups are also junkies. Second, it is related to criminal practices; blackmail is the vicious means by which the group keeps a tight grip on all its initiates. Third, it is related to violence. Murder is made necessary because of the potential leakage of secret information or incriminating evidence and it is also justified for sacrifice. Generally the victim is only a chicken or a cat, but sometimes it is a human—a child, a tramp whom no one knows or a prostitute whom no one cares to report missing. One wonders how many of the grizzly, unsolved murders in recent years can be traced to such Satan groups. Evidence outside the scope of this book makes this a grim probability.

The case of Charles Manson and his Family needs no such discreet treatment because of its wide publicity. Ex-convict, self-styled prophet, calling himself God, Jesus and Satan, drawing around him his community which he called Satan's slaves or the Family, Manson has a mentality very close to the medieval "Man in Black" who reportedly ordered sacrificial killings and rewarded his followers with sex. In fact, the various influences behind him show the logical terminus of so many of the fringe trends of our generation. Lawlessness, the use of drugs, the Eastern notion that he was beyond good and evil, the involvement in Satanist worship—all were fatally combined in one single man and ripened under the Californian sun into the virulent horror which so shook society.

On a far less serious level, the high-school vogue, rock group names, album titles and song numbers express such ideas more superficially. One group calls itself the Black Sabbath, and the Rolling Stones entitled their album *Their Satanic Majesties* and named a song "Sympathy to the Devil." With some it is merely trendy, but others soon find themselves out of their depth.

Generally speaking, there are four ways of becoming involved in Satanism. The first is by heredity; it is passed on by families that practice these rituals. *Rosemary's Baby* describes this. Often it ends in death-bed tragedies if members of the family do not want to accept the gift passed down, for the person dying cannot rest until it is passed. This is called the diabolical succession. The second way is devil's subscription, the blood ritual counterpart to Christian baptism, whereby one sells his soul to the devil in a black magical baptism. The third way is by occult experiments. With the bookstores full of "how-to" books, such as *Guide to the Supernatural,* many are browsing in these, taking them home, trying their own experiments and finding themselves slowly submerging. The fourth way is occult transference, the black magical equivalent of the Christian "laying on of hands" in which the power is passed from one person to another.

The Christian and the Occult

The historic Christian position on the occult is clear, practical and courageous, but this cannot be said for the greater part of liberal theology, which is embarrassed by the resurgence of the occult and its bold claims for supernatural reality. It must either deny its liberalism or be pushed to an even further extreme of sceptical rationalism. I have often noted that when the existential reality of the demonic is most vividly evident, the people most visibly shaken are atheists. It is not just that their naturalistic system bursts at the seam, unable to explain the evidence; rather, they feel their inability to help those in trouble. It is almost a choice: Deny the phenomena or join the cult. Bishop Pike's career shows what it means to be impaled successively on both horns of the dilemma. The same sad comment could be leveled at much of the Christian church today, among both those who are theologically liberal and those who are ostensibly orthodox but for whom the reality has been lost in empty repetition of "rite words in rote order" as James Joyce described it. As Jesus said in a different context, their problem is that they know neither the Scripture nor the power of God.

First, the Bible emphatically affirms the reality of the occult world. The Christian description of the universe as abnormal applies not only to the seen world which has fallen but also to an unseen world in which there is a devil and evil spirits who in their own rebellion against God have an active influence in the world and affairs of men. The Apostle Paul wrote, "For our fight is not against human foes, but against cosmic powers, against the authorities and potentates of this dark world, against the superhuman forces of evil in the heavens."[21] Modern spiritism and Satanism (when they are not mere fraud and when they do not rely on purely psychological factors) actually tap and harness the forces of this occult world.

In the account of the temptation in Genesis 3, Eve is promised, "You will be like gods knowing both good and evil."[22] Satanism and black magic are the final antithesis to trust and obedience to God; they offer a knowledge and power which are superhuman, and therefore are ostensibly on a par with God but actually under the aegis and authority of the devil.

Intriguingly, parapsychology recognizes this double nature of magic with its desire for knowledge and hunger for power. It makes a basic distinction between Psi gamma phenomena (from the Greek word γιγνώσκω, "to know") and Psi kappa phenomena (from κινεῖν, "to move"). So the Bible clearly affirms the reality of the occult. As "occult" it is hidden and unseen but no less real than the world which we call natural because seen.

Second, it is equally plain that the Bible affirms that the reality of the occult does not give it legitimacy. The Old and New Testaments are united in rejecting it as wrong, although real. The Old Testament rejects the occult and calls for the clarity of community based on the character of God. Israel was called to be a national community with a difference, because they knew and worshipped a God whose character had a difference. Syncretism and synthesis, either with their neighbors or with trading merchants, were sternly forbidden. Any resort to occult practices, spiritism, fortunetelling, omens, talismans, diviners or magic was categorically differentiated from the freedom of open trust in God and emphatically denounced as a denial of God and a sign of social disintegration and degradation.[23] Fundamentally, involvement with the occult is an insult to God in the light of who he is. The Levitical law explicitly legislates, "Do not resort to ghosts or spirits . . . I am the Lord your God."[24] From this standpoint the occult is an offense against the first commandment. If God is God, he must be recognized as God and respected as God. Magic is not primarily a question of the reality of demons, but of the character of God.

The New Testament further develops this rejection of the occult. With the incarnation of Jesus Christ, power over the demonic forces is a keynote of the arrival of the new kingdom and an establishment of a new order. The kingdom of God is primarily one of restoration; the blind see, the lame walk, the lepers are cured, the deaf hear, the dead are raised, the poor hear good news declared to them, the shackles are removed and the prisoners are released. While much of the opposition to this new kingdom of Christ was human–priests, scribes, establishment and tradition–Jesus clearly saw that occult powers were behind this opposition, unmasked openly in the demoniacs, who represented society's fringe failures and the limitations of religious humanism.

Seeing these powers as the hub of his opposition, Jesus said, "If it is by the finger of God that I drive out the devils, then be sure the kingdom of God has already come upon you."[25] Looking towards future generations, Jesus predicted that his followers would, if they believed, perform greater signs than even he had.[26] Paul, anticipating the consummation of the kingdom, describes it as a time when all the occult forces will be disarmed by Christ and the earth will be seen to be God's.[27]

The call to Christians is twofold. Knowing the reality of these things within the context of the greater reality of God, we can have no time for the shallow, superficial stupidity of much modern occultism where it is hoax. But where it is real, it stands as a challenge to God's character and man's freedom, and it is time to demonstrate the greater power and genuine freedom that are ours in Christ.

As we face the reality of this, other features of biblical teaching sharpen critical discernment and clarify the Christian's superior power. First, the Bible teaches the double character of such power as a sign. The miraculous need not be divine; it can also be demonic. If Moses can demonstrate certain signs, so can the Egyptian conjurers.[28] In the New Testament the word *σημεῖον* or *sign* is used both of the divine miracles of Christ and of the demonic miracles predicted as a mark of the world's end times, when many counterfeit signs will be performed, testing the faith of genuine believers.[29] Jesus warns of false messiahs,[30] Paul soberly predicts the coming of a supremely lawless man,[31] John gives his apocalyptic vision of the Great Beast, of occult forces and of false prophets—all these underline the double character of power as a sign.[32] Reality is not to be mistaken for legitimacy. In a day of contentless religious experiences, the appeal of powerful spiritual phenomena is far wider than their legitimacy.

Interestingly, the word used for sorcery predicted in this context in Revelation is the word *φαρμακεία*, from which we get our word *pharmacy* or *drugs.*[33] It is far from fanciful to interpret this as a prediction of the prevalence of drug-inspired sorcery at the end times. The apostle John warns in his letter that we must test the spirits to see whether or not they are truly from God.[34] In our day, when healing, fortunetelling and speaking in tongues are so in vogue, there must be neither naiveté nor total scepticism, but a critical discernment made possible within the Christian framework.

Such a discernment should lead to a wisdom of balance. The fact that there is genuine power does not mean that all power is genuine. Nor does the fact that there is false power mean that all power is false. He who most strongly exposes the counterfeit should most warmly appreciate the genuine and vice versa. For every counterfeit phenomenon under occult power, there is also a genuine counterpart under the Holy Spirit. Biblical prophecy often included extrasensory perception made possible by the Holy Spirit, whether rational or ecstatic. Biblical healing or exorcism is extrasensory influence made possible in the power of the Spirit. Angels in the Bible are spiritual beings, unseen and supernatural, but as real as the occult forces of evil.

The closely related questions of diagnosis and counseling are too detailed and complex for this general discussion. But with no hesitation, I will emphatically say that in Jesus Christ can be found complete liberation from any occult bondage. Christ does liberate, and when he does, the word *liberation* no longer seems empty religious rhetoric, for it points to a dynamic freedom of new life. This last sentence is not written lightly; it is based on the experience of people I personally know. Whether the bondage involved is dark, suicidal depression, severe alcoholic addiction or strange features like an inability to float in water, liberation in the name of Christ has brought unmistakable, decisive freedom for change and growth.

Paul, evoking the image of the Roman conqueror's triumphal procession, wrote of Jesus, "On that cross he discarded the cosmic powers and authorities, . . . he made a public spectacle of them and led them as captives in his triumphal procession."[35] The same power of Jesus Christ is still active and available today.

If we can see the encircling eyes threateningly pressing in around us, as the fires of Christian culture burn low, we can surely feel the tragedy of a generation which has set out on a road of shining idealism but still remains so far from its destination. The counter culture is still in the order of myth and the pathway to its present position is debris-strewn with broken and abandoned ideals. As the occult matures from a fad into a phenomenon, it too spirals downward towards the dark, the dangerous and the depressing. Combining with acid and rock music, it is withdrawing into itself, finding its only hope in an esoteric and apocalyptic rapture for the spaced-out elite. Audaciously counterfeiting Christian eschatology, much of the movement is becoming heavy with spiritual vibrations, experiencing latter-day rock festivals like Satanic Pentecosts and preparing the faithful to wait the final hope in the Starship ("People! Needed Now. Earth getting too thick. Move on out to the cool and the dark. . . . Embarkation date: Mill 4 [App. 1989-9] . . . Starship Foundation.")[36] Is this to be taken as serious or satirical? History will cast its own verdict, but the end of the spiral is a far cry from the rumbustious early Beats, the dedicated freedom riders, or the euphoric psychedelic rishis.

Seen in the mind's eye, our generation can be visualized as caught in a gigantic, unlit, circular enclosure. Around the dark frontiers pace the sentries—philosophers, poets, artists, thinkers, each grappling with the great unknown beyond, wrestling with the absurdities within, many of them counting their own lives as dice in the last throw of the game. Pressing after them are the young, the brave, the committed, the idealistic, fated either to take their place on the precarious, lonely frontier or to fall back frustrated and bewildered. Back in the middle live the great majority, self-sufficient and self-contained, afraid to follow the questioning line of their fears, unwilling to pursue the hard discipline of any alternative.

The question of this alternative is the subject of the next chapter.

9/The Ultimate Trip?

"In the end it is religion that constitutes the strength of this generation, and not, as I used to think, their morality, political will and common sense."
Paul Goodman

"Can man make gods for himself? They would be no gods!"
Jeremiah

"These which are given out as teachings are not. . . . They are illusions, fulfilments of the oldest, strongest and most urgent wishes of mankind."
Sigmund Freud

"Take away the life lie from the average man, and you take away his happiness."
Henrik Ibsen

"Man inhabits, for his own convenience, a homemade universe within the greater alien world of external matter and his own irrationality. Out of the illimitable blackness of that world the light of his customary thinking scoops, as it were, a little illuminated cave—a tunnel of brightness, in which, from the birth of consciousness to its death, he lives, moves, and has his being. . . . We ignore the outer darkness; or if we cannot ignore it, if it presses too insistently upon us, we disapprove of being afraid."
Aldous Huxley

"Much of what has happened in the past twenty or so years has challenged my basic beliefs, but I still adhere to them."
James Wechsler

"Now people are saying, let's hear the truth. We haven't heard it in a long, long time."
Jaime Robbie Robertson[1]

Is our age passing from civilization to barbarism? Civilization is all too fragile. Always the result of human consciousness and its confidence, it is never the product of its achievements, however glorious, or its institutions, however solid. The West today, its self-confidence sagging, its vitality ebbing, its order eroded, knows only introspection, lethargy, traditions. Prone from exhaustion, a prey to its own fears, it is in danger of being overwhelmed by the anxiety, apathy and anger of a humanity strangled within it. Thus it is vulnerable to the frustration and fury of those enraged by the betrayal of its meaning.

This is the West of our time. The loss of center can no longer be disguised. The infinite polarizations are only illustrative features of this disintegration. The striptease of humanism and the abortion of the counter culture should now be accepted as facts germane to any discussion of the future direction of our society. No new flights of romantic idealism must be allowed. Such solutions are extravagant and futile indulgences against the constant better judgments of history. A civilization which is collapsing can never be repaired in the abstract. But does this mean that Western man is doomed to a paralyzed contemplation of his dilemmas, caught between the Scylla of romantic optimism and the Charybdis of realistic pessimism? Is there no alternative to resigning ourselves with Theodore Roszak to the belief that, "if the resistance of the counter culture fails, I think there will be nothing in store for us but what anti-utopians like Huxley and Orwell have forecast"?[2] Is there no Third Way?

I believe there is, and I am writing with the intense conviction that this Third Way is to be found in the re-examination and rediscovery of the truth of historic Christianity—in a Reformation of its truth and in a Revival of its life, neither being valid or possible without the other, but both together opening the path to significant new premises that will reshape culture. This Third Way—this higher humanism—can be realized in a personal and communal relationship to the living God who is infinite and personal. To know him as Creator is significance, to know him in revelation is clarity of knowledge, to know him as personal is fulfillment, to know him in character is order and values, to know him in grace is freedom, love, joy, peace and adoration. But this is not the experience of modern man in his encounter with Christianity. The usual taste ranges from bland to bitter. Nor was it always mine. So now it is necessary to indicate what I mean and to clarify this unmistakably by indicating what I do not mean.

Much contemporary Christianity, having missed its way, has attempted to rediscover it in a flashy display of trendy relevance or to stop the clock and enjoy the frozen atmosphere of a more favorable historical climate. Either way, reality is increasingly submerged in ritual or relevance in rhetoric.

The Image of the Church

The sociological image of the church is the first barrier to serious attention. "Man enters a spiritual ice-age," diagnoses Arthur Koestler, "and the established churches can no longer provide more than Eskimo huts where their shivering flocks huddle." We are in fact swinging from the Arctic of atheism to a spiritual hothouse climate in which the exotic and the eccentric come into their own, but the general characterization still holds good. Some have observed that the reactions to the crisis of faith were different in Europe and the United States. When the crisis came in Europe and there was less to believe, people felt there was no point in going to church. Attendance dropped drastically, and the outlines of truly believing communities were more starkly delineated. But in the United States, when the crisis came and there was less to believe, churchgoing became all the easier and churches became community centers, part and parcel of the American way of living.

A catalogue of criticisms is lengthy and justifiable: the poverty of leadership (one pew often representing more faith than a host of pulpits); the vacuousness of public statements; the encroachment of technological streamlining spiritually camouflaged as stewardship campaigns; the undignified leapfrogging from inner city to suburbia, exposing the bourgeois nature of Christians; and so on. But all relate to unreality in language and life. Hypocrisy is the unfortunate product of hollowness, the vacant grin lingering after the cat has disappeared. The justifiable impatience of any perceptive atheist is caustically summarized in Adrian Mitchell's poem, "The Liberal Christ Gives an Interview":

I would have walked on the water
But I wasn't fully insured.
And the BMA sent a writ my way
With the very first leper I cured.

I would've turned the water into wine
But they weren't giving licenses.
And I would've died and been crucified
But like—you know how it is.

I would've preached a golden sermon,
But I didn't like the look of the Mount.
And I would've fed fifty thousand,
But the Press wasn't there to count.

And the business men in the temple
Had a team of coppers on the door.
And if I'd spent a year in the desert
I'd have lost my pension for sure.

I'm going to shave off my beard
And cut my hair,

Buy myself some bullet proof
Underwear
I'm the Liberal Christ
And I've got no blood to spare.[3]

If for many the sociological image of contemporary Christianity is tarnished, the intellectual status is even worse. Faith is considered emotional or psychological but rarely intelligible or credible, and hardly a question of truth. Cycling into Oxford, England, one morning, students noticed imposing posters urging them to join the Oxford Inter-Collegiate Christian Union. As they looked closer, the subscription price was listed—their intellectual integrity. In tiny letters came the publisher's name, the Humanist Association. That truth is merely relativistic, subjective, existential is the universal premise underlying modern man's examination of Christianity. "Feeling is the deeper source of religion," said William James. "We must . . . bid a definitive goodbye to dogmatic theology."[4] Freud's conclusion was no less forceful: "These, which are given out as teachings, are not . . . end results of thinking; they are illusions, fulfilments of the oldest, strongest, and most urgent wishes of mankind."[5] It appears, therefore, that Christians may be using theology as a metaphysical filibuster and that they are masking the emptiness of their faith by a skillful and acrobatic process of rationalizing, evading or dismissing genuine intellectual questions as if they were diversionary smoke screens for deeper moral problems. Describing the present situation R. D. Laing says, "Many people are prepared to have faith in the sense of scientifically indefensible belief in an untested hypothesis. Few have trust enough to test it. Many people make-believe what they experience."[6]

Such charges are often all too true. Modern Christianity has carelessly laid itself open so that its most vulnerable flank is exposed. If there are not sufficient grounds for its claims to truth, it is no more than another experiential option, a trip, not truth. Of these two crucial weaknesses, the intellectual is more serious than the sociological, for in fact it is the reason for the latter. Social obsolescence is the consequence of the failure to understand that particular shift in the concept of truth which is the hallmark of modern thinking. Unless this is remedied even the various attempts to brighten the image of the church will fail, and nothing will be left but trendy variations on the theme of relativism. This inability to come to grips with modern truth and give a reply that is specifically Christian and distinctively different can be seen at several places.

The Intellectual Stance of the Church

Liberal Protestant and progressive Roman Catholic theology is one part of the church that suffers from this deficiency of truth. Heavily stressing the leap of faith, decreeing a divorce between facts and faith, turning history into myth, removing all solid ground for reasonable belief, the liberals and progressives have reduced the credibility of faith to radical uncertainty. Whether it is Karl Barth with his distinction between the Bible as the Word of God and the Bible containing the Word of God; Rudolf Bultmann with his assertion that Easter faith is intact even if the bones of Christ are found in a grave today; or more recent theologians with similar theories—all have an insoluble problem of meaning. That is, under the close scrutiny of questions such as, "What do you mean?" or "What basis do you have for saying it?" their replies tend to tail off toward the vacuous, the trivial or the absurd. Meaning is no longer what God means about himself to man, but rather what man means as he searches for God and expresses himself in human terms. But such language is purely symbolic. Like an arrow it tries to puncture the ceiling of infinity beyond which God, if there is a God, is the unknowable other. Below the ceiling man may struggle, search and strive, but meaning is always beyond and man is left with what T. R. Miles has called "silence qualified by parables." This "radical uncertainty" is little different from open doubt, and such a cliff-hanging belief is brave only to the believer. Preferable by far is the cold-blooded realism of Freud, who commented on such unverifiable beliefs, "Just as they cannot be proved, so they cannot be refuted."[7] Liberalism can provide no firm answer to the question, How do we know? However sophisticated its semantics are, faith is always in danger of being eaten up by epistemological uncertainty or by relativism.

The second place where this deficiency of truth can be seen is in the extreme fundamentalism of the older variety. It is ironic that, although fundamentalists are implacably opposed to liberalism, their extreme reaction shows the same weakness. They too stress the leap of faith and make irrationality almost a principle, dismissing the serious questions of seeking modern men as intellectual smoke screens or diversions to conceal deeper personal problems. All this masks a desperate intellectual insecurity, barely disguised by the surrounding hedge of taboos to preserve purity. The strident intolerance of much guilt-driven evangelism betrays the same insecurity. In these circles, much that is taught has to be unlearned in the wider school of life, and it is not surprising that universities are littered with dropouts from such groups. Their non-rational, subjective faith is cruelly punctured by varsity-level questions, and many manage to survive only by resorting to a severely schizophrenic faith which they hold to be true religiously but not intellectually, historically or scientifically.

The reason for this is simple. Contemporary Christianity has consciously and subconsciously betrayed its basis of faith by failing to understand the shift in the concept of truth and by not replying with an eye to the basic premises of modern thought. For modern man to speak of absolutes in the area of morals, universals in the area of reason and objective truths in the area of theology or metaphysics is not just mistaken, it is meaningless. But if the swing from absolutes to relativism, from objectivity to subjectivity, from the universals to the existential is a hallmark of modern thinking, then both liberalism and fundamentalism have made equally mistaken though opposite reactions. Liberalism from the rise of Higher Criticism onwards has not understood Christianity on its own premises. Instead, its distinguishing feature has been the attempt to baptize biblical theology in whatever naturalistic secular philosophical presuppositions were current. No liberal theology is ever a New Theology. It is merely secular premises shifted to the religious dimension. This explains why new theologies become passé so quickly, for they have no life beyond the life span of their parent philosophy. Certain theologians could be aptly described as "theological fashion models." Usually to detect the Hegelian, existentialist or idealistic premises behind a particular new theology is to be able to predict its relevance and to plot its rise and fall. Whatever liberal theology appears to gain by its momentary up-to-dateness, it loses ultimately in its capitulation by compromise. By mixing biblical and secular premises, it can never be anything but irrational.

Extreme fundamentalism is equally irrational though for different reasons. Pride in purity of doctrine drives fundamentalists to scorn the very suggestion of compromise or capitulation, but the basic deficiency of truth is just as marked. Their mistake has been to fight the battle where it is no longer being fought, quixotically tilting at the windmills of yesterday. They ignore Martin Luther's reminder that to fight at any point except where the battle is currently raging is a waste of time. Not understanding the modern premises of relativism and its spread geographically, culturally and intellectually, extreme fundamentalism has found itself socially marooned. Cut off from the general culture and even from its own children, it is intellectually and socially isolated on a middle-class island of its own making. Failing to understand the difference between being dismissed as meaningless and being rejected as mistaken, their voice is strangely old-fashioned even when they speak out. They defend the Bible as the Word of God but fail to appreciate the sting of the liberal position that this is not so much mistaken because of details but meaningless because of premises. They point to the resurrection of Jesus as evidence for the truth of Christianity but fail to see that the dilemma of the existentialist is not whether the resurrection was history or not but whether if it occurred it was not just one more freak event in an irrational universe. Discussing the possibility of miracles with a consistent materialist, they fail to understand that the problem is not the amount of evidence but the prior theoretical commitments which veto the possibility of meaningfulness. This failure to understand not only results in a failure to communicate but stiffens into an intellectual stance that is at best nonrational and at worst incredible or absurd. Such faith is intellectually hemophiliac. One need only prick its finger in order for it to bleed to death.

This deficiency of truth is not limited to liberalism or extreme fundamentalism; it is also a running thread in more recent movements within the church. Certainly Christians need to express their unity and heal their divisions, but the tendency of ecumenism has been to stress unity at the expense of truth rather than unity on the basis of truth. Certainly Christians need a deep and genuine spiritual experience, but the tendency of the charismatic movement has been to stress experience at the expense of truth rather than experience within the framework of truth. The net effect of all these movements—liberalism, extreme fundamentalism, ecumenism and the new pentecostalism—whatever their positive values, has been to devalue truth, blur the uniqueness of the Christian faith and leave historic Christianity shorn of its greatest strength—its claim to be true.

The Jesus Revolution

At this point some may say, But what of the Jesus Revolution? Surely here is a movement qualified to stand spart from bourgeois Christianity, specifically biblical and anti-humanist and coming out of the heart of the counter culture. Such an estimate is typical of a widespread Christian appraisal of the movement so far, but in my view this is both uncritical and naive. Much of the Jesus Movement represents this same deficiency of truth, and its weakness may prove the most flamboyantly expensive so far.

First, it is important to see that the movement is in no sense a genuine Revival in anything approaching its entirety. Rather it is one portion of a considerably larger swing to a new religious era. Dostoevsky's prediction of moral permissiveness was given religious direction by G. K. Chesterton's dictum that when God is dead, people do not believe in nothing; they believe in anything. Both tie in with Oswald Spengler's vision of a generally fervid religiosity which would mark the decline and fall of the West. Atheism, with its termini in mechanistic science, rationalistic philosophy and technological objectivity is losing its ice-age grip, and the present thaw is seeing a spectacular resurgence of religious aspirations. *Time* which had presided over the announcement of the demise of God (cover, April 8, 1966) suddenly realized that God-is-dead theologians were only seismographs recording shock waves from earlier secular philosophy. Three and a half years later, switching to the cultural scene, *Time* found itself asking, "Is God coming back to life?" (cover, December 26,

 1969).

There is a religious renaissance, but it is dangerous to mistake this for Revival. Gary Snyder, Jack Kerouac and early Beat Zen showed the rumblings of this new religious soul. Long before the Jesus Movement it found substantial expression in the swing towards the East and later in the religious use of psychedelics and later still in the trend towards the occult. *Time* put the Jesus Movement in line with the great American revivals of George Whitefield and Jonathan Edwards, quoting a minister who describes it as "the most genuine revival of our lifetime."[8] This infatuated and uncritical enthusiasm illustrates an interesting feature of modern society. A decade ago the general complaint was that the older generation did not understand. Now they are pathetically desperate to understand and have exchanged an unthinking criticism for an uncritical naiveté. Bewildered by a rapidly changing society, excessively fearful of becoming out of date, the older generation is increasingly relying on young people and their trends to act as geiger counters against the perils of cultural obsolescence.

Of course it would be equally wrong to return to the unthinking criticism of earlier days. Too many critiques of the movement either prejudge the issue or make sweeping generalizations from limited data. Two examples of this are James Nolan's politically biased "Jesus Now: Hogwash and Holy Water" (*Ramparts*, August 1971) with its open anti-Christian hang-up, or Richard Gelwick's insidious unfounded insinuations that the Jesus Revolution is anti-Semitic (*The Christian Century*, May 10, 1972). Such articles are in the worst possible taste, and tell us more about the writers than the subject under review.

But it is true that if unqualified enthusiasm is curtailed by seeing the movement against its cultural background, it is dimished even further by a closer examination of the movement itself. Rather than an amorphous whole it could be classified in several categories. The first group comprises those with a genuine Christian faith, expressed in a fresh and free life style. Where they also attain a spiritual balance and an intellectual maturity, this is the Jesus Movement at its highest and most hopeful. Deeply based in its convictions, practicing a love stronger than slogans, fired by a powerful vision for society, their coffee houses, hot lines, drug centers and their "Christian houses" have provided hope for many, expressed socially and evangelistically. What it seems that preachers have only been talking about for years people are really experiencing, and the genuinely communal expression of Christian love speaks into the vacuum created by the failure of homes and churches.

A second group includes those who are perhaps sincere Christians but tend to be totally subjective in faith, separatist in their purity and unwise in their enthusiasm. Strangely they are lapsing into the very same mistakes which an older generation of Christians made and which served to turn off our own generation. Stressing the Bible, they isolate it from cultural relevance and call for withdrawal from society. Universities are evil, movies are worldly, short skirts are prohibited, books are proscribed, work is discouraged and sometimes a spirit of fanatical absolutism and complete dependency is fostered. With many a new extreme chiliasm is rearing its head, escapist as always in its tendency. They may well be sincere Christians, but they show an immaturity that cannot be explained by inexperience and a folly that cannot be excused by enthusiasm.

The third group is the most dubious of all. This comprises a wide range of people both Christians and others whose claim to be Christian time alone will clearly expose as spurious. For some, Jesus is simply a hero symbol, a fellow rebel in the common cause against existing systems. For some he is the ultimate trip, beyond marijuana and LSD, safe, satisfying and spiritual. For some he is the soul man. But in today's wildly indiscriminate climate, the spurious flourishes with the authoritarian, and the shallow with the heretical. Typical of the worst in this are elements of the Children of God, a highly authoritarian, exclusivist and judgmental sect with a heavy persecution complex. Beginning in Texas, they are now spreading all over the world. Initiates join the communes and submit to dictatorial control. They are forbidden to go home again, their mail is censored, their phone calls monitored, their privacy overruled and their possessions pooled. From their "outposts" they fan out in "prophet buses" under the direction of the secret-identity leaders and conduct a high-powered proselyting, with strong-arm corralling tactics of evangelism. The ugliness of their style, the stupidity of their simplistic literalism and the repugnance of their methods display their harshness. At least the SDS, Haight-Ashbury or the Rock Festivals took some dignified time to expose the logic of their folly. The lower end of the Jesus Movement represents almost instant folly.

At the opposite pole from this religious authoritarianism is the religious anarchy represented by the wandering bums and dropouts, thinly disguised as self-styled apostles and prophets—ego-trippers whose arsenal of styles includes the Jesus language. Another is the admixture of what in clearer times would be recognized as heretical, such as "The Way" in Ohio. Even the occultist group "The Process" has been mistaken for part of the Jesus Movement.

The movement as a whole presents three grave dangers. The first is confusion. Without a strong understanding of truth, there is a constant tendency towards contentless faith and counterfeit experience. The former makes for a weakness in faith and communication, while the latter means that the spurious will thrive with the genuine. There is, of course, much genuine spiritual experience in the movement, but there is also much that is simply psychological, and some that is demonic. This is true of healing, prophecy and speaking in tongues. Even that which is genuine is sometimes made an end in itself rather than being channeled into growing maturity or constructive public concern. If this contentless super-subjectivism or instant spirituality is allowed to continue, the chaos will soon be extreme. Those who once tripped on drugs and now trip on Jesus will find some new trip, and in the swing away not only will the spurious be discredited but the genuine as well. The whole movement could disband.

In many ways the present situation parallels the early enthusiasm stirred up by Jesus himself, but his reaction was quite different: "Many gave their allegiance to him when they saw the signs that he performed. But Jesus for his part would not trust himself to them. He knew men so well, all of them."[9] Avoiding the extremes of both cynicism and naiveté, he was not deceived by a passing trend. Instead, stressing content, challenge and cost, he divorced the genuine from the spurious and so found his true disciples. The test of truth, the challenge of content, is the crying need today.

The second danger is commercialism. Far too much of the Jesus Movement is unwitting faddism; the fate of the Beats, Hippies, Rock Festivals, and radicals should be clear warning. In this direction the Jesus shirts, bumper stickers, posters, watches, buttons, the endless slogans, the Jesus cheers and even Jesus jockey shorts and bikinis—all devalue the genuine reality of the inner meaning and debase it to the level of another California-born neophiliac fashion. Sadly the movement itself is not free of this shoddy hucksterism. Soon the real message will be rendered innocuous, and society will reach a saturation point. There are many signs that this is already happening. One is strongly tempted to sigh for the good old-fashioned days of clear, hard-headed atheism. God-words and Jesus-phrases are in vogue, but no words are emptier or more liable to misinterpretation.

The twin dangers of confusion and commercialism come together in the Broadway production of *Jesus Christ Superstar.* Speaking to audiences who know little of the Bible and less of history, it cashes in on the current spiritual fervor with its blend of skillful rock, abysmal theology and astute business acumen, spawning further confusion and making Christian symbolism the copyright property of grasping businessmen. Their exploitation of religion makes them twentieth-century counterparts of those whom the Jesus of history drove out of the temple in his moral outrage.

The third danger, more far-reaching than the Jesus Movement, is that religions are now open to control as tools of modern manipulation. This is a problem common to many religions outside Christianity, and within Christianity to all those movements which lack a clear statement of truth. Such religions can become so vacuous and meaningless that they leave themselves open to manipulation and become a source of potential danger. This needs considerably more elaboration. There is a growing recognition that the social values of religion are necessary. A nation with monolithic religious ideals is more easily governed, as G. B. Shaw recognized when he said, "Government is impossible without a religion."[10] Reviewing his career as an analyst, Carl Jung wrote, "Among all my patients in the second half of life,—that is to say, over thirty-five—there has not been one whose problem in the last resort was not that of finding a religious outlook on life. It is safe to say that every one of them fell ill because he had lost that which the living religions of every age have given to their followers and none of them has been really healed who did not regain his religious outlook."[11]

In many areas the religious resurgence coincides conveniently with the growing recognition of religion's sociological value, especially when there is no embarrassingly stubborn content and theology shrivels to "God is what you take seriously without any reservations" (Tillich).[12] The danger of this should be apparent to anyone sensitive to the warning bells heralding totalitarianism. Writing of the period of the decline of the Roman Empire, Edward Gibbon remarked that religions were commonly held by the people to be equally true, by the philosophers to be equally false and by the magistrates to be equally useful. This cynical triple-tiered toleration of religion was part of the cement of Roman totalitarianism. Few people realize that during the war Himmler was working furiously on the rudiments of a new Nazi religion, culled eclectically from the world's great religions of the past, but summed up in the person of Hitler himself. Some predict that within fifty years the USSR may also be using religious language, not with any belief that religions are true but simply as useful sociological cement. Consequently, while Julian Huxley could say, "Evolutionary man can no longer take refuge from his loneliness by creeping for shelter into the arms of a divinised father-figure,"[13] later humanists maintain that even though there is no God, man functions better on the basis that there is a God. So the belief or beliefs continue, but the spiritual introspection and preoccupation prevent anyone from seeing that religion is now only soma, a modern opiate for the people.

Christianity: Psychological Truth?

So far our analysis has been negative. We have only seen what true Christianity, the Third Way, is not. We must go one step further along this line and clearly illustrate that Christianity must not be mistaken for modern forms of religious or psychological truth. If I had stood in Cambridge in 1700 and said, "I believe in God," few people would have misunderstood what I meant. Whether or not they agreed with me that there was a personal God, most would have understood plainly that I was asserting faith in a God who was objectively there, as opposed to not being there. In other words, a discussion would have centered around whether or not I was mistaken. But if I stood in Cambridge today (and more particularly in Cambridge in the United States, in the William James Building) and was foolish enough to stop short after saying "I believe in God," people would not only disagree with what I was saying, but most would understand something very different from what I meant. I would still mean, "I believe in a God who is objectively there," but because of the relativistic grid of their premises most would hear me as saying, "I believe in a God whom I need as a father-figure or as a psychological crutch, that is, I believe in something only psychologically true for me."

Christianity, however, must not be mistaken for this modern form of psychological truth. In his short book, *The Future of an Illusion,* Sigmund Freud clearly stated that Christianity is only an illusion arising from the need of man who feels his helplessness against inner and outer forces. Man creates, Freud argued, the illusion of a father-figure as a shelter and comfort, either so that his civilization may have an answer to the questions of nature and fate or so that the individual may have an answer to the weakness of his civilization. For Freud there were no truth claims behind a religious doctrine: "Society is very well aware of the insecurity of the claim it makes on behalf of its religious doctrines."[14] This means that a courageous man should renounce religion, expose it as the collective neurosis it is, venture into "hostile life and strive for a new religion through science."[15] Yet, despite this critical view, Freud still admitted that religion is "perhaps the most important item in the psychical inventory of a civilisation."

Carl Jung is supposedly less openly opposed to religion than Freud, restricting himself to the phenomena of religion as distinguished from its metaphysics. In terms of particular religious beliefs like the resurrection, Jung would say that it is unimportant whether the resurrection is historically true or false because the resurrection in the psychology of the believer is all the truth that matters. "Psychology is only concerned with the fact that there is such an idea, but it is not concerned with the question whether such an idea is true or false in any other sense. It is psychologically true inasmuch as it exists. Psychological existence is subjective insofar as an idea occurs only in one individual but it is objective insofar as it is established by a society."[16]

This means that Jung, although apparently less opposed to religion than Freud, is in fact equally critical of the basis of Christianity, for Jung's "psychological truth" is little different from Freud's "illusion." The Jungian criterion for validity (or objectivity of truth) is social acceptance, and that, of course, is relative. It is not that Freud is opposed and that Jung is favorable, one dismissing it as an illusion and the other allowing it as a psychological truth, but that in neither case does psychoanalysis aim at anything more than the understanding of the psychological reality behind the thought systems. Both are close to Spinoza's statement: "What Paul says about Peter tells us more about Paul than about Peter." As Eric Fromm points out, for psychoanalysis, "the problem of religion is not the problem of God but the problem of man."[17] The residual result is the commonly accepted though erroneous conclusion that psychoanalysis denies the possibility of anything other than the psychological reality behind religious beliefs. This is the silent but mistaken premise behind much modern psychology. It is important to notice that Freud admitted he was not discussing truth claims of religions, only their psychic origins. He actually stated that the fact that an idea satisfies a wish does not necessarily mean that the idea is false. Eric Fromm explicitly admits this too: "The criterion of validity does not lie in the psychological analysis of motivation but in the examination of evidence for or against a hypothesis within the logical framework of the hypothesis."[18]

Here is the crux. Can the truth claims of historic Christianity be verified? Is there an answer to the failure of humanism? An alternative to the abortion of the counter culture? A solution to the cultural crisis of Western man? Or as O. H. Mowrer asks, "Has evangelical religion sold its birthright for a mess of psychological pottage?"[19] Is Christianity like other religions, neither true nor false but simply better or worse? In speaking of God, is there an alternative to the sheer silence of atheism or the mere symbolism of mysticism? Is there a God who is truly there, who speaks and who speaks clearly?

Can Christianity Be Verified?

This question of verification is doubly important. On the one hand, it is a natural question for any searcher and not just a necessary answer to the sceptic's taunt. Any believer desires cash value reality for his faith. No one likes to be short changed. Questions are not necessarily smoke screens for moral problems. Faith turns on whether these things are so or not. The believer must know not only what he believes but why he believes. The natural question has grown into an urgent question. At the very moment when we are recognizing the possibilities of manipulating a contentless religion, modern psychology and philosophy pronounce that this is all that Christianity is or ever can be. If so, Christianity too is an ideal element in the twenty-first century religious amalgam. Outside of its claim to be true, Christianity has neither answers nor integrity and no one should deceive himself by settling for less.

We must, therefore, answer the specific charges which

deny it, and then substantiate what we mean by truth and show the areas where these claims can be verified. The alternative is that as Christians we are merely "day-dream believers" or, as an acid head said to me, "If you can't stand by that truth, put LSD in the communion wine and join the rest of us on a trip!" It is not enough to look into the blackness of twentieth-century thinking and affirm faith as an answer; this too would be a leap of faith. Nor is it enough to look at modern presuppositions with their unhappy conclusions and then look at Christian ones and say we believe because they are different and better; the leap of faith encore! Christian presuppositions must not simply be different or even somewhat better. They must relate to the reality of what is in a way that can be seen to be true.

Two problems are raised by this challenge. First, is such a concept of objective truth meaningful in theory? Second, even if it is meaningful in theory, is such a concept verifiable? The issue of the meaningfulness of the Christian concept of truth leads us to a discussion of premises. The current veto on Christian faith stems from modern epistemology, whether reflected in psychology or philosophy, and the root is the premise of relativism. It is absurd for a finite man, beginning with himself as his reference point and refusing all outside revelation, to claim knowledge of anything approaching a universal, an absolute or an objective truth. Such a claim would not just be mistaken but meaningless. Properly speaking, all knowledge is only relatively true.

Let me illustrate this: Imagine that I am on the phone, speaking simultaneously to someone in the Sahara and someone in the Arctic. If my friend in the Sahara were to ask me, "What's the weather like in Switzerland?" and I replied, "The weather is warm," my statement would not be absolutely true. In relation to the Arctic it would be true, but in relation to the Sahara it would be false. In short, the statement would be only relatively true; it would need qualification. Because finite man starts from his own point in history and is limited by the understanding of his own mind and the scope of discovery of his own generation and tradition, any knowledge he gains of the universe beyond him can be only relatively true because he cannot relate his statement of truth to all the factors which he has not yet discovered.

All finite human knowledge is only a slice of the larger cake of discoverable truth. Such a philosophic quest is like the old story of blind men describing an elephant after feeling its various parts. Reliability is severely limited by relativity. Absolute truth is the monopoly of inifinite knowledge. This leaves man with the Herculean task of finding a universal which will give meaning to the particulars. The agony of his failure is writ large from Leonardo da Vinci to Jean Paul Sartre. But *if* God is there, and for the moment that is all I am saying (yet something hardly unexpected within the Christian premises), then he is a God, personal and infinite, who contains the knowledge of the whole world and not just one slice of the cake. If such a God speaks in self-disclosure that is both encounter and proposition, then because he is the infinite reference point, such revelation allows the possibility of "true" knowledge that can be accepted by man even if he does not have "exhaustive" knowledge. The meaningfulness is a question of the premises. To limit oneself to the premises of modern man is to court the despair of modern man, to choose despair not as a moment but as a way of life.

But it is not enough for Christian premises to be different or even meaningful. We must ask the second question, Are they verifiable? If they are not verifiable, faith is a presuppositional idealism, resting on a denial of history and floating in a fact-free vacuum. But there must be no divorce between premises and evidences.

Premises without evidences are unsupported; evidences without premises are insufficient.

Here we face the challenge of modern empiricism, rooted in the Renaissance dilemmas of knowledge and in the philosophical tradition of Locke, Berkeley and Hume, but developed expressly in logical positivism and linguistic analysis. Initially they challenged theology and verification. Based on the premise that the meaning of a statement is related to the method by which its truth can be tested by the senses, the sharpest formulation was the verification principle of A. J. Ayer: Only what can be empirically verified through the senses is to be accepted as true. All statements purporting to be true must be analyzed so that the false can be exposed.

There are three kinds of sentences. Analytical sentences are those in which the content of the sentence adds nothing not already implied in the original premises, e.g., "All men are mortal." If there is a man, he is mortal; the sentence simply analyzes what is already inherent in the idea of man. In this category are included logic, symbols and tautologies. The second category comprises synthetic statements, those which add something not already implied intrinsically and which therefore need to be tested in reality, e.g., "Some men are fat." While all men are mortal, some men are fat and some are thin, some have blue eyes and some have brown. Such sentences are not true by virtue of definition and so need to be tested by reference to the phenomenal world. Metaphysical sentences, the third category, neatly include all those that are not in either of the other two. Such sentences, neither analytical nor synthetic, are not open to testing and so are in the area of "non-sense." This for Ayer includes all ethics, metaphysics and theology.

Ayer's analysis descended like a guillotine on historic Christianity. Going beyond normal agnosticism and atheism, it completely dismisses the subject as meaningless. For Ayer, it is impossible for a sentence both to be significant and to be about God. More simply, the word *GOD* is now less significant than the word *dog.* The latter is verifiable. The former is not.

At first it seemed as if any objective basis for faith was undermined forever. Some positivists were embarrassed that history and science were also undermined, but most welcomed the principle as the most systematic annihilation of metaphysics. But a simple objection was quickly seen—the very principle itself is not open to verification. To accept as truth only that which can be tested by the senses is a statement which cannot itself be tested by the senses. It contains a whole nest of metaphysical assumptions. Properly speaking, Ayer should admit that his principle is only an empirical generalization and that his positivism can be established only on non-positivist grounds. The positivist has no right to say that his sense data are true data because he proceeds only by presupposing what is proper to his conclusions, which is just what he will not allow others to do. Paul Helm puts this delightfully, "The history of logical positivism can be read as the history of attempts to construct a net with meshes so sized and shaped as to allow through the most awkward scientific mackerel while catching the least metaphysical sprat."[20] Not surprisingly the positivist approach was later admitted by Ayer to be a "blind alley."

His argument is no more than a sophisticated philosophical version of the anti-theistic argument of Yuri Gagarin. Emblazoned on the walls of the anti-God museum in Leningrad are Gagarin's stirring words proclaimed upon re-entry from space, roughly translated: "I have been out in space and didn't see God; therefore there is no God." Such reasoning is foolish, but it illuminates an ancient insight: A viewpoint is important because it determines what one sees, not necessarily what there is to be seen.

Christianity and Falsification

This first challenge of theology and verification is now modified and refined to the challenge of theology and falsification. The weakness of the verification principle is its failure to understand that all "proof" is really the "openness to disproof." Without universals, which modern man correctly denies are possible on the basis of his premises, thought is shut up to the exploration of particulars. Universals alone could give absolute proof. If only particulars are available, what we call proof is really openness to disproof. So the challenge of falsification proceeded from the basic premise that the meaning of a statement is related to the possible denial of its negation. If anyone claims that a particular statement is true, the question then comes, What will he allow to stand against it as its disproof? What counterevidence can be brought to show whether or not it can be falsified, so that one may know whether the statement relates to the reality it purports to? The statement "It is raining" is clearly incompatible with the absence of falling water, but how are theological statements falsifiable? It is all very well to say that theological statements are different, but are they true? Or falsifiable? If so, where is the area of disproof? Do theological statements really refer to reality, or is theology just silence qualified by parables? (Or pious rhetoric, or just hot air?) If "It is raining" is incompatible with the absence of falling water, with what is "God is love" incompatible? I can make the statement, "The Bengali father loves his child" and it is easily open to disproof in the observable urgency (or lack of it) with which he searches for food or medicine. But if I say, "The heavenly father loves the Bengali child," what, as a Christian, do I allow to stand against it, so that my statement is not dismissed as vacuous "non-sense"?

At this point, the introduction of immortality (the claim that the falsification comes in an "after life") is irrelevant, for a concept such as immortality may be verifiable if it is true but it is not falsifiable if it is false. So the Christian wins both ways! If Gagarin's saying was an over-simplification of the first challenge, then the alleged reply of a United States astronaut is an over-simplification of the second: "I didn't see God either, but both of us would have if we'd stepped out of our space suits!" This is cheating, for while the statement may be verifiable if it is true, it is not falsifiable in this present life if it is false, and there is no way of collecting the bets! So unless Christians can answer the challenge of falsification, how can they avoid the suspicion that theological language is merely a refinement on "Keep smiling," the religious man's "having your cake and eating it" or a spiritual "double-think"?

The challenge is well distilled in Anthony Flew's and John Wisdom's classic parable of the invisible gardener:

> Once upon a time two explorers came upon a clearing in the jungle. In the clearing were growing many flowers and many weeds. One explorer says, "Some gardener must tend this plot." The other disagrees, "There is no gardener." So they pitch their tents and set a watch. No gardener is ever seen. "But perhaps he is an invisible gardener." So they set up a barbed-wire fence. They electrify it. They patrol with bloodhounds. (For they remember how H. G. Wells' *The Invisible Man* could be both smelt and touched though he could not be seen.) But no shrieks ever suggest that some intruder has received a shock. No movements of the wire ever betray an invisible climber. The bloodhounds never give cry. Yet still the Believer is not convinced. "But there is a gardener, invisible, intangible, insensible to electric shocks, a gardener who has no scent and makes no sound, a gardener who comes secretly to look after the garden which he loves." At last the Sceptic despairs, "But what

> remains of your original assertion? Just how does what you call an invisible, intangible, eternally elusive gardener differ from an imaginary gardener or even from no gardener at all?"[21]

Wisdom's point is that what starts as an assertion is thus reduced step by step to an altogether different status, to the expression of a picture preference. As Flew concludes, "A fine brash hypothesis may thus be killed by inches, the death by a thousand qualifications."[22] The same challenge has been applied to many areas of theology, including prayer and miracle, with the express aim of showing that what starts as a factual assertion is gradually reduced to a particular religious way of looking at things.

If this is so, once again Christian truth is devoid of meaning. The objection to this principle is not that it is faulty, like the verification principle, but that it is not operable in all areas. Falsifiability draws a line *within* meaningful language not *around* it. It is not a comprehensive criterion of meaning but a limited criterion of some meaning. To limit meaningfulness to empirical and analytic (and therefore falsifiable) statements is an insult to the rich complexity of the tool box of language. A living language has many types of statement—scientific, historical, moral, aesthetic, legal, sociological—and it is always a mistake to reduce statements of one sphere to statements of another sphere. The principle of falsifiability is thus valuable but strictly limited.

For example the principle of falsifiability cannot intrude into the area of subjectivity. As soon as an observer becomes observed, there is a shift from the subjective to the objective, so it would be impossible to put out an empirically observable, objective disproof on the subjective without killing it. On the surface, love and murder are incompatible, but the sentence "Othello loved Desdemona" is not incompatible with the sentence "Othello strangled Desdemona" because jealously is the subjective link between love and murder. The more inscrutable the motivation the less observable the falsification. The ambiguity of love is well expressed in Elizabeth Barrett Browning's love poem, "Proof and Disproof."[23] The subjectivity of human personality must always remain a partial mystery, beyond objective reductionist explanation.

To say this does not mean that objectivity and subjectivity are disjuncts. If they were, we would be caught again between positivist objectivism and irrational subjectivism. Human knowledge has both objectivity and subjectivity as its complementary poles. Thus the principle of falsification, though limited, is operable in some areas. Meaningfulness in language and trustworthiness in relationships are obviously not dependent on constant and complete openness to falsification or there would be reduced meaningfulness and no personal subjectivity. Yet meaning and trustworthiness are not unrelated to falsifiability in objective areas. If a man's character is consistent, and if in general his statements relate accurately to a reality that is observably falsifiable, then he may be considered trustworthy. In man's language and relations there are often times when a particular statement cannot be immediately falsified, and one is thrown back on the more basic grounds of knowing why the speaker is trustworthy. Seen with this necessary limitation, the principle of falsification and the view of reality which it implies are both welcomed by the Christian. If it is vital to guard the mystery of God's personality at some points, this is no more than one would ask for human personality, although on a higher scale because of God's infinity. But if, when God does speak, his words have no relation to external reality, we must dismiss them as psychological fabrication or nonsense.

Basil Mitchell's parable of the resistance fighter, written in reply to John Wisdom, opens an avenue of approach and leads into the vital question of where an adequate, durable faith can be truly grounded.

> In time of war in an occupied country, a member of the resistance meets one night a stranger who deeply impresses him. They spend that night together in conversation. The Stranger tells the partisan that he himself is on the side of the resistance—indeed that he is in command of it, and urges the partisan to have faith in him no matter what happens. The partisan is utterly convinced at that meeting of the Stranger's sincerity and constancy and undertakes to trust him.
>
> They never meet in conditions of intimacy again. But sometimes the Stranger is seen helping members of the resistance, and the partisan is grateful and says to his friends, "He is on our side." Sometimes he is seen in the uniform of the police handing over patriots to the occupying power. On these occasions his friends murmur against him: but the partisan still says, "He is on our side." He still believes that, in spite of appearances, the Stranger did not deceive him. Sometimes he asks the Stranger for help and receives it. He is then thankful. Sometimes he asks and does not receive it. Then he says, "The Stranger knows best."[24]

A Christian recognizes the problem of pain, for instance, as counting against a complacent belief in a good God, yet he will not allow it to count decisively against faith. This raises a question: At what point should he say, "The Stranger is not on our side" (which would be non-faith), or should he continue to say, "The Stranger has his own reasons which I don't know"? The latter is faith, but it need not be blind, for the length of time during which one maintains faith depends on his original estimate of the trustworthiness of the resistance leader and the character of later evidence.

The core concept of Mitchell's parable is highly suggestive in pinpointing the nature of Christian faith, although it can be interpreted in two ways, one of which is counterproductive. Many liberal theologians seem to suggest that the duration of maintaining faith depends on the depth of the initial encounter understood solely as experience. If the intellect cannot handle God, who is known only in encounter or crisis, then truth (i.e., grounds for trustworthiness) is totally subjective, outside the area of conceptual knowledge or verbalization. The depth of trust depends on the depth of the experience. The fallacy of this is plain. Even in human relations depth of trust does not depend on the depth of experience but on the character of the person with whom one has an experience. A faithful but frigid housewife is more "trustworthy" because of the nature of her character than the most passionate prostitute. If the grounds for faith are not partly falsifiable objectively but are only a subjective and transient experience, then we still have a faith indistinguishable from tripping and explicable as merely psychological. Moreover, in a day of spiritual counterfeit and confusion, there is no way to know whether what we are experiencing is God, an "angel of light," an acid trip or a theologian's hoax.

The second possible interpretation highlights the nature of faith as understood by historic Christianity. Seen this way the length of time during which one maintains faith depends on the trustworthiness of the character originally encountered. Even in the agony of his torment Job could say,

> But in my heart I know that my vindicator lives
> and that he will rise last to speak in court; and
> I shall discern my witness standing at my side
> and see my defending counsel even God himself.[25]

Even in his agony his faith was not totally blind but it was agonizing because the very presence of pain is ambiguous in the abnormal fallen world. His faith at that point was blind; he did not know "why." But his faith was not totally blind because he knew why he trusted the God who knew "why." The basic rationality of faith is at the initial point of faith. Is there sufficient evidence, open to falsifiable observation, which can give me strong grounds for believing that God is there and that he is who he says he is? Here is the heart of the question. Of course, many people become Christians for lesser reasons than the fact that they fully understand Christianity to be true. But it is vital for Christianity (if it is true) that, for whatever reason he becomes a Christian, a man can think it through afterwards to the point where he knows "why" he believes "what" he believes.

For the Christian the validity of the principle of falsification is welcomed as a genuine test of the integrity of faith and calls for an openness in every falsifiable area which can confirm or contradict God's basic trustworthiness.[26] As with the trustworthiness of human personality, what is at stake is the validity of God's revelation or self-disclosure. What God is exhaustively in himself is mystery. What he is towards us is his self-disclosure, and this must always be open to two questions: Is it consistent with itself? Does it square with falsifiable reality wherever it touches the phenomenal world of man, history and the space-time continuum? The Christian claims that wherever God's self-disclosure touches the world at these points, it is not only open to falsification but in fact is not falsified; rather it answers questions where no other revelation, hypothesis or guess can probe. This is not only the nature of the Christian's faith; it is the very reason why he came to believe.

God's Self-Disclosure

In parenthesis, we need to stress two points which should be obvious but if not well understood will once again weaken the Christian case. First, what is included in the idea of God's avowed revelation or self-disclosure? There are four parts to this.

The first two include God's self-disclosure in the external universe and in the personality of man. These together comprise a general revelation; they are pointers to God's existence and character, but lack clarity and sufficient definition. The last two include the Bible, seen as the Word of God, and Jesus Christ, the supreme revelation of God in human focus. These comprise special revelation and convey God's self-disclosure with clarity and sufficiency. Any failure to see all four of these areas as part of God's self-disclosure leads to one of two errors. A first mistake is the scholastic attempt, based on rationalistic premises, to argue the way to God intellectually, solely by the use of general revelation without special revelation. Such theistic proofs are failures in themselves. Even if successful, they do not point to the God of the Bible but to an abstract Aristotelian Prime Mover. The second and rather different error common to much evangelicalism has been to base the whole Christian truth claim in the area of special revelation, so that even when presented forcefully it is in a total intellectual and cultural vacuum for anyone not familiar with the Bible. A more adequate approach is to see that the four parts together–what God says in the world, in man, in the Bible and in Christ– are all aspects of his self-disclosure, of what he is "towards us." If Christianity is true, all of these must be falsifiable where they touch history, man and the space-time continuum.

The second question in parenthesis is this: What is implied when a Christian claims that his faith is true? This should need no elaboration at this stage, only the re-emphasis that the Bible implies a truth which is absolute and objective, in the sense that it is related to the final reality of what is. The simple phrase "telling the truth" implies that a description in words (semantic symbols) relates accurately to events. The truth told can easily be accepted as true, without necessarily being exhaustively true. Similarly, truth as implied by Christianity is not a mere symbol, nor a map, nor a picture preference which Freud could explain as an illusion or Huxley could commend as sociological cement. By contrast with other religious truth, Christianity must not be accepted because of any blind authority and certainly not because "the church says so." Technically Christianity is not even true because the Bible says so but rather because God who is the ultimate screen of truth has said so. God's ultimacy as "He Who Is" is clearly expressed to Moses in the revelation "I am who I am," implying that the final derivation and definition of meaning is what God means. This is apparently similar to but basically different from Eastern conceptions. An Indian guru, Ma Anandamayee, is believed by her many disciples to be an incarnation. When I asked her who she thought she was, her enigmatic reply was, "I am whoever you think I am."

These two parentheses should both heighten the clarity of the Christian claim to truth. Christianity asks for no special favors for a faith that is true and non-true at the same time. It stands or falls as true or false, open to falsification in the way that any scientific statement or philosophical problem is proved or disproved. The invitation to examine its trustworthiness could be illustrated like this: If you were to visit our community and had to follow a map which I had drawn up to describe the land between the Geneva airport and the little Alpine village in which I live, the truth of my map and my trustworthiness would be quickly discernible. If, as you went, you discovered that Lac Leman was on your left rather than your right and that Montreux came before Lausanne and not after, you would soon conclude that my map was not true to the reality of the Switzerland you found. The "truth" of the map would be erroneous and my trustworthiness would be at stake. Perhaps you might conclude that I was careless, malicious, ignorant or even drunk or stoned when I drew it, but, whatever the conclusion, the inaccuracy of the map would impair my trustworthiness. On the other hand, if the map was accurate (i.e., true) then my trustworthiness would be vindicated within the small limits of the significance of the test.

To put the challenge more strongly still, we could take two men, A and B, blindfold them and take them to a large gymnasium inside of which we had placed several high, hard hurdles in random positions all around the gym. We then ask each man to form a mental picture of the way he imagines the room has been laid out and to write down his projections. A simple test of "truth" of their projections would be to push them both into the room, still blindfolded, and ask them to run for ten minutes without hitting the hurdles. If by any chance A's picture exactly accorded with the reality of the room's layout, he could run blindfolded for hours without ever hitting a hurdle. But to the degree that, say, B's picture was faulty, he would be liable to bruise his shins! What we would be doing is pushing both to the logic of their prior projections of reality. That is, we would be verifying or falsifying their maps of reality.

If Christianity is true, it is not just a word game, a semantic system of religious symbols. It claims to speak of the reality of that which is, so much so that if any other faith, philosophy or psychology differs from Christianity, it does not simply differ from it in terms of words; it differs from the reality of what is as well. And to that degree it is liable at some point to falsify itself. This is the silent presupposition behind the public challenge of Elijah to the prophets of Baal. In a situation of potential paranoia, he never lifted his hands in holy horror, insecurely calling on the nation to return to God. Instead, believing that God was there, he presupposed that Baal was not there. The quickest disproof was to open Baal's prophets and predictions to falsification and so push them to the logic of their presuppositions. Carefully Elijah chose common ground between him and the other prophets—the common ground of prayer—and gave Baal the first chance. When Baal's ability to intervene had been openly falsified, he proceeded to show that God was there. The huge crowd, understanding the contest, fell on their knees saying, "The Lord is God, the Lord is God."[27]

This is not the place for a full examination of the significance of each of the four areas of revelation. What follows is only a sketchy outline. Nor am I attempting to spell out the full Christian truth-claims or the exact manner of their openness to falsification. Such a discussion might well be taken as an attempt to "prove" God's existence in the rationalistic sense. God's existence not only *cannot* be proved, it *should* not be attempted. God is not the final point of a ten-point proof but the one on whom all meaning rests. All I am pointing out is that to the man whose own premises (world view) have given no coherent meaning the Christian premises not only offer a basis for meaning but also offer falsifiable evidence to substantiate those premises. This openness-to-examination is the fundamental mentality of historic Christianity. I am only stressing this and indicating various avenues of approach. Certainly these go only so far in themselves, but the point is that even that distance is further and more clear than most today admit or realize is possible.

General Revelation: The World and Man

First, there is the broad area of general revelation beginning with God's self-disclosure in the external universe. The revelation content here is at its lowest and least certain, but it should not be ignored. Whether we like it or not, all of us live in the external universe, and at some point we must take it as real either for normal living or as the basis for scientific research. Few ask why this is or what is their own basis for treating it as such.

 The Christian view of the universe stresses two points of fundamental importance—its reality and its rationality, both stemming from who God is and the nature of his creative work. It would be wrong to imagine that only Christians have this view of the reality and rationality of the universe, but it is important to see that Christianity gives a basis for living in the universe in a way man needs in order to be meaningful. As mentioned earlier, many have explicitly related the rise of modern science to the Christian milieu. The reality and rationality of the universe allows for a uniformity of natural causes, as compared with random relativity. Interestingly, as the frontiers of modern science are being pushed back further and further from mechanistic science and closer to mysticism, many are moving towards a mystical view of God as an explanatory basis for their scientific procedures and discoveries. Towards the end of his life Einstein was reported to have said, "God does not ask me to play dice with the universe." He often compared the universe to a well-constructed word puzzle in which many possible words might theoretically fit but in actual fact only one does.

This is far from even hinting that Christianity is "proved" by modern science, for, as we have seen, this sort of proof is neither possible nor desirable from general revelation alone. But what we can see is that certain non-Christian views do not clear even this first hurdle, and many which do are strikingly deficient in any specific basis. Among those which fail are the Eastern view of maya and various bizarre Western views expressing a random relativity which makes for fine theory but uncomfortable living.

Even within the respectable citadels of Neo-Darwinism, there appears to be a growing cleavage. Some fasten on the *mechanism* of evolution with unrelenting toughness and Stoic resignation towards its cold reductionist end. Others from Darwin himself to Arthur

Koestler are in intellectual revolt against such implications too bleak to accept. Rebellion against the indifference of the cosmos is not uncommon during the later years of a man's life.

Darwin was troubled by a horrid doubt towards the end of his life: "Can the mind of man, descended as I believe from the lowest animal, be trusted when it draws such grand conclusions?" A loyal Darwinian, David Lack, expresses this well: "Darwin's 'horrid doubt' as to whether the convictions of man's evolved mind could be trusted applies as much to abstract truth as to ethics. . . . The armies of science are in danger of destroying their own base. For the scientist must be able to trust the conclusions of his own reasoning. Hence he cannot accept the theory that man's mind was evolved wholly by natural selection, if this means, as it would appear to do, that the conclusions of the mind depend ultimately on their survival value and not on their truth, thus making all scientific theories, including that of natural selection, untrustworthy." Many others who do not succumb to this "horrid doubt" smuggle in their own mystically affirmed meaning often by personifying nature.

The second area under general revelation is the personality of man. Again, what Christianity claims is true of man as revealed by God must be open to the possibility of falsification. No real science ignores the observer, but this is the Achilles' heel of many views of man, from naturalistic science to Eastern religions to various psychologies. We have already seen something of the inevitable failure of humanism, determinism and Hinduism and their final inability to explain man adequately. What is man to make of his own observation of himself expressed in his history, drama, poetry, love-making, war-making, cave paintings, funerary rites? Is the significance—freedom, love, individuality, personality—real or is it illusory? Can these all be explained as mechanistic? Is it all such a metaphysical hassle that dissolution of personality is the only solution? Serious attention to the Christian view shows its sensitive understanding of man's aspirations (by virtue of his creation in the image of God) balanced by a realistic recognition of his alienations. His sense of individuality, his striving for communication and love—all that it means to be personal—these areas are not explained by mechanistic conditioning nor are the aspirations fulfilled by humanism or the East. The constant challenge is: Which of these views of man best accords with the way man must live to be human?

Again I would stress that I am not saying that only Christians live like this, for this would be arrant nonsense as well as arrogance; but what I am saying is that if Christianity is true only Christians have a sufficient basis for living the way all men must live to be meaningful. Outside of this basis there is always a tension between the way a man must live to be meaningful as a man and the logic of his presuppositions, silent or explicit.

In his latest play *Jumpers* Tom Stoppard depicts this tension cleverly as he explores the central argument between, first, those who believe in absolute values and, second, those who are relativists in morals, utilitarians in politics, and atheists or at least agnostics. The moral of the play seems to be that the former are humane, and therefore human, in a way the latter are not. But as Professor Ayer points out in his intriguing review (a philosopher reviewing a philosophical play that pokes fun at philosophers), "Even logical positivists are capable of love."[28]

Exactly. No one would suggest otherwise. All men *as men* are capable of love. But on what basis? Certainly not that of logical positivism. Perhaps Professor Ayer is a *Jumper* twice over—once by virtue of his philosophical gymnastics, as Stoppard shows, a second time by virtue of this particular leap of faith—as he affirms the possibility of love without any basis.

For Ingmar Bergman this tension is often the creative source of his artistic vitality. In many of his films the absence of God is more real than the presence of men, but Bergman never faces the "danger point" in the logic of his premises. In *Winter Light* it is the despairing suicide of Jonas which is consistent but which is portrayed without compassion. By contrast Tomas the priest, though he doubts, is unable to tear himself away from the dead corpse of his faith. There is no reality left in his theology, but there is still ritual in his ministry and routine in his life. Similarly Bergman has admitted that only his life habits and familiar surroundings keep him from the brink of catastrophe. Artistically he may portray a world of alienation—silence, nameless diseases, incompetent doctors, undecipherable foreign words, fragile human relationships, hopeless metaphysical quests and black eight-legged spiders—but practically there is always the cushion of convention.

In the eighteenth century the French *philosophe* Diderot had cursed his own philosophy which mocked his aspirations of love and reduced love itself to a blind encounter of atoms. Writing to Sophie Volland, whom he loved, he raged, "I am furious in being entangled in a confounded philosophy which my mind cannot refrain from approving and my heart from denying."[29]

I have already mentioned the haiku poem by the Japanese poet Issa, "The world is dew, the world is dew, and yet, and yet."[30] The logic of Buddhism is summed up in the first three words while the logic of the man, the husband, the father, the personality is summed up in the words, "and yet, and yet." Between the two lies the great divide of modern man's thought. For many, to see this has been a moment of truth; it has led them on to ask afresh if what God claims to say about man accords with the way man is in reality.

This is no new argument. Basically it was the apologetic of the prophet Isaiah to his generation as he attacked them for their worship of idols. His disgust was not merely aesthetic or moral or even religious, centering on the nature of the idols as objects. His disgust was also human. Their tragedy and foolishness was that they themselves as humans were not even fulfillable on the basis of their own integration point. Their alienation was self-chosen; their aspirations were higher than the idols they worshipped. Paul's argument on the Areopagus in Athens was in a similar tenor, and this is a necessary charge today: Twentieth-century man is not fulfillable on the basis of his own views of himself.[31] For many sensitive modern men, to live out the logic of their presuppositions is to accept alienation as a way of life.

Special Revelation: Christ and the Bible

If general revelation is open to falsification, so is special revelation. This needs specially to be stressed as both Jesus Christ and the Bible are in danger of being turned into religious symbols beyond the need for verification, defended obscurely in circular reasoning. This is far from their own mentality and more a by-product of modern religious faith. While it is only the universal (God) which as a premise gives any meaning at all to the claims of the particular (Jesus), it is the particular (Jesus) which substantiates the universal (God).

Once more, space prevents a full treatment of the evidences of the truth-claims of Christianity as represented in the Bible and in the personality and life of Christ. All I can do here is to show briefly that modern "faith" is something externally imposed on the Bible; it has no part in the biblical mentality. If what the Bible says is true, it is open to scrutiny, to examination, to falsification; no one is asked to believe in it as anything other than credible.

Supremely this is so of the incarnation and the life of

Christ himself. No one is asked to believe in the gentle Jesus meek and mild of the Sunday school myth; or in Nietzsche's Christ with his strong "eternity corruption," oppressing the poor; or in "Jesus Christ Superstar" with his tortured doubts and personality problems. The falsification of such views is not that they are repugnant to Christianity but that they are not borne out by the objective evidence of the life of Christ. The essence of the incarnation is God becoming man, shattering the invisibility of Wisdom's gardener and opening himself to falsification on every level. Those who saw Jesus saw nothing but a man, five feet six inches or six feet or whatever height you like, but a man. In Jesus, God so became man that, after three years of living with Jesus—seeing him, hearing him, touching him, walking with him—the disciples were forced to fall at his feet and say, "My Lord and my God!"[32] Nor was this burst of faith irrational. Did not the converging web of prophecies tie in? Were they genuine fulfillment or were they rigged? Was Christ's life consistent with his claims for himself, or is there evidence of megalomania or fraud? Were his life, death and resurrection seen by reliable, original eye-witnesses, or were they later fabrications? In the area of his consistency Jesus said himself, "Which of you can prove me in the wrong?"[33] No one dared pick up the challenge. In the area of openness to falsification Jesus said to Thomas, "Reach your hand here and put it into my side."[34] The resurrection was not a mystical symbol like a Salvador Dali painting, but a historic event in the space-time continuum, presenting to the original eye-witnesses a type of evidence which would have satisfied A. J. Ayer in his most empirically skeptical mood. This was the Jesus of history, whose life and claims forced the conviction that he was God become man. In fact, it is the "other Christs" invented by the media and the artists that are highly selective and eventually only an imaginary reconstruction or half-truth. The radical

 Christ of Pasolini's film, *The Gospel according to St. Matthew,* the socialist Christ of much liberal activism, the Hindu Christ—these are not so much anti-Christian as unhistorical.

Openness to falsification is the general mentality of the whole Bible, though there are degrees of falsifiability. The writer of the Letter to the Hebrews says that the origins of the universe are beyond verification; it is only by faith that we can accept that God created, but this should surprise no one, and there should be equal humility from non-Christians in regarding evolution only as a hypothesis and not as a proven fact.[35] Obviously too, the evidence of the resurrection was open to firsthand falsification in its own time but to us the falsification is once removed, and involves the evidence for the reliability of the records. But this is a qualification common to all historical evidence. And one must remember that only within the premises which this evidence substantiates does any history finally have meaning.

This mentality can be seen throughout the whole Bible. When people came to Moses asking how they could distinguish between genuine and false prophecies, his reply was simple. "If you ask yourselves, 'How shall we recognize a word that the Lord has not uttered?', this is the answer: When the word spoken by the prophet in the name of the Lord is not fulfilled and does not come true, it is not a word spoken by the Lord."[36] The initial test of the genuine prophecy was that it would come true. Centuries later, Jeremiah expressed the same view: "If a prophet foretells prosperity, when his words come true it will be known that the Lord has sent him."[37] Moses added a further test to distinguish the legitimate successful prophecy from the illegitimate demonic success (Deut. 13:1-5) but the implied view of truth is the same. There is a correlation between truth and historical reality. This mentality is present in the New Testament also. Luke introduces his Gospel narrative as "authentic knowledge" of "events that have happened among us" witnessed "by the original eyewitnesses," and he claims to write as one "who has gone over the whole course of these events in detail."[38] In his preface to Acts, Luke speaks in similar vein of "ample proof."[39] Paul in his defense before King Agrippa turns to Festus and says, "What I am saying is sober truth. . . . I do not believe that he can be unaware of any of these facts for this has been no hole-and-corner business."[40] Later, writing to the church in Corinth, Paul says bluntly, "If Christ was not raised, then our Gospel is null and void, and so is your faith."[41] Such faith is worlds apart from the feeble faith of liberalism, and Paul would have nothing but scorn for a certain seminary in the United States where, it is said, only one professor believes in God and none believes in a historical resurrection. Peter, writing to new Christians who had not seen Jesus, assures them, "It was not on tales artfully spun that we relied when we told you of the power of our Lord Jesus Christ and his coming; we saw him with our own eyes."[42] Similarly, John writes, "We have heard it; we have seen it with our own eyes; we looked upon it, and felt it with out own hands; and it is of this we tell."[43] In the specific context of coming to faith, John writes at the end of his Gospel, "These are written that you may believe that Jesus is the Christ, the Son of God."[44]

The force of this is inescapable. Historic Christianity and biblical faith allow no discontinuity between facts and faith, between credence and credibility. Such faith must not be reduced to anything less than a full conviction of truth. It is not to be confused with a Byzantine symbol, an Eastern orthodox ikon, a Dali painting or modern psychological truth. If Jesus was a man, he sweated as we do. When he was crucified, the cross was real in the sense that you could run your hands along it and catch splinters. When he rose from the dead, if there had been alarm clocks, they would have been going off in the city at the same hour. This is the nature of the truth of which Christianity speaks.

The Logic of One's Choice

If this is so, two conclusions follow. First, a Christian can and must affirm the rationality of his faith. Faith is not rationalism, in the sense that it is reason alone finding God (for this is still positivism or humanism), yet it is rational in the sense that a searching mind can closely examine the claims of revelation and come to the conviction that they are the truth of what is. On the one hand, between the searching and the believing, there is no discontinuity of reason but rather a strong continuity so that faith is not irrational or non-rational; on the other hand, faith is more than rational in the sense that it is rational only to the limits of the validity of reason. Becoming a Christian is an authentic choice of a whole man; it involves his reason, his emotions and his will; it is in this sense that faith is more than rational. Furthermore, what an individual does in coming to believe is only his part of salvation. God counters this with forgiveness and his gift of the Holy Spirit; the Christian community marks it by a welcome to the fellowship. But the point is clear. Christian faith is not a leap in the dark, nor faith in faith nor faith in blind authority, and it is far from radical uncertainty. It is the firm conviction that the self-disclosure of God in Jesus Christ is the ultimate truth of what is. It is a reasonable decision after rational reflection.

Naturally this means that the Christian should be a man with an absolute integrity towards truth in every discipline. He will ignore no serious question, he will keep abreast of contemporary issues and face problems squarely, tackling some immediately and placing others in cold storage until he has the time and strength to wrestle them through. Seen one way this will mean that faith is eminently sane. Yet, being not only rational but personal, it will never be cold, dry and static but growing. A Christian will grow in relationship to God, his understanding of the Bible will deepen, his alienations will begin to heal, his personal aspirations will begin to be fulfilled, and his appreciation of nature and the universe will widen. A Christian must not succumb to the temptation of imagining that God is no more certain than his defense of God. This is only an inverted positivism given a subtle twist by the ego. The whole range of peace, joy, love, hope, forgiveness, wonder, adoration and bliss—part of the believer's subjective final verification—lies open to the Christian whose faith rests on God himself rather than on his own defense of God or even his own experience of God.

The second conclusion concerns a non-Christian considering faith. Christianity should not be accepted as another trip or psychological crutch. Its sole claim for consideration, its unique difference and supreme strength in the twentieth century, is its claim to be true. Nonetheless, anyone searching must decide on the basis of the facts available. The evidence for Christian truth is not exhaustive, but it is sufficient. Too often Christianity has not been tried and found wanting; it has been found demanding and not tried. The clarity and sufficiency of the Christian claims have objectivity but not neutrality. They compel choice. It is perfectly legitimate for a girl to ask many questions of someone who proposes to her; love may be blind, but certain questions are natural. Yet at some point she must make up her mind or she will be an old maid—men do not like to be still answering questions at the age of eighty-four!

In the same way there is often a watershed between sincere questions and diversionary questions. A man may ask too many questions of God. Too many think they have closed the discussion by saying they are atheists, but they fail to realize that this defines only that which they do not subscribe to. What do they subscribe to as a world view? The challenge of verification cuts two ways. Equally we might ask, what does the atheist allow to stand against his disbelief? What does the humanist allow to stand against his faith? Usually to turn the table like this,however gently, is to meet surprise or indignation and sometimes a series of evasions, death by a thousand qualifications once more!

More seriously still, the man who rejects Christianity should remember that he is not just rejecting a religious picture preference but the claim to be the truth of what is. If a genuine consideration and mature choice (as opposed to a shallow acquaintance or social prejudice) leave him convinced that this is not so, he should make doubly sure that his own premises do square with reality.

The dilemma of many men is illustrated by the story of the man taken to a psychiatrist by his friends because he claimed he was dead. By establishing the assertion that dead men do not bleed, the psychiatrist hoped to prove the unfortunate fallacy of his patient's notion, so he asked the man to read lengthy medical tomes and took him to autopsies for six months. Eventually, the patient was convinced intellectually that dead men do not bleed. Then the psychiatrist took the man's hand and with a sharp razor made a little cut in one finger. Blood appeared and the patient went ashen gray and exclaimed, "Good heavens! Dead men bleed after all!"

It is quite possible to have such a closed circuit of unsound presuppositions that wider reality is finally ignored and all experience must be pressed through this constricting circle of premises. Henrik Ibsen expressed this in his play, *The Wild Duck*: "Take away the life lie from the average man and you take away his happiness."[45] Aldous Huxley also recognized it as a common human necessity which all share but few admit: "Man inhabits, for his own convenience, a homemade universe within the greater alien world of external matter and his own irrationality. Out of the illimitable blackness of that world the light of his customary thinking scoops, as it were, a little illuminated cave—a tunnel of brightness, in which, from the birth of consciousness to its death, he lives, moves, and has his being. . . . We ignore the outer darkness; or if we cannot ignore it, if it presses too insistently upon us, we disapprove of being afraid."[46]

This is the same tension, with several variations, we have noticed all along between realistic pessimism and romantic optimism, between mysticism which achieves nothing and Marxism which achieves too much, between what a man says and who a man is. Perhaps man should cease to think, but then he would settle for an appalling complacency on the eve of global disaster. Yet if he thinks, he is drawn to the brink of intellectual and social dilemmas from which he cannot escape. So he creates his own faiths, dogmatic, non-verifiable and Freudian, and sticks to them doggedly despite all counter evidence. In a debate at Hunter College in the fifties, James Wechsler, then editor of *The New York Post,* announced, "Much of what has happened in the last twenty or so years has challenged my basic beliefs, but I still adhere to them."[47]

It was in this same context nearly twenty centuries ago that Paul of Tarsus charged the culture of his day with monumental folly—mistaking the fool*proof* in the sense of ignoring rules so plain as to defy misinterpretation, refusing to understand what they had no right to misunderstand. Looking at the men of his day in Athens, on Mars Hill, Paul charged that they were not fulfillable on the basis of their own views of themselves. This is in fact the most crucial challenge which historic Christianity throws into the cultural arena today.

In the erosion of Christian culture, post-Christian man has turned from the truth of God but still twists

10/The Third Race

"The Christians are distinguished from other men neither by country, nor language, nor the customs which they observe. For they neither inhabit cities of their own, nor employ a peculiar form of speech, nor lead a life which is marked out by any singularity. . . . They dwell in their own countries, but simply as sojourners. As citizens, they share in all things with others, and yet endure all things as if foreigners. Every foreign land is to them as their native country, and every land of their birth as a land of strangers. . . . They are in the flesh, but they do not live after the flesh. They pass their days on earth, but they are citizens of heaven. They obey the prescribed laws, and at the same time surpass the laws by their lives. They love all men, and are persecuted by all. . . . They are poor, yet make many rich. . . . To sum up all in one word—what the soul is in the body, that are Christians in the world."
Letter to Diognetes, c. A.D. 150

"My previous discussions did not take proper account of that whole aspect of Christianity which is uncompromising, ornery, militant, rigorous, imperious and invincibly self-righteous."
Alan Watts

"The world expects of Christians that they will raise their voices so loudly and clearly and so formulate their protest that not even the simplest man can have the slightest doubt about what they are saying. Further, the world expects of Christians that they will eschew all fuzzy abstractions and plant themselves squarely in front of the bloody face of history. We stand in need of folk who have determined to speak directly and unmistakably and come what may, to stand by what they have said."
Albert Camus

"To shame what is strong, God has chosen what the world counts weakness. He has chosen things low and contemptible, mere nothings, to overthrow the existing order."
Paul of Tarsus[1]

Ours is supremely a generation of talkers and travelers. An epitaph for the counter culture might well read: When all is said and done, much more will have been said than done. It remains to be seen whether our generation has the discipline to match its vision and the courage to stand by its convictions. So far, with much protest betrayed by posturing, with radicalism tapering off into rhetoric, with force generated mostly by frustration, with dialectical somersaults alone disguising the logic of failure, there is little to show for a decade of activism but a series of sorry spirals that plunge from idealism to despair. This is hardly the making of a genuine counter culture.

Nor should we have any illusions that the Christian alternative will be easy. Christians, by virtue of the truth they hold, stand even more uncompromisingly against the cultural stream. But their stance in relation to the broader culture is not the immediate problem. The major problems are internal. The Christian community needs first to put its own house in order, to struggle to regain its integrity and clarity from its compromise with the present confusion. In the light of this task there are three possible reactions which we must avoid. They may look like plausible solutions, but each would lead only to an impasse similar to the one we already face.

What Not to Do

The first is to use an analysis such as the one in this book to bolster a critique of all that threatens to disrupt the status quo. This reaction, which lacks integrity and panders to lazy thinking, is not limited to politically conservative and Christian circles. It is certainly not my intention that this critique of the counter culture should be used as a "put down" in the name of maintaining any established position. The failures of the counter culture are stressed only so that they need not be made again; lessons are emphasized only to be learned. On no account must the Christian community return to the cultural captivity of the past two hundred years. It dare not continue under the intellectual and social domestication of Western society, where its spirituality is exorcised, its sensitivity blunted, its ethical authority muted and its anaemic lifelessness exposed. It cannot be content with a "simple" gospel comfortably divorced from social justice, or with a "social" gospel that dilutes the historic content of faith. It must recognize that any deficiency of truth—whether from unfortunate ignorance (extreme fundamentalism), misguided desires for relevance (liberalism), or a desirable motivation towards unity (ecumenism) or towards spirituality (neo-pentecostalism)—can only leave historic Christianity shorn of its strength and reduced to the status of a harmless folk myth. Only he may dare pronounce a damning critique of the counter culture who is prepared, so far as he is able, to follow the challenging imperative of God's call in the coming years.

A second mistake is equally disastrous. While many Christians managed unwittingly to postpone the disappearance of the Silent Generation and to preserve the climate of the fifties in the sixties, others were roused earlier by the radicals and played a prominent part in later protest. However, now that the counter culture is losing its momentum, it is many of these latter who are exhibiting a similar disarray, expressing the same frustration, demonstrating the same paralysis of initiative, following the same trends to escapist communes or to a spiritual Consciousness III. This is a sure sign that their radicalism was spurious. It had no specific Christian base, only an exchange of slogans, and thus it has become a hollow lingering echo of radical protest. Peer-persuasion is no part of the Christian's call. The day the radical falters is the day the Christian radical must demonstrate his staying power.

A third mistaken reaction is to create an illusion of

radicalism which is really only a new spiritual chic. Cashing in on the current religious vogue, majoring in the recent genius for pretending that rhetoric is reality, preoccupying itself with a proliferating Christian free press, there is a subtle danger of creating a new Christian subculture, long-haired instead of short, but equally narcissistic and self-contained. All these various reactions are blind alleys, and their pursuit will only perpetuate the church's cultural captivity.

The Third Race

What is needed is nothing short of Reformation and Revival, a rediscovery of the Truth of God by his people and a renewal of the Life of God within his people. This is our crying need individually and corporately, but both are the prerogative of God. A culture rivalling Rome for inhumanity, ahead of Assyria in catalogues of cruelty, surpassing Sodom and Gomorrah for its perversions, dare not plead for justice. That would mean only the silence of God, the judgment of being left to the consequences of our settled choice. The possibility or probability of Revival is beyond the scenarios of futurology, but it is exactly in these non-humanist hands that the future of Western civilization lies. If Reformation and Revival do not come, then the Christian community must assert its regained integrity and clarity in being a loyal Remnant. Whether as a spearhead in a new Reformation or as a Remnant in a post-Christian culture, no one should have any illusions about what will be involved. There is a tendency to idolize Revival, a tendency which is often symptomatic of the selfish desire for a short-cut return to the benefits and enjoyment of a Christian consensus. For the true Christian the Golden Age comes only when Christ returns; it is never to be identified with any of the great purple passages of Christian history, either past or future. Similarly, there is a tendency to romanticize persecution, forgetting that often it was only by God's mercy that persecution stopped short of genocide and so acted as catharsis and not extinction. But whether the call is to be a loyal Remnant or to witness a Revival and a Reformation, there must be a rigorous practice of Truth and Love.

Increasingly the lines of culture are being redrawn to resemble a situation strikingly similar to the one faced by the early church. On one side the early Christians faced the obvious threat of totalitarian Roman power, while on the other they faced the more insidious threat of gnosticism in all its amorphous, many-headed guises. If there is no Reformation, this could soon be the Western Christian's prospect again. It was exactly in this situation that the early Christians were first recognized as "the Third Race."[2] Used first as a taunt by Aristides, and taken up by Celsus, it was an insult which became an insight, an aspersion which was transposed into an aspiration. Across the recognized divisions of the first-century world they were a community which refused to be classified or categorized. Neither Romans nor Greeks nor Barbarians, neither Jews nor Gentiles, neither masters nor slaves, neither male nor female, neither rich nor poor, they were a healing community, they were one in Christ, they were a Third Race. All classification by nation, race, ideology, religion or class structure denoted a previous reality now transcended by Christian truth.

The early Christians were not revolutionary because they roused the slaves against their masters; this they never did. They were ultimately far more revolutionary, because in Christ they transcended the old distinctions altogether. To set slave against master would only have allied Christ to Spartacus, Marx and Mao. To transcend the very distinction is to make Christian freedom the true liberation. "There is no question here," wrote Paul, "of Greek and Jew, circumcised and uncircumcised, bar-

barian, Scythian, slave and freeman, but Christ is all, and is in all."[3]

Today it is this very difference which is at once the promise and the problem of Christianity, its offer of hope and its occasion for hurt. Alan Watts is not entirely wrong when he speaks of "that whole aspect of Christianity which is uncompromising, ornery, militant, rigorous" and then continues, "Only such a unique 'impossible' religion could be the catalyst for the remarkable developments of human consciousness and self-knowledge which distinguish Western culture since 1500."[4] It is this difference, the uniqueness of Christian truth, which makes a difference and this truth is the only hope for a Third Way.

How often in the contemporary discussion a sensitive modern man knows that he cannot accept either of the polarized alternatives offered to him! Left versus right, radical versus establishment, Marxist versus Anarchist, idealist versus pragmatist, practical revolution versus mystical revolution of consciousness, optimism with no basis versus realism verging on despair, activism versus escapism—all these are polarizations born of the loss of center, of the death of absolutes. In Christianity, however, there can be a Third Way, a true middle ground which has a basis, is never compromise and is far from silent.

This practice of Christian truth will have many consequences for Christians, both individually and corporately, ranging from an inevitable certainty of conviction to a sufficiently based and well-balanced spirituality. But I will mention only two prerequisites that are indispensable for the integrity of Christianity in the context of the declining Western culture. In neither case will I attempt to spell out detailed answers to specific problems; rather I will try to draw out some of the guiding principles presupposed by the practice of Christian truth.

The first prerequisite is that this concept of Christian truth be practiced in terms of constructive Christian radicalism. Martin Luther was once described as a man climbing the ancient steeple of a medieval cathedral; struggling up, tired and groping, he reached out his hand to steady himself, laid hold of a rope and was startled to hear above him the clanging of a bell. The radical is often the man who stumbles on truths so deep that the immediate implications are quite beyond his understanding but through his discovery they echo throughout the world. Such is a common experience of those who come to grips with the searching and surprising Word of God, whose timelessness suddenly relates to specific times. Certain implications of this must be thought through.

First, Christian truth gives legitimacy to the concept of constructive Christian radicalism. Few terms are so empty and abused today; misleading to some, unfamiliar to others. To avoid all misunderstanding let me stress at once that I am not using the term *Christian radicalism* in the sense of what is currently fashionable as either political radicalism (the extreme left wing) or theological radicalism (the God-is-dead theology). In the long run neither of these is genuinely radical nor constructive, and both, including the theological version, are specifically non-Christian. Sadly there are signs that a new wave of Christian radicalism, rightly breaking with the automatic equation of conservative theology and conservative politics, is becoming motivated as much by anti-establishment disaffiliation as by clear Christian principles.

Thus a definition is vitally necessary to avoid the pitfall of spiritual chic, making Christian radicalism into rhetoric again. Obviously as one thinks of change, there must be criteria for analysis, both to fault what is wrong and to redefine what is desired. Frequently Marcuse claims that empiricism is a philosophical truth which can only bolster the status quo, with its insistent stress on that which empirically is. By contrast, he claims that true revolution is possible only on the basis of dialectics which transcend the present reality to proclaim: "That which is, cannot be true." What he fails to see is that neither modern empiricism nor the dialectic is strong enough to give adequate criteria for radical critique and a basis for a genuine revolutionary alternative. Both have impressive strengths and critical weaknesses. The strength of idealism is its power to transcend present reality in the name of its transcendent truth and therefore to judge that which is wrong intellectually, socially or morally. The strength of empiricism, however, is its rigorous critique which exposes the vacuous claims of much unverifiable idealism, whether in shallow propaganda or serious ideology. Both also have their weaknesses. Empiricism without imagination tends towards the acceptance of that which is, the status quo, whereas the dialectic without any basis or definition tends towards mere ideology.

The necessary balance between the two is made possible in the practice of Christian truth. On the one hand, Christian truth is unashamedly transcendent, for there is always a dialectical tension between that which God made and meant the world to be and that which man has made and marred the world into being. Thus Christian truth transcends present reality in terms of its view of who man is, what morals are, what solutions are possible. Each is made possible in the transcendent truth of who God is. William Wilberforce found the eighteenth-century African enslaved by the British slave trade; a contemporary American Christian may find his fellow man dehumanized by a determinist framework in psychology, a depersonalizing technological environment or a dishonest manipulation by the media. In every case his basic reaction must be the same. What the

 Christian sees man to be and do by virtue of his being in a fallen world, he judges by the transcendent truth of who man was, is and could be by virtue of his being created in the image of God and his being offered renewal in Jesus Christ. Hence Christian truth is not one-dimensional. It stands against and above, judging the present situation in the name of God.

Isaiah, prophesying the Messianic liberation proclaims, "He shall not judge by what he sees nor decide by what he hears"[5] and continues to show that God's criteria are his own standards of justice and have no necessary relation to the empirical or sociological analyses of the day. Accordingly, Christian truth provides the strength of the dialectical, transcendent truth, but, unlike idealism, it has a falsifiable basis and clear definition and so should never become an ideology. Consequently it has the strength of the empirical, and its truth, although transcendent, can never become totally "other." Christians should, therefore, be constantly showing a substantial reality in their practice of truth.

The radical nature of Christianity's transcendent truth is also evident in the way in which Form is seen to be related to Freedom. Repeatedly we have seen the necessity for a balance of Form and Freedom. If Form dominates Freedom, society swings towards authoritarian control, but if Freedom dominates Form, society tends towards anarchic chaos. But how can human society maintain this necessary balance? For the Christian—with his concept of truth as the description of ultimate reality, "that which is" (whether who God is or who man is)—Freedom (either personal or social) will be possible only within the Form which God made man to enjoy and within the values by which he made man to live. Outside of this (and potentially in a fallen world we are all constantly outside of this) two results always occur. First, whenever Freedom is taken for granted, it hardens into a grating Form. Second, whenever all Form is rejected in the name of total Freedom, the situation generates an even uglier Form than the one earlier rejected.

Thus, the cycle of history, seen from the Christian point of view, constantly confronts men with false forms—tired traditions, constricting crusts that cover and conceal the original freedom they preserved. With the original freedom lost and the original form hardened beyond repair, the process is constantly recycled. In a fallen world there is no possibility of maintaining a true equilibrium between Form and Freedom; so man is faced with a constant cyclical clash of reaction and revolution. Seen this way, there are four agencies of change. The first is the radical whose role is not *to tear up by the roots* but *to cut through to the root* ("radix") of the situation and so expose the cancerous growth of false forms that have choked off the original truth. The second agent is the rebel who attacks the false forms. The third is the revolutionary who overturns the false forms. The last is the reformer who is entrusted with the task of producing a renewal of true Freedom within Form. Within the Christian framework this whole process is called Reformation and Revival—a renewed Freedom within a reconstructed Form.

In the present climate, it is the radical, the rebel and the revolutionary who are in vogue, partly because negation is much easier than affirmation and partly because modern man lacks an alternative basis which is a prerequisite to reformation. Unfortunately, today reform is relegated to being a kind of patchwork prevention prior to revolutionary crisis. But unless reform culminates in revolutionary change, the radical's role is totally negative and the goals of revolutionary change are betrayed. Nonetheless, within the Christian framework, the role of the constructive Christian radical is legitimate.

Second, the practice of Christian truth ought inevitably to lead to constructive radicalism. The crusty conventions of contemporary society, resisting the process of change and preventing the true fulfillment of man in society, are obvious. Change is inevitable, for history and humanity are mobile and dynamic. A static society is impossible. Thus any reactionary or conservative attempt to maintain the status quo is not only naive but dangerous, and in the long run counterproductive. The most foolish reaction to revolution is the attempt to stifle the forces behind it and thus succeed only in preserving the false forms that constrict freedom and demand change. With some form of change inevitable, it is tragic that much of the West generally and much of the Church particularly are the main reactionary forces in the world, attempting to prevent change both at home and in other parts of the world. A different cultural order is on the way. The only question is: Which way will the new order go? Defense of the traditions and conventions that linger from a long-eroded Christian culture will mean the identification of Christianity with these defunct institutions. Ultimately it will lead to the rejection of Christianity in the West. Moreover, if society is chafing at such forms and is pregnant with the natural course of change, the abortion of this change will lead to a frustrated violence brought on as much by those attempting to prevent change as by those seeking it. All this makes the practice of true Christian radicalism an absolute necessity.

The Logic of Christian Premises

Third, there is a close relationship between radicalism and the Christian concept of reality. If Christianity is true, its truth is, as we have seen, the truth of what is. Understood at this depth, Christian truth is the most radical thing in all the world, for it is the root definition of what ultimate reality, beneath all forms, traditions and conventions, truly is. Here lies the uniqueness of Christian radicalism: It is beaten out by the hammer of transcendent truth on the anvil of empirical reality. Such radicalism is the reverse side of apologetics, for, if apologetics pushes the non-Christian to the logic of his premises, radicalism pushes the Christian to the logic of *his* premises. The consequences are profound. The premise of both Christian apologetics and Christian radicalism is that Christian truth describes root reality so that any form, idea, ideology, custom or morality inconsistent with this must be challenged. It is plain that in a day of relativism, contemporary radicals suffer from value vertigo. Since they have no conception of absolutes or objective truth, they are condemned to cut through false forms only to expose a swamp of subjectivity. That is, they cut "through" false forms but never "to" any solid roots. By contrast the Christian community, when it is in living touch with the God of truth, is never other than contemporary. The moment it simply relies on its forms, it is overtaken. False radicalism is, of course, insufficient and must be exposed. Both the shallow radicalism so typical of many tea-cup causes within the church and the highest non-Christian radicalism lack a true radix; they can only perpetuate the old cycle. To the degree that any radicalism is off center in relation to the true form, it produces only a new but false form. To prevent being off center, the Christian radical will be a man of God and a man of God's Word. The Scripture will be his script of truth. What God says in the Bible will be both necessary and normative to him in all his thought and action. Without this, Christian radicalism will merely be the momentary avant garde, speciously modern, but eventually destructive, wielding a dangerous weapon that will rebound like a boomerang. A vital warning is necessary: Christian radicalism can only be practiced in the context of a personal relationship to God, who himself is the truth. While this truth may be spelled out at times in human, moral terms, such truth is only true because it is spoken by the God who is himself the truth. This means that no principle—even a high or a radical principle—must ever be elevated into being an absolute in itself. God's Being (and his expression of this in character) is the only absolute before which the Christian radical lives. Any attempt to elevate a relative principle, aim or situation to an absolute is highly dangerous. Theologically it is the creation of a new form of idolatry; politically it is the beginning of a new ideology. There are grave perils in the current tendency to make change, revolution or radicalism ends in themselves. It is not only naive (for the new can be worse than the old), it is dangerous (for it fosters ideologies that are totalitarian).

Radicalism and Creativity

Fourth, constructive Christian radicalism is closely related to human creativity. Is it only a coincidence that certain modern thinkers furthest from the reality of what is, in terms of the external universe and the humanness of man, eventually stifle their own creativity by their own views? Take, for example, Marcel Duchamps. He was decidedly radical in his iconoclastic aversion to empty traditions. But in his radical opposition to these he was pushed towards a nihilism that stifled his own creativity. This is a partial explanation of his later, more unproductive years. Radicalism "sans radix" is not conducive to creativity. But the very opposite is true for the Christian because his radicalism is intensely human and extremely close to basic concepts of human creativity.

Arthur Koestler has suggested that there are three types of human creativity. The first is the scientific discovery or the "AHA!" reaction; the second is artistic creativity or the "AH!" reaction; and the third is comic inventiveness or the "HA HA!" reaction.[6] Basic to each of these is the fact that human creativity is not creation *ex nihilo* but rather a discovery of the connection between things. Each proceeds by combining truths unrelated till then, or by seeing an analogy where no one had seen it before. Koestler points out that probably the writer of the Song of Solomon was the first man to see the Shulamite's neck as the tower of ivory, but his combination of symbols produced poetry. In the same way William Harvey was the first man to see the heart of a fish in terms of a mechanical pump, and his connection of ideas furthered science. Perhaps some cartoonist was the first one to see a man's nose in terms of a cucumber, but it was the collision of ideas which led to humor. The Christian concept of radicalism is very close to this. Cutting through to the root where God's truth shows the reality of what is, it is often the nature of this radicalism to bring together the inner coherence, connections and consistency of truth not seen by others because concealed by false forms. It is the release of this "new" truth which unleashes a fresh freedom that cracks the stale forms. Nonetheless, in the course of time the new freedom is also taken for granted and it hardens into a form which grates. As we look back in history, therefore, what was revolutionary in its own time appears familiar to us in the driver's mirror of hindsight.

This is true of many periods of intense intellectual, cultural and religious innovation. From the radicalism of Stephen in the New Testament to the Reformation wrestlings of Martin Luther to the social outrage of William Wilberforce in decadent eighteenth-century England, the highest examples of Christians in history have illustrated this call to a Christian radicalism. It is the duty of the modern Christian to examine the forms and order of contemporary society, to look at its government, law making, cities, education, entertainment, morals, values, propaganda, art and literature, and to examine these in the light of God's truth. Undoubtedly there will be implications which will ring out a bell that can never be silenced. Just as Luther pulled on his rope and was surprised to hear the bell pealing forth above him, so the full import cannot be spelled out at the moment of radical discovery. Some attempts to develop particular programs, parties and policies are actually premature attempts at such spelling out. What is called for on every level, however, is a total confrontation between Christian truth and the prevailing consensus.

The basic issue of humanness is a clear example. It is not the fact that other views are different that forces the Christian to take exception. It is rather that these other views fail to describe the reality of man and so dehumanize him in consequence. The concerned Christian cannot, for example, agree with the Eastern view of man, especially in light of the low value it places on human identity and individuality. He cannot accept determinism with its undermining of the basis for significance, sapping initiative, responsibility and guilt (both psychological and legal). He cannot allow the humanist to pass unchallenged, for his view fails to account for the aberrations in man. Man, by virtue of his fallen nature, needs checks and balances. When a man is guilty, he needs to be confronted with his guilt; when he is weak, he needs help; when he is in sorrow, he needs comfort. The list is endless, but in every encounter the Christian must not only be heard to say that man is made in the image of God, he must be seen to practice this truth.

The Christian community must affirm that human identity is valuable. It must affirm that human aspirations are valid and that a substantial fulfillment of them is possible. It must affirm that man's dilemmas are real and that a substantial resolution is possible. As they build homes, administer hospitals and run their businesses, Christians must struggle for human environments in cities and communities. In every area, from integrity in advertising to morality and justice in national defense, humanness in living must be demonstrated. The effects of this will be cultural, social, moral, political, educational and aesthetic; they will permeate the fabric of society at every level. If any new order is achieved, any "re-formation," then it will be important to recognize that these new forms are themselves not final and that, however closely they approximate Christian principles, they must not be absolutized.

Sometimes, as the Christian radical probes contemporary issues, his truths will force him to ask questions that are deeper and more searching than the particular current statement of the issue. Discussing abortion, he will grapple with the crucial question of when a fetus is human, but will also delve deeper to point out that the widespread demand for abortion today accurately mirrors the low view of life, love, relationships and sex. Discussing capital punishment, he will avoid the mistake of stressing only what the Bible teaches, at the expense of the reason why, so missing an essential point. The discussion of capital punishment in Genesis presupposes (and demands) a high view of man. Murder is the ultimate violence, because each human life is inviolable. In Genesis, capital punishment is the expression of a high view of man, not a mere sanction which by itself can compensate for the lack of such a view. Contemporary society, whatever its propaganda, has so cheap a view of man in practice that the retention or reintroduction of capital punishment acts only as a negative deterrent. Thus, neither the abolition nor the retention of capital punishment speaks to the heart of the dilemma. The basic problem is really one of humanness rather than of humaneness. In such situations, the radical nature of Christian truth may be even more profound than we realize.

It is as the Christian community understands and begins to practice this constructive Christian radicalism that it will gradually be seen for what it is–The Third Race. Renewal will shake off the dust of centuries; it will transcend the divisions of denominations; it will distinguish Christianity both from the establishment and from the revolutionaries; it will give strength to intellectual conviction and mature responsibility to social involvement.

Christian Compassion

The second prerequisite is that Christian truth be practiced with concerned Christian compassion. Without it, many could well suspect that what is being suggested is the ground plan for a new Crusade or worse, a new Inquisition. Nothing could more betray the very meaning of Christianity. God alone is the absolute. No principle dare be absolutized. If it is, it becomes totalitarian, and to get rid of it, men will overreact with force and we will have once again the ugly horror of violence. Christian truth must not be turned into a new fascist faith. Actually, any honest examination would quickly show that dogmatic fanaticism is more frequently a result of the insecurity of truth: He who has lost his aim must redouble his efforts! He who lacks certainty must shout louder!

By contrast, it is the very strength of Christianity that allows it to be gentle without being sentimental, tender without being trite, sacrificial without being melodramatic. Such compassion is not a front, nor a public relations exercise, but an expression of the heart of Christianity. But compassion too requires clear definition today, for its difficulty as an ideal as well as its relation to the vacuous modern absolute of love tends to leave it gasping for air in a heavily pragmatic climate. Eventually it becomes limp and lifeless, and connotes only watery sentimentality.

Two years ago, I had an opportunity to visit Iraq. I recall how, while walking from the ruins of ancient Babylon to the nearby remains of the alleged Tower of Babel, I was musing on the meaning of Babel. This was the city proto-typical of historical confusion. Suddenly I was struck by a billboard standing between Babylon and the ruins of Babel, its message aptly expressing the chaos of modern communication: *Coca Cola!* The "big" words like *God, freedom, love* and *man* mean whatever men make of them and the world is divided by their definitions. The only universal words in our time are the crass words like *Coca Cola.* Sadly, compassion too has fallen under the shadow of this cloud. So it is important to define *compassion* carefully.

True Understanding

The life of Jesus illustrates the three vital elements of compassion in action. The first element is true understanding. John noted that although many believed in Jesus, "Jesus for his part would not trust himself to them. He knew men so well, all of them, that he needed no evidence from others about a man, for he himself could tell what was in a man."[7] In human relationships, there are often two extremes. The first is naiveté, believing that all men will treat us well. The naive man tries to love all men and be open to all men but finds himself taken for granted, taken for a ride; therefore he swings to the opposite extreme of cynicism, suspecting low motives in the best of actions, wanting to control a relationship or not have it, speaking at people and not with them. But Jesus, who had a realistic understanding of who men are, was able to look the worst of human life in the face without shock or recoil and to touch men at their seamiest without any sense of having dirtied his fingers. And thus he was able to be open to men. The reference point for his trust was his Father, not men; yet, understanding perfectly who men were, he did not veer to the other extreme of cynicism. He remained open without being naive.

Compassion is born from true understanding. Matthew noted that Jesus had compassion on the crowds because "they were like sheep without a shepherd, harassed and helpless."[8] Jesus did not see these people as a priest or politician might have seen them, merely as sheep to be fleeced financially or penned into political folds. Rather he saw them as sheep without a shepherd and from that understanding was born his compassion. His was a compassion which respected the individuality of each sheep, for, as we learn elsewhere, if one sheep out of a hundred was missing, he would search for that one outsider.[9] And, while he spoke of insiders too in terms of sheep, he stressed his intimate knowledge of each: "My own sheep listen to my voice; I know them and they follow me."[10] Thus the metaphor of sheep does not reduce an individual to a member of a crowd or become a powerful image to press a political point. Rather, it depicts a genuine compassion based on a real understanding of men.

Of course, no Christian can understand men as Jesus did. Our knowledge is limited by finiteness and impaired by sin and a selfish perspective. But we do know something of who man is and what compassion means. Compassion means that we have two cross hairs in the sights of our understanding: the fact that man is a being created by God in the image of God and the fact that man is fallen and lives in a fallen world. Where the two lines cross is the center of the sphere of compassion. Without this dual conception there can be no compassion. Ignorance of either one of them is often behind the fear and prejudice which stifle compassion.

Once after I had spoken to a small group in a home and had stressed the need for compassionate understanding of those involved in the counter culture, a woman thumped on the table and exclaimed, "I will never have compassion on these people!" The reason was plain. Her right-wing stance and her instinctive reaction in terms of this political position meant that she had no real understanding which could lead to specific Christian compassion. For her the counter culture simply existed as a threat to the status quo, and she reacted with shock and distaste. To be effective, Christian compassion must be informed. A Christian must be a man of careful study, intelligent prayer, wide thinking and penetrating analysis. He must know the whys and the wherefores so that he will not react emotionally or defensively but with maturity. Such spiritual understanding is the first element of compassion.

Outrage

The second element of Christian compassion is outrage. If we see what is wrong as God sees it, we will feel about it as God feels. Two striking words used of Jesus are particularly relevant here. The first is the Greek word σπλαγχνίζομαι which is translated rather too weakly in English as *compassion.* This is not a classical word but its roots are in classical usage, where σπλάγχην describes those inner parts of man which are the seat of the deepest emotions. Thus the later word *to be moved with compassion* does not describe ordinary pity or *mere* compassion, but an emotion which moves a man to the very depths of his being.

In normal Greek usage another word—ἐλεέω (to show mercy)—was in popular currency, emphasizing either the high position from which someone showed mercy or the low plight of the man to whom mercy was shown. The word σπλαγχνίζομαι, on the other hand, cannot be understood apart from its root meaning derived from the classical Greek word for "guts" or the seat of the visceral emotions. It denotes a gut reaction, an intense visceral emotion, the deep feelings of man for man which clutch at the stomach, and it also suggests strong anger at the situation which has reduced the man to his present circumstances.

This word is used only by Jesus in his parables or of Jesus in the descriptions by his disciples. Jesus tells of a forgiving master who had *compassion* on the debtor who was unable to pay his debt, of the father of the prodigal son whose *compassion* made him run to welcome him home, of the Samaritan whose *compassion* made him go to the rescue of the wounded traveler on the Jericho road.[11] Describing Jesus the disciples record that he was *moved with compassion* when he saw the crowds as sheep without a shepherd or as hungry out in the desert.[12] Similarly, in relation to individuals, it is recorded that Jesus had *compassion* on the leper who came to him for healing, on the two blind men who cried out for mercy,[13] and on the bereaved widow at Nain whose son had just died.[14] In each case what is seen is a gut reaction, the deep feeling of Jesus for his fellow men as well as a controlled anger at the external forces which had trapped the individuals in their particular predicament.

A second striking word used to describe Jesus is the word *ἐμβριμάομαι* (deeply moved). John uses it twice in his account of Jesus at the tomb of Lazarus.[15] This deep emotion is usually interpreted in relation to the verse "Jesus wept." Certainly as he stands at his friend's grave with Lazarus' two mourning sisters, Mary and Martha, this is not unnatural. But the Greek word has a twist which the English unfortunately fails to convey. Weeping, or sorrow, does not exhaust what is meant by Jesus' being "deeply moved," for Jesus knew Lazarus would be alive and standing beside him in a matter of moments. Where is the sorrow in that? The Greek gives us a clue to what is really involved here, for the root meaning of *ἐμβριμάομαι* is to "snort in spirit." It was used by Aeschylus to describe the Greek stallions before battle, rearing up on their hind legs, pawing the air and snorting before they charged. Similarly, Jesus "snorted in spirit": He was moved deeply in the sense of a furious inner anger. Entering his Father's world as the Son of God, he found not order, beauty, harmony and fulfillment, but fractured disorder, raw ugliness, complete disarray—everywhere the abortion of God's original plan. Standing at the graveside, he came face to face with a death that symbolized and summarized the accumulation of evil, pain, sorrow, suffering, injustice, cruelty and despair. Thus while he was moved to tears for his friends in sorrow, he was also deeply moved by the outrageous abnormality of death.

Such examples are not only seen in the life of Jesus but are a recurring theme throughout the Bible. Young Moses was outraged as he "went out to his people and looked on their burdens, and he saw an Egyptian beating a Hebrew, one of his people."[16] His reaction was immature, for he took the law into his own hands. But his outrage was natural as he saw the injustice of the Hebrew's being beaten by an Egyptian slave driver. Later in Israel's history the newly elected King Saul heard of an atrocious insult and threat leveled against part of his kingdom. Recording what happened, the historian says, "The spirit of God came mightily upon Saul when he heard these words, and his anger was greatly kindled."[17] There is no mistaking the direct relationship between the inspiration of God's Spirit and the arousing of Saul's anger.

Later still in the time of the prophets, as Israel's national decadence brought in its wake virulent social injustice and inhumanity, the outrage of the prophets is searing: "Listen to this, you cows of Bashan . . . who oppress the poor and crush the destitute."[18] Amos was furious as he saw the poor sold for the price of a pair of shoes. Again, what is evident is the awesome dichotomy between what God made and meant man to be and what man had made and marred the situation into being. With the transcendence of the truth of God on the one hand and the reality of the fallen world on the other, genuine outrage is the legitimate response. Listen to Jesus, speaking about the commercial exploitation of the temple: "Scripture says, 'My house shall be a house of prayer'; but you have made it a robbers' cave."[19] The transcendent truth is the house of prayer it was meant to be and the reality is the robbers' cave it had become: The response is outrage. Listen also to Amos, gathering indignant fury from the same tension,

> Can horses gallop over rocks?
> Can the sea be ploughed with oxen?
> Yet you have turned into venom the process of law
> and justice itself into poison.[20]

Finally, we will note a passage in Isaiah, where outrage is specifically attributed to God himself. After a catalogue of immorality, injustice and violence Isaiah concludes, "The Lord saw, and in his eyes it was an evil thing, that there was no justice; he saw that there was no man to help and was outraged that no one intervened."[21] Genuine outrage is not just a permissible reaction to the hard-pressed Christian; God himself feels it. And so should the Christian in the presence of pain, cruelty, violence and injustice. God, who is the Father of Jesus Christ, is neither impersonal nor beyond good and evil. By the absolute immutability of his character he is implacably opposed to evil and outraged by it. So, for the Christian to live with moral neutrality is to betray his faith. Nor dare we content ourselves with stirring reminders of the heroes of yesterday. We must not simply think of men like Wilberforce and Shaftesbury, only to warm our hands over the fires of their memories, insulating ourselves against the bleak failure of inaction today. Sadly, outrage has become the monopoly of existentialism and the New Left, the one an authentic rage against metaphysical absurdity, the other an authentic radicalism confronting social injustice. Because it lacks this element of outrage, the modern church needs to be reminded that if her life and institutions are being strangled by a dying culture, then she is choking on the very truths which she has herself betrayed.

Identification

The third element of Christian compassion is identification. The Latin root for "compassion" is parallel to the Greek root for "sympathy"; both refer to deep fellow feelings "with" or "alongside" someone. Identification is at the heart of the incarnation. As God became Man in Jesus, he was no Whitehall or Pentagon chief, making quick flying inspections of the front line, but one who shared the foxholes, who knew the risks, who felt the enemy fire. No other God has wounds. It is because God identified so fully with us that we know him and can trust him. On the contrary, it was exactly because Moses failed to identify with the Hebrew that his early outrage was a failure. Arriving on the scene the day after his revolutionary act of liberation, he was rudely rebuffed by the very Hebrew he had come to help: "Who set you up?"[22] But forty years later, having chosen "rather to share ill-treatment with the people of God than to enjoy the fleeting pleasures of sin,"[23] he was able to identify with them, share their marches, their hunger, their fighting, their problems. His tempered courage and mature meekness signalled the greatness of his leadership. He was trusted because he identified with those he led.

Prophesying the coming of Christ, Isaiah even predicted that a strange mistake would be made about the Messiah. His generation would reckon him as a man punished by God because he had so identified himself with men that he actually bore "our griefs and carried our sorrows."[24] This identification is at its deepest and most mysterious in the cry of desolation from the cross: "My God, my God, why hast thou forsaken me?"[25]

 Much of this mystery is beyond understanding, but one thing it does mean is that at the supreme moment of his dying Jesus so identified himself with men and the depths of their predicament and agony that no man can now sink so low that God has not gone lower.

It is when Christians have at least partially entered into the profundity of identification that the Christian community has been at its most human and most sensitive and that its message has been most credible and compelling. When the young English missionary, Hudson Taylor, sailed to China in the nineteenth century, he found people wrestling with many problems—corruption, famine, education, medicine, opium. It was to the Chinese as whole men and not just as "souls" that his message came, and it was carried by a compassion that identified with their dress, habits, customs and culture to such a degree that he scandalized his Western friends. The same cannot be said of all missionary enterprise, for much of it comes embarrassingly close to a cultural imperialism of the worst sort. (West Africans studying in English universities speak scornfully of "Cadillac Christianity.")

The paternalism and hypocrisy of such cultural transplants is as hollow and suspect as much foreign aid. During the 1968 election, Richard Nixon stated during a political commercial in Ohio, "Let us remember, the main purpose of American foreign aid is not to help other nations but to help ourselves."[26] Christians who are unwilling to identify themselves with those they seek to help run the risk of similar suspicions and misinterpretations. From the revolutionary perspective of the Third World, Fanon comments, "We must put the D.D.T. which destroys parasites, the bearers of disease, on the same level as the Christian religion which wages war on embryonic heresies and instincts, and on evil as yet unborn. The recession of yellow fever and the advance of evangelization form part of the same balance-sheet. . . . The Church in the colonies is the white people's Church, the foreigner's Church. She does not call the native to God's ways, but to the ways of the white man, of the master, of the oppressor. And as we know, in this matter many are called but few are chosen."[27] And Gandhi once gently rebuked certain missionaries in Calcutta: "I miss receptiveness, humility, willingness on your part to identify yourselves with the masses of India."[28]

If there is understanding, if there is outrage, if there is identification, then Christian compassion fired by love can be forceful, practical and effective, and need not run through the fingers like watery sentiment. With this compassion Christians can live true to the calling of God and true also to the crying needs of modern man. The practice of truth and love in such constructive radicalism and such concerned compassion beggars description and its consequences defy the imagination. What is involved in the fullness of knowing God, a profound gratitude in knowing substantial healing and the deepening wonder at personal fulfillment. Even this in the area of personal significance is only the beginning; it is followed quickly by wider communal significance and eventually by even wider cultural consequences. Certainly not because of what they have, nor even because of what they do, but primarily because of who they are under God, the Christians in the world, by their life, their life styles, and their life-giving answers can become the Third Race.

Is It Possible?

As we draw to a close I might include a postscript, partly to round things off and partly to anticipate two natural reactions that are bound to follow. The first reaction will be from those who say, So what? Can anything really be done? I have often seen people deeply stirred by the terrible dilemmas of modern society and excited by the relevance of a related Christianity only to be paralyzed by the thought of their own next step or contribution. This malaise of immobility, this dearth of discipline is a blight upon our generation.

The practice of Christian truth means, among other things, the practice of individual significance, a tiny yet earthshaking concept that must be asserted against the tide of cultural influences. Modern determinism in its biological, psychological and historical forms saps the sense of identity. Dwarfed by the vast complexity of the universe, towered over by technology and its environment, men see themselves reduced to insignificance, and their initiative is drained. Beguiled by the East or lured into the self-containment of Consciousness III, men lose their sense of individuality. Inaction becomes elevated into a principle. The result is a generation suffering from cultural failure of nerve.

But if God is God and man is made in his image, then *each* man is significant. *Each* man's action can cause ripples that never cease. The Third Race is not a super race, a master race, an elite of the wise, the strong and the bold. Its heroes are not "great" men. They are ordinary *men* who do great things because they reckon on God's being with them. They have no time for the prevalent mentality of "All or Nothing!"—another variation on the romanticism-pessimism oscillation. Better the significant "Something" than the illusory "All" or the frustrated "Nothing." Such human significance is not easily measured. The odds were very much against David as he faced Goliath, but the difference between him and the rest of the Israeli army paralyzed on the sidelines was his affirmation of his significance under God. Theodore Roszak's estimate of the early Christians echoes the arrogant scorn of their Graeco-Roman contemporaries: "absolute nobodies, the very scum of the earth . . . a handful of scruffy malcontents."[29] But under God, it was such nobodies who were still there when the Roman Empire disintegrated. In the fourth century A.D., Athanasius stood against the world, but because of the lonely courage of his stand, the basic truths of who God is were preserved. Kenneth Clark reminds us that in the sixth century Western Christianity survived only by clinging precariously to places like Skellig Michael, a tiny pinnacle of rock eighteen miles from the Irish coast, rising 700 feet from the stormy sea, and was thus "saved by its craftsmen,"[30] an historical footnote that is encouraging to the vital new movement of craftsmanship within Christian circles.

Paul Goodman reminds us that the source of the sixteenth-century Reformation was the tiny University of Wittenberg which today would be considered an insignificant junior faculty, only fifteen years old, with a total complement of one hundred and whose professors' average age was only in the twenties.[31] Goodman's parallel is particularly telling. Unlike many, he compares the present situation not with the birth of the early church but with the situation in 1510 when Luther went to Rome on the eve of the Reformation. This was the period between the Renaissance and the Reformation when there was protest and re-evaluation everywhere. Renaissance humanism with all its brilliance had burst on the West, bringing with it not only the highest in art but also unrest, chaos, violence and disruption. It was into that situation that the Reformation came with an equal emphasis on the arts but also on order, freedom and a high value for man. The present erosion of the Christian culture means the removal of the last restraining influence of the Reformation. The striptease of humanism is simply the logic of the Renaissance held in check by the Reformation for four centuries but now exposed in all the extremes of its consequences. If the struggles of the last twenty-five years presuppose the tensions and questions of preceding centuries, it is little wonder that the counter culture is not equal to its task.

 Christianity proved itself a genuine counter culture once before. It is the hour for the Third Race once again.

The second reaction will be from those who will say, How come? All this is very well in theory, but how can it be translated into action? As Bertrand Russell remarked in one of his more tolerant moods, "The Christian principle, 'Love your enemies' is good. . . . There is nothing to be said against it except that it is too difficult for most of us to practise sincerely."[32] His emphasis was not strong enough. The Christian life is not just difficult for man; it is impossible. But it is exactly here that humanism leaves off and Christianity begins.

That is also why only this uniquely "impossible" faith—with a God who is, with an Incarnation that is earthy and historical, with a salvation that is at cross-purposes with human nature, with a Resurrection that blasts apart the finality of death—is able to provide an alternative to the sifting, settling dust of death and through a new birth open the way to new life.

References

chapter 1: the striptease of humanism

1/ Friedrich Wilhelm Nietzsche, *The Gay Science,* 125, in *The Portable Nietzsche* (New York: The Viking Press, 1954), p. 96; C. G. Jung, "Epilogue," *Modern Man in Search of a Soul* (New York: Routledge Books, 1933); Bertrand Russell, *Has Man a Future?* (Harmondsworth: Penguin Books, 1961), p. 110; Federico Fellini, *Fellini's Satyricon,* ed. Dario Zanelli, trans. Eugene Walters and John Matthews (New York: Ballantine Books, 1970), p. 269.

2/ Quoted in Kenneth Clark, *Civilisation* (London: John Murray Ltd., 1971), p. 104.

3/ Quoted in ibid., p. 101.

4/ Peter Gay, *The Enlightenment: An Interpretation* (New York: Alfred A. Knopf, Inc., 1966), p. 44.

5/ Ibid., p. 417.

6/ Michael Harrington, *The Accidental Century* (Harmondsworth: Penguin Books, 1967), p. 31.

7/ Gordon Childe, *Man Makes Himself* (New York: Mentor Books, 1951).

8/ Julian Huxley, ed., *The Humanist Frame* (London: George Allen and Unwin Ltd., 1961), p. 44.

9/ Ibid., p. 7.

10/ Algernon Charles Swinburne, "Hymn of Man."

11/ J. Huxley, p. 6.

12/ Ibid., p. 26.

13/ Harrington, p. 35.

14/ Heinrich Heine, quoted in Walter Kaufmann, *Nietzsche: Philosopher, Psychologist, Antichrist* (New York: Meridian Books, 1956), p. 375.

15/ Nietzsche, *The Will to Power,* 1-2, quoted in Kaufmann, p. 103.

16/ C. S. Lewis, *Christian Reflections* (London: Geoffrey Bles Ltd., 1967), p. 82.

17/ Frantz Fanon, *The Wretched of the Earth,* trans. Constance Farrington (Harmondsworth: Penguin Books, 1967), p. 251.

18/ Ibid., p. 21.

19/ Letter of Aldous Huxley to Sibylle Bedford quoted in *Time,* May 4, 1970.

20/ J. R. Platt, *The Step to Man* (New York: John Wiley & Sons Ltd., 1966), p. 196.

21/ Norman O. Brown, *Life Against Death* (London: Sphere Books Ltd., 1968), p. 267.

22/ See discussion in Nigel Calder, *Technopolis* (London: MacGibbon & Kee Ltd., 1969), pp. 98-99.

23/ Arnold Toynbee, "Changing Attitudes towards Death in the Modern Western World" in Arnold Toynbee and others, *Man's Concern with Death* (London: Hodder and Stoughton Ltd., 1968), p. 125.

24/ Arthur Koestler, *The Ghost in the Machine* (London: Hutchinson & Co. Ltd., 1967), p. 15.

25/ Viktor E. Frankl, "Reductionism and Nihilism" in *Beyond Reductionism,* ed. Arthur Koestler and J. R. Smythies (London: Hutchinson & Co. Ltd., 1969), p. 398.

26/ Mortimer J. Adler, *The Difference of Man and the Difference It Makes* (London: Holt, Rinehart & Winston Ltd., 1967).

27/ Quoted in T. M. Kitwood, *What Is Human?* (Downers Grove, Ill.: InterVarsity Press, 1970), p. 49.

28/ Nietzsche, *Ecce Homo,* IV, 1, as quoted in Kaufmann, pp. 83-84.

29/ Harrington, p. 26.

30/ Koestler, p. 313.

31/ Fanon, pp. 251-52.

32/ Harrington, p. 36.

33/ Sigmund Freud, *Civilization and Its Discontents,* Standard Works of Freud, 21 (London: The Hogarth Press Ltd., 1961), p. 91-92.

34/ Albert Camus, *The Rebel,* trans. Anthony Bower (Harmondsworth: Penguin Books, 1962), pp. 243-44.

35/ Nietzsche, *The Gay Science,* 125.

36/ Quoted in Gay, p. 65.

37/ Quoted in Kitwood, p. 54.

38/ Erich Heller, *The Disinherited Mind* (Harmondsworth: Penguin Books, 1961), p. 75.

39/ Nietzsche, *Thus Spake Zarathustra,* IV, 14, in *The Portable Nietzsche,* p. 409.
40/ Nietzsche, *Thus Spake Zarathustra,* I, 11, in *The Portable Nietzsche,* p. 160.
41/ Fyodor Dostoevsky, *The Possessed* (New York: Signet Classics, 1962), pp. 384-85.
42/ Camus, *The Rebel,* p. 199.
43/ Fyodor Dostoevsky, *The Brothers Karamazov* (Harmondsworth: Penguin Books, Inc., 1968), p. 733.
44/ Quoted in Camus, *The Rebel,* p. 58.
45/ Quoted in ibid., p. 62.
46/ Quoted in ibid.
47/ Quoted in ibid.
48/ Heller, p. 76.
49/ Nietzsche, *Zarathustra's Prologue,* 4, in *The Portable Nietzsche,* p. 126.
50/ Jean Paul Sartre, *Nausea* (Harmondsworth: Penguin Books, 1965), p. 191.
51/ Sartre, *Being and Nothingness,* trans. Hazel E. Barnes (London: Methuen, 1957), p. 566.
52/ Samuel Beckett, *Waiting for Godot* (London: Faber and Faber Ltd., 1956).
53/ Samuel Beckett, *Krapp's Last Tape* (New York: Grove Press, Inc., 1958).
54/ Yoko Ono, *Grapefruit* (London: Peter Owen Ltd., 1970).
55/ Paul Simon, *The Paul Simon Songbook,* C.B.S. 62579.
56/ Jean Luc Godard, *La Chinoise,* filmed 1967.
57/ Quoted in H. R. Rookmaaker, *Modern Art and the Death of a Culture* (Downers Grove, Ill.: InterVarsity Press, 1970), p. 174.
58/ Jacques Ellul, *The Technological Society,* trans. John Wilkinson (New York: Alfred A. Knopf, 1970), p. 321.
59/ Chores and Roy Medvedev, *A Question of Madness* (New York: Alfred A. Knopf, 1971).
60/ "Psychoadaptation, or How to Handle Dissenters," *Time,* September 27, 1971, p. 45.
61/ Ibid., p. 44.
62/ Quoted in Harrison Salisbury, "Introduction," *The Prison Diary of Ho Chi Minh* (New York: Bantam Books, 1971), p. ix.
63/ Fyodor Dostoevsky, *The Idiot* (New York: Bantam Books,

 1958), p. 71.

64/ Jerzy Grotowski, *Towards a Poor Theatre* (New York: Simon and Schuster, 1968), p. 123.

65/ Erich Fromm, *The Sane Society* (New York: Routledge Books, 1956).

66/ R. D. Laing, *The Politics of Experience* (Harmondsworth: Penguin Books, 1967), p. 24.

67/ Ibid., p. 24.

68/ David Cooper, ed., *The Dialectics of Liberation* (Harmondsworth: Penguin Books, 1968).

69/ Malcolm Muggeridge, *Tread Softly for You Tread on My Jokes* (Glasgow: William Collins Sons & Co. Ltd.), p. 28.

70/ Ibid., p. 29.

71/ Christopher Booker, *The Neophiliacs* (Glasgow: Fontana, 1970), p. 70.

72/ Ibid., p. 44.

73/ Ibid., p. 339.

74/ Ernst Fischer, *The Necessity of Art,* trans. Anna Bostock (Harmondsworth: Penguin Books, 1963).

75/ Lewis Feuer, "What Is Alienation? The Career of a Concept," *New Politics,* Spring 1962, pp. 116-34.

76/ Fischer, p. 80.

77/ Erich Fromm, *Marx's Concept of Man* (New York: Frederick Ungar Publishing Co., 1961).

78/ Hermann Dooyeweerd, *A New Critique of Theoretical Thought,* 4 vols. (Grand Rapids: The Presbyterian and Reformed Publishing Co., 1957); *The Twilight of Western Thought* (Nutley, N.J.: Craig Press, 1960).

79/ Francis A. Schaeffer, *The God Who Is There* (Downers Grove, Ill.: InterVarsity Press, 1968); *Escape from Reason* (Downers Grove, Ill.: InterVarsity Press, 1968).

80/ J. R. Rushdoony, "Preface," Dooyeweerd, *The Twilight of Western Thought,* p. 9.

81/ Camus, *The Rebel,* p. 16.

82/ Nietzsche in a letter to Gersdorff, November 7, 1970, quoted in Erich Heller, p. 70.

83/ Ibid., p. 181.

84/ Fromm, *Sane Society,* p. 360.

85/ Laing, *The Politics of Experience,* p. 118.

chapter 2: utopia or oblivion

1/ Clark, p. 345; Timothy Leary, *The Politics of Ecstasy* (New York: Paladin, 1970), p. 293; Teilhard de Chardin, *The Future of Man,* trans. Norman Denney (New York: Harper & Row, 1964), p. 151; Gordon Rattray Taylor, *The Biological Time Bomb* (London: Panther Books Ltd., 1969), p. 245; Joan Baez, "The Hitchhikers' Song," *Blessed are . . .* (New York: Vanguard Recording Society, Inc.), VSD-6570/1; Brown, p. 267; Bob Dylan, "Desolation Row," from *Highway 61 Revisited,* CBS, SBPG 62572.

2/ Bertrand de Jouvenel, *The Art of Conjecture* (London: Weidenfeld & Nicolson, 1967), pp. 18-19.

3/ Herman Kahn and Anthony J. Wiener, *The Year 2,000* (New York: MacMillan, 1967).

4/ Desmond King-Hele, *The End of the Twentieth Century?* (London: MacMillan, 1970), p. 11.

5/ Ibid., p. 1.

6/ Ibid.

7/ Ibid., p. 7.

8/ Alvin Toffler, *Future Shock* (New York: Random House, 1970), p. 15.

9/ Ibid., pp. 14-15.

10/ Ibid., p. 171.

11/ Gordon Rattray Taylor, *The Doomsday Book* (London: Thames and Hudson Ltd., 1970), p. 48.

12/ Calder, p. 241.

13/ See Calder, "Athanatical Riddles," *Technopolis,* p. 240.

14/ Toffler, p. 203.

15/ Aldous Huxley, *Brave New World* (New York: Vanguard Press, Inc., 1952), pp. 11-15.

16/ Toffler, p. 221.

17/ Ibid., p. 222.

18/ Marshall McLuhan in a discussion with Malcolm Muggeridge and Norman Mailer, *The Realist,* October, 1968.

19/ Paul Goodman, "The New Reformation," *The New York Times Magazine,* September 14, 1969, p. 33.

20/ Quoted in Victor Ferkiss, *Technological Man* (New York: Mentor Books, 1969), p. 80.

21/ See B. F. Skinner, *Beyond Freedom and Dignity* (New York: Alfred A. Knopf, 1971) and *Walden Two* (New York: MacMillan, 1962).

22/ Skinner, *Walden Two,* p. 288.
23/ Skinner, *Beyond Freedom and Dignity,* p. 200.
24/ Ibid., p. 215.
25/ Lewis Mumford, *The Story of Utopias* (New York: The Viking Press, Inc., 1962), pp. 4-5.
26/ Edwin Warner, "A Voyage to Utopia in the Year 1971," *Time,* January 18, 1971, p. 19.
27/ Richard R. Landers, *Man's Place in the Dybosphere* (Englewood Cliffs, N.J.: Prentice-Hall, Inc., 1966).
28/ Quoted in Ferkiss, p. 84.
29/ Quoted in ibid., p. 84.
30/ Quoted in ibid., p. 85.
31/ From a letter to Mme. Georges-Marie Haardt, quoted in Teilhard de Chardin, p. 7.
32/ Ibid., pp. 156-58.
33/ Ferkiss, p. 28.
34/ Ibid., p. 222.
35/ Ibid., pp. 173, 201-02.
36/ Ibid., p. 56.
37/ Toffler, p. 4.
38/ Carl G. Jung, *Memories, Dreams and Reflections* (Glasgow: Fontana Books, 1967), p. 263.
39/ Toffler, p. 3.
40/ Ibid., p. 430.
41/ Ibid., p. 285.
42/ Isaac Asimov, "The End," *Penthouse Magazine.*
43/ Bertrand Russell, *Nightmares of Eminent Persons* (Harmondsworth: Penguin Books, 1962).
44/ Teilhard de Chardin, p. 300.
45/ Brown, p. 267.
46/ Quoted in Calder, p. 60.
47/ King-Hele, p. 24.
48/ Paul R. Ehrlich, *The Population Bomb* (New York: Ballantine Books, Inc., 1968), p. 21.
49/ Quoted in Taylor, *The Biological Time Bomb,* p. 58.
50/ Quoted in Taylor, *The Doomsday Book,* p. 249.
51/ "Dying Oceans, Poisoned Seas," *Time,* November 8, 1971, pp. 74.
52/ Ibid., p. 76.
53/ Quoted in Taylor, *The Doomsday Book,* p. 118.

54/ "Dying Oceans, Poisoned Seas," p. 76.

55/ Quoted in Taylor, *The Biological Time Bomb,* p. 20.

56/ Calder, p. 92.

57/ Quoted in Toffler, p. 382.

58/ Taylor, *The Doomsday Book,* p. 279.

59/ Toffler, p. 25.

60/ Ellul, *The Technological Society,* p. 430.

61/ David Price of the U.S. Public Health Service speaking in 1959, quoted in Taylor, *The Doomsday Book,* p. 13.

62/ Ferkiss, p. 34.

63/ Quoted in Taylor, *The Doomsday Book,* p. 102.

64/ George Wald, "Generation in Search of a Future," excerpts, *The New Yorker,* March 22, 1969, pp. 29-31.

65/ S. G. F. Brandon, "Time and the Destiny of Man," *The Voices of Time,* ed. J. T. Fraser (London: Allen Lane The Penguin Press, 1968), p. 157.

66/ Taylor, *The Doomsday Book,* pp. 298-99.

67/ *Newsweek,* August 17, 1970, p. 9.

68/ Stephen Spender, *The Year of the Young Rebels* (New York: Random House, 1969), p. 179.

69/ Todd Gitlin, "The Politics and Vision of the New Left," *Radical Education Project,* mimeograph, San Francisco, pp. 2, 5.

70/ Included in Paul Jacobs and Saul Landau, *The New Radicals* (Harmondsworth: Penguin Books, 1967), p. 156.

71/ Joan Baez, "The Hitchhikers' Song."

72/ *Chicago III,* CBS, S66260 (United Kingdom, 1971).

73/ L. Clark Stevens, *EST: The Steersman Handbook: Charts of the Coming Decade of Conflicts* (Santa Barbara: Capricorn Press, 1970), p. 34.

74/ Ibid., p. 93.

75/ Ibid., p. 131.

76/ Koestler, *The Ghost in the Machine,* p. 339.

1/ Jack Kerouac, "Beatific," *Encounter,* August 1959; Leary, quoted in *The Marijuana Papers,* ed. David Solomon (London: Panther Books Ltd., 1969), p. 156; Theodore Roszak, *The Making of a Counter Culture* (New York: Anchor Books, 1969), p. xiii; John Lennon, quoted in "James Taylor: One Man's Family of Rock," *Time,* March 1, 1971, p. 45.

2/ Quoted in John Clellon Holmes, "Nothing More to Declare," *Listener,* June 27, 1968, p. 841.

3/ Norman Mailer, *The White Negro* (San Francisco: City Lights Books, Inc.).

4/ Kerouac, p. 60.

5/ Allen Ginsberg, *Village Voice Reader* (New York: Black Cat Books, 1963), p. 311.

6/ Quoted in Solomon, p. 429.

7/ Quoted in Jack Newfield, *A Prophetic Minority* (New York: Signet Books, 1967), p. 31.

8/ Jeff Nuttall, *Bomb Culture* (New York: Dell Books, 1968), p. 104.

9/ Kerouac, p. 57.

10/ Ibid., p. 58.

11/ C. W. Mills in *Anvil and Student Partisan,* Vol. 9, No. 1, 1958.

12/ Ibid.

13/ Quoted in Piet Thoenes, "The Provos of Holland," *Nation,* April 17, 1967, p. 494.

14/ Nuttall, p. 193.

15/ Allen Ginsberg in a speech at the Arlington St. Church, November 1966, quoted in *International Times* (London), January 1967.

16/ Allen Ginsberg in *Esquire,* July 1960, p. 87, quoted in Toffler, p. 274.

17/ Jacques Ellul, *Violence: Reflections from a Christian Perspective* (London: SCM, 1970), p. 120.

18/ *International Times* (London), June 2, 1967.

19/ Quoted in Newfield, p. 25.

20/ C. W. Mills, *Power, Politics and People* (London: Oxford University Press), p. 24.

21/ *New Left Review,* September-October, 1960.

22/ Quoted in Newfield, p. 47.

23/ Ibid., p. 48.
24/ Jacobs and Landau, p. 158.
25/ Quoted in "Portrait of a Young Radical," *Newsweek*, September 30, 1968, p. 66.
26/ Herbert Marcuse, *A Critique of Pure Tolerance* (London: Cape, 1969), p. 134.
27/ Quoted in Newfield, p. 19.
28/ In a speech by Carl Oglesby at the Washington Peace March, November 27, 1965.
29/ *Time,* February 22, 1971, p. 10.
30/ Quoted in Newfield, p. 157.
31/ *Time,* October 18, 1971, p. 51.
32/ Samuel McCracken, *Commentary,* October 1972, p. 61.
33/ Nuttall, p. 252.
34/ From a letter to *Modern Utopians,* quoted in *Whole Earth Catalog: An Evaluation and Access Device for What Is Worth Getting and Where and How to Get It,* ed. Stewart Brand, Inc. (Berkeley: Portola, 1970).
35/ Letter to *The Tribune* (London), August 28, 1961.
36/ "The Capital," *Time,* September 28, 1970, p. 9.
37/ Peter Buckman, *The Limits of Protest* (Panther Modern Society, 1970), p. 16.

chapter 4: one dimensional man

1/ Rousseau in *Emile,* quoted in B. F. Skinner, *Beyond Freedom and Dignity,* p. 40; Paul Goodman, *Growing Up Absurd* (New York: Random House, 1960), p. 169; Marshall McLuhan, *Understanding Media* (New York: McGraw-Hill Book Company, 1964), p. 46; Mario Savio, quoted in Jacobs and Landau, p. 69; William H. Whyte, *The Organization Man* (Harmondsworth: Penguin Books, 1956), p. 12; Herbert Marcuse, *Eros and Civilization* (Boston: Beacon Press, 1966), p. 91.
2/ Marshall McLuhan, *War and Peace in the Global Village* (New York: Bantam Books, 1969), p. 126.

3/ Toffler, p. 324.

4/ Nuttall, p. 9.

5/ Marcuse, *Eros and Civilization,* p. 13.

6/ Marshall McLuhan, *The Gutenberg Galaxy* (London: Routledge & Kegan Paul Ltd., 1962), p. 31.

7/ Quoted in Fischer, p. 83.

8/ David Riesman, *The Lonely Crowd* (New Haven: Yale University Press, p. 123).

9/ Whyte, p. 123.

10/ Ibid., p. 16, 18.

11/ Ibid., p. 33.

12/ Goodman, *Growing Up Absurd,* p. 4.

13/ Ibid., p. 11.

14/ Ibid., p. 12.

15/ Ibid., p. 123.

16/ Ibid., pp. 159-60.

17/ Ibid., p. 169.

18/ C. W. Mills, *White Collar* (London: Oxford University Press, 1951), p. xv.

19/ Ibid., p. xii.

20/ Ibid., p. xviii.

21/ Ibid., p. xv.

22/ C. W. Mills, *The Power Elite* (London: Oxford University Press, 1956), p. 9.

23/ Ibid., p. 361.

24/ Ibid.

25/ Herbert Aptheker, *The World of Cyril Wright Mills* (New York: Marzani and Monsell, 1960), p. 170.

26/ Quoted in Joe McGinniss, *The Selling of the President* (Harmondsworth: Penguin Books, 1970), p. 26.

27/ Ibid., p. 35.

28/ Quoted in Newfield, p. 23.

29/ Marshall McLuhan, *The Medium Is the Massage* (New York: Bantam Books, 1967), p. 41.

30/ Ibid., p. 26.

31/ McLuhan, *Understanding Media,* p. 46.

32/ McLuhan, *War and Peace in the Global Village,* p. 37.

33/ McLuhan, *Understanding Media,* p. 329.

34/ Ibid., p. 45.

35/ Herbert Marcuse, *One Dimensional Man* (London: Sphere

Books, 1968), p. 9.
36/ Ibid., p. 12.
37/ Ibid., p. 14.
38/ Ibid., p. 19.
39/ Ibid., p. 159.
40/ Ibid., p. 141.
41/ Ibid., p. 86.
42/ Ibid., p. 77.
43/ Quoted in Jacobs and Landau, p. 69.
44/ Roszak, p. 6.
45/ John Wilkinson, *Introducing Jacques Ellul* (Grand Rapids: Wm. B. Eerdmans, 1970), p. 168.
46/ Ellul, *The Technological Society,* p. 21.
47/ Ibid., p. 19.
48/ Ibid., p. 22.
49/ Ibid., p. 99.
50/ Quoted in Calder, p. 1.
51/ Ellul, *The Technological Society,* pp. 84-85.
52/ Ibid., p. 93.
53/ Ibid., p. 94.
54/ Ibid., p. 97.
55/ McLuhan, *The Medium Is the Massage,* p. 12.
56/ Ellul, *The Technological Society,* p. 100.
57/ Aldous Huxley in his 1946 Foreword to *Brave New World,* pp. 11-15.
58/ Ellul, *The Technological Society,* p. 125.
59/ Ibid., p. 318.
60/ Ibid., p. 417.
61/ Goodman, *Growing Up Absurd,* p. 231.
62/ Whyte, p. 10.
63/ Kenneth Kenniston, "Youth, Change and Violence," *American Scholar,* Spring 1968, p. 239.
64/ R. D. Laing, "The Obvious," *The Dialectics of Liberation,* ed. David Cooper (Harmondsworth: Penguin Books, 1968), p. 32.
65/ Alasdair MacIntyre, *Marcuse* (Glasgow: Fontana/Collins, 1970), p. 66.
66/ Ibid., p. 71.
67/ Riesman, p. 220.
68/ Toffler, pp. 127, 233.
69/ Ibid., p. 130.

70/ Ibid., p. 236.

71/ Alexander Solzhenitsyn, *For the Good of the Cause* (London: Sphere Books, 1971), p. 97.

72/ Toffler, p. 284.

73/ Ibid., p. 383.

74/ Oswald Spengler, *The Decline of the West, I, Form and Actuality,* trans. C. F. Atkinson (New York: Alfred A. Knopf, 1926), p. 37.

75/ Camus, *The Rebel,* p. 146.

76/ Quoted in James Joll, *The Anarchists* (London: Methuen & Co. Ltd., 1969), p. 85.

77/ Quoted in ibid., p. 110.

78/ Quoted in ibid., p. 105.

79/ Marcuse, "Political Preface 1966," *Eros and Civilization,* p. 11.

80/ Marcuse, *Eros and Civilization* pp. 90-91.

81/ Quoted in Roszak, p. 116.

82/ Psalm 115:8.

chapter 5: violence—crisis or catharsis

1/ Fanon, *The Wretched of the Earth,* p. 74; quoted in Ellul, *Violence: Reflections from a Christian Perspective,* p. 130; Mao Tse-tung, "Problems of War and Strategy" (November 6, 1938), *Selected Works,* 2 (Peking: Foreign Languages Press), p. 224; quoted in Ira Einhorn in *Psychedelics,* ed. Bernard Aaronson and Humphrey Osmond (New York: Anchor Books, 1970), p. 451; Norman Mailer, *Miami and the Siege of Chicago* (New York: Signet Books, 1968), p. 194; Koestler, *The Ghost in the Machine,* p. 339.

2/ Platt, p. 200.

3/ Joseph Heller, *Catch-22* (New York: Dell Books, 1962), p. 253.

4/ Quoted in Karl Mannheim, *Ideology and Utopia: An Intro-*

duction to the Sociology of Knowledge (London: Routledge & Kegan Paul Ltd., 1966), p. 196.

5/ Georges Sorel, *Reflexions sur la violence* (Paris: M. Riviere, 1950), p. 389.

6/ Desmond Morris, *The Naked Ape* (New York: Dell Books, 1967), p. 120.

7/ Konrad Lorenz, *On Aggression*, trans. Marjorie Kerr Wilson (New York: Bantam Books, 1967), pp. 26-27.

8/ Ibid., p. 230.

9/ Ibid., p. 290.

10/ Koestler, *The Ghost in the Machine*, p. 267.

11/ Ibid., p. 298.

12/ Ibid., p. 339.

13/ Freud, *Civilisation and Its Discontents*, pp. 113-14.

14/ Brown, p. 93.

15/ Ibid.

16/ Ibid.

17/ Quoted in L. Clark Stevens, p. 110.

18/ Quoted in Hannah Arendt, *On Violence* (London: Allen Lane The Penguin Press, 1970), p. 9.

19/ McLuhan, *War and Peace in the Global Village*, p. 97.

20/ Ibid., p. 123.

21/ Eldridge Cleaver, *Soul on Ice* (London: Jonathan Cape Ltd., 1969), p. 49.

22/ Camus, *The Rebel*, p. 147.

23/ Mills, *The Power Elite*, p. 171.

24/ Quoted in Ellul, *Violence: Reflections from a Christian Perspective*, p. 130.

25/ Mao Tse-tung, p. 224.

26/ Arendt, p. 9.

27/ Fanon, *The Wretched of the Earth*, p. 252.

28/ Ibid., p. 251.

29/ Sartre, "Preface" in ibid., p. 22.

30/ Ibid., p. 17.

31/ Fanon, *The Wretched of the Earth*, p. 66.

32/ Ibid., p. 68.

33/ Ibid., p. 73.

34/ Ibid., p. 74.

35/ Sartre, "Preface" in ibid., p. 18.

36/ Ibid., pp. 18-19.

37/ Ibid., p. 20.

38/ Frantz Fanon, *Black Skin, White Mask* (London: MacGibbon & Kee Ltd., 1968), pp. 10-11.

39/ Quoted in David Caute, *Fanon* (Glasgow: Fontana/Collins, 1970), p. 85.

40/ Arthur Schlesinger, Jr., *Violence: America in the Sixties* (New York: Signet Books, 1968), p. 19.

41/ Quoted by Krishan Kumar, *The Listener,* July 3, 1969, p. 1.

42/ Virginia Adams, "Psychology of Murder," *Time,* April 24, 1972, pp. 54-59.

43/ Mailer, *Miami and the Siege of Chicago,* pp. 15, 194, 223.

44/ Quoted in Ellul, *Violence: Reflections from a Christian Perspective,* p. 21.

45/ Ibid., p. 49.

46/ Ibid., p. 75.

47/ Matthew 5:21-22.

48/ R. D. Laing, *The Politics of Experience,* p. 11.

49/ Matthew 26:52.

50/ Camus, *The Rebel,* p. 146.

51/ Roszak, p. 296.

52/ Karl Popper, "Utopia and Violence," an address delivered to the Institut des Arts in Brussels, June, 1947, reprinted in *Conjectures and Refutations* (New York: Basic Books, Inc., 1963), p. 355.

53/ Matthew 26:52.

54/ Genesis 15:16.

55/ See 2 Kings 21:9; Isaiah 28:2, 11; Ezekiel 33:23-29; Habakkuk 1:1, 5, 12.

56/ Matthew 5:38-44.

57/ Matthew 18:21-35.

58/ Matthew 18:35.

chapter 6: the east, no exit

1/ Rudyard Kipling, "The Ballad of East and West"; Laing, *The Politics of Experience,* p. 136; Aldous Huxley, *Island* (Harmondsworth: Penguin Books, 1961), pp. 219-20; quoted in Alan Watts, *Beat Zen, Square Zen and Zen* (San Francisco: City Lights, 1959), p. 10; Charles Manson, *Rolling Stone Magazine,* June 25, 1970; Buddhagosa, "Path of Purity," *Man in Buddhism and Christianity* (Y.M.C.A. Publishing House, 1954), p. 119.

2/ Kipling, "The Ballad of East and West."

3/ Quoted in Watts, *Beat Zen, Square Zen and Zen,* p. 3.

4/ Quoted in McLuhan, *The Medium Is the Massage,* p. 143.

5/ McLuhan, *The McLuhan Dew-Line,* Vol. 1, No. 12, June 1969, p. 7.

6/ Laing, *The Politics of Experience,* p. 136.

7/ Hendrik Kraemer, *World Culture and World Religions* (London: Lutterworth Press, 1960), p. 18.

8/ For much of this section I have relied heavily on D. S. Sarma, *The Renaissance of Hinduism* (Benares, 1944).

9/ Quoted in R. C. Zaehner, *Hinduism* (London: Oxford University Press, 1962), p. 199.

10/ Ibid., p. 221.

11/ Alan Watts, *The Way of Zen* (Harmondsworth: Pelican Books, 1962), p. 9.

12/ From "Winter Light" in *Three Films by Ingmar Bergman* (New York: Grove Press, Inc., 1970), p. 87.

13/ Laing, *The Politics of Experience,* p. 35.

14/ Quoted in H. D. Lewis and R. L. Slater, *The Study of Religions* (Harmondsworth: Pelican Books, 1969), p. 163.

15/ D. S. Sarma, "Nature and History of Hinduism," *The Religion of the Hindus: Interpreted by Hindus,* ed. Kenneth W. Morgan (New York: Ronald Press Co., 1953), p. 11.

16/ Quoted in R. C. Zaehner, *Mysticism: Sacred and Profane* (London: Oxford University Press, 1961), p. 169.

17/ See Lynn White, Jr., "The Historical Roots of Our Ecological Crisis," *Science,* March 10, 1967, pp. 1203-07.

18/ Aldous Huxley, *Island,* pp. 219-20.

19/ See Francis A. Schaeffer, *Pollution and the Death of Man: The Christian View of Ecology* (Wheaton, Ill.: Tyndale House Publishers, 1970).

20/ Aldous Huxley, *The Doors of Perception* (London: Chatto and Windus Ltd., 1954), p. 50.

21/ Alan Watts, *Beyond Theology: The Art of Godmanship* (New York: Meridian Books, 1967), p. 32.

22/ Alan Watts, *The Joyous Cosmology* (New York: Vintage Books, 1962), p. 92.

23/ *The Bhagavad Gita,* trans. Juan Mascaro (Harmondsworth: Penguin Books, 1962), p. 50.

24/ Quoted in Zaehner, *Mysticism: Sacred and Profane,* p. 169.

25/ From *An Encyclopedia of Religion,* ed. Vergilius Ferm (New York: The Philosophical Library, 1945), p. 707.

26/ R. C. Zaehner, *The Convergent Spirit* (London: Routledge & Kegan Paul Ltd., 1963), pp. 184-85.

27/ Quoted in Zaehner, *Mysticism: Sacred and Profane,* p. 178.

28/ Watts, *Beyond Theology,* p. 68.

29/ *The Bhagavad Gita,* p. 53.

30/ Buddhagosa, p. 119.

31/ Watts, *Beyond Theology,* p. 49.

32/ Laing, *The Politics of Experience,* p. 113.

33/ Meher Baba, *Discourses* (Sufism Reoriented, Inc., 1967), 1, p. 23.

34/ Lewis Carroll, *Alice in Wonderland and Through the Looking Glass* (Glasgow: Collins Classics, 1954), p. 186.

35/ Teilhard de Chardin, pp. 46-47.

36/ Ibid., p. 52.

37/ Ibid., p. 54.

38/ Ibid., pp. 54-55.

39/ Ibid., p. 46.

40/ Ibid., p. 60.

41/ Arnold Toynbee and others, *Man's Concern with Death,* p. 184.

42/ Watts, *Beat Zen, Square Zen and Zen,* p. 10.

43/ Alan Watts, *This Is It* (New York: Pantheon Books, Inc., 1958), pp. 30, 36.

44/ Dostoevsky, *The Possessed,* p. 224.

45/ Harold G. Henderson, *An Introduction to Haiku: An Anthology of Poems and Poets from Basho to Shiki* (New York: Doubleday Anchor Books, 1958), p. 124.

46/ Quoted in Zaehner, *Mysticism: Sacred and Profane,* p. 170.

47/ Zaehner, *Convergent Spirit,* p. 36.

48/ R. C. Zaehner, *Foolishness to the Greeks* (London: Oxford

University Press, 1953).
49/ Watts, *Beyond Theology*, p. 160.
50/ Ibid., p. xii.

chapter 7: the counterfeit infinity

1/ Aldous Huxley, *Brave New World*, p. 54; Ken Kesey, quoted in Tom Wolfe, *The Electric Kool-Aid Acid Test* (New York: Bantam Books, 1969), pp. 120, 342; Leary, quoted in Solomon, p. 155; Charles Baudelaire, *Les paradis artificiels* (Paris: Poulet-Menassis, 1860); Baudelaire, quoted in Solomon, p. 221.
2/ Leary, *The Politics of Ecstasy*, p. 57.
3/ *The Times* (London), July 15, 1967.
4/ Leary, *The Politics of Ecstasy*, p. 55.
5/ Martin Mayer, "Getting Alienated with the Right Crowd at Harvard," *Esquire*, September 1963.
6/ Baudelaire, *Les paradis artificiels*.
7/ Aldous Huxley, *The Doors of Perception*, p. 49.
8/ Baudelaire, *Les paradis artificiels*.
9/ Charles Reich, *The Greening of America* (New York: Random House, 1970), p. 353.
10/ Leary, *The Politics of Ecstasy*, pp. 141, 57.
11/ William Blake, "The Marriage of Heaven and Hell."
12/ William James, *Varieties of Religious Experience* (New York: Mentor Books, 1958), p. 298.
13/ Colin McGlashan, *The Savage and Beautiful Country* (London: Chatto and Windus Ltd., 1966), p. 122.
14/ For much of the information in this section I have relied on Solomon, *The Marijuana Papers*.
15/ R. Gordon Wasson, *Soma: Divine Mushroom of Immortality* (New York: Harcourt Brace Jovanovich, Inc., 1969).
16/ An excerpt from "The Seraphic Theater," quoted in Solomon, p. 222.

17/ Quoted in Robert S. De Ropp, *Drugs and the Mind* (New York: Grove Press, Inc., 1967), p. 86.

18/ H. J. Anslinger, "Traffic in Opium and Other Dangerous Drugs," *Government Report,* December 31, 1938.

19/ Allen Ginsberg, "First Manifesto to End the Bringdown," quoted in Solomon, p. 270.

20/ From the Summary by George B. Wallace, Chairman of the Report, quoted in Solomon, p. 384.

21/ Baudelaire, quoted in Solomon, p. 222.

22/ "The Hay-Wain," along with other famous paintings of Bosch, such as "The Garden of Delights," is in the Prado Museum, Madrid.

23/ Quoted in De Ropp, *Drugs and the Mind,* p. 55.

24/ Quoted in ibid., p. 57.

25/ Quoted in Aaronson and Osmond, pp. 461-62.

26/ Aldous Huxley, *The Doors of Perception,* p. 17.

27/ Quoted in "She Comes in Colours," *Playboy,* September 1966.

28/ This one sentence is the entire foreword to Leary, *The Politics of Ecstasy.*

29/ Leary, *The Politics of Ecstasy,* p. 136.

30/ Quoted in *Playboy,* September 1966.

31/ Quoted in Roszak, p. 167.

32/ Ibid.

33/ Leary, *The Politics of Ecstasy,* pp. 299-300.

34/ From "The Mind Alchemists," BBC TV program, 1967.

35/ Quoted in Wolfe, pp. 93, 95.

36/ See Leary, "Poet of the Interior Journey," *Psychedelic Review,* No. 3, reprinted in *The Politics of Ecstasy,* p. 146.

37/ Leary, *The Politics of Ecstasy,* p. 87.

38/ Ibid., p. 98.

39/ This was claimed by Leary in an interview with Paul Krassner, *Realist,* September 1966.

40/ Sidney Cohen, *The Beyond Within: The L.S.D. Story* (New York: Atheneum, 1966), p. 209.

41/ *California Law Review,* January 1968, pp. 74-85.

42/ Robert S. De Ropp, *The Master Game* (London: Allen and Unwin, 1969), p. 48.

43/ Ibid., p. 44.

44/ Quoted in De Ropp, *Drugs and the Mind,* p. 67.

45/ Leary, *The Politics of Ecstasy*, p. 37.

46/ See Leary, "The Politics, Ethics, and Meaning of Marijuana," in Solomon, pp. 154-75.

47/ Leary, quoted in Solomon, p. 173.

48/ For a discussion on the non-drug analogues to the psychedelic state, see Aaronson and Osmond, pp. 277-320.

49/ Maharishi Mahesh Yogi, *The Science of Being and the Art of Living* (New York: Signet, 1963), pp. 46-49.

50/ For a discussion of this, see Cohen, p. 50.

51/ Aaronson and Osmond, p. 367.

52/ Leary, *The Politics of Ecstasy*, pp. 24, 115.

53/ Watts, *The Joyous Cosmology*, p. 48.

54/ Leary, *The Politics of Ecstasy*, p. 57.

55/ James, p. 298.

56/ Leary, *The Politics of Ecstasy*, p. 164.

57/ Zbigniew Herbert, *Selected Poems* (Harmondsworth: Penguin Books), p. 41.

58/ Leary, *The Politics of Ecstasy*, p. 106.

59/ Ibid., p. 109.

60/ Ibid., p. 231.

61/ Ibid., p. 193.

62/ Aaronson and Osmond, pp. 477-78.

63/ Reich, p. 350.

64/ Roszak, p. 160.

65/ Aldous Huxley, *The Doors of Perception*, p. 13.

66/ Leary, *The Politics of Ecstasy*, p. 69.

67/ Arthur Rimbaud, *Oeuvres completes* (Paris: Bibliotheque de la Pleiade, 1954), p. 221.

68/ Aaronson and Osmond, p. 184.

69/ U. A. Asrami, "Synthesis of Science and Mysticism," *Main Currents La Modern Thought*, 20, September-October 1963, quoted in Cohen, pp. 242-43.

70/ Leary, *The Politics of Ecstasy*, pp. 223, 164.

71/ James, p. 326.

72/ Zaehner, *Mysticism: Sacred and Profane*, p. 17.

73/ Martin Buber, *Between Man and Man* (New York: The Macmillan Company, 1965), p. 24.

74/ Meher Baba, "God in a Pill?" a pamphlet published by Sufism Reoriented, Inc.

75/ Leary, *The Politics of Ecstasy*, p. 29.

76/ Watts, *The Joyous Cosmology*, p. 47.
77/ Ibid., p. 6.
78/ Leary, *The Politics of Ecstasy*, p. 28.
79/ Watts, *The Joyous Cosmology*, pp. 58, 70-71.
80/ Leary, *The Politics of Ecstasy*, p. 182.
81/ Ibid., p. 224.
82/ Watts, *The Joyous Cosmology*, p. 224.
83/ Leary, *The Politics of Ecstasy*, p. 245.
84/ Carlos Castaneda, *The Teachings of Don Juan: A Yaquí Way of Knowledge* (Berkeley: University of California Press, 1968), p. 26.
85/ De Ropp, *The Master Game*, pp. 11-12.
86/ Watts, *The Joyous Cosmology*, p. 61.
87/ Leary, *The Politics of Ecstasy*, p. 179.
88/ Rimbaud, p. 225.
89/ Wolfe, p. 289.
90/ Leary, *The Politics of Ecstasy*, p. 40.
91/ Acts 9:5.
92/ Acts 9:5.
93/ Acts 26:14.

chapter 8: the encircling eyes

1/ C. S. Lewis, *The Screwtape Letters* (London: Macmillan, 1961), p. 3; Marshall McLuhan, quoted in "Astrology: Fad and Phenomenon," *Time*, March 21, 1969, p. 48; Laing, *The Politics of Experience*, p. 109; Karl Jaspers, *General Psychopathology* (Manchester: Manchester University Press, 1962), pp. 417-18; Rimbaud, quoted in Ellul, *Violence: Reflections from a Christian Perspective*, p. 164; 1 Corinthians 4:20.
2/ See Arthur Koestler, *The Roots of Coincidence* (London: Hutchinson, 1972) and Sheila Ostrander and Lynn Schroeder, *Psychic Discoveries Behind the Iron Curtain* (Hemel Hempstead·

Prentice-Hall, 1970).
3/ Pennethorne Hughes, *Witchcraft* (Harmondsworth: Penguin Books, 1965), p. 210.
4/ Ibid., p. 217.
5/ C. S. Lewis, *The Screwtape Letters,* p. 3.
6/ "Astrology: Fad and Phenomenon," *Time,* March 21, 1969, p. 56.
7/ James, p. 327.
8/ Laing, *The Politics of Experience,* pp. 109-10.
9/ Quoted in *Time,* March 21, 1969, p. 48.
10/ "That New Black Magic," *Time,* September 27, 1968, p. 42.
11/ Ibid.
12/ Kurt E. Koch, *Between Christ and Satan* (West Germany: Evangelization Publishers, 1967), p. 16.
13/ Ibid., p. 14.
14/ Ibid., p. 27.
15/ See Montague Summers, *The History of Witchcraft and Demonology* (New York: Barnes and Noble, Inc., 1965).
16/ See Margaret A. Murray, *The Witch-Cult in Western Europe: A Study in Anthropology* (London: Oxford University Press, 1921).
17/ See Roszak, Chapter 8.
18/ Koch, p. 103.
19/ Jaspers, pp. 417-18.
20/ Raphael Gasson, *The Challenging Counterfeit* (Plainfield, New Jersey: Logos International, 1966), p. 23.
21/ Ephesians 6:12.
22/ Genesis 3:5.
23/ See Deuteronomy 18:9-13; Leviticus 20:6, 27.
24/ Leviticus 19:31.
25/ Luke 11:20.
26/ John 14:12.
27/ 1 Corinthians 15:24-28.
28/ Exodus 7:8-13.
29/ For examples of "sign" as divine, see Mark 16:17; John 2:23, 4:54, 6:2, 9:16, 11:47; Acts 4:16.
30/ Matthew 24:24; Mark 13:22,
31/ 2 Thessalonians 2:9.
32/ Revelation 13:13, 16:14, 19:20.

33/ Revelation 9:21, 17:23.

34/ 1 John 4:1.

35/ Colossians 2:15.

36/ Album insert to *Blows Against the Empire,* RCA Victor SF8163.

chapter 9: the ultimate trip?

1/ Paul Goodman, "The New Reformation," p. 147; Jeremiah 16:20; Sigmund Freud, *The Future of an Illusion* (London: Hogarth Press, 1961), p. 30; Henrik Ibsen, *The Wild Duck,* Act V; Aldous Huxley, "Introduction," *D. H. Lawrence: Selected Letters,* selected by Richard Aldington (Harmondsworth: Penguin Books, 1950), p. 10; James Wechsler, quoted in *The Village Voice Reader* (New York: Grove Press, 1963), p. 239; Jaime Robbie Robertson of "The Band," quoted in a handout accompanying *Stage Fright,* E.M.1., EA-SW 425.

2/ Roszak, p. xiii.

3/ Adrian Mitchell, "The Liberal Christ Gives an Interview," *Out Loud* (London: Cape Goliard Press, 1969).

4/ James, pp. 329, 341.

5/ Freud, *The Future of an Illusion,* p. 30.

6/ Laing, *The Politics of Experience,* p. 118.

7/ Freud, *The Future of an Illusion,* p. 31.

8/ Rev. John Bisagno, quoted in "The New Rebel Cry: Jesus is Coming!" *Time,* June 21, 1971, p. 63.

9/ John 2:23-25.

10/ G. B. Shaw, *Androcles and the Lion* (Baltimore: Penguin Books, 1951), p. 108.

11/ Carl Jung, *Psychotherapists or the Clergy?* quoted in Booker, p. 323.

12/ Tillich, quoted in Harrington, p. 130.

13/ Julian Huxley, p. 19.

14/ Freud, *The Future of an Illusion,* p. 26.

15/ Ibid., p. 49.

16/ Carl Jung, *Psychology and Religion* (New Haven: Yale University Press, 1957), p. 3.

17/ Erich Fromm, *Psychoanalysis and Religion* (New York: Bantam Books, 1967), p. 109.

18/ Ibid., p. 12.

19/ O. Hobart Mowrer, *The Crisis in Psychiatry and Religion* (London: Van Nostrand Reinhold Company Ltd., 1961), p. 60.

20/ Quoted in Elaine Storkey, "Faith, Verification and Falsification," an unpublished paper, p. 3.

21/ Antony Flew, "Theology and Falsification," *New Essays in Philosophical Theology,* ed. Antony Flew and Alasdair MacIntyre (London: SCM Press, 1955), p. 96.

22/ Ibid., p. 97.

23/ Elizabeth Barrett Browning, "Proof and Disproof," *The Complete Works of Elizabeth Barrett Browning* (Boston and New York: Houghton Mifflin Company, 1900), pp. 212-13.

24/ Quoted in Flew and MacIntyre, p. 103.

25/ Job 19:25-27.

26/ This must not be mistaken as suggesting that a Christian view of truth and knowledge rests on the validity of Karl Popper's falsification principle or necessarily supports the falsification principle as valid. Rather, it is my view that to the degree any theory of knowledge has a genuine and valuable insight into the nature of reality (as opposed to also containing assumptions that are either false or unwarrantable on its own premises)—to that degree Christian truth is open to satisfying the challenge of its criteria. With empiricism the insight centers around the nature and necessity of evidence.

27/ 1 Kings 18:39.

28/ Review by A. J. Ayer, *Sunday Times* (London), April 9, 1972.

29/ Quoted in Gay, p. 64.

30/ Henderson, p. 124.

31/ Isaish 44:12-21; Acts 17:22-34.

32/ John 20:28.

33/ John 8:46.

34/ John 20:27.

35/ Hebrews 11:3.

36/ Deuteronomy 18:21-22.
37/ Jeremiah 28:9.
38/ Luke 1:1-4.
39/ Acts 1:3.
40/ Acts 26:25-26.
41/ 1 Corinthians 15:14.
42/ 2 Peter 1:16.
43/ 1 John 1:1.
44/ John 20:31 (RSV).
45/ Ibsen, *The Wild Duck,* Act V.
46/ Aldous Huxley, "Introduction," *D. H. Lawrence: Selected Letters,* p. 10.
47/ Quoted in *The Village Voice Reader,* p. 239.

chapter 10: the third race

1/ *Ante-Nicene Christian Library, I: Apostolic Fathers,* trans. A. Roberts, J. Donaldson and F. Crombie, ed. A. Roberts and J. Donaldson (Edinburgh: T. and T. Clark, 1867), pp. 307-08; Watts, *Beyond Theology: The Art of Godmanship,* p. xii; Camus, quoted in *The Post-American,* Vol. 1, No. 1, Fall 1971, p. 1; 1 Corinthians 1:27-28.
2/ See Adolph Harnack, *Mission and Expansion of Christianity in the First Three Centuries,* Book 2, Chapter 7.
3/ Colossians 3:11.
4/ Watts, *Beyond Theology: The Art of Godmanship,* pp. xii-xiii.
5/ Isaiah 11:3.
6/ Koestler, *The Ghost in the Machine,* pp. 193-95.
7/ John 2:24-25.
8/ Matthew 9:36.
9/ Luke 15:1-7.
10/ John 10:27.
11/ Matthew 18:33; Luke 15:20; 10:33.

12/ Matthew 9:36; 14:14.

13/ Mark 1:41; Matthew 20:34 (RSV).

14/ Luke 7:11-17, especially v. 13.

15/ John 11:34, 38.

16/ Exodus 2:11-12 (RSV).

17/ 1 Samuel 11:6-7 (RSV).

18/ Amos 4:1.

19/ Luke 19:45-46.

20/ Amos 6:12.

21/ Isaiah 59:15-16.

22/ Exodus 2:14.

23/ Hebrews 11:25 (RSV).

24/ Isaiah 53:4 (RSV).

25/ Matthew 27:46.

27/ Fanon, *The Wretched of the Earth,* p. 32.

27/ Fanon, p. 32.

28/ Quoted in Zaehner, *Hinduism,* p. 224.

29/ Roszak, pp. 43-44.

30/ Clark, p. 9.

31/ Goodman, "The New Reformation," p. 153.

32/ Bertrand Russell, *History of Western Philosophy* (Bloomfield, N.J.: Simon and Schuster, 1945), p. 579.